Cool Careers
FOR
DUMMIES®
3RD EDITION

by Marty Nemko, PhD

Foreword by Richard N. Bolles

BICENTENNIAL
1807
WILEY
2007
BICENTENNIAL

Wiley Publishing, Inc.

Cool Careers For Dummies,® 3rd Edition

Published by
Wiley Publishing, Inc.
111 River St.
Hoboken, NJ 07030-5774
www.wiley.com

WILEY

About the Author

Marty Nemko has several cool careers. In his 20th year as career coach, he's served more than 2,500 clients. *U.S. News & World Report* called him "Career coach extraordinaire." The *San Francisco Bay Guardian* named him "The Bay Area's Best Career Coach." He enjoys a 97 percent client-satisfaction rate.

He's Contributing Editor for career issues at *U.S. News & World Report* and career columnist for *Kiplinger's Personal Finance Magazine* and for the *Mensa Bulletin.* Before going national, his column appeared in the Sunday *Los Angeles Times* and *San Francisco Chronicle.*

He's the author of 500+ well-published articles and five commercially and critically successful books, including the *All-in-One College Guide,* a consumer advocate's guide to choosing, getting into, finding the money for, and making the most of college.

He's in his 18th year as producer and host of *Work with Marty Nemko,* on a National Public Radio affiliate in San Francisco.

He's hosted a nationwide PBS pledge-drive special, *Eight Steps to a Better Worklife,* and been a repeat guest on major TV and radio shows, including the *Today* show and *CNN Headline News Comcast Local Edition,* on which he now appears daily. He has been the primary interview source for dozens of articles, including those in *The New York Times, Washington Post,* and *Wall Street Journal.*

He holds a PhD from the University of California, Berkeley, and subsequently taught there.

He's the hybridizer of six commercially introduced *no-spray* roses; they don't require spraying for disease.

Believe it or not, he finds time for hobbies. In 2006, he starred in a San Francisco Bay Area production of Neil Simon's *Broadway Bound,* in which he played the cheating husband opposite his real-life wife. At that show, he also played the pre-show music on the piano. (He has played more than 2,000 professional jobs as a pianist.) In summer 2007, he directs the play *Same Time Next Year.*

Marty's first job: New York City taxicab driver.

Marty's Web site, www.martynemko.com, offers 500+ of his published articles for free. If you want to be coached, by phone or in person, by Marty or one of his personally selected and trained associates, e-mail him a brief description of your situation at mnemko@comcast.net.

Dedication

To my parents. As teenagers, they were wrested from their home in Poland and into concentration camps. After the war, they were placed on a cargo ship and dropped in New York City with no money, no family, no education, no English, but plenty of Holocaust scars. Despite it all, they succeeded. For them, work — even though they didn't have cool careers — was their healer. They are my inspiration.

Author's Acknowledgments

To the thousands of my clients and callers to my radio show who taught me much of what is in this book.

To Paul and Sarah Edwards, for their significant contributions to the self-employment chapter.

To the book's wise reviewers: Jim Gonyea, career forums host on America Online; Marilyn Maze, director of career products for American College Testing; the queen of online career searching: *The Riley Guide*'s Margaret Riley Dikel; and a guy who painstakingly reviewed every word of this edition, my colleague Steve Piazzale.

To other people whose ideas enrich these pages: Michael Scriven, Greg Stock, Warren Farrell, Michael Edelstein, Bob Karr, David Brodwin, Allan Gold, David Wilens, Rick Newman, Miriam Weinstein, Jeffrie Givens, Becky Washington, Arthur Jensen, Harvey Davidson, Walter Block, Libby Pannwitt, Lynaire McGovern, Jared Taylor, Julie Petrie, Jackie Strellis, Robin Happy, and the dean of career experts, the author of *What Color Is Your Parachute,* Dick Bolles.

Thanks, John Jones, for your reassurances.

To the good people at Wiley: Editors Lindsay Lefevere, Georgette Beatty, and Sarah Faulkner for being consummate professionals while always friendly and tactful. I especially appreciate Lindsay's telling me, before I started writing this edition, that I was one of the best *For Dummies* authors. That motivated me to try to live up to her expectations. I have had a number of publishers, and you guys are, by far, the best. Consumer Dummies rocks!

And finally, my dear wife, Barbara Nemko, not just for having contributed a great chapter to this book and offering suggestions on the rest of this manuscript, but for being a model for all of us to aspire to. I love you, forever.

Publisher's Acknowledgments

We're proud of this book; please send us your comments through our Dummies online registration form located at www.dummies.com/register/.

Some of the people who helped bring this book to market include the following:

Acquisitions, Editorial, and Media Development

Project Editor: Georgette Beatty

(Previous Edition: Norm Crampton)

Acquisitions Editor: Lindsay Lefevere

Copy Editor: Sarah Faulkner

(Previous Edition: Neil Johnson)

Technical Editor: Steve Piazzale, PhD

Editorial Manager: Michelle Hacker

Editorial Assistants: Erin Calligan Mooney, Joe Niesen, Leeann Harney

Cartoons: Rich Tennant (www.the5thwave.com)

Composition Services

Project Coordinator: Heather Kolter

Layout and Graphics: Carl Byers, Stephanie D. Jumper, Heather Ryan

Anniversary Logo Design: Richard Pacifico

Proofreaders: Aptara, John Greenough, Jessica Kramer,

Indexer: Aptara

Publishing and Editorial for Consumer Dummies

    Diane Graves Steele, Vice President and Publisher, Consumer Dummies

    Joyce Pepple, Acquisitions Director, Consumer Dummies

    Kristin A. Cocks, Product Development Director, Consumer Dummies

    Michael Spring, Vice President and Publisher, Travel

    Kelly Regan, Editorial Director, Travel

Publishing for Technology Dummies

    Andy Cummings, Vice President and Publisher, Dummies Technology/General User

Composition Services

    Gerry Fahey, Vice President of Production Services

    Debbie Stailey, Director of Composition Services

Contents at a Glance

Foreword ....*xix*

Introduction 1

Part I: Finding Your Cool Career, Right Here.................7

Chapter 1: Your Cool Career Journey 9
Chapter 2: The Cool Careers Yellow Pages 15
Chapter 3: The 35 Most Revealing Questions About You...........................159
Chapter 4: Making Your Career Choice...173

Part II: Training for That Cool Career 187

Chapter 5: Degree-Free Career Preparation 189
Chapter 6: Degree-Based Career Preparation 201

Part III: Landing That Cool Job 213

Chapter 7: Creating the Right Mindset for Job Seeking 215
Chapter 8: 30 Days to a Cool Job...223
Chapter 9: Crafting the Right Resume in Less Time 245
Chapter 10: Impressive Interviewing 263

Part IV: Making Any Career Cooler 281

Chapter 11: Making the Most of Any Job...283
Chapter 12: Light My Fire, Please! Overcoming Procrastination...................311
Chapter 13: The Keys to Successful Self-Employment 329

Part V: The Part of Tens 343

Chapter 14: Top Ten Career Musts for Women.....................................345
Chapter 15: Top Ten Career Musts for Men 351
Chapter 16: Top Ten (Or So) Career Musts for Everyone 357

Appendix: The Cool Career Finder..............................363

Index 371

Table of Contents

Foreword...xix

Introduction 1
   About This Book..1
   Conventions Used in This Book 3
   What You're Not to Read 3
   Foolish Assumptions 3
   How This Book Is Organized...4
      Part I: Finding Your Cool Career, Right Here...................4
      Part II: Training for That Cool Career 4
      Part III: Landing That Cool Job 5
      Part IV: Making Any Career Cooler.................................5
      Part V: The Part of Tens..5
   Icons Used in This Book 6
   Where to Go from Here..6

Part I: Finding Your Cool Career, Right Here 7

   Chapter 1: Your Cool Career Journey 9
      Julie Seeks a Career: A Cautionary Tale 9
      Taking Your Own Journey 12
         Discovering your cool career..13
         Finding the best training for your needs 13
         Getting a cool job 14
         Making the most of your new career 14

   Chapter 2: The Cool Careers Yellow Pages 15
      What Makes a Cool Career Cool? 15
      Using the Cool Careers Yellow Pages 16
         The categories 16
         The icons 17
         Taking the road less traveled...18
      Work with People 18
         Bringing people together...28
         Sales-oriented work..29
         Other people-oriented careers 32

Work with Data 35
    Scientific data 35
    Computer data 43
    Business data 46
Work with Words 50
Work with Things 56
    Artistically Done 56
    Structured procedures 60
Work with People and Data 71
Work with People and Words 82
    Public speaking 82
    Training and teaching 84
    On the creative side 88
    Getting political 90
    One-on-one 90
Work with People and Things 92
Work with Data and People 94
    Technically Speaking 94
    Crunching numbers 96
Work with Data, People, and Words 100
Work with Data and Things 105
Work with Data, People, and Things 108
    Healthcare 108
    Other specialties 111
Work with Data, Things, and People 113
Work with Words and People 118
Work with Things and People 125
Work with Things and Data 134
Work with Things, People, and Words 140
A Guide to the Future 143
    Computers and technology 143
    Health and science 149
    Politics, culture, and economics 152

Chapter 3: The 35 Most Revealing Questions About You **159**

Making the Process Easier 160
Examining Your Values 160
Taking Stock of Your Abilities and Skills 161
Eyeing Your Interests 162
Considering Self-Employment 165
Answering Big-Picture Questions 167
The Virtual Career Coach: Integrating Head and Heart 169
    Step 1: List your career musts 170
    Step 2: See whether the careers you
        picked satisfy your career musts...............................170
    Step 3: Note other careers suggested by your career musts........170

Step 4: Add careers from the 35 Most Revealing Questions 171
Step 5: Pick one or more careers that may actually work.............171
Step 6: Find out more 171

Chapter 4: Making Your Career Choice **173**
Reading about a Career 173
Why read before phoning or visiting?...174
What's the best stuff to read? 174
Contacting People in the Field..176
"Okay, okay, but whom do I contact?" 176
"What should I say?" 177
Visiting a Workplace 178
Knowing what to do during a visit 179
Taking a virtual visit 179
Getting Serious about a Career 179
Finding the Courage to Commit 180
When you don't know enough about a prospective career 180
When no career seems attractive enough...181
When you're afraid that you'll fail...182
A Final Check: Is Your Choice Right for You? 185

Part II: Training for That Cool Career 187

Chapter 5: Degree-Free Career Preparation **189**
The Bad and the Good about Pursuing a Degree.................................189
Lousy reasons to get a degree..190
Good reasons to get a degree 190
More reasons to save your tuition money 191
You U. — Often a Better Way 193
Planning Your You U. Education..195
Finding a mentor 195
Figuring out what to learn 196
Surveying sources of courses 196
Scoping out other learning tools 198
Convincing Employers to Hire You without That Degree 198
Engaging in Lifelong Learning...200

Chapter 6: Degree-Based Career Preparation **201**
Choosing the Right Program...201
Identify your career niche..201
Identify programs in your niche..202
Finding the Right College or Grad School..203
Getting in 206
Getting into killer colleges 207

Finding the Money 208
Comparing the Deals 209
Making the Most of the School You Choose 210
    Find good teachers..210
    Read first 211
    In class, stay active 211
    Choose your advisor well..211
    Look for one-on-one opportunities 211
    Adapt assignments to fit you 211
    Build relationships with potential employers 212
    Don't take crap 212
    Succeeding in school after 40 212

Part III: Landing That Cool Job 213

Chapter 7: Creating the Right Mindset for Job Seeking 215

Staying Upbeat..215
    Pretend that you're going to the mall 215
    Picture the benefit...216
    Be playful yet persistent...216
    Fake it 'til you make it 216
    Be real 217
    Be in the moment 217
    Have six balls in the air 217
    Breathe..217
    Get support 218
Shrugging Off Fear of Rejection and Failure 218
    Make a solid effort, and you won't be a loser................218
    Recognize that you have skills 219
    Ask yourself "What would God think?" 219
    Think of your contacts as library books 220
    Know that batting .050 is good enough 220
    Stay cool 220
    Pretend that rejection is a blessing...............................220
    Envision the worst that could happen 220
    For folks who are 40-plus: Be proud of your experience.............221
    Help yourself cure a deep-rooted fear of rejection 221
Getting That Chip off Your Shoulder 222

Chapter 8: 30 Days to a Cool Job **223**

Finding the Time to Search 223
Day 1: Craft a Winning Resume and Research Your Field 224
    Creating your resume 225
    Studying your field of interest 225
Day 2: Concoct Your Pitch and Identify Your Target Employers 226
    Coming up with a winning pitch 226
    Targeting specific employers 227
Day 3: Research Your Target Employers 228
Days 4–5: Contact Your Network 228
    Knowing how much networking time you need 229
    E-mailing contacts in your network 229
    Succeeding on the phone 230
Day 6: Contact Leads 231
    Making contact when you have cold feet 231
    Getting through..232
    Speaking to a lead 234
    Following up 235
Days 7–8: Answer Want Ads the Smart Way 236
    Answering want ads: An underrated job-search method............236
    Deciding how much to use the want ads 238
    Starting to answer ads 239
Day 9: Contact Your Target Employers..240
Days 10–11: Follow Up 242
Days 12–30: Interview and Land That Cool Job 242
    Interviewing 243
    Negotiating 244
What If, After 30 Days, You Got Zippo?..244

Chapter 9: Crafting the Right Resume in Less Time **245**

Spending a Limited Amount of Time on Your Resume..........................245
Step 1: Write Your Name and Contact Information................................246
Step 2 (Optional): Write Your Objective..247
Step 3: Choose Your Format: Attributes or Chronological 248
Step 4: Select a Specific Resume to Use as a Model 250
Step 5: Draft a Resume that Builds on Your Model Resume 250
    Listing impressive accomplishments 250
    Including transferable skills..253
    Compensating for an imperfect work history..........................253
    Phrasing carefully to get your resume
        past the computerized gatekeeper..................................255

Step 6: Write the Education Section 256
Step 7: Decide on Optional Sections 258
Step 8: Write the Personal Section..................................258
Step 9: List Your Highlights at the Top..........................258
    Option 1: A summary of accomplishments....................258
    Option 2: A paragraph of attributes.........................259
    Option 3: Your human story.................................259
Step 10: Get Feedback..259
Step 11: Create an Unformatted Version of Your Resume.....................260
Step 12: Stop Obsessing and Start Celebrating 261

Chapter 10: Impressive Interviewing **263**

Getting Ready for an Interview...263
    Study 263
    Prepare...264
    Practice..265
Eighteen Ways to Create Chemistry in an Interview 266
    Check your body chemistry....................................266
    Dress one notch above 266
    Arrive early..266
    Help yourself relax 267
    Try to have a good time from the get-go 267
    Establish the first-date mindset.............................267
    Make the most of the first ten seconds 268
    Avoid turn-off mannerisms.....................................268
    Really try to understand the employer's needs 269
    Be yourself, but be your best self 270
    Really listen and watch......................................270
    Talk the right amount 271
    Ask one or more power questions early in the interview..........271
    Stay connected with all your interviewers 272
    Bring up one weakness early on................................272
    Mirror the interviewer 273
    Reveal a bit about your personal life.........................273
    Know the secrets to video interviewing........................273
Other Keys to Wowing Interviewers 273
    Don't just say you can do it — prove it 273
    Maximize the good part of the interview 274
    Fit the job description to your strengths 274
    Success at 40-plus 275
    Offer to fill other needs if you sense
        you're a poor match for the job............................276
After the Interview: When the Job Is Often Won or Lost 276
    The Interview Report Card.....................................276
    Ahead-of-the-pack thank-you letters...........................277

References 278
The end game...278
Handling Job Offers and Rejections...................................279
You got the job offer!...279
Someone else got the job, but all's not lost 280

Part IV: Making Any Career Cooler *281*

Chapter 11: Making the Most of Any Job **283**

Managing Your Boss 283
Tailoring the job to fit you...284
Developing wonderful communication skills.......................285
Maintaining a Moderate Workload......................................287
Working at home...287
Time-efficiency, no matter where you work.......................288
Keeping Your Job Interesting..289
Compose a mission statement...289
Propose a special project...289
Develop a mentoring relationship....................................290
Find a fun hobby...290
Weave your hobby into your job......................................290
Make a lateral move 291
The World's Shortest Stress Management Course.................291
Stop rushing..292
Be accepting..292
Conserve your emotional energy units 292
Find support from someone fun.......................................293
Decorate your workspace with flair..................................293
Get permission to bring your pet to work...........................293
Watch for early signs of stress.......................................293
Think less and act more 294
Take three breaths and leave..294
Be in the moment 294
Winning at Office Politics without Selling Your Soul 295
Staying Current the Smart Way 297
The Three-Minute MBA: The World's Shortest Management Course....299
Enjoying Success at Every Career Stage 300
When you're just starting out..300
When you're mid-career 302
When you're in your final years on the job.........................303
Assessing Your Chances of Getting Ahead 307

Chapter 12: Light My Fire, Please! Overcoming Procrastination . . .311
In the Beginning: How People Develop a Habit of Procrastination........312
The World's Shortest Course in Overcoming Procrastination..............313
Cures for Every Imaginable Excuse 315
The fear-of-failure excuse 315
The live-for-today excuse 317
The spacey procrastinator's excuse 318
The perfectionist's excuse #1 319
The perfectionist's excuse #2 319
The fear-of-imposing excuse 320
The fear-of-success excuse 320
The adrenaline addict's excuse 321
The resent-authority excuse 321
The don't-have-time excuse 322
All-Purpose Procrastination Cures 322
Doing your work without becoming stuck.......................322
Getting unstuck when all else fails 324
Advice for the Incurable Procrastinator 327

Chapter 13: The Keys to Successful Self-Employment 329
But What about the Downsides of Self-Employment? 330
What Are the Six Musts for Successful Self-Employment?....................331
Coming up with a good idea 331
Putting your toe in the water...332
Creating your mini business plan....................................333
Having an entry plan that keeps the cash flowing.........334
Acting like the CEO you are..338
Getting business to come to you 339
But What If I Fail? 341

Part V: The Part of Tens 343

Chapter 14: Top Ten Career Musts for Women 345
Being Who You Are 345
Being Self-Effacing...346
Negotiating for Fair Pay..346
Competing Healthily 347
Balancing Work and Family...347
Harnessing Your Hormones 348
Getting Physical...349
Dressing Wisely 349
Flirting to Advantage 350
Dating in the Workplace without Disaster 350

Chapter 15: Top Ten Career Musts for Men 351

Consciously Decide Whether You Want
to Be the Primary Breadwinner 351
Consider Nontraditional Careers 352
Use the Power of Deep Connection 352
Temper "Male Energy" 352
Be Tactful and Listen Well...353
Mind Your Health 354
Flirt with Your Antennae Out...354
Don't Date Your Supervisee 355
React to Reverse Discrimination......................................355
Be Proud to Be a Man 356

Chapter 16: Top Ten (Or So) Career Musts for Everyone 357

Become a Master Communicator......................................357
Work Hard 358
Don't Overvalue Money..358
Prize Integrity 358
Become Beloved...359
Avoid Saboteurs 359
Ask for What You Want...360
Conquer Procrastination...360
Control Your Anger 361
Get a Mentor; Be a Mentor 361
Date Delicately...362
Always Look Forward 362

Appendix: The Cool Career Finder **363**

Index...**371**

Foreword

· ·

*T*here's a big, big world out there, with a lot of things to choose from. But you already know that, or you wouldn't be reading/browsing/eyeballing this book about cool careers. Hmmmm.

In the matter of choosing a career, there are thousands of possibilities for you to explore. You want, of course, to find someone who can cut the number of possibilities down to manageable size. Welcome to *Cool Careers For Dummies*, a veritable encyclopedia. It's just what you were looking for.

Encyclopedias of careers come in two forms. One form is that of a book or some related database. The other form is that of a person. Yep, some people are "walking encyclopedias." They know more about all the options that are available out there than ten other people put together. If you want to read a book that is a kind of all-encompassing encyclopedia of your options, be sure — always — that it is first of all written by a person who is a walking encyclopedia.

Marty Nemko, the author of this book, is just such a person. I have known Marty for years, and I am always amazed at all the things he knows, and knows about. Just read his "Yellow Pages," and you will see. The scope of his knowledge is breathtaking. He knows big facts and also little facts that no one else seems to know.

A walking encyclopedia isn't just concerned with information. A good walking encyclopedia is concerned with something deeper that I think we must call "wisdom." It involves selection, evaluation, matching, discrimination (in the good sense of that word), and large gobs of graciousness. Yep, that's Marty.

Read this book. Use this book. Study this book. You're in good hands, I guarantee you.

Richard N. Bolles, Author

*The 2007 What Color Is Your Parachute? A Practical Manual
for Job-Hunters & Career-Changers*
(9 million copies in print, updated annually)
The best-selling job-hunting book in the world

Introduction

A number of years ago, I heard about a little-known career called child life specialist. When children must go to the hospital for an extended stay, they're assigned a child life specialist to help them adapt to living without their parents.

When I told a client about this career, something happened that had rarely occurred with previous clients: her eyes lit up.

That helped me realize what people most want from career counseling: new options. So, I started collecting cool careers. Every time I heard of an interesting career, I added it to the list. I included unusual careers as well as neat niches within the popular careers. One example: lawyers who specialize in outer space issues. Plus, I included low-risk/high-payoff ideas for self-employment. After a few years, my list contained more than 500 careers.

This book contains a quick scoop on each of those careers. Each scoop focuses on the non-obvious insider information about that career and ends with a great Web site and/or book in case you want to learn more about that career.

The book also gives you, for free, the strategies that my private career counseling clients pay me big bucks for. These approaches have been the most helpful in choosing a career, in landing a job, and in making the most of it. I developed many of these strategies because, for many people, the standard career advice wasn't working.

And that's the book in a nutshell. Its ideas have helped many, many people find a cool career, including folks who were quite stuck. Whether you're looking for your first real job, thinking about changing careers, or considering self-employment, I know this book will help you — a lot.

About This Book

Although the previous editions of *Cool Careers For Dummies* received uniformly gratifying reviews, from the day the second edition was published, I've been working to ensure that this third edition is even better. In this edition, I do the following:

- ✔ Pack the book with advice aimed especially at people just starting out — two years on either side of graduation — and add plenty of tips for mid-career people and for Boomers.

- ✔ Provide new guidance for career searchers who simply don't have an overriding passion or skill.

- ✔ Add, to the *Cool Careers Yellow Pages* in Chapter 2, new, rewarding, viable careers and drop some that no longer measure up. Also, I enhance or update 95 percent of the career scoops that were in the previous edition.

- ✔ Completely rewrite the section on ahead-of-the-curve careers in the *Cool Careers Yellow Pages*. It's filled with ideas on how to get in on the ground floor of the next Big Things.

- ✔ Revise the *35 Most Revealing Questions* in Chapter 3 so that they're even more likely to reveal what you really want in your career.

- ✔ Improve the advice in Chapter 4 for the many people who have a hard time making the final decision — "Yes! This is the career I want to pursue."

- ✔ Improve Chapter 8, which distills what really works into a doable step-by-step plan.

- ✔ Add secrets to creating a winning resume in Chapter 9 — even if your work history isn't ideal.

- ✔ Enhance Chapter 11 on making any job better. Even more important than landing a good job is making the most of it. This chapter provides a step-by-step plan for making even a humdrum job much better. To whet your appetite, here's one component: "The 3-Minute MBA: The world's shortest management course."

- ✔ Streamline Chapter 12 on how to conquer procrastination.

- ✔ Add two new chapters about the top ten career truths for women and men (Chapters 14 and 15). Being a guy, I wasn't sure I was the right person to write the former, but I found the right person. She's a huge career success; for example, she was named her region's Schools Superintendent of the Year. Plus, she's a straight shooter, willing to tell you the things a woman normally tells only her own child. Oh, I should also mention that she's my wife: Dr. Barbara Nemko.

- ✔ Create special lists of great careers in the *Cool Career Finder* (the Appendix) for liberal arts graduates, Boomers, offshore-resistant job searchers, and even slackers.

Conventions Used in This Book

I use a few conventions to make your experience with this book as easy as possible:

- *Italics* highlight new terms and emphasize words.

- **Boldface** text indicates the keywords in bulleted lists and the action part of numbered steps.

- To draw your attention to Web sites, I set them in `monofont` — a font that looks like it came out of a typewriter.

- These days, even some cool sites have addresses so long they stretch to Kansas — well, at least beyond the end of the line. In those cases, I don't insert a hyphen to indicate the break. So, when using one of those Web addresses, just type in exactly what you see in this book. Pretend the line break doesn't even exist.

What You're Not to Read

I'd love to see you read every word in this book, but if you twist my arm, I have to admit that some of the words are less important than others:

- Sidebars, which are shaded in gray, are useful stand-alone material, but the world won't end if you skip them.

- The 500-plus career intros in the *Cool Careers Yellow Pages* in Chapter 2 are arranged in categories, such as careers with people. If your idea of nirvana is to work in isolation, you can certainly skip that section. Just read the sections that appeal to you.

- You can easily find and succeed in your cool career without reading the paragraphs marked with an Unconventional Wisdom icon. But they're mind-expanding and you probably won't find those ideas anywhere else.

Foolish Assumptions

Because you're reading this book, I assume

- You're still unsure what you want to be when you grow up — even if you already have gray hair. This book will help you get clear.

✔ You're not aspiring to a low-level job. This isn't the book for high school dropouts exploring options in manual labor. All work is worthy. Indeed, people willing to work on low-paying, boring, low-prestige jobs deserve great respect. But this isn't the book for them.

✔ You're reasonably intelligent, somewhere between bright and brilliant. Don't be fooled by the *For Dummies* title. These books are for intelligent people who don't want a drawn-out, painful learning experience. They want the important information, and they want it fast and enjoyable. That's what I try to give you.

✔ You're not easily offended. I sometimes write politically incorrect things. I'd rather offend you with the truth than anesthetize you with lies.

How This Book Is Organized

The chapters in this book are organized into five parts.

Part 1: Finding Your Cool Career, Right Here

Whether you've never had a career before or want to dump your old career for a new and improved one, this part is for you.

First, follow your heart. Browse the 500-plus careers in the *Cool Careers Yellow Pages* in Chapter 2 and simply pick out one or more that make your heart beat a little faster. Don't feel like browsing all 500? There's a quicker approach. I divide the careers into categories to make it easier to home in on the ones that are right for you.

Next, use your head. I ask you to list what's really important to you in a career. Don't know? Answer the *35 Most Revealing Questions* in Chapter 3.

Finally, blend head and heart. This part concludes with a virtual career coach. It simulates what I do with my private clients so that your final career choice makes sense *and* feels good.

Part II: Training for That Cool Career

Choosing a career is one thing; succeeding at it is something else. Often, a key to success is to be trained well. In this part, I show you how to find the right training for you and how to make the most of it. If a university seems like the right choice, I show you how to maximize your chances of admission to a great program and how to reap the maximum benefit from your training. But often, you can learn more at what I call *You University,* a custom mix of mentoring, articles, tapes, and live or online classes. I even show how You U. "graduates" can get hired over candidates with more degrees.

Part III: Landing That Cool Job

The standard advice — network, network, network — simply doesn't work for lots of people. They either don't have many contacts to network with or they're uncomfortable with schmoozing. This part shows you an effective way to land the job even if the thought of networking gives you the creeps and you don't have a 500-name Rolodex. For my clients, this approach has been invaluable. From creating a winning resume to knock-their-socks-off interviewing to staying motivated, this part covers it all.

Part IV: Making Any Career Cooler

When you buy a suit, it probably looks just okay off the rack. To really make it look good, it needs to be tailored and accessorized. The same is true with your career. This part shows you how to make any job better by tailoring it to your strengths and by using wise approaches with your boss and co-workers.

And if you're a procrastinator, you probably won't be after you finish reading Chapter 12. (Don't tell me you'll read it next year.)

Another approach to making your career cooler is to become self-employed. Chapter 13 takes the exciting but scary thought of being your own boss and shows you how to maximize your chances of success.

Part V: The Part of Tens

Many good ideas don't require long explanations. So here's where I plunk lots of good ideas that are self-explanatory: the top ten career truths for men, women, and everyone.

Finally, there's the appendix. It's called *The Cool Career Finder* — a way for you to find careers in nearly 20 categories, such as Cool Careers for Liberal Arts Grads, Offshore-Resistant Careers, Boomer-Friendly Careers, Make a Difference Careers, and even Cool Careers for Slackers.

Icons Used in This Book

There are some ideas I really don't want you to miss, so I mark them with one of these icons:

This book is filled with tips. These are important good ideas.

Bigger than a tip, these are key strategies for finding and landing a cool career.

Many people procrastinate on their career search if it's drudgery. So, over the years, I've kept track of approaches that are fun yet effective, and I put many of them in this book. This icon makes sure you don't miss them.

This icon lets me brag. These are the ideas I'm most proud of.

Avoid these common pitfalls and you probably won't bomb out.

Where to Go from Here

No need to read the book from start to finish. I write it so that you can skim the Table of Contents and simply start reading from the place that most intrigues you. For example, perhaps you'll want to start by browsing the *Cool Careers Yellow Pages* in Chapter 2 or by answering the *35 Most Revealing Questions* in Chapter 3. Of course, I believe you'll enjoy and profit from reading every word. (That's what every author thinks.) If you don't, e-mail me. I promise to respond and maybe incorporate your suggestion into the next edition.

Part I
Finding Your Cool Career, Right Here

The 5th Wave

By Rich Tennant

"When choosing a career I ignored my heart and did what my brain wanted. Now all my brain wants is Prozac."

In this part . . .

You've probably tried to choose your career — unsuccessfully, or you wouldn't have bought this book. The approach in this part was developed for people like you. I give you plenty of options to explore in the Cool Careers Yellow Pages and ask you 35 revealing questions to help you match a career to your talents, interests, and values. By the time you finish reading this part, chances are, you'll have found your cool career — and had fun in the process.

Chapter 1

Your Cool Career Journey

In This Chapter

▶ A morality tale on career planning

▶ Previewing your own career journey

*I*n this chapter, I give you an overview of what works as you find and enjoy your own cool career, but first, I show you what doesn't work.

Julie Seeks a Career: A Cautionary Tale

Sure, some people come out of the womb knowing what they want to be when they grow up — the 5-year-old violin prodigy comes to mind. But most people aren't so lucky — and they don't get much help.

Some parents tell you, "It's your life. You decide." Other parents go to the other extreme, expecting you to follow in their footsteps: "Hazardous waste disposal is a great career." Before you even learn how to tie your shoes, they're pushing: "Come on, let's visit Daddy's toxic waste dump."

In high school, you take a career test that asks what you're interested in. How the heck are you supposed to know? If you're like most teens, you spend most of your school life studying such career irrelevancies as the symbolism in *Romeo & Juliet,* quadratic equations, and the slave ships of 1628. After school, you play soccer and are forced to take piano lessons — a skill for which only your mother thinks you have talent. You spend summers at Camp Kowabonga, during which your career exploration consists of observing your counselor go postal. How in the world are you supposed to validly answer test questions about your career interests? It's little surprise that many high school students laugh at their career test results: forest ranger, funeral director, or "You could pursue a wide range of careers."

Many students remain undaunted. They figure that career clarity will come in college. Trouble is, most colleges proudly proclaim that their courses are *not* for career preparation but for general education. Worse, college courses are taught by professors — people who have deliberately opted out of the real world. So, many college students' career sights are limited.

As college graduation approaches, panic often sets in and the same students who procrastinated endlessly trying to ensure that they made the perfect career choice suddenly force themselves into a decision, often based on very little information. Their entire reasoning often fits on a bumper sticker:

- ✔ "I want to help people, so I'll be a doctor."
- ✔ "I'm lousy in science and I like to argue, so I'll go to law school."
- ✔ "I want to make a lot of money, so I'll go into business."
- ✔ "I don't know what I want to do, so I'll get a master's in something."

None of these reasons would work for Julie. She was sick of school. So she headed to her college's career center where she was pointed to a career library and encouraged to "explore."

That's inadequate guidance for most people. Julie did, however, fall into a job. Her cousin was the janitor at Western Widget Waxing, Inc., and put in a good word for Julie: "She has always been interested in widgets." Julie wrote a letter to Western Widget Waxing, Inc., that began, "I believe I'm well-suited for a career in the widget waxing industry." She got an interview. She wore that conservative suit she swore she'd never wear and told old WWW, Inc., that ever since childhood, she spent much of her spare time waxing widgets. She got the job.

Within days of starting at WWW, Julie realized that widget waxing wasn't all it was cracked up to be. Now what? Not surprisingly, WWW's human resources manager told Julie only about options in widget waxing. "Well, Julie, you *are* on track to becoming a widget waxing supervisor, and down the road, I think you have the potential to become a widget waxing director." On seeing Julie's face go flat, the manager tried, "Well, you could join our sales department. Would you like to sell widget waxing? How about the accounting department? Shipping? Well, what *do* you want, Julie?" That was the problem. Julie hadn't a clue.

In desperation, Julie decided to seek help from a professional — even though it used up the money she'd been saving for that vacation. "What's a thousand bucks if it can land me a cool career?"

Alas, when Julie showed up at her appointment with the career counselor, there were those tests again.

> **Counselor:** Well, Julie, on the Myers-Briggs Type Indicator, you're an INFP. That means you're an intraverted, intuitive, feeling perceiver.

> **Julie:** So what should I do for a career?

> **Counselor:** Julie, you can't rush this. That would be premature foreclosure. We need to review the results of the Campbell Interest and Skills Survey. You're an RIC. That stands for realistic-investigative-conventional. Let's interpret that.

> **Julie:** So what should I do for a career?

> **Counselor:** Well, Julie, use the information you've learned about yourself from the Myers-Briggs Type Indicator and from the Campbell Interest and Skills Survey by exploring in the career library.

> **Julie:** Noooooooh, not again!

Instead, Julie returned to Western Widget Waxing, Inc.

Too often, career counseling is like psychoanalysis: You gain insight into yourself but your life is no better.

One day, Julie heard about a book called *Find Your Career Joy While Doing What You Love and the Money Will Come While Your Flower Opens*. So off Julie trotted to the bookstore, and although daunted by the book's thickness and its 66 worksheets, she figured it was only $19.99 — the cost of two movie tickets. Such a deal. Julie bit.

Five years later, our hero was still on worksheet #4. Her father, her friends, and even her hairstylist were asking her, "Well, Julie, what *are* you going to be when you grow up?" Julie decided to get serious. She pulled out her aging copy of *Find Your Career Joy While Doing What You Love and the Money Will Come While Your Flower Opens* and actually managed to complete all 66 worksheets. This gave her a complete inventory of her skills, interests, values, job requirements, personality attributes, and inter-ocular focal length.

But doing all that still didn't tell Julie how to figure out which career fits best.

I swear I'm not exaggerating. Even the best-selling career guides don't take you through that crucial next step: showing you which careers fit your skills, interests, and values. The guides state or imply that if you do all their worksheets, you'll somehow divine your dream career.

Julie cried, and Julie stayed on at Western Widget Waxing, Inc. "Maybe I *am* meant to be in widget waxing," she told herself. She worked hard, and indeed the human resources manager's prediction came to pass. Julie became director of Widget Waxing. But still she wasn't happy.

Then Julie was sure she found a solution: the computer. WWW, Inc., benevolent firm that it is, bought a career-finding software program and made it available to its employees. Julie was first in line. A couple of hours and voilà, 15 best-fit careers popped out. Some of the careers made sense but didn't excite her enough to make her quit her now-comfortable job at WWW to go back and get retrained for a profession she wasn't even sure she'd end up liking better. After all, Julie had become a director and was vested in WWW's retirement plan. A few of the generated careers did excite Julie, but they were careers that excite too many people — TV broadcasting, for example. So what if Julie would love to anchor the nightly news? So would half the continent.

Although Julie didn't know it, many computer programs often fail for another reason. They eliminate careers if the career seeker lacks even one ostensibly necessary skill or personality trait. In the real world, many careers don't have such rigid skill and personality requirements. Take book editors, for example. Some succeed primarily because of their aesthetic sense, others because of their feel for the bottom line. And aren't some editors introverts, others extroverts? Even if Julie lacked a key attribute, if she found a career that excited her, she may well have been willing and able to put the energy into compensating for her weakness. But the computer program never gave her the chance.

Krishna Rama (*nee* Julie) now resides at the Harmonic Transcendent Monastery in Berkeley, California, hoping to find career nirvana through meditation.

All jokes aside (at least for the moment), despite taking career tests, plowing through fat career guides, and/or meditating, many people end up falling into their careers more by chance than by choice. Not a good way to ensure career happiness. There has to be a better way.

There is. Read on.

Taking Your Own Journey

There are two ways to use this book. You can simply flip to a chapter that intrigues you and start there. Or you can let me be your virtual career coach. After reading the overview in the following sections, just turn the page and I'll take you by the hand and walk you through what, for most people, is the most successful way to go from career clueless to career contentment. Reading this book all the way through simulates what my private clients pay me big bucks for.

Discovering your cool career

Here's what you and I can do together to start your journey:

1. Our first hour or two will be especially exciting. In browsing Chapter 2's *Cool Careers Yellow Pages,* you discover fascinating information about 500 cool careers and self-employment opportunities. Even on the off chance that none of those 500 appeal to you, you understand the world more richly than you ever have before. But chances are good that one or more careers will call out to you.

2. I ask you the *35 Most Revealing Questions* in Chapter 3. Over my 20 years as a career counselor/coach, I've tried zillions of questions to tease out my clients' core skills, interests, values, and desires. These 35 are the ones that have been most revealing.

3. By this point, you likely have come up with one or more careers that intrigue you. Not so fast. Before committing to a career, you deserve to know more about it. So, in Chapter 4, I show you the smartest ways to learn more about a career. If, after that, you're still unsure, I help you gain the courage to make a decision.

If, after completing these three steps, you're still unsure of what career to choose, I've learned, over the years, that it's far wiser to choose the best of the options you've considered than to wait on the sidelines hoping for something better to come along. By choosing something, and then getting the best training, and doing a competent job search so that you can unearth a good job offer, you'll probably be further along on the path toward a cool career than if you took more career tests, visited a career library yet again, or even worked with a career counselor/coach like me.

Finding the best training for your needs

In Chapters 5 and 6, I show you how to choose the right training program and make the most of it. Feeling like an expert is more central to believing you're in a cool career than the career itself. I've seen people who have ostensibly cool careers — for example, actors — who are miserable, because deep down, they're not sure they're that good. On the other hand, I've seen plumbers who think they're in a cool career, largely because they know they can handle virtually any problem they're likely to face.

Getting a cool job

The part of career-finding that most people hate is looking for a job. Some people will procrastinate until they're homeless instead of sitting down to start the job hunt. So, in the next part of our journey, I do everything I can to make that job search easy and pleasant. I start, in Chapter 7, by helping you get into the right mindset — by the time you're through, you'll practically laugh at getting rejected. In Chapter 8, I lay out the plan, step by step. I show you how to create a great resume in just a few hours (see Chapter 9), and the secrets of impressive interviewing — even if you've been slacking on your parents' sofa for the last two years. (Chapter 10 has the full scoop on interviewing.)

Making the most of your new career

The last step in your journey is probably the most important. Choosing your career carefully and then not making the most of it is like giving the gas station attendant $20 but putting only $10 of gas in your tank. I show you how to take your off-the-shelf career and tailor and accessorize it to fit you. And I equip you with skills critical in nearly every career: for example, people skills so outstanding that you become beloved (see Chapter 11), overcoming procrastination (see Chapter 12), and the art of being entrepreneurial (see Chapter 13).

Okay. Onward to what may be one of your life's most exciting journeys.

Chapter 2

The Cool Careers Yellow Pages

● ●

In This Chapter

▶ Using the *Cool Careers Yellow Pages* effectively

▶ Discovering many great career options

▶ Finding out what's on the leading (but not bleeding) edge

● ●

*T*he first step in finding your career may be the most fun: browsing the *Cool Careers Yellow Pages*. It gives you a fast yet substantive introduction to more than 500 good careers, including many unlikely suspects.

What Makes a Cool Career Cool?

Competition for a spot in the *Cool Careers Yellow Pages* was fierce. First, a career had to be one of the following:

✔ A popular career

✔ A little-known niche within a popular career

✔ A little-known career

✔ A self-employment opportunity that seems to have a high reward/risk ratio

I narrowed down the careers further by selecting the highest scorers overall on these criteria:

✔ Potential to make a difference in society

✔ Potential for at least a middle-class income

✔ A good job market

Using the Cool Careers Yellow Pages

You have three options when you peruse the *Cool Careers Yellow Pages:*

- **The Very Busy Person's Approach.** To make it easy to home in on the right career for you, I divide the career profiles into categories. Scan the careers in the category that seems to best fit you (for example, *careers with people and words*), read the profiles of just the few careers that jump out at you, and pick the career that seems most on-target. A tentative career in ten minutes! (Of course, even the busiest person should check that career out in greater detail. So, each career's profile ends with one or more Web sites or books that enable you to do that.) Most of those books are too specialized to be carried in your local bookstore, but most are available at www.amazon.com.

  You can also learn a lot about a career simply by googling the career name and the word "careers." So, for example, if you want to know more about a career in geology, just enter "geology careers" into the search engine at google.com.

  Want another superbusy person's approach to homing in on the right career? This book's appendix contains special lists of careers: for example, the careers most likely to impress your family, easy-to-transition-into careers, careers that are too much fun to be work, those offering the surest routes to big bucks, and the careers most likely to improve society. You could start by browsing the careers on one of those lists.

- **The Busy Person's Approach.** Zoom into a couple of categories and read just those profiles. A tentative career in 20 minutes!

- **The Wisest Approach.** The career profiles are short and pleasant to read, so it's wise to read 'em all. Who knows? Your dream career could be in a category you wouldn't have picked. Besides, at the risk of immodesty, I'm confident you'll enjoy reading this chapter and learn a lot about the world in the process. A woman who had bought this book's second edition for her son e-mailed me to say she couldn't stop reading the *Cool Careers Yellow Pages* even though she wasn't looking for a career.

The categories

A career can require skill with *people,* with *data,* with *words,* and/or with *things.* In the *Yellow Pages,* I categorize the careers accordingly. For example, the attorney profile is in the "Words/People" category. Most attorneys must excel at using words and must also have good people skills.

Puhleeze, don't treat a career's category as gospel. The individual job you land may be different. For example, one lawyer may mainly write contracts, in which case he doesn't need exceptional people skills. Another reason not to take the categories too seriously is that many careers fall on the border between two categories. They could easily fit in another category.

The icons

Sometimes, a picture is worth 1,000 words. Not so with these pictures; thcy'rc worth maybe three or four.

Each career profile is accompanied by an education icon. It represents the typical minimum that an average employer requires. Some job openings require more than that minimum, but, occasionally, a candidate is impressive enough to be hired with less. Before choosing a career, verify the current education requirements in your locale.

 No degree required. Training may involve an on-the-job program, an apprenticeship, or a certificate program.

 Some college required, usually a two-year degree.

 Bachelor's degree required.

 Master's or other post-bachelor's — but not doctoral — education required.

 Doctoral degree required.

Some icons denote things other than education requirements:

 Careers marked with this icon have significant self-employment potential.

 A career in which being older is often a plus.

 Careers marked with this icon are profiled in-depth in the Occupational Outlook Handbook, an authoritative government source available in most libraries, and online at www.bls.gov/oco.

Taking the road less traveled

The *Cool Careers Yellow Pages* covers the popular professions, such as doctor, lawyer, and psychologist, but as you know, those careers require years of graduate school. Many people in those fields believe their education failed to prepare them for their career despite the enormous cost and years of effort. Before committing to all that schooling, know that many people find great career satisfaction and acceptable income in similar careers that don't require you to spend so many of your peak years behind a student desk. Examples:

- ✔ Aspire to be a doctor? Physician assistants and nurse practitioners realize most of a doctor's benefits: They command a healthy salary, get to diagnose and treat patients, and because they rarely treat serious illnesses, most of their patients get well.

- ✔ Leaning toward the law? Consider becoming a mediator: less confrontational work, fewer ethical temptations, and shorter training.

- ✔ See yourself as a psychologist? Personal coaches not only train for a shorter time but because they deal with healthier people, they also see more progress.

- ✔ Aspire to be an executive? It's a long hard road. And in today's flatter hierarchy, an ever-smaller percentage of aspiring executives ever get past middle management. That often means long hours and little power. Instead, consider owning your own small business, where you get to instantly catapult yourself from schlepper to CEO (with no MBA required).

So in addition to the popular high-status professions (which *are* covered in the *Cool Careers Yellow Pages*), consider checking out the *Yellow Pages'* many other careers.

Okay, enough preliminaries. Enjoy.

Work with People

Caretaking and coaching

Mediator. Traditionally, the way that divorcing husbands and wives avoid killing each other is by hiring two attorneys and letting the lawyers slug it out. That's expensive, adversarial, and often, just plain yucky. An ever-more popular alternative is to hire a mediator. Don't like divorce mediation? Tackle employment cases — before going to trial, most wrongful termination suits must be mediated. Lawyers generally are chosen to mediate complicated fact-centered disputes while counselor-types more often are used when emotional issues are at the core. Whether a lawyer or counselor, a really good mediator needs the listening skills of a suicide counselor, the patience of Job, the wisdom of Solomon, and, alas, the marketing skills of P. T. Barnum. *Mediation Information:* www.mediate.com *Meditation Resource Center:* www.nolo.com/resource.cfm/catID/B21C6122-6654-468C-83A6D0B4B74D37CD/104/308/239.

Geriatric Care Manager. Imagine you have aging parents living in another city. They need help dealing with the healthcare system, finding someone to look in on them, or completing paperwork. You'd help out if you were local, but you're not. An answer? Hire a geriatric care manager. *U.S. News* tells of geriatric care manager Pat Gleason. She "has dozens of 'adopted' grandparents. As she makes the rounds to private homes and nursing facilities in Texas, she is showered with hugs and kisses from clients she helps with the problems of aging. It may be a woman recovering from a broken hip who needs help making her home easier to navigate, or a widower having trouble rebuilding a social life . . . One job perk, she says, is free history lessons, such as the stories she heard from a 104-year-old about crossing the Oklahoma Territory in a covered wagon." Don't want to be self-employed? Some hospitals and HMOs also hire geriatric care managers. *National Association of Professional Geriatric Care Managers:* www.caremanager.org.

Psychotherapist/Psychologist. Not long ago, experts thought that schizophrenia, autism, and depression were caused by bad parenting. So countless patients and their families were subjected to years of fruitless psychotherapy. Now, it's clearer that these and many other psychological problems have largely physiological roots. That will increase the need for physicians trained in psychology but reduce the need for psychologists focused on the psyche. Nevertheless, for now at least, demand for psychotherapists remains solid. More health plans are covering psychotherapy visits because it's tough to cope with life's ever-greater demands and because new therapies *are* more effective. For example, brief solution-oriented therapy, sometimes combined with new drugs, is rapidly replacing prolonged analysis of childhood angst. New trend: e-counseling. Compared with in-person or by-phone counseling, the client can take more time to reflect on the therapist's questions. *Wikipedia entry:* en.wikipedia.org/wiki/psychotherapy. *Jeffrey Kottler's book: What You Never Learned in Graduate School: A Survival Guide for Therapists.*

My experience getting a PhD in educational psychology from Berkeley and then teaching at four different graduate schools has convinced me that psychologist training programs have been padded into doctorate-length marathons: It's not because there's so much that aspiring psychologists need to know, but because universities make more money the longer students are in school.

And grad students are free or low-cost research slaves for professors. If you're considering a career as a psychologist, ask yourself whether you want to endure that. Then consider whether a career as a personal coach (which I cover later in this chapter) may be less demanding and more fulfilling.

That said, the following niches, which don't attempt to radically remold people the way traditional psychotherapy does, are, in my view, among the most likely to be rewarding:

(Neat Niche) **Relationship Acceptance Therapist.** Couples counseling apparently works best when it helps partners learn to accept each other as they are instead of trying to change each other. (This makes sense. How easy is it to make *you* change?) A study found that after just six months of acceptance therapy, 90 percent of couples considering divorce reported "dramatic" increases in satisfaction and none split up. *Andrew Christensen's book: Reconcilable Differences.*

(Neat Niche) **Men's Therapist.** The number of therapists for women and people of color have long been increasing. Now men are starting to seek counselors specializing in men's issues. *Mensight magazine: www.men sightmagazine.com. The National Men's Resource: www.menstuff.org. Glenn Good's book: The New Handbook of Psychotherapy and Counseling with Men, Revised Edition.*

(Neat Niche) **Infant Mental Health Counselor.** This career emerged because more and more children are born with severe mental or physical problems, or into homes with parents ill-equipped to be parents. The infant counselor advises parents on how to bring up a challenging baby while retaining their sanity. *The Infant Mental Health Specialist: www.zerotothree.org/ vol21-2s.pdf. World Association for Infant Mental Health: www.msu.edu/ user/waimh.*

(Neat Niche) **Money Counselor.** Some people hoard money, others spend it too fast; Boomers can't discuss it with their aging parents. Enter the money counselor. In my favorite incarnation of this career, you first help your client understand the cause of his money problem and, in turn, develop a plan to cure it. Then, if the client is deeply in debt, you negotiate for him, asking creditors for reductions in interest and penalties. Sometimes, creditors will even pay you a percentage of any debt payments you submit to them. *Myvesta: www.myvesta.org. National Foundation for Credit Counseling: www.nfcc.org. Olivia Mellan's book: The Advisor's Guide to Money Psychology.*

(Neat Niche) **School Psychologist.** This can be a great job: nine-month year, high status, no undue stress. Typical project: Johnny is doing lousy in school. What should school and parents do? In comes the school psychologist: Observe the kid; test him; pow-wow with parent, teacher, kid, and special education teacher; and write jargon-filled report. School psychologists may also conduct parenting workshops and screen students for gifted students programs. *National Association of School Psychologists: www.nasponline.org. Kenneth Merrell's book: School Psychology for the 21st Century.*

Alas, programs for gifted students are being dismantled. Why do slow learners have the right to special, expensive instruction, and psychological and other services, but gifted students, with so much potential to contribute to society and who often flounder without attention, increasingly get zilch?

(Neat Niche) **Consulting Psychologist.** A dentist is losing patients and terrifying others. Maybe she's just a bad dentist, but it could be she doesn't know the art of calming patients. A consulting psychologist teaches the dentist how to calm her patients. Another example: a psychologist may teach a lawyer how to tease out honest responses from clients and deponents. *Society of Consulting Psychology: www.apa.org/divisions/div13.*

(Neat Niche) **Sports Psychologist.** A golfer has trouble concentrating. A pitcher freaks out under pressure. Teammates hate each other's guts. Enter the sports psychologist. *The American Psychological Association's Division of Sports Psychology: www.psyc.unt.edu/apadiv47. Robert Weinberg's book: Foundations of Sport and Exercise Psychology, 4th Edition.*

(Neat Niche) **Forensic Psychologist.** Is he sane enough to deserve the death penalty? Rehabilitated enough to be released into society? Competent enough to manage his own affairs without a conservator? More worthy of being the custodial parent? Was the death a disguised suicide to let the beneficiaries cash in on an insurance policy? Forensic psychologists address those sorts of questions. *The Forensic Psychologist: www.geocities.com/athens/7429/forensicpsychprep.html.*

College Student Advisor. In years past, professors advised the students, but colleges have realized that professors are more interested in and knowledgeable about their own research than about what courses Jill should take. So, many colleges now hire counselor types to advise undergraduates. Sometimes, it's just a matter of reviewing a transcript and suggesting courses, but with the amount of career-planning and personal malaise that many college students feel, it often goes well beyond. *National Academic Advising Association: www.nacada.ksu.edu. Virginia Gordon's book: Academic Advising.*

Personal Coach. Do you like to help others but would rather deal with problems easier to address than reconstructing a personality? Personal coaching is some combination of goal-setting advisor, time-management consultant, motivator, sounding board, confidant, dream-builder, image instructor, and cheerleader — everything but going back and discussing the childhood causes of one's malaise. The emphasis is on problem solving — what are you going to do to solve this *now?* Some psychotherapists, who practice cognitive or rational-emotive therapy, do those things, but personal coaches can be adequately trained in far less time. Alas, coaches must market heavily to get clients — there seems to be a coach under every rock. Coaching is increasingly done by phone. Some even coach via e-mail for the clients who prefer having time to reflect on the coach's question before answering. *International Coaches Federation: www.coachfederation.org. Coach U: www.coachu.com. Choice magazine: www.choice-online.com. Julie Starr's book: Coaching Manual.*

(Neat Niche) **Career Coach/Counselor.** Here, I get to write about my own career. The part I like best is helping people make the most of their current jobs — I'm successful with nearly all those clients. Unfortunately, most people hire a career counselor to help them get a different job. And here I have mixed feelings. With students and new college graduates, it's still fine. I help them identify new options and develop a plan to get hired, and it usually works. But many older people come in wanting to change careers, and my success rate and that of other career counselors I've spoken with is low. Few midlifers who say they want a new career end up being willing to put in the time and effort necessary to make it happen. The third type of client wants help landing a job. I find this work a little boring because it's mechanical: cranking out a resume and teaching the client how to win the job-hunt game. More important, I dislike that part of my job because I believe it actually makes the world a worse place: My task is basically to make my clients look their best to employers. That gives my clients an unfair advantage over uncoached candidates who may in fact be more qualified. So I refer most such clients to a hand-picked colleague.

That said, a lot of things are great about my job. I work one-on-one in a peaceful environment — my home. I get to hear people's life stories — fun. I get to wear many hats: counselor, idea generator, marketer, cheerleader, chastiser. I improve people's worklives and often help them make a bigger difference in the world than they otherwise would have. If you want to be a career counselor, here's what it takes: You must be credible yet not intimidating, and optimistic yet realistic. You must also be a perceptive listener, know a lot about the world of work, be able to motivate people to act, and know how to use the Internet's myriad career resources. Private practice can work if you're willing to self-promote, especially if you pick a niche: teachers, lawyers, middle-age men, whatever. If you're averse to marketing yourself, some of the best jobs are at college career centers. *The book you're reading constitutes a summary of my style of career coaching. A book presenting a more traditional approach is Howard Figler's and Richard Bolles's Career Counselor's Handbook. National Career Development Association: www.ncda.org.*

(Neat Niche) **Time Management Coach.** When someone asks, "How are you?" the answer is as likely to be "Swamped" as "Fine." Enter the time-management coach — the person who tries to help wring 25 hours from a 24-hour day. Many people and employers willingly pay for that kind of advice. Marketing tip: Conduct time-management seminars in workplaces. That generates a fee and helps you recruit individual clients. Start preparing for this career by doing the equivalent of writing a term paper. Read a few books and articles on time-management, do a Web search, and write down potentially useful strategies so that you have plenty of different strokes for different folks. Then do a few freebie consultations for friends. *First, check out the time-efficiency section of this book in Chapter 11. Stephen Covey's book: The 7 Habits of Highly Effective People. Alec MacKenzie's book: The Time Trap. Google "time management coaching" to get a sense of what various time management coaches do.*

(Neat Niche) **Simplification Coach.** More people are recognizing that overly materialistic, hypercomplicated lives make for a worse existence. Some people may have no choice, like the 55-year-old executive with a stay-at-home spouse and a fat mortgage who's still paying for two kids in college. Even if a person has a choice, it's tough to get off the treadmill. Most people are conditioned to try (rarely successfully) to buy their way into happiness. A simplification coach can help. You help your clients evaluate every aspect of their lives: "If you opted out of the materialistic lifestyle, could you pursue a career you'd enjoy more? Will that home remodel truly be worth the hassle, cost, and resultant financial insecurity? Should you build in more time for just relaxing? Would your child benefit from a less packed after-school schedule? *Michael Sheffield's Simplicity Coaching: www.simplicitycoaching.com. Linda Pierce's book: Simplicity Lessons.*

(Neat Niche) **Parenting Coach.** Whether they have a newborn or an adult child who just moved back home, many parents worry that they're not good enough at parenting. They don't want a therapist; they just want help in getting their pride and joy to not drive them crazy. You can market to individual parents, for example, by offering free seminars at PTA meetings. Too, school districts and social service organizations may hire parenting coaches. Subniches: sleep consultant, potty trainer, adult child slacker coach. *Search "parenting coaching" at google.com to get a sense of what different parenting coaches do.*

(Neat Niche) **Shyness Coach.** Many people are painfully shy. Coaching them is a largely untapped market. You role-play stressful situations with clients and help them realize that the worst-case scenario isn't so bad or so likely. New evidence suggests that shyness often has a physiological component, so improvement may be modest, but even that is often worthwhile. *Wikipedia entry: en.wikipedia.org/wiki/shyness.*

(Neat Niche) **Dating Coach.** You start by helping your clients figure out who the right sort of romantic partner for them would be and where such people are most likely to be found. Next, you help them with initial interactions: for example, writing a match.com ad or teaching them the art of flirting in a supermarket. Role-play the first date, and then "double date" with them, debriefing afterward. Finally, help them develop the ability to turn a great first date into a serious relationship. *David Wygant's book: Always Talk to Strangers. Romy Miller's book: Understanding Women: The Definitive Guide to Meeting, Dating and Dumping, If Necessary. Ellen Fein's book: Rules II. Joy Browne's book: Dating For Dummies, 2nd Edition.*

(Neat Niche) **Image Coach.** "Are you a winter, spring, summer, or fall?" As an image consultant, you may start by picking out their clients' colors, but you'll probably move on to helping them select their clothes, makeup, and maybe even posture and interaction style. New subniche: Teaching people the art of walking into a meeting or party. Image consultants are popular because primping up one's image is a relatively painless way to get an edge at work and at play. The freshly divorced, for example, are often eager to present a new persona. Market your services by offering seminars for singles groups or for an organization's employees. Or convince a corporation's HR department to hire you to spruce up all employees who want an image assessment and upgrade. Neat niches: enginerds, singles older than 50, those who wear plus sizes, employees in a specific field. *Association of Image Consultants International:* `www.aici.org`.

(Neat Niche) **Executive Coach.** Many executives are just a beat off. They're a bit too intense, too detail oriented, too something. Companies or the executives themselves hire coaches to help underperforming execs get into the rhythm. You may help them on such matters as posture, body language, speaking style, etiquette, nonverbal communication, running a meeting, and business protocol. *Harvard Business School's article on executive coaching:* `hbswk.hbs.edu/archive/4853.html`. *Stephen Fairley's book: Getting Started in Personal and Executive Coaching.*

(Neat Niche) **Retirement Coach.** Boomers are entering retirement age, many with trepidation. They may need to plan on living another 30 years but have only saved for a fraction of that. Work is central to their identity and even with a bit of part-time work and volunteering, they worry they'll feel out-to-pasture. Couples in retirement suddenly find themselves spending more time together and may not like each other so much anymore. Enter the retirement coach, who may assist in financial planning, helping the client figure out how to fill days, and/or readjusting to seeing the spouse 24/7. *Jan Cullinane's book: The New Retirement.*

Organizer. Work and homelives are increasingly complicated and cluttered, so it's no surprise that the demand for organizers is growing. Marketing tip: Contact HR directors at nearby businesses. Suggest they hire you to do "organizing makeovers" for any employees who feel they need it. Repeat business is likely because, generally, once a slob, always a slob. Tell your clients that, just as they get their teeth cleaned regularly, they need you to clean house (don't forget the garage) regularly. Since 1993, membership has more than doubled in the *National Association of Professional Organizers:* `www.napo.net`. *Julie Morgenstern's book: Organizing from the Inside Out.*

Doula. The most exhausting period in many women's lives is labor and childbirth, and the first weeks after birth. Throughout, the *doula* is there to provide pain-decreasing techniques from breathing techniques to different positions, from massage to aromatherapy. Doulas also provide much needed emotional support and advice for moms (and dads?) before, during, and sometimes after the birth. Some evidence suggests that doula-assisted births result in shorter labor, fewer Caesarean and forceps births, and less need for pain medications. Doulas of North America has seen membership grow from 85 in 1992 to 6,000 today. *Doulas of North America:* www.dona.com.

Literary, Artist's, or Performer's Agent. Most artistic types aren't entrepreneurial. Left to their own devices, they'd hang out, practice their craft, and the checks would somehow arrive in the mail. The agent's job is to make that happen. Agents help polish the sample product, pitch it to prospective buyers, and negotiate the deal for 10 to 15 percent of the take. Why is being an agent a cool career? You get to pick out and then champion the talented people you want to represent, work closely with them to ensure their product is well packaged, and help them reach as large an audience as possible. Plus, being an agent requires no formal credentials. Most agents learn the business as an agent's assistant or as a talent buyer — acquisitions editor for a publishing company, for example. *North American Performing Arts Managers and Agents:* www.napama.org. *Association of Authors Representatives:* www.aar-online.org. *Tony Martinez's book: An Agent Tells All.*

Social Worker. Many people and families just can't make it without help. A child is abused; an older adult has Alzheimer's disease; a single parent with eight children, on top of it all, gets AIDS. Few jobs are more intimate and human than the social worker's. Despite the frustrations and low pay, most social workers who make it past the first two years like their jobs. After all, part of their job is to give away cash, rent subsidies, child-care, food stamps, health services, job training, and other resources, compliments of taxpayers. And pay isn't as bad as it used to be, averaging about $50,000. Social work remains one of the last professions with excellent job security: More than half of social workers work for the government, it's not a job that can be sent offshore, and it's hard to foresee the need for social workers declining. Many social workers are, however, employed by HMOs or private agencies such as the Red Cross, or are in private practice. This is one of the many careers in which the training requirements have been ratcheted up: Now, a master's degree is usually required. *National Association of Social Workers:* www.socialworkers.org. *The New Social Worker Online:* www.socialworker.com. *Linda May Grobman's book: Days in the Lives of Social Workers.*

Employee Assistance Professional. Workers show up with problems: drug abuse, prone to violence, in financial disarray, or with eldercare needs. Employee assistance professionals coordinate programs to help. On the prevention side, EAPs may establish physical fitness programs, sponsor workshops on time management or career planning, and even arrange carpools. *Employee Assistance Professional Association:* www.eap-association.com. *Mark Attridge's book: The Integration of Employee Assistance, Work/Life, and Wellness Services.*

Victim Assistant. Imagine that you've just been assaulted. Upon reporting the crime — if you're fortunate — you're introduced to a victim assistant. This person provides you with emotional and practical support all the way through trial and is your liaison with the district attorney. Victim assistants work for social service agencies, courts, or in private practice. *Victim-Assistance Online: www.vaonline.org. National Association for Victim Assistance: www.try-nova.org.*

Bail Bond Investigator (Bounty Hunter). Few tasks are riskier than going after criminals on the run. Believe it or not, the police are often too busy to find them. That's where bail bond investigators come in. First, you must track down leads. Computers help, but the ability to find snitches is key. (One woman bailed her grandson out of jail by posting her house as a bond, but he skipped town, and guess who turned him in? Dear ol' grandma.) An unsurpassed adrenaline rush comes in the actual chase and takedown — many people who skip bail won't go back to jail without a fight. So, it's not surprising that successful bail bond investigators can earn a six-figure income. (I wouldn't do it for seven figures.) *Premiere Bounty Hunter School and Training Center: www.beabountyhunter.com.*

Child Life Specialist. Imagine that your child is told she has a serious illness and must suddenly move from home into a hospital for a long stay filled with painful treatments. The child life specialist's job is to help children adapt to living without their parents and to psychologically prepare them for scary medical encounters. Child life specialists also help ensure that these kids get an education and a bit of fun in their lives. *Child Life Council: www.childlife.org. Richard Thompson's book: Child Life in Hospitals.*

School Guidance Counselor. The modern version of this job is much more complicated than dealing with kids kicked out of class for chewing gum. School counselors may coordinate sex education, health awareness, career counseling, gang violence prevention, and on-site social work services. And yes, counselors still spend a lot of time telling Johnny that he better shape up or else. The quality of these jobs varies. Some end up being more clerk than counselor. *American School Counselor Association: www.schoolcounselor.org. John Schmidt's book: A Survival Guide for the Elementary/Middle School Counselor.*

Nanny. The training is short; the task is doable, often pleasurable; and you may get to work in an environment most people only dream about: a wealthy person's home. That's not a bad combination, even if the pay is low. If you're good with kids, you won't have trouble finding a job. With the increase in single parents, and with two-parent families working full time, even many middle-class people find that a nanny is a must. The key to enjoying nannyhood is to get hooked up with a great family. Attending nanny school maximizes your chances. Why? Because many desirable families search for their nannies by contacting nanny schools. *International Nanny Association: www.nanny.org. Jo Frost's book: Supernanny: How to Get the Best from Your Children.*

Child-Care Center Owner. As the number of single parents and families with two working parents grows, so does the need for child-care centers. To succeed, worry less about creating a fancy facility or even having lots of toys and equipment. What's key is to be or hire a child-care provider(s) with that ineffable ability to make children love them. Of course, child-care providers must also be responsible and have an ever-watchful eye — young children can do all sorts of dangerous things. My mother told me that as a toddler, I had a habit of eating carpet fuzz. *National Child Care Information Center: www. nccic.org. National Association of Child Care Professionals: www.naccp.org.*

Personal Assistant. According to *the New York Post,* a typical day in the life of Olympia Dukakis's personal assistant consists of rendering a second opinion on a movie contract, dropping off her dry cleaning, picking up her dog's gourmet dog food, and suggesting ideas for marketing Dukakis's salad dressing. Salaries range from $30,000 to $100,000, plus perks like concert tickets and traveling first class. Of course, not just celebrities need assistants. These days, just about any busy person could use one. Niches: executives, college presidents, wealthy widows, and your run-of-the-mill busy middle incomer. Sometimes, the job may be more like an office assistant — word-processing a report, coordinating a project, and handling the bookkeeping — but Beth Berg made a good living with none of that. She started "Dial a Wife." She plans the meal, waits for the plumber, takes Junior (and his friends) to soccer, perhaps plants your herb garden, and even does the initial house hunting. Sounds like a traditional wife, but she gets paid $50 an hour. Berg's first ad simply said, "Buy time." *Dionne Muhammad's book: Beyond The Red Carpet: Keys To Becoming a Successful Personal Assistant.*

(Neat Niche) **Virtual Assistant.** This is an option for someone who wants to, at home, use administrative skills, such as word-processing, database management, Internet searching, travel arranging, and bookkeeping. Of course, virtual assisting is especially appealing if you have a disability, you want a portable business because your spouse's career requires frequent moving, or simply because you love the idea of being able to play in your garden during the day. There's no commute and no office politics. A *Newsweek* article describes this career as an administrative assistant without a boss looking over your shoulder. *International Virtual Assistants Association: www.ivaa.org. Training: www.assistu.com.*

Concierge. Marcia's concierge service, operating in the lobbies of residential and office buildings, helps inhabitants with life's mundane tasks, such as picking up dry cleaning, returning videos, and taking cars in for oil changes. Marcia can often get employers to pay for her services because they know that many employees sneak time off work to take care of life's necessities. In hiring Marcia, the boss gets full use of the employees and grateful workers as a bonus. *Wikipedia entry: en.wikipedia.org/wiki/concierge. Article, How to Be a Personal Concierge: www.entrepreneur.com/startingabusiness/ businessideas/startupkits/article37930.html. You're a What? Corporate Concierge: www.bls.gov/opub/ooq/2002/spring/yawhat.htm*

Bringing people together

Personnel Recruiter. Forget about the image of the recruiter coming onto campus to recruit applicants. Today's recruiter starts before jobs are even advertised. He develops ongoing relationships with the sorts of people the employer is likely to hire. For example, a company that uses Java programmers may routinely post tips and tricks on online Java discussion groups to elicit positive feelings toward the recruiter. When a job opens, the recruiter posts it on the Web and sets up software to screen applicants. Increasingly, he conducts interviews by phone, online, or even webcam. Job growth is fastest in temp agencies. *Wikipedia entry:* `en.wikipedia.org/wiki/recruiter`. *Michael Foster's book: Recruiting on the Web.*

(Neat Niche) **Employment Interviewer.** You've been on the other side of the table: "Mr. Job Applicant, why do you want to work for this company?" You think, "Because I'm desperate. I'll work anywhere." You answer, "Because I'm impressed with your fine line of products." How'd you like a career in which *you're* the interviewer? Employment agencies hire interviewers to screen applicants, prep them for interviews, and then pitch them to prospective employers. Don't like the selling part? Work for a company or the government. Your job is simply to match applicants with the available openings. *Pierre Mornell's book: 45 Effective Ways for Hiring Smart.*

(Neat Niche) **Executive Recruiter (Headhunter).** This is one of the few jobs that requires no formal education yet can yield a six-figure income. You work for a private agency engaged by companies to lure top execs from other firms. What makes this a neat niche is that you get to work with accomplished people, and you can earn big money if you can persuade enough HR managers to let you conduct their employee searches. You must also be able to sniff out top-flight execs, determine whether they're compatible with the client company's culture, and if so, convince them to take a job with another company. *Keith Kulper's article:* `www.kulpercompany.com/newsletters/executive_search_consulting_demy.html`.

School-to-Work Coordinator. Some schools are finally realizing that they graduate too many students ill equipped for real-world jobs. So high schools are hiring school-to-work coordinators. A coordinator may arrange for teachers to visit local workplaces. Some teachers, on seeing what it takes to succeed in today's workplace, change what they do in the classroom. School-to-work coordinators may also help students in career planning by bringing community members to schools to talk about their jobs, and arranging student job shadowing and internships. *National Tech-Prep Network:* `www.cord.org/ntpn`.

Casting Director. Would you find it fun to cast a sitcom? An epic motion picture? A feminine hygiene commercial? Casting director is one of those little-known but fun Hollywood careers. Here's how casting works: You write a breakdown (a list of all the needed characters), e-mail it to agents, and wait for submissions (photos and resumes). Then you pick people to audition.

Casting Director Lisa Pirriolli says, "Casting is perfect for people who were unpopular in high school and this is their way of getting back at all the people who didn't ask them out." The bad news: You usually have to start as a volunteer. *Casting Society of America:* www.castingsociety.com. *Janet Hirshenson and Jane Jenkins's book: A Star Is Found.*

Sales-oriented work

Salesperson. When you hear the word "salesperson," what's the first word that comes to mind? Pushy? Although those types are around, many successful salespeople don't fit the stereotype. They are, however, self-starters who are pleasantly persistent and good at listening to the customer and explaining how a product can solve the customer's problems. They aren't reluctant to ask for the sale. A career in sales is one of the few routes to high income without college. Sales offers flexible hours and, if you're an outside sales rep, a chance to travel. Plus, it's nice to know that your income is directly related to your performance: The more you sell, the more you make. The problem is it's tough to know how much you'll sell. Even good salespeople will fail if the product, territory, or commission rate stinks. (Before accepting a job, ask one of the company's other salespeople about those three things.)

Many salespeople are surprised to find that they actually spend less than half their time selling. They answer technical questions, write proposals, take care of problems with product or delivery, and write reports to management. The Internet is eliminating many sales jobs — an intelligent Web site can do a better job of selling than many salespeople at a fraction of the cost and is available 24/7. But at least until the next edition of this book is written, jobs for good salespeople should be available. *Wikipedia entry:* en.wikipedia. org/wiki/sales. *Louise Kursmark's book: Sales Careers. Tom Hopkins's book: How to Master the Art of Selling.*

Many salespeople tell me that, sooner or later, they find sales to be unfulfilling. After all, if the product was that good, it would usually sell itself or merely require somebody earning $12 an hour to take orders or explain the product. When salespeople earn a good living, it's often because they're able to convince prospects to buy something they wouldn't have in the absence of a sales pitch. Some of my clients do like selling: They enjoy "the thrill of the kill" (closing the sale), promoting a product they believe in, the money, and the competition against their sales quota or fellow salespeople. But reflective people, I believe, may want to avoid a career as salesperson.

(Neat Niche) **Sales of E-mercials.** As you bid a not-fond farewell to blinking ads, you alas must say hello to Internet commercials now that more people have high-speed Internet connections. Getting in on the ground floor of this nascent niche may be as lucrative as the ad salespeople who started selling TV spots in the 1950s.

(Neat Niche) **Big-Ticket Item Sales.** Examples: golf courses, airplanes, sky-scrapers, and custom software. Custom software? The software that banks use to back up their data costs each bank hundreds of thousands of dollars.

(Neat Niche) **Green Product Sales.** Environmentalism is the world's newest religion. That means that green products, from solar panels to pollution control systems to lumber made from sawdust and plastic milk containers, are becoming an ever-easier sell.

(Neat Niche) **Sales of Instruments and Consumables to Biotech Companies.** The biotech industry is booming and its companies use lots of costly items.

(Neat Niche) **Industrial Sales.** I like this because it's under-the-radar — no one grows up thinking, "When I grow up, I want to sell conveyer belts." That means the competition is less and the pay is better. And, for the right person, it can be fun — getting to visit all sorts of manufacturing plants and helping them solve their problems. *Manufacturer's Agents National Association: www.manaonline.org. Don't miss its quiz for future agents.*

(Neat Niche) **Electrical Components Sales.** Electrical parts aren't sexy, but demand for these components is high and few salespeople have the technical expertise to sell them effectively. That means higher salaries. An engineering background is a plus and sometimes a must.

(Neat Niche) **Financial Services Sales.** Thirty-somethings worry about saving for their children's obscenely expensive college education. Older people are becoming ever-more desperate to figure out how their tiny nest egg will last their lifetime. So, financial "consultant" (sales) careers at banks and other financial service companies should be lucrative.

(Neat Niche) **Security Sales.** Employees and customers often view employers as Bad Guys and are increasingly willing to — let's be blunt — rob them. Of course, your basic off-the-shelf theft remains popular, but there are new, more complicated schemes, such as selling the company's customer database to competitors or starting a company that utilizes the previous employer's core technology that's been tweaked just enough to avoid getting caught or at least sued. And of course, there are the increasingly popular hack attacks, rendering a company's computers inert. Add to those the growing terrorism threat and it's easy to see why companies and the government are willing to spend more on security.

I predict that one of the decade's best-selling security products will be "intelligent video." (See, for example, www.objectvideo.com.) These are video cameras with an attached computer that can discern illegal activity. Governments, especially in high-crime areas, are installing intelligent video cameras on buses, in schools, even at stop signs. (You wouldn't fail to come to a full and complete stop every time, now would you?) Companies such as retailers and banks will increasingly use intelligent video for loss prevention. And of course, Homeland Security can install them to increase border security.

 College Admissions Recruiter. The United States has almost 5,000 colleges and vocational-technical schools, 97 percent of which must recruit to fill their classrooms. Your title may be College Admissions Counselor, but a more accurate description is salesperson. You must be able to soft-sell — sell without appearing to be selling. This is a great job for anyone who likes to travel and talk with teens and parents. A sense of humor and a repertoire of clean jokes go far. *National Association for College Admission Counseling:* www.nacacnet.org.

Don't confuse a college admissions *recruiter* with a college admissions *counselor*. The recruiter is hired by a college to recruit students to that college, whereas the college counselor's job is to help students find a college matching their needs.

 Fundraiser/Development Specialist. You may wonder, "Why the term 'development'?" Because a nonprofit organization *develops* prospective donors into actual donors — ideally, big donors. For example, your alma mater attempts to develop you in the beginning by e-mailing you invitations to free or low-cost events designed to make you feel closer to the college — to remind you of the good old days, even if, in fact, they weren't so good. Half-price tickets to the football game, a glossy alumni magazine and e-zine with stories designed to make you feel close to the college, and dinners with speeches by the campus's best professors are all part of the cultivation process. Then, when you're feeling warm and fuzzy about dear ol' State U, the college starts with the solicitations — usually with e-mail campaigns and telemarketing banks. Plus, if according to the alumni questionnaire you completed, you're a potential big donor, the college assigns an already-donating alumnus with similar interests to individually solicit you. A development office keeps precise records of how much you donate. The more you donate, the more they ask for the next time. A development officer's crowning achievement is convincing you to put the organization in your will.

Development jobs tend to divide into *cultivators* and *harvesters*. *Cultivators* coordinate fundraising events, maintain donor databases, and write pitch pieces and grant proposals. *Harvesters* are the direct pitchers. They must have the ability to get wealthy people to trust them quickly, to ask for large sums of money without blinking, and to endure rejection. Knowledge of wills and trusts is helpful. If you're older and polished, a career as harvester may work because many donors fit that description. Former sales managers make especially good fundraising executives. *Association of Fund Raising Professionals:* www.afpnet.org. *Chronicle of Philanthropy:* www.philanthropy.com. *Ilona Bray's book: Effective Fundraising for Nonprofits.*

(Neat Niche) **Fundraiser for Arts Organizations.** Fundraising for the theater, the symphony, and so on, lets you spend time around artistic types without having to fight the long odds against making a living on stage. *Karen Hopkins's book: Successful Fundraising for Arts and Cultural Organizations: Second Edition.*

Auctioneer. "$100 bid, now two, now two, will ya give me $200? $200 bid, now three, now three, will ya give me $300?" When you think of auctioneers, you may think of one thing: fast talkers. But there's more: Auctioneers must enjoy selling and be masters at creating a sense of urgency while using a sense of humor. Acting skills can help. *Note:* The auctioneer chants not just because it keeps the audience interested, but because it makes things go quickly. At an average household estate auction, the auctioneer's chant helps sell an average of 60 items per hour. Tobacco auctioneers may sell 500 to 600 lots per hour! Half of auction events are real estate and business liquidations, but auctions are used to sell everything from forests to amusement parks. It's becoming better known that auction fever leads to high prices, so good auctioneers are selling high bids. And you don't need a lot of school to start chanting. Only one-third of auctioneers have a college degree. Many auctioneers learn on the job, while others attend short training programs. *National Auctioneers Association:* www.auctioneers.org.

(Neat Niche) **Fundraising Auctioneer.** Many nonprofit groups, from elementary school PTAs to United Way, have fundraising events. Auctions can raise big bucks, but most are conducted by amateur auctioneers. That usually results in lower bids than with a professional. *Richard O'Keef Fund-Raising Auctions:* www.letsdoanauction.com.

Other people-oriented careers

Producer. Whether it's a hip-hop concert, a TV news segment on legalizing prostitution, a local production of *Brighton Beach Memoirs,* or a DVD virtual trip to Tahiti, few things are more fun than coming up with an idea and putting the pieces together so it becomes a reality. That's what a producer does. I'm not talking just about hiring the actors and behind-the-camera crew. I'm talking about solving countless problems like this: In the book, *Gig,* producer Jerry Bruckheimer tells of having spent a million dollars designing space suits in which the actors in the movie *Armageddon* could breathe. In the middle of the shoot, Ben Affleck fell to the floor, suffocating in his space suit. The oxygen system had stopped working. Someone had to cut it open. No harm was done except that it stopped production, and for every lost minute, hundreds of people must be paid — an expensive meter always is running. Bruckheimer said, "So there's a little set story for you. And there are a million of those."

How to become a producer? David Wolper, producer of *Roots,* the Los Angeles Summer Olympics, and the Jacques Cousteau National Geographic specials, believes that if you're a go-getter, producing isn't rocket science. Just find a cool idea you'd like to make happen, get a team of experts to agree to participate if funding is available, tap all the talented unemployed film production people you know (they're around), and then pitch well-off people to fund it. *Producers Guild of America: www.producersguild.org. Lawrence Turman's book: So You Want to be a Producer.*

(Neat Niche) **Expo/Show Producer.** As an expo producer, you may put on a bridal show, a plastic manufacturer's convention, an art fair, or a conference on nanotechnology. Identify a need, get lots of exhibitors and enough attendees to keep them happy, and you may be able to make a year's income in a few months. *International Association for Exposition Management: www.iaem.org. International Festivals and Events Association: www.ifea.com.*

(Neat Niche) **Game Producer.** According to Jill Duffy, managing editor of *Game Developer* magazine, you needn't be a supertechie. Game producers are more likely to hire the programmers and artists, keep track of the budget and milestones, set up meetings, and keep people motivated. Less competitive points of entry: games for cellphones or so-called *casual games,* which are quick games such as the classic Tetris and my favorite, Bookworm. The hardcore PC and PS3 games are the sexiest and therefore hardest-to-get-into niche of the market, but the casual game segment is, in fact, the fastest growing. *Game Developer Magazine: www.gdmag.com. Dan Irish's book: The Game Producer's Handbook.*

Event Planner. This is similar to being a producer without the financial risk. Someone else is the producer, and she pays you a fee. This career is the compulsive's dream — with endless details to get right, all by an immovable deadline, plus a Nervous-Nelly client usually adding to the stress. To boot, you frequently must give up your nights and weekends. To tell you the truth, I can't imagine why anyone likes this career, but many people do. Indeed, event planning is among the more aspired-to careers among my female clients. That's the only reason it's included in this book. (They say they like working on projects with a definite beginning and end, that it's aesthetic and people-oriented, and that it doesn't require much technical knowledge.) The good news is that it's a huge field. The meeting industry, predominantly conventions and expos, has a national market of more than $80 billion! Other niches: corporate parties and product rollouts. *Meeting Professionals International: www.mpiweb.org. International Special Events Society: www.ises.com. Judy Allen's book: Event Planning.*

(Neat Niche) **Reunion Planner.** "I can't believe it. Back when we were in school, he was skinny!" High school reunions are intriguing events but who has time to send invitations, take reservations, hire bands, find food, arrange hotels, line up child-care, plan activities, and — most challenging — dig up all those missing class members? The reunion planner. Tracking down long-lost folks, mainly using online databases, adds a detective component to an already fun job. *National Association of Reunion Managers: www.reunions.com.*

(Neat Niche) **Wedding Planner.** Thirty years ago, there were no wedding planners, but as couples marry later in life, many lives are too full to handle all the details of a wedding (like how to make the Elks Club look like the Ritz). *National Association of Wedding Professionals: www.nawp.com. Carley Roney's book: The Knot Ultimate Wedding Planner.*

(Neat Niche) **Convention, Trade Show, or Expo Planner.** Planning these events offers big bucks in exchange for big headaches. *Professional Convention Management Association: www.pcma.org.*

Trial Consultant. This field has certainly evolved from its start, when a few activist social scientists tried to help Vietnam war protesters win their cases. Then, hiring a trial consultant became de rigueur for celebrity defendants: If OJ Simpson hadn't retained a trial consultant, who knows where he'd be living today? Dr. Phil met Oprah Winfrey when she hired his trial consulting firm to aid in her defense. Now, trial consultants are frequently used by all sorts of well-heeled clients.

You probably think of trial consultants as helping to pick a jury, but they also coach witnesses and conduct mock trials and focus groups to try out different strategies. Beware if you're the defendant and the other attorney has retained a trial consultant. This is a cool career for lawyers who don't want to argue, psychologists who don't want to listen to patients' problems all day, and market researchers who'd rather deal with people than data. *American Society of Trial Consultants: www.astcweb.org. Amy Posey's book: Trial Consulting.*

Temp Agency Owner. Alas, many full-time jobs are being replaced by temp positions. How can you capitalize? Start a temp agency. You can't compete with mega-agencies such as Manpower or Olsten, so pick a profession in which it's tough to find good employees — especially a field you know a lot about. Examples: nurses, association executives, disabled employees, short-order cooks, medical records technicians, pharmacists, escrow personnel, and robotics engineers. If you're successful, you can consider franchising your operation. *American Staffing Association: www.americanstaffing.net.*

Relocation Consultant. You're moving to a new city. What's the best neighborhood to live in? Which are the best schools? Where should your husband look for a job? A relocation specialist living in that city can help you. Based on answers to a questionnaire about your wants and needs, the relocation consultant points you in the right direction. It's like having a wise, local relative. How do you get a job as a relocation consultant? Approach the local offices of national real estate chains or the human resources of large, locally-based corporations. *Employee Relocation Council: www.erc.org.*

Personal Care Facility Owner. Many aging Boomers can't stand their varicose veins, wrinkles, and fading eyesight. And because the surgeries have become easier, more people are lining up. Personal care surgery clinics have been popping up for a while now, but the need, especially in small cities, may not be saturated. Don't worry, you needn't be a doctor. You can be the entrepreneur who opens the clinic, does the marketing, and hires the doctors to staff it.

Work with Data

Scientific data

Biologist. No field has done more to improve life. In the last decade alone, people working in biology/biotechnology have developed

- Food crops that can grow in a previously infertile section of Latin America that covers 800,000 square miles — an area larger than the size of Mexico. Thousands of formerly starving people now can eat.

- A method to identify a criminal (DNA analysis) that is thousands of times more accurate than conventional methods.

- Breakthrough drugs — like new proteins that lessen the effect of heart attacks, and drugs that greatly extend the life span of people with HIV. Currently, 300 biotech drug products and vaccines are in clinical trials targeting cancer, Alzheimer's disease, heart disease, diabetes, multiple sclerosis, AIDS, and arthritis.

I attended a presentation by five Nobel Prize winners. One of the few things they agreed on was that the field that will make the greatest impact on humankind in the coming decades is molecular biology/biotechnology. When most people think of biology, they think of *macro*biology: studying different animals and plants. I recall, in college, seeing cute pictures of endangered furry creatures. Indeed, many people choose to major in biology with such visions in mind. But fact is, if you're considering a career in biology, know that most of today's biology careers focus on molecules. From here forward, biology is mainly math. Actually, the name "biologist" is now misleading. Today, most biologists are part biologist, part chemist, part mathematician, and part programmer. They spend a majority of their time on the computer. Those with a whole-animal biology background will usually be limited to positions as lab assistants or high school biology teachers.

An oversupply of biology PhDs makes competition fierce for PhD-level jobs in biotech unless your background includes computer science, mathematics, or engineering. Even then, a low-paying one-to-two-year postdoc is usually required. The good news is that associate-, bachelor-, and master-level jobs are available at biotech and pharmaceutical firms. True, you aren't top banana, but you can have interesting opportunities, such as running experiments, perhaps assisting in designing them and writing them up, and even co-presenting at conferences. In short, you can derive many of the benefits of a PhD with less school and less difficulty landing a job. *Careers in Biology: www.emporia.edu/biosci/carebiol.htm. American Institute of Biological Sciences: www.aibs.org/careers. Nancy Rothwell's book: Who Wants to be a Scientist?*

(Neat Niche) **Genomics Biologist.** Now that the human genome has been sequenced, genomists are starting to discover what each gene does. Genes have been discovered that control everything from shyness to obesity. These discoveries, of course, are key to enabling the use of gene therapy to prevent and cure diseases and to enhance human potential. Progress has been amazing. A number of years ago now, Princeton University researchers inserted a gene into a mouse. As a result, the smart mouse, nicknamed Doogie (for the precocious TV doctor, Doogie Howser), dramatically improved its memory and that of his offspring. This gives hope for curing Alzheimer's disease and mental retardation, and, if society decides it's ethical, to improve normal people's memory and that of their children. In the 1967 movie, *The Graduate,* Dustin Hoffman got a career tip: plastics. Today, if I were to give such a tip, it would be genomics. *BayBio: www.baybio.org. BioSpace: www.biospace.com. American Society of Gene Therapy: www.asgt.org.*

(Neat Subniche) **Proteomics Biologist.** Genes work by expressing (generating) proteins. Those proteins are the actual building blocks of human function and of disease. Learning how to fix defective proteins will result in many cures. For example, scientists at Zycos Corp. identified a protein that is expressed in nearly every major cancer but not in normal tissue. *Wikipedia entry: en.wikipedia.org/wiki/proteomics.*

(Neat Niche) **Bioinformatician (Computational Biologist).** Scientists used to study drug candidates one at a time. Now, they can assess a pharmacological characteristic of 500,000 compounds in days. An individual person's genome can be identified within hours. Such advances usher in a new era of personalized medicine. But all these studies generate an extraordinary amount of data that must be stored and available in a user-friendly format for interpretation. Who makes this happen? Bioinformaticians. These combination molecular biologists, mathematicians, and computer programmers promise to be the coming decades' most important behind-the-scenes heroes. Biotech research companies, universities, and federal agencies are hiring them. *Information: www.bioinformatics.org.*

(Neat Niche) **Plant Geneticist/Botanist.** Plant geneticists have created high-protein grain that has saved countless lives in developing nations. Less dramatic, orchids used to be affordable only for the wealthy. Now, thanks to plant cloning and tissue culture, you can buy a world-class orchid for 20 bucks. (Now if they only figured out how to make them easy to grow.)

More important, plant geneticists play a key role in figuring out how humans develop from one cell into highly differentiated adults. This understanding is crucial to preventing and curing diseases. Although some of this research can be done only on animals, much can be done ethically and inexpensively using plants. As a plant lover who likes intellectual challenges and wants to make a difference, if I were starting over, this may be the career I would choose for myself. *Botanical Society of America:* www.botany.org.

(Neat Niche) **Agricultural Scientist.** Are you a science type who doesn't want to be in a lab all day? An ag scientist's job is to find better ways to grow crops. You may work on a better way to control downy mildew on rose bushes or the glassy-winged sharpshooter on grapes or to keep oxalis weeds from taking over broccoli fields — all with minimal impact to the environment. Rather than work on control, you may work on prevention: developing plant varieties genetically engineered to be resistant to pests and disease. The largest employers are the government and university extension services. *American Society of Agronomy:* www.agronomy.org.

(Neat Niche) **Entomologist.** Locally or in remote jungles, you may gather and study data on the thousands of new insect species discovered each year. Which are threats? Allies? How to deal with them? Or you may visit a farm infested with some little terror and figure out how to nuke it without nuking the rest of us. *Entomology Society of America:* www.entsoc.org.

 Epidemiologist. With the world ever-smaller, diseases can spread fast. And with bioterrorism an ever-increasing risk, those diseases can be man-made as well as natural. Epidemiologists may track and predict an outbreak's spread and develop plans for its mitigation. Think avian flu. Or using a combination of hard science and social science methods, they may help governments develop plans and policies to help prevent conditions such as obesity or AIDS. The most responsible positions usually require a doctorate. *American Public Health Association:* www.apha.org/public_health/epidemiology.htm.

 Pathologist. These detectives of the microscopic try to figure out what, if anything, is abnormal in a person's cells or bodily fluids. Clinical pathologists do that to help an individual patient while investigative pathologists do it to help solve crimes. (CSI fans know what I'm talking about.) *Careers in Pathology:* www.aamc.org/students/cim/pub_pathology.htm.

(Neat Niche) **Cytotechnologist.** You're the cancer detector. You examine biopsied cells using microscopes and chemical tests to see what's up. Obviously, this is a career for someone who is careful. A mistake can be devastating. This career usually requires only a bachelor's degree. *American Society for Cytopathology:* www.cytopathology.org.

 Terrorism Expert. Alas, terrorism is likely to provide plenty of job and consulting openings. This profile's heading, of course, subsumes many different specialties. For example, governments and companies hire people to try to smuggle terrorist weapons onto planes, into ports, and into supposedly secure buildings. Other specialties: extremist religious sects and cults; political extremist groups; unaffiliated terrorism-prone individuals; countries likely to spawn terrorist groups or state-sponsored terrorism; prevention of conventional, biological, chemical, cyber, nuclear, or radiological (dirty nuke) attacks; food supply protection; water supply protection; public venue (for example, arenas or trains) protection; port security; and corporate and community preparedness planning.

The feds hire the most terrorism experts, but so do states, cities, and mid-to-large companies. Also, some jobs may be available at disaster-related nonprofit organizations such as the Red Cross. *A first step to learning more about any of those specialties is simply to google them. If you're interested in a career in port protection, google such terms as "consultant 'port protection'" and "expert 'protecting ports.'" The portal to federal terrorism-related jobs:* www.usajobs. opm.gov/homeland.asp. *The portal to state offices of Homeland Security:* www.alarm.org/homeland/Homeland_Security.htm

> (Neat Niche) **Biological Weapons Deterrence Specialist.** Biological weapons are far more dangerous than even nuclear weapons. An airborne-communicable biovirus released on just a single subway car could decimate the nation. And bioweapons are far more portable than nuclear weapons — enough airborne-communicable bioviruses to destroy the United States can fit in a vial. The National Academy of Science worries even more about custom-created bioviruses — there isn't time to develop an antidote every time a new one is created. The need for deterrence experts is obvious, the federal budget for it has grown, and the field is far from saturated. Hey, if you're intelligent, please get into this career. You could save our lives. *Wikipedia entry:* en.wikipedia.org/wiki/Biological_warfare. *Seminal CIA/National Academy of Sciences formerly classified document, The Darker Bioweapons Future:* www.fas.org/irp/cia/product/ bw1103.pdf#search=%22bioweapons%22.

I believe it is impossible to foil all such attacks, and thus, the wisest, although certainly not foolproof, approach is to attempt to understand and work with terrorist groups so they're less likely to want to destroy us.

Hydrologist. Tom Stienstra, author of *Sunshine Careers,* reminds us that without water, we have nothing. Hydrologists ensure that water is as safe as possible. They gather data and then make water-saving proposals to corporations or government agencies. Although some hydrologists work in labs, many have offices in the great outdoors. Hydrology is one of the few outdoor professions that pays a middle-class living and may require, for an entry-level position, only a bachelor's degree. Can you picture yourself hiking into wilderness areas to take and analyze water samples, sneaking in reveries by a flowing stream? Just remember, many hydrologists spend a lot of time in front of a computer and at the water's source: frigid mountains and glaciers. A master's or doctoral is typically required for hydrology's higher-level positions. *Great*

Lakes Careers: `www.greatlakeseducation.org/careers/hydrologist.` `html.` *American Institute of Hydrology:* `www.aihydro.org.`

Environmental Analyst. Typical project: In an area with higher-than-normal cancer rates, environmental analysts look for aberrations in the composition of the air, soil, and water, and then play detective and try to figure out whether any of those are causing the problem. If analysts find unexpected chemicals, they check to see whether local companies are culprits. Environmental analysts are hired by federal, state, and local environmental protection agencies or through consulting firms. *National Association of Environmental Professionals:* `www.naep.org.`

OOH

Meteorologist. Believe it or not, they're getting better at predicting the weather — not only tomorrow's but also next year's. This has profound implications. For example, imagine you're a farmer and you know how wet and warm the next season will be. You can pick the perfect crop for that weather. You can be a meteorologist even if you're too shy to be on the nightly news. Meteorologists also work in agriculture, for cruise lines, ski resorts, the Department of Defense, and airlines. Meteorology is for the math and computer person who doesn't want to be a programmer. Because predicting the weather requires integrating information from around the globe, a foreign language is a plus. Of course, it helps if you're fascinated with the weather. Half of the meteorologists are hired by the National Weather Service, which often requires a master's, and a PhD if you'd enjoy improving weather prediction. *National Weather Service career portal:* `www.weather.gov/careers.php.`

OOH

Geologist. The career for people with and without rocks in their heads. Many geologists — petroleum geologists, for example — don't even see the rocks they're studying because they're so far below the earth's surface. These geologists use computer data to answer one question: Where should we drill for oil? Guess wrong and the company loses millions. Guess right and you're a genius. You, of course, have lots of cool tools — like gamma ray detectors — to help you guess right. Much of the work is outdoors and can be in remote locations for long periods, so it's a lousy choice if you value family life and a stable work environment. Most of the unexplored oil locations are abroad, so if you can speak a foreign language and are willing to relocate, job opportunities should be ample. The growth area in U.S. geology jobs is in cleaning up ground-based pollution. What luck: Most of the oil is far away and the pollution is right here. New employers of geologists are seismic data brokering companies, but the largest employers are oil companies and the U.S. Departments of Agriculture, the Interior, and Defense. *About.com's geology portal:* `geology.about.com.`

(Neat Niche) **Planetary Geologist.** Is there life on Mars? Can we introduce life onto Venus? The answers may lie on and beneath the planet's surface. Enter the planetary geologist. He may look at samples retrieved from space missions or simply look at photographs of planets, moons, and comets. Fewer than 1,000 planetary geologists are employed in the United States.

Most work for universities and NASA. A PhD in planetary geology is a must. *American Astronomical Society:* `www.aas.org`.

Geophysicist. Usually, the earth doesn't move. That is, unless you're in love or there's a volcano or earthquake. Geophysicists focus on the latter two in these neat niches. *American Geophysical Union:* `www.agu.org`.

(Neat Niche) **Volcanologist.** When will a volcano erupt? Volcanologists better not guess wrong. If they predict an imminent gusher and nothing happens, many people have been needlessly terrified and evacuated. If the volcanologist says, "No problem," and it blows, you have a fried community. According to *Time,* "Volcanology may be the most dangerous science since those vast laboratories can explode at any moment with a force equal to thousands of atom bombs." The United States has fewer than 200 volcanologists, and most have a PhD. I include very few careers with such poor prospects of landing a job and that require so much training, but despite the danger, *volkies* really love their career, so I couldn't resist. Volcanologists spend a lot of time in exotic places studying a fascinating phenomenon. Their work can save lives and property, and because children are so fascinated with volcanoes, they visit many schools, usually leaving an auditorium full of wide-eyed kids. *Article, Do You Want to Become a Volcanologist:* `volcano.und.edu/vwdocs/how_to.html`. *For a contrarian perspective:* `www.popsci.com/popsci/science/806ffb24a5f27010vgnvcm1000004ee cbccdrcrd/5.html`. *Dick Thompson's book: Volcano Cowboys.*

(Neat Niche) **Seismologist.** So, you think seismologists predict earthquakes. Sorry, bub. Most seismologists earn their livings *creating* earth vibrations. Why would they do that? One reason is that it's a good way to determine where to drill for oil. Other seismologists figure out how to prevent mining disasters — and what to do when they guess wrong. Of course, some seismologists do get involved with earthquakes. They may help design a plan to make a building earthquake resistant, and try to predict when and where the next Big One will strike. Unfortunately, to date, despite all the PhDs hacking away at it, dog barking still seems to predict earthquakes as well. *U.S. Geological Survey's Earthquake careers portal:* `earthquake.usgs.gov/learning/topics.php?topicID=42&topic=Careers`.

Chemist. Yes, you get paid to play with a grown-up's version of a chemistry set, but it's a lot more complicated than mixing two potions and seeing whether the mixture turns green. You need lots of advanced math in this field. The job market isn't great for pure chemists because many jobs today require a chunk of biology or physics along with the chemistry. Drug companies and materials manufacturers do hire some chemists, with lead positions requiring a master's or doctorate. Try not to blow up the lab, huh. *Chemical careers:* `www.chemistry.org/portal/a/c/s/1/acsdisplay.html?DOC=vc2%5c 3wk%5cwk3.html`.

(Neat Niche) **Food Scientist.** How can we make a better tasting frozen pizza? Can we make a hot dog that tastes good without cancer-causing nitrites? How can chicken processors reduce pyelobacteria, which sickens thousands of people each year? Food scientists work for food-processing companies to make better foods, and increasingly, for government agencies to ensure that the foods you eat don't make you puke. *Institute of Food Technologists:* `www.ift.org`. *Article, You're a What?: Flavorist:* `www.bls.gov/opub/ooq/2004/winter/yawhat.htm`

(Neat Niche) **Toxicologist.** Toxicologists found the source of the 2006 e-coli spinach outbreak. How? The DNA of fecal matter on the lettuce matched that found on one farm. The Texas A&M toxicology home page warns that such incidents are far from rare: "Hardly a week goes by without hearing about a chemical that may threaten our health: pesticides in the food we eat, pollutants in the air we breathe, chemicals in the water we drink. Are these chemicals really dangerous? How much does it take to cause harm? Toxicologists answer these questions." The terrorism threat is further increasing the demand for toxicologists. A doctorate is typically required for high-level jobs. *Society of Toxicology:* `www.toxicology.org`. *Wikipedia entry:* `en.wikipedia.org/wiki/toxicology`.

Physicist. Want to figure out how the universe began? Create nano-sized machines to cure disease? Develop the science behind the next generation of fuel cells or medical imaging machines? How about study things with no conceivable practical application, like string theory? I listened to an entire NPR show on that and all I know is that string theory has something to do with groups of quarks (things much smaller than electrons) acting like guitar strings. I think I'll leave that to the physicists. *American Physical Society career site:* `www.aps.org/jobs`.

(Neat Niche) **Photonics.** Your job is to figure out how to move photons (elemental particles of light) so they do some good. And indeed, they can. They're used in missile defense, correction of poor sight, welding, barcode scanners, and fun stuff like laser light shows, holograms, and tattoo removal. Well, that doesn't sound like much fun. *Wikipedia entry:* `en.wikipedia.org/wiki/photonics`. *Optical, Laser and Fiber Optics Resource:* `www.photonics.com`

Statistician. Where should a gold-mining company explore for gold? In what districts should a politician campaign hardest? Should the pitcher intentionally walk the batter? A statistician helps answer such questions. Yeah, you can lie with statistics, and not everything can be reduced to probabilities, but statistics often lead to good decision making. Not a bad payoff for one's career efforts. Florence Nightingale said that statistics is the most important science in the whole world: for upon it depends the practical application of every other science. *The American Statistical Association:* `www.amstat.org`.

(Neat Niche) **Biostatistician.** You answer questions such as "How effective is a new drug? How sure are we that this specific gene expresses this specific protein across an entire population? What are the chances of a side effect among pregnant women?" Among the many job openings for statisticians I've seen lately, by far the most are for biostatisticians. *Wayne Daniel's book: Biostatistics, 8th Edition.*

(Neat Niche) **Sports Statistician.** Were you the kid who calculated the likelihood of this or that happening during the game? This may be your dream career. Sports statisticians are numeric journalists, creating interesting stats that enrich a journalist's article or broadcaster's reporting. Or your job may be to keep track of numbers that help a coach decide which players to play and which to bench.

Can you make a living as a sports statistician? Alas, probably not. Most sports statisticians work for free or peanuts. Want to try to beat the odds? Hone your craft by being a high school or college team's statistician. Don't record just the basics; be creative. For example, in the game's final minutes when the outcome is in doubt, Biff completes 40 percent fewer passes than he does in the rest of the game — Mr. Choke — while Rick completes 20 percent more passes — Mr. Clutch. If you prove yourself at the high school or college level, send work samples — especially that creative stuff — to producers of pro sports TV shows. Their names are mentioned or listed at the end of the game. You may even send your material to the Elias Sports Bureau, which produces stats for Major League Baseball, the NFL, and the NBA. *American Statistical Association:* www.amstat.org/sections/sis/career/index.html.

 Cryptanalyst. The government has just intercepted a secret message from a terrorist organization. Cryptanalysts decode it. A Web site contains thousands of customers' credit card numbers. Cryptanalysts encode it to deter hackers. In short, cryptanalysts make and break secret codes. Most cryptanalysts have a PhD in math — a secret decoder ring won't quite do. *Wikipedia entry:* en.wikipedia.org/wiki/cryptography. *Society for Industrial and Applied Mathematics:* www.siam.org.

 Cancer Registrar. Because most cancers don't have a single foolproof cure, many treatment protocols are tried for each type of cancer. One way to figure out which methods work best for whom (for example, African-Americans in their 60s with leiomyosarcoma and diabetes) is to accumulate treatment records of every cancer case. Most HMOs, insurance companies, and government agencies do that, and the person in charge is the cancer registrar. (Might I ask why there isn't a worldwide or even a national database?) This person doesn't just enter submitted information into the database; he often speaks with the physician and even the patient for clarification. May you never get a call from a cancer registrar. *National Cancer Registrar's Association:* www.ncra-usa.org.

Computer data

Computer Programmer. You get to work on puzzles with a real-world application. For example, you may start with a problem such as how to monitor the amount of electricity Minnesota uses per second. You figure out how that can be calculated and then use a programming language to "teach" the computer how to calculate it. That part, for really bright people, tends to be challenging, fun, and addictive. But after the basic program is written, major tedium usually follows. Debugging often means days of staring at screens full of numbers, trying to divine which ones are wrong. Another plus, however, for this career is that programming tools are getting ever better. Of course, that means that today's programming languages are tomorrow's dinosaurs, so to be happy and successful as a programmer, you must relish the idea of continually reeducating yourself. The current hot languages are Java, C, C++, Visual Basic.NET, and PHP.

Alas, with so many programmers in low-cost countries such as China and India willing to work for a pittance, the average U.S. programmer may soon have a hard time convincing employers she's worth a middle-class salary. *IEEE Computer Society: www.computer.org. Francis Glassborow's book: You Can Do It!: A Beginners Introduction to Computer Programming. Harry Henderson's book: Career Opportunities in Computers. Info Tech Employment's book: Software Programmer - Consultant - Network Engineer - Application Developer Career & Job Guide.*

(Neat Niche) **Wireless Device Programmer.** Entire cities such as San Francisco and Philadelphia are becoming giant wireless hotspots. Cell=phones have ever-more features, such as full-motion video and wireless Internet capability. And as Boomers age, they demand wireless technology to help them through their dotage. For example, researchers are developing an implantable microchip that monitors an outpatient's vital signs and broadcasts anomalies and the patient's location to his physician. Wireless jobs are available if you know Java, VXML (for voice recognition), and WML. *Experts Exchange, Wireless Programming: www.experts-exchange. com/Programming/Wireless_Programming.*

(Neat Niche) **Virtual Reality Programmer.** You write software that's the ultimate training method: putting students in a virtual duplicate of the actual situation — military officers in war zones, doctors in surgery, schoolchildren learning what to do in case of fire, and astronauts in spaceships. And of course, virtual reality is the goal of video games — witness how eyetracking is starting to replace game controllers. Soon, controller cramp from pressing "Shoot" 10,000 times may become a thing of the past. *Wikipedia entry: en.wikipedia.org/wiki/virtual_reality. Virtual Reality Resources: vresources.jump-gate.com.*

(Neat Niche) **Education/Training Programmer.** Do you like the idea of creating software that helps students learn more while having fun? Although teacher unions are unlikely to trumpet this, evidence is growing that students learn more from good, simulation-centered or even so-called drill-and-kill software than from a live teacher. Parents and corporate training departments buy the most education software, but schools are increasingly being dragged along. *Encyclopedia of Educational Technology:* coe. sdsu.edu/eet. *Educational Software Cooperative:* www.edu-soft.org.

(Neat Niche) **Web Programmer.** The job is usually to take the blueprint from a Web site designer and bring it to life. Increasingly, Web programmers specialize in either the front- or back-end. Front-enders develop the site's interface, where a sense of the artistic and what humans will like are key. Back-end specialists work on such matters as integrating a database into the site or ensuring that the site is compatible with multiple browsers. Whether front- or back-end, you need to at least be proficient in Java and PHP. If your site needs to access information from a database, you need to know SQL scripting. On the artistic side, common tools include Adobe Illustrator, Photoshop, Flash, and 3DS Studio Max. But no programmer's toolkit is complete without the skills to optimize the site's search engine placement. *The Web Guild:* www.webguild.org. *Search Engine Watch:* www.searchenginewatch.com.

(Neat Niche) **Game Programmer.** Of course this sounds cool. The question is, how do you get hired? Most developers still learn on their own, but there are a growing number of university-based training programs. *Game Developer* magazine's site has a list. When you create a cool sample program, send it to game companies. Easy way to find them: read reviews of games on www.gamespot.com. They usually include the name of the developers. Then use google.com to find their Web site, and e-mail your creation to them. *Game Developer magazine:* www.gdmag.com. *International Game Developers Association:* www.igda.org.

(Neat Niche) **Computer Security Programmer.** The Feds consider computer systems one of terrorism's most likely targets. In addition, from both inside and outside an organization, hackers steal information from computers to make money or to try to disrupt a company just for the heck of it. This produces an ever-stronger demand for security programmers to foil the thieves. Also, corporations, the FBI, and the Department of Justice hire these cybersleuths to search the Net to nab software pirates. The Business Software Alliance estimates that nearly one in two software applications is pirated. *Wikipedia entry:* en.wikipedia.org/wiki/ Computer_Security. *Rick Lehtinen's book: Computer Security Basics.*

Newsletter Publisher. According to the Newsletter Publishing Association, 50 percent of new newsletters succeed, a higher percentage than other small businesses. And your chances are even better if you do things right:

- ✔ Choose a narrow niche. It's easier to sell 1,000 newsletters for home health nurses than 100 for nurses.

- ✔ Choose a topic that has an endless stream of new information that your target readers crave. Sample titles: *Citywide Wi-Fi Update, Power Plant Financing, Proteomics This Week, Currency Options Insider, iPhone News,* and *Employment Law Digest.* Or focus on creating custom newsletters for nonprofits or clubs.

- ✔ Be sure an existing publication doesn't meet the need.

- ✔ Focus on your online edition. Distribution costs are much lower than print.

- ✔ To market a newsletter successfully, make the most of such e-marketing tools as Google's AdWords.

Specialized Information Publishers Association: www.newsletters.org. *Newsletter-clearinghse:* www.newsletter-clearinghse.com *The Newsletter Factory:* www.nlf.com *Carol Eyman's book: How to Publish Your Newsletter. Mike's Marketing Tools:* www.mikes-marketing-tools.com *Cheryl Woodard's book: How to Start and Run a Successful Newsletter or Magazine.*

Employee Background Checker. When one of former San Francisco Mayor Willie Brown's key employees was caught lying on his resume, His Honor shrugged, "Everyone lies on their resume." Alas, he's not wrong. Depending on which study you believe, 33 to 45 percent of job applications contain "creative writing" — a degree never completed, a claim of no criminal record, or an inflated work history. As job and tenant applicants seem ever more likely to stretch the truth and government regulations tighten about what can and can't be asked, companies increasingly turn to pre-employment checkers to verify information on resumes and to contact former employers. The Internet enables you to learn an awful lot about an applicant in just a few minutes. Yet companies routinely pay more than $100 per background check. This is a low-investment home business that would seem to have a high probability of success. *National Association of Professional Background Screeners:* www. napbs.com *A leader in this field, Employment Screening Resources:* www. esrcheck.com *Lester Rosen's book: The Safe Hiring Manual: The Complete Guide to Keeping Criminals, Imposters and Terrorists Out of Your Workplace.*

Business data

Actuary. How much should an insurance company charge each employee of the Western Widget Company for health insurance? That's a typical question asked of an actuary. Actuary is a good career for someone who wants a career that applies math to practical decisions, and that offers salaries that often reach six figures. More good news: You can achieve the highest level of actuary (Fellow) without a graduate degree. You do have to pass a series of arduous exams for which you can study at home or take classes at local actuary clubs or at universities. *Society of Actuaries:* www.beanactuary.org.

Economist. This is another career for the math-centric person who wants to do something that's at least potentially practical. Economists answer such questions as, "How will our company be affected if the minimum wage goes up?" "What are the costs and benefits of legalizing gambling in this county?" "What has happened to solar cell production and why?" In other words, economists predict and analyze production and consumption trends to help governments and companies make policy. Problem is, people's actual behavior often doesn't follow the predicted model. I'm always amused when I read a panel of blue-ribbon economists' predictions. They rarely agree. Nevertheless, a master's or doctoral degree is often required. *List of Economics Careers:* business.baylor.edu/Steve_Gardner/CAREERS.HTM

(Neat Niche) **Environmental Economist.** You figure out the economic impacts of activities such as a proposed new Wal-Mart in your community, an environmentalist-proposed policy to build no new freeways (enacted in the San Francisco Bay Area), or passing a law prohibiting U.S. oil companies from purchasing oil from Venezuela. *Environmental Economics Career Information:* aec.msu.edu/ee/careers.htm

(Neat Niche) **Forensic Economist.** You claim that your business partner ruined your business. How large were the damages? A forensic economist can tell you. Your spouse got run over by a car. How much should you get? An estimate will come from a forensic economist. Your spouse needn't die for you to need a forensic economist. You're divorcing her. How much alimony do you need to pay? A forensic economist would be happy to tell you — for a nice fee. *Article: Forensic Economists:* finance.monster.com/articles/forensic. *National Association of Forensic Economics:* www.nafe.net.

Expense Reduction Consultant. A perfect career for a cheapskate. Your job is to review a business's buying decisions: phone service, office supplies, printing, insurance, shipping — everything — making sure they're buying as wisely as possible. *A franchise:* www.ercfranchise.com

Government Procurement Consultant. The nation's largest customer is the government — and it may be willing to pay $85 for a screw. That's the sort of customer that all businesses love, but most companies don't know how to get the government to buy from them. Your job is to teach them. *The U.S. Small Business Administration's Government Contracting Division:* www.sba.gov/GC. *Scott Stanberry's book: Federal Contracting Made Easy, 2nd Edition.*

 Credit Risk Manager. This isn't a sexy job, but it's high paying and in demand. Credit risk managers work for organizations that extend credit: credit card companies and other corporations, universities, even government agencies. Your job is to figure out who should get credit and how much. You must be computer-savvy and have at least a bachelor's degree in statistics, economics, computer science, math, or operations research. Six-figure salaries are possible after three to ten years of experience. *National Association of Credit Management:* www.nacm.org.

 Securities Analyst. Would you find it fun to figure out whether a company's stock or bond is a bargain? That's what securities analysts do. They're mathematical detectives who interview company employees and crunch a lot of numbers. *Articles from the New York Society of Security Analysts:* www.nyssa.org/Content/NavigationMenu/career_development/reference_center/nyssa_publications/becoming_a_security_analyst.htm

 SEC rules prohibit trading based on information before it's released to the public, but how can government regulators keep insiders from buying the stock early — not in their own name, but in a friend's?

> (Neat Niche) **Portfolio Manager.** After you've been an analyst for a while, the big step up is to portfolio manager. Pension funds, mutual funds, and large companies hire portfolio managers to decide which securities to buy and dump. *Chartered Financial Analyst Institute:* www.cfainstitute.org.

 Want to play with other people's money but don't see yourself getting the MBA or CFA certification that's usually required of a portfolio manager? See the financial planner profile in the later "Work with People and Data" section.

 Web Store Owner. If you keep it simple, you have a reasonable shot at earning at least a sideline income, as they say, earning income while you sleep.

 ✔ Sell on both your site and on eBay. Pick a niche: fish tanks, Japanese netsuke, whatever you love or know a lot about. Don't pick anything perishable, like African violets. A newbie won't be able to anticipate sales well enough — you'll likely have a house full of dead plants.

✔ Try to get a self-explanatory name for your site. So, if you want to sell netsuke, go to a domain registration site (my favorite is www.godaddy.com)

and find something close to `netsuke.com`, which is taken. That site offers suggestions. For example, `bestnetsuke.com` is currently available. Good enough.

✔ Next step: Create and host your site at `store.yahoo.com`. Not only is its site-creation software sophisticated yet idiot-resistant, but your site will also be well-placed on Yahoo!'s search engine. An alternative: an eBay store: `pages.ebay.com/storefronts/start.html`.

✔ Keep your site simple: It must load quickly, enable you to find what you want quickly, and check out quickly. Forget cutesy graphics — they look amateurish and slow things down. Speed sells.

✔ To maximize traffic to your site, try to make it the definitive one in your niche. For example, if you're selling window boxes, make sure your site has a great selection of fairly priced ones. Yes, you need a JPEG picture of each, but each should be small enough that the pages load quickly. To increase traffic further, build an e-mail list: Invite visitors to sign up to get an RSS feed or regular e-mails about your site's new features and products; publicize your site on your Facebook, MySpace, or linkedin profile; post a promotional video on You Tube; give live and teleclass/Webinar workshops (collecting the names of attendees); write an article for an on-target publication (including a tag line with your Web site, of course); and/or start a visitor forum on the site.

Scott Fox's book: Internet Riches. Rick Segel's book: The Essential Online Solution. Entrepreneur magazine's eBay Center: `www.entrepreneur.com/ebusiness/index.html`. *Cheryl Russell's book: eBay Income.*

(Neat Niche) **Sell information online.** "Special reports" (a more lucrative term for "article") are fast and cheap to produce. Can't write? Hire someone to do it. How to find one? Just enter "freelance writer" into the search engine at `google.com` and dozens of writers' names, complete with sample work, appear. What topic? Yeah, yeah, if possible, write about what you're passionate about, but don't forget about practicality. To help predict what topics will sell, look at Amazon.com's current bestselling nonfiction books and Google's most searched terms (listed at `www.google.com/press/zeitgeist.html`). Get that "special report" onto your site fast or it will be yesterday's news. *Stephanie Chandler's book: From Entrepreneur to Infopreneur.*

 eBay Trading Assistant. Many people want to sell their stuff on a one-time or ongoing basis but don't have the skills to write copy, take great photos, ship efficiently, and so on. Wanna do it? *eBay's Guide to Getting Started:* `pages.ebay.com/tahub/index.html`.

(Neat Niche) **eBay Marketing Consultant.** What items will sell? Where and for how much should you acquire product? How should you pitch it? What should the opening bid be? What are competitors doing? How much should you charge for shipping? Should you ship yourself or outsource that task? Many eBay sellers just go on gut instinct. Can you do better? *Janelle Elms's book: The 7 Essential Steps to Successful eBay Marketing.*

Adventure/Eco Travel Organizer. More and more people are deciding that the vacation they want isn't a week at a Hilton. They want to go back to nature. Hiking, bird watching, whitewater rafting, and other forms of recreation have seen double-digit growth since the early 1980s according to the United States Forest Service. And in the search for the exotic, markets are building for the likes of dog sledding, hang gliding, sky diving, mountain climbing in the Himalayas, and exploring Antarctica and the Brazilian jungle. The market for adventure and travel is getting crowded, so nichecraft is particularly important here. For example, activist travel is on the rise. *About.com's adventure travel portal:* `adventuretravel.about.com` *International Ecotourism Society:* `www.ecotourism.org`.

(Neat Niche) **Student Travel Service.** Set up on or near a local college campus and focus on low-cost adventures. For example, set up mini Peace Corps–like experiences, in which groups of students assist villages in so-called developing nations. *About.com's student travel portal:* `student travel.about.com`

Exporter. In the movie *Back to the Future*, Michael J. Fox goes back in time and so has no trouble predicting the future. Exporters have it almost as easy. Many fads, such as the now hot and soon likely cold iPod lanyards, become hot overseas a year or two later. Think of a product in the United States that came and went recently. *(Wikipedia has a list of faded fads of the 21st century:* `en.wikipedia.org/wiki/2000s_fads_and_trends`. *Also, see Google zeitgeist of previous years' most searched froogle items:* `www.google.com/press/zeitgeist/archive.html`.*)* Xbox 360 may be an example. Want to sell it in another country? By the time you set up your business, that country's demand should be ramping up. *Kenneth Weiss's book: Building an Import/Export Business, 3rd Edition.*

Export Agent. Most companies want to expand their market, but few small ones know the ins and outs of exporting: how to find the right foreign buyers, and how to deal with them and with shippers, customs agents, and with all the regulations. The good news is that you don't need a degree, and you can learn what you need to know quickly. Start with the resources here. A *Money* magazine report concluded that, among all home-based businesses, export agents are among the most likely to generate high income. *Fun Careers: Export Agent:* `www.funcareers.com/categories/ot/sa-exprt/Export_ Agent.html`. *John Jagoe's report: How to Become a Successful Export Agent. U.S. Commerce Department's export Web site:* `www.tradeinfo.doc.gov` *(it has vast resources, even including an entire Web site on how to export to Iraq).*

Appraiser. Yes, there's the mundane sort of appraising businesses, machinery, and real estate. But some appraisers are more like professional treasure hunters, sifting through collections of coins, stamps, jewelry, antiques, or art, and figuring out whether there's booty among the ordinary. You can find oddball niches too: appraising race horses and Lionel train collections, for example. As businesses turn over more quickly and the population ages, the need for appraisers is increasing: in estate planning, or in divvying up the pie after the fact. And because big bucks are at stake, you may be well paid. *American Society of Appraisers: www.appraisers.org. Appraiser's Net: www.appraisers-net.com.*

Work with Words

OOH

Writer. Self-expression — it's a powerful driver for many people, including me. My life gains meaning when I know that others will read what I have to say. And written self-expression has particular power because there's time to be more reflective than when speaking. Although your odds of making a living as a novelist or poet aren't much better than the chances of Al Qaeda embracing Israel, neat writing niches exist that may allow you to write without having to eat ramen three times a day. For example, in addition to traditional writing jobs such as journalist, new writing careers have emerged in recent years — for example, eBay listing writer and professional blogger. In most writing careers, you must write not only well, but also quickly: a few publishable pages per day is a rule of thumb. *Writer's Resource Center: www.poewar.com. About.com's portal for freelance writers: freelancewrite.about.com. Elizabeth Foote-Smith's book: Opportunities in Writing Careers, Revised Edition. David Trottier's book: The Freelance Writer's Bible.*

(Neat Niche) **Professional Blogger.** Sun Microsystems CEO Jonathan Schwartz says, "My blog has become my single most effective vehicle to communicate to all of our constituencies." Few CEOs blog, but ever-more companies are hiring bloggers to add an edgier and more human tone to their Web site. Make money from your own blog by selling products and/or advertising. Vlogs (video blogs) will soon become the norm, so learn how to stream video. *The Professional Blogger blog: www.problogger.net. The story of one professional blogger: weblogs.about.com/od/bestofblogs directory/a/elisacamahort.htm To learn how to stream video and audio: streamingmediaworld.com/series.html.*

(Neat Niche) **Film Critic.** Here's how to increase your chances of making a living at this long-shot career — without having to get a film studies degree. Step 1: Study *Christopher Null's book: Five Stars! How to Become a Film Critic, the World's Greatest Job.* Step 2: Watch a movie. Step 3: Write a review with a distinctive style. Step 4: Show your review to three trusted people. Step 5: Make revisions as a result. Step 6: Repeat Steps 2 through 5 with at least

100 films. Be sure to include some classics. Step 7: Send your half dozen favorite reviews to at least 30 employers of film critics. Also post them on `amazon.com` and `imbd.com`.

(Neat Niche) **Web Writer.** Your writing must be concise; generally laced with bullets, punchy anecdotes, and statistics; and packed with fresh content — the Web operates at warp speed. Web writing is the ideal career for someone with a supermarket full of knowledge about one field, the ability to quickly track down additional tasty morsels, and then boil them all down into a quick but satisfying snack. *Writing for the Web:* `crofsblogs.typepad.com`.

(Neat Niche) **Medical Writer.** Writing *Preparing for Your Hysterectomy* is a typical assignment for medical writers. Many medical writers translate prevention practices and treatments into plain English. Who'll hire you? Medical Web sites (such as HealthWatch or WebMD), HMOs and other health insurers, hospitals, clinics, and publications that appeal to older readers. If you have a strong science background, biotech and pharmaceutical companies may hire you to produce regulatory documents. To me, the latter sounds less cool, but I hear the money's good. *Article:* `healthcare.monster.com/articles/writestuff`.

(Neat Niche) **Politician's Writer.** Most politicians, from the town councilperson to the president, need writers. Political writers craft copy for the pol's site, fundraising letters, speeches, and see-how-much-I'm-doing-for-you newsletters. One approach to landing a job is to write a fundraising letter for your favorite local politician, and then send it as a sample.

(Neat Niche) **Industry Publications Writer.** Ever thought of writing for *Pizza Today?* It's a magazine for people in the pizza biz. Thousands of trade rags exist and, because it's not sexy work, tend to pay writers well.

(Neat Niche) **Ghostwriter.** Here's a back-door route into ghostwriting, a cool gig. Contact celebrities, especially those who have been outside the headlines for a few months — last year's hero is usually afraid he's had his 15 minutes of fame. Ask the person whether he'd like you to write a book about him. If he agrees, develop a proposal together and send it, probably through an agent, to publishing houses. When the book comes out, the star is listed as the author in huge type and your name is Lilliputian, if it appears at all. The name of Hilary Clinton's ghostwriter for *It Takes a Village,* Barbara Feinman, never appeared on the book. Celebrity ghostwriting may be the fastest route to a well-paying, if secret, book deal. *Eva Shaw's book: Ghostwriting. Jennie Erdal's book: Ghosting.*

(Neat Niche) **Copywriter.** This job offers one of the surer routes to a non-starving writing career. Many copywriters think first about ad writing, but also consider company annual reports, Web or mail order catalog copy, consumer information booklets, and restaurant menus. The key to being a good copywriter? Being able to put yourself in the readers' shoes: "What would make the reader act?" *Article, Principles of Copywriting for the Web:* `www.provenanceunknown.com/edit/basics.html`. *Steve Slaunwhite's book: Start & Run a Copywriting Business.*

(Neat Niche) **Technical Writer.** In this in-demand niche, you develop user manuals, articles about new products, instruction booklets, press releases, and online help files. It's often a high-pressure job because you're brought on after the product is completed and everyone's eager to get it on the market. *Online Technical Writing Textbook:* `www.io.com/~hcexres/ textbook`. *Writer's Workshop on Technical Writing:* `www.writerswrite. com/technical`. *Society for Technical Communication:* `www.stc.org`.

(Neat Niche) **Writing Coach.** So many writers and wannabe writers have trouble: coming up with the right idea, structuring their work, dealing with writer's block, craving feedback on their work, or requiring editing help. Even if you can't make a middle-class living as a writing coach, it could well be one ring in your three-ring-circus writing career. *To get a sense of what they do and how they market themselves, google "writing coach."*

OOH

Journalist. If you can land a decent-paying job, journalism is a great career. You have opportunities for creativity, you're often learning something new, and you feel you make a difference. Many factors, however, make it ever-more difficult to find a journalism job that pays a middle-class salary. Print and broadcast organizations are merging or folding, and many remaining ones are using more nationally syndicated content. Thousands of bloggers, vloggers, and other citizen journalists are doing journalism for free, and before long, online search engines will provide on-demand custom "newspapers," based on information from multiple news organizations.

Like a career in acting or film directing, journalism is one of those job aspirations that often results in poverty. I was on a top floor of the Time-Life Building talking with four editors from one of Time-Warner's major magazines, and everyone agreed how obscene it was that colleges continue to welcome more and more journalism majors even though only a small fraction will ever make a middle-class living in the field. Indeed, a 2006 *Wall Street Journal* op-ed said, "In 2005, newspapers cut 2,000 jobs; this spring more people graduated from journalism school than ever before."

So why is journalism on the list of cool careers? Because it's so rewarding that it's worth considering — if you love interviewing and digging up information, and are excellent at cranking out clear prose rapid-fire. To increase your chances of landing a good job, specialize; science, technology, or ethnic specialists may have an edge. *Wikipedia entry:* `en.wikipedia.org/wiki/ Journalism`. *Stephen Warley's book: Vault Career Guide to Journalism and Information Media.*

Many articles and TV news segments are slanted more than the Leaning Tower of Pisa. Even in prestigious media outlets, too many journalists select stories mainly so they can sell their viewpoint (for example, anti-George Bush). They cram each article full of support for their position, carefully nuancing every word, adding just enough balance to make it look fair. Biased coverage is the main reason the media is distrusted. You may never completely control your biases, but the public trust demands that you make your best effort.

(Neat Niche) **TV Newswriter.** You write the words that those public-idolized puppets called TV news anchors read, down to the segues between stories. You have to write concisely and with edge. *Ted White's book: Broadcast News Writing, Reporting, and Producing, Fourth Edition.*

Book/Magazine/Web Site Editor. The fun part of being an editor is finding great projects, convincing your editorial/publication board to say yes, and then helping the author to mold the project into something wonderful and salable without deflating the author into inaction. But getting into this field is tough, and your first jobs are usually low paying with long hours. If you insist on the book business, consider moving to the Big Apple, where 90 percent of the business is located. One rarely considered starting place is as an agent's assistant. You read unsolicited submissions (called the slush pile), and make connections with editors. Scan acknowledgments in recent books to find beloved agents. In magazines, try to get a first job as a fact checker or researcher. *Wikipedia entry:* en.wikipedia.org/wiki/editing. *American Society of Magazine Editors:* www.magazine.org/careers. *American Society of Newspaper Editors:* www.asne.org. *Diana Athill's book: Stet.*

(Neat Niche) **Web Site Editor.** A Web site wants to be *sticky,* stimulating return visitors. Web editors are in charge of making that happen. One part writer, one part editor, one part businessperson, the Web editor comes up with content ideas for the site (a four-part series, a weight-loss tracker that requires you to check in, and so on), recruits writers, polishes submissions, and works with the tech person to make them Web-ready. *Association for Internet Professionals:* www.association.org.

(Neat Niche) **Copy Editor.** Many people write, but to get their writing into publishable form often takes some doing. That's why print and online publishers hire copy editors. Writers who want to maximize chances of publication also hire copy editors to polish their drafts into publishable shape. *American Copy Editors Society:* www.copydesk.org.

(Neat Niche) **Resume Writer.** Even many confident people find having to write their resume scary. "One page or two?" "How can I sound good without bragging?" "What about that employment gap when I was hitchhiking cross-country?" Enter the resume writer, a wordsmith who helps people present their best selves while resisting the temptation to overinflate. It's a good career for writers who enjoy interviewing people and can quickly convert that interview into a concise, logical resume. Linking yourself to an employment Web site, outplacement firm, or headhunter attracts more clients and work. So does conducting a resume seminar at job fairs and job-seeker support groups; sending postcards to seniors at local colleges (student directories are usually made public); and specializing in military personnel moving to civilian life, medical, legal, or technical professionals, or the physically handicapped (getting referrals from a local department of rehabilitation). *Resume software: ResumeMaker Professional, downloadable from* www.resumemaker.com. *Professional Association of Resume Writers:* www.parw.com.

Librarian. If you picture a mousy bookworm, update your stereotype. Today's librarian is a sociable computer whiz whose job increasingly focuses on helping patrons retrieve obscure information from mountains of electronic and print resources. This is an underrated career. Most librarians enjoy helping patrons dig up information. They learn in the process and keep up-to-date on the latest books and online resources. Librarians who specialize in medicine, other sciences, law, or engineering make more money. *American Library Association Library Resources:* www.ala.org. *Priscilla Shontz's book: The Librarian's Career Guidebook.*

(Neat Niche) **Private Librarian.** Hospitals, government agencies, prisons, magazines, TV and radio station news departments, and research departments of corporations and nonprofit organizations have libraries. Would you ever have thought Revlon had a library? The Brookings Institute? The United States Air Force? *Newsweek* magazine? Most large law firms? All hire librarians. I recently gave a talk to 100 special librarians. Most of them love their careers. *Special Libraries Association:* www.sla.org.

(Neat Niche) **Information Retriever/Independent Search Specialist.** You're already overwhelmed with information, and it's going to get worse. Your savior is the information retriever, who for a fee, goes beyond what a librarian has time to do. Retrievers search the Net and databases such as Dialog and Nexis and phone interview the right people, providing you with a digest of the best information. The information mountain is so overwhelming that information professionals specialize, for example, in genomics, engineering, mergers and acquisitions, politics, or digital art. How do you get clients? Pick your specialty, give talks at its professional association, and write for its publications. *Association of Independent Information Professionals:* www.aiip.org.

Information Abstractor. Would you enjoy synthesizing articles into a paragraph or two? Can you do it quickly? In an hour, an abstractor must abstract two to three articles. If you can do that, you'll be in demand because of the need to distill that relentless information explosion. Major hirers: Web sites, corporations needing to distill material for scientists and executives, and publishers of research abstracts. You'll be particularly in demand if you have content expertise in law, medicine, engineering, chemistry, or real estate. *Article: How to write an abstract: www.ece.cmu.edu/~koopman/essays/abstract.html. National Federation of Abstracting & Information Services: www.nfais.org.*

 Indexer. An index can make the difference between a book and a good book. Peter Farrell, author of *Make Money from Home,* calls a good index, "a minor work of art but also the product of clean thought and meticulous care." That work of art must usually be done quickly — publishers usually give indexers manuscripts just a few weeks before publication. Indexing is a self-employed occupation that requires a person with the odd combination of enjoying the solitary work of creating an index and the ability to go out, ask for business, and insist on reasonable compensation: $3 to $4 per manuscript page or $30 to $40 an hour. A degree may not be necessary. *American Society of Indexers: www.asindexing.org. Susan Holbert's Indexing Service (she has indexed 100 books and offers impressive-sounding training): www.abbington.com/holbert.*

 Ethicist. Dilemma: Robots can now create robots. Efficient yes, but could they eventually create a man-destroying army of robots? Probably not, but to avoid the risk, should research on robot-creating robots be illegal? If these practices are made illegal, will that only transfer control of the technology to terrorist groups and rogue nations? Such dilemmas, along with more common ones, like when should doctors stop treating a dying patient, fill the ethicist's inbox. *American Society of Law, Medicine, and Ethics: www.aslme.org.*

  Radio Guide Publisher. Why are there so few radio guides? TV guides are ubiquitous, yet few radio guides exist. When getting into your car, wouldn't you like to know what music is playing on which station? Who's debating whom on talk stations? To make a living as publisher of a radio guide, get local radio stations to e-mail you their program listings — they should be eager because you're offering them free publicity. Then sell the listings for newspapers or local Web sites to publish. For additional income, publish an advertising-funded radio guide to distribute free at supermarkets. *New York Online Radio Guide: www.nyradioguide.com.*

  Graphologist/Handwriting Analyst. You can find handwriting analysts at more than just carnivals. Police departments, attorneys, and employers also use graphologists to catch forgers or to verify who wrote the ransom note. Bonus: Graphologists can be the center of attention at a party. *Wikipedia entry: en.wikipedia.org/wiki/Graphology. The Handwriting Analysts Group: www.handwriting.org.*

Work with Things

Artistically done

   Magician. Oh to pull a rabbit out of a hat, saw a woman in half, or link the solid rings. And to do it in Vegas or L.A.'s Magic Castle, America's centers of magic. But it requires years of practice, plus showmanship and a sense of humor. Alas, most magicians don't end up in Vegas. To have even a chance of conjuring up a living at magic, you probably must convince corporations to hire you for their parties and trade shows. You'll also have to fill in with street shows in tourist areas, in train or bus stations, and at parades, and with private parties for kids and adults like me who continue to be fascinated with prestidigitation, welcoming it as a low-tech escape from a too-fast, too-serious world. Despite the liabilities, few careers are as, well, magical. *International Brotherhood of Magicians:* www.magician.org. *Jim Steinmeyer's book: Hiding the Elephant.*

  Specialty Cake Baker. Most bakers are poorly paid production machines. Special-occasion cake bakers are an exception. You must be an artist, offering delicious masterpieces unavailable at your basic bakery. It should be the kind that when the bride and groom look at wedding pictures, they smile and say, "That was *some* cake!" If I wanted to become a cake baker, I'd look in my Yellow Pages under "wedding services" and visit wedding cake makers until I found a baker of superlative cakes who was willing to let me apprentice. Alternative: Ask local restaurants whether they want you to bake cakes for them. You think restaurants want to bake in-house? At a very fancy hotel's Sunday buffet brunch, I saw someone take the last piece of cheesecake. I asked a server whether there might be any more. He reached under the table and pulled out a bakery box with another cheesecake. Sandra Gurvis, in her book *Careers for Non-Conformists,* suggests that for cake bakers, a high metabolism and/or health club membership helps counteract the inevitable taste tests. *Bo Friberg's book: The Professional Pastry Chef.*

   Artist/Graphic Artist. Get real. If you have visions of hanging out in your loft, splattering paint on some enormous canvas, congratulations — you have a cool hobby. *The Princeton Review* profile of artist careers reports that "as a purely self-expressing career, 90 percent of artists make under $1,000 per year on their art." If you expect to make a living as an artist, know that 75 percent of the art available in the United States is produced by the ad industry. Much of the rest appears on Web sites. And almost all is computer-generated art produced by people with excellent freehand drawing skills enhanced by the computer. You must make good friends with Adobe Illustrator, Photoshop, and possibly 3ds Max and Maya. The good news is that demand for computer artists is growing. More good news: In production art, degrees don't count; your portfolio does. Send it to art directors at ad or design/marketing agencies — and don't forget the small houses. Oh, one more sad truth: Only a third of people who start a career in graphic arts last five years.

If I *was* trying to make a living as a fine artist, I'd drive samples around from gallery to gallery seeing whether they would take my work. I'd also create a commercial line of work that took me just an hour or two per piece to make and see whether I could sell them at craft fairs at a price that would yield me a decent hourly rate for my time. I'd create a Web site that sold my stuff while also serving as an online brochure. Finally, I'd schmooze relentlessly in the art world. In no field is the aphorism, "It's not what you know, it's who you know," more true. *About.com's graphic design portal:* `graphicdesign.about.com`. *Graphic Artists Guild:* `www.gag.org`. *ACM SigGraph:* `www.siggraph.org`. *World Wide Web Artists' Consortium:* `www.wwwac.org`. *Long list of artist careers:* `www.khake.com/page42.html`.

Many art schools' Web sites, brochures, and salespeople paint an overly optimistic picture of career prospects. For example, a site may tout a few suc-cessful graduates. They don't address *the* question: Of every 100 students who start attending your school, what percentage earn enough money from their art even to pay for their education, let alone earn a middle-class living? If you're interested in art school, ask the admissions representative that question. The usual answer is, "I don't know." If the percentage was high, I bet they would know.

(Neat Niche) **Animator.** An architect develops a blueprint for a house, but the customer is nervous. Will it really be livable? So an animator develops a walk-through animation of the premises. Now the customer can do as many virtual walk-throughs as he likes before the first nail is hammered. This is just one of the new opportunities for animators. Now computers can, at moderate cost, do animations sophisticated enough to appeal to adults that previously were impossible at any price. Science and industry, TV, films, Web sites, and video games have jumped on the animation band-wagon. Downsides are low pay and highly structured work — this isn't the career for freewheeling artists. Also, much animation work is now offshored to low-cost countries. Top animation schools: California Institute of the Arts and Toronto's Sheridan College. *Animation World Network:* `www.awn.com` *David Levy's book: Your Career in Animation.*

(Neat Niche) **Special Effects Artist.** Create impossibilities that appear before your very eyes in movies or computer games. Have kinky black hair transform in seconds into straight blond tresses, a 70-year-old's face morph into a teenager's, a lovely day degenerate into Armageddon. *Key software: Maya and SoftImage. Letter to an aspiring special effects artist:* `www.fxsupply.com/features/careers.html`.

(Neat Niche) **Jewelry Maker.** Most jewelry makers like creating only unique pieces. They dislike repeat production and marketing. If that's you, do you need to outsource those? *Tip:* The easiest sort of jewelry to make is strung beads. Too, some people make a good living just setting stones. *Article, Jewelry career options:* `www.ganoksin.com/borisat/nenam/career.htm` *Jewelry making blog:* `www.bloglander.com/jewelrymaking`. *About.com's jewelry portal:* `Jewelry.about.com` *Joanna Gollberg's book:*

The Art & Craft of Making Jewelry. Stone setting portal: www.ganoksin. com/borisat/directory/library/subject/15/1.

(Neat Niche) **Textile Designer.** So many of my female clients wax rhapsodic about their love of fabric, color, and design. For them, textile design is a dream career: computer-centric, yet still enabling you to touch, feel, and intuit what looks beautiful not only to you but also to users. *Surface Design Association: www.surfacedesign.org. Marypaul Yates's book: Textiles: A Handbook for Designers.*

(Neat Niche) **Muralist/Faux Finisher.** If you can't get a government grant, convince local merchants to hire you to paint inspiring murals on graffitied buildings, in restaurants, in apartment house or office building lobbies, on freeway underpass walls, even on billboard-sized signs. Faux finishing is the art of making a surface — usually a wall — look like something else, such as marble or leather. It's less sexy than mural painting, but potentially offers more gigs. *The Ultimate Resource for the Faux Finisher: www.muralsplus.com. Rebecca Pittman's book: How to Start a Faux Painting or Mural Business.*

(Neat Niche) **Commission Artist.** If you can create paintings that look good on the walls of corporate buildings or rich people's living rooms, place an ad in a magazine that your potential clients read (for example, corporate executives may read *Forbes,* and wealthy people may read *Town and Country*). Include a few samples and text such as, "Create a gallery-quality painting to your specifications for a fraction of the cost." *Article, Making Art on Commission: www.artbusiness.com/privcom.html.*

Technical Illustrator. Three of the words I most dread are *some assembly required.* The "easy instructions," despite the drawings created by technical illustrators, usually don't help. Maybe you'll do a better job. Technical illustrators tackle projects more important than my patio furniture. They may, for example, create drawings of the inner workings of a rocket engine. *Article: www.adda.org/content/view/41/46. Society of Illustrators: www.society illustrators.org.*

(Neat Niche) **Biomedical Visualization Specialist.** This field, formerly known as medical illustration, has come a long way. Thanks to software and imaging equipment, medical illustrators are no longer limited to what they can draw by hand. For example, they now use computer-generated brain maps to demonstrate differences between a Nobel Prize winner and a developmentally delayed person or between the parts of the brain that are activated when thinking about math or about sex. *Information: www.ahs.uic.edu/bhis/programs/bvis.php.*

(Neat Niche) **Ocularist.** You paint artificial eyes, typically in front of patients, so you can match their other eye perfectly. So, in addition to art skills, you need an empathic personality. I'd guess that with the right patient, a Cyclops or pirate quip or two may make the process more pleasant. *American Society of Ocularists:* `www.ocularist.org`.

(Neat Niche) **Forensic Artist.** Forensic artists create those composite drawings of criminal suspects, reconstructions of dead or maimed victims to use in solving crimes, and computer-generated drawings, slides, and videos that attorneys use to present their cases. Because each situation is different, because you're not a robot, and because the stakes are high, you have a shot at being a nonstarving artist. *Neville's Forensic Art World:* `www.forensicartist.com`

Conservator. A conservator's idea of bliss is restoring old paintings, furniture, autographs, books, and musical instruments to their former glory. A combination painter, refinisher, and chemist (watch those fumes!), most conservators are hired by major museums, libraries, and archives, and in the restoration of historic properties. Alas, few jobs are available. *American Institute for Conservation of Historic and Artistic Works:* `aic.stanford.edu`. *National Trust for Historic Preservation:* `www.nationaltrust.org`.

Cinematographer. It seems that everyone wants to be a film director, but what are the odds of making a living at it? Think lottery. How can you derive many of the benefits of directing with fewer people competing for jobs? Try cinematography. Like directors, cinematographers direct on film sets. The major difference is that rather than directing people, they direct the cameras. *American Society of Cinematographers:* `www.cinematography.com`. *Blain Brown's book: Cinematography.*

Lighting Designer. This is another backdoor into a film or theatrical career. Lighting designers are hired not only in film and theater, but also for trade shows, and for lighting major buildings — hotels, corporate lobbies, museums, concerts, and theme parks. *International Association of Lighting Designers:* `www.iald.org`.

Foley Artist. Remember the sounds of the steamy sex scenes in the last movie you saw? They probably were created by a foley artist making dispassionate love to his own wrist. That crunching snow as the avalanche rescuers try to save the day? Walking on cornstarch in a burlap bag. Foley artists create sounds that are easier to record than those made during an actual shoot. The good foley artist must be an *audile:* able to look at an object and imagine what type of sound it produces. Take, for example, that horror flick in which a character's guts are pulled out: It's raw chicken. *Article and links:* `www.skillset.org/film/jobs/post_production_sound/article_4768_1.asp`.

Exhibit Designer/Builder. Many artistic types who like to sling a hammer dream of becoming film or theater set designers, but that market is extraordinarily tight. But exhibit designing/building, a similar field, is less known and therefore easier to break into. You build the equivalent of theater sets for trade shows, expos, and museums. *Exhibitor magazine:* `exhibitoronline.com`. *Exhibit Designers and Producers Association:* `www.edpa.com`.

Holographer. Looking for a career that melds art and science? Wanna make something cool? Try holography. Holographs are no longer just 1960s psychedelia; the field is growing. Holographs are used in new-product promotion, on ID and credit cards, in movie special effects, and even in medical diagnosis. Holograms may even be used as a replacement for digital memory storage, because they can store data in three dimensions, rather than just two. Although some holographers learn on the job, others attend a special school, such as the one at *The Museum of Holography: www.holographiccenter. com. HoloWorld: www.holoworld.com. P. Hariharan's book: Basics of Holography.*

OOH

Tool and Die Maker. This is one metal artist who can expect to earn a living. Working from a blueprint or instructions, you develop the prototype tools and dies for metal or plastic products — from coins to wrenches. Although you need artistic skills, you get lots of help from designers. Tool and die designing and cutting are computer assisted. No college is required. Most die makers learn as apprentices. For you, could this be a career to die for? (Groan.) *Precision Machined Products Association: www.pmpa.org.*

Perfumer. Come up with a fragrance that smells great and different — that's what perfumers do when new perfumes, soaps, laundry products, shampoos, lotions, or candles are created. Most perfumers learn their art in an extensive apprenticeship. Procter and Gamble offers a prestigious one. Entrants to that program typically have a master's degree, yet half of perfumers have no degree at all. *Article: careers.nsta.org/pdfs/perfumer.pdf. Perfumer and Flavorist magazine: www.perfumerflavorist.com. Perfumers World: www.perfumersworld.com (offers online training, including a free introductory course). Mandy Aftel's book: Essence and Alchemy.*

Structured procedures

Computer Chip Layout Designer. This job essentially requires you to fit New York City onto a postage stamp. It sounds harder than it is. But like a chip — a potato chip — it's addictive. You can find yourself working 24 hours straight because, "I'm getting it. I'm getting it. It's almost done." You take engineer's specs for the 10,000-device chip, and feed that information into a computer program that lays it out for you. Unfortunately, the computer layout invariably has errors that you have to fix by hand. That's where the art comes in. Your job is to cram those devices in as tight as possible and still get the chip to work. *David Comer's book: Fundamentals of Electronic Circuit Design.*

Neon Sign Maker. How'd you like a career of twisting colored glass into special shapes? Tom Unger of Krypton Neon says you have a reasonable shot at making a living if you make neon signs for sign shops. Training is on-the-job. Don't worry, you needn't be a Rembrandt. An artist creates the design. Your job is to bend the glass to match the design. *Links: www.neonshop.com/ neonweb.*

Sailboat Captain. Some people seem to have the sea gene — they feel they are meant to be around water. If that's you, you can make a living at it if you really put your mind to it. Government regulations require extensive on- and off-boat training, which can cost almost as must as a yacht — and take as long as building one by hand. After you're licensed, pick a niche: Want to transport yachts? Move to Hawaii and take tourists on scuba trips? Take 'em on a history buff's trip down the river or whale watching off the California coast? All are possible, but only if you develop a serious marketing plan and have a personality that can win over everyone from your customers to hotel concierges. *John Rousmaniere's book: The Annapolis Book of Seamanship: Third Edition.*

 Harbor Pilot. This is a sailor's job that doesn't require long stints away from home. Your job is to dock ships or take them — the world's largest moveable man-made objects — out to sea. You start as a $50,000-a-year deck hand or engineer and move up to captain. If you're talented and a relentless networker, you may get to be a harbor pilot and earn a solid six-figure salary. Why do they earn so much? Because even experienced sea captains don't have the skills to navigate all sorts of vessels through the shallow, tricky waters of ports. And sometimes, after steering the ship to sea, they must climb down from the ship and into a small boat to get back to harbor. The job market for the top-paying jobs is tight as the tightest sail, but jobs that pay a middle-class salary are aplenty: fear of oil spills has resulted in regulations requiring most large ships to be towed into dock, often by a tug, but sometimes simply by advising the ship captain. Some tug operators and aspiring harbor pilots get their experience by working on party or fishing boats or by attending a two-year maritime program, such as that at the National Maritime Academy or one of the five state maritime Academies: California, Maine, Massachusetts, New York, and Texas. *Article, You're a What? Harbor Pilot:* www.findarticles. com/p/articles/mi_m1155/is_n4_v31/ai_6812807.

 Heart-Lung Perfusionist. In open-heart surgery, the surgeon can't work on the heart if blood is squirting all over the place. So a machine is hooked up to an artery to receive the blood. The machine then, like a heart and lungs, pumps blood and air back into an artery on the other side of the heart and lungs, and circulation continues. Meanwhile, the heart is relatively bloodless so the surgeon can work. The surgeon hooks up the blood vessels and the perfusionist runs the machine. Sounds straightforward, but talk to any perfusionist and he'll mention one word: stress. One mistake can be one too many for a bypass patient. Only calm people with a high tolerance for stress do well. They must also be mature enough to accept the great responsibility of this work. The big upside of this career is that you're intimately involved in saving people's lives. Perfusion is the smallest healthcare profession with only 3,200 practitioners in the United States. *Heart Pumper:* www.heartpumper.com. *American Society of Extra-Corporeal Technology:* www.amsect.com.

 Prosthetist/Orthotist. An amputee walks in. You're going to make his artificial limb or brace. You must be able to work face-to-face with amputees and create limbs and braces with great precision. After all, you're preparing a device on which that person's ability to use hands or feet depends. Extensive training is required, but many of the schools are public so it doesn't — pardon the expression — cost you an arm and a leg. *Orthotics and Prosthetics Careers: www.opcareers.org.*

 Pedorthist. A person needs special shoes — not because she has to match a dress, but rather because her feet are deformed from disease or injury. A podiatrist (foot doctor) sends her with a shoe prescription to a pedorthist, who examines and measures her feet and then designs or modifies shoes to fit. Demand for pedorthists exceeds supply, and training normally takes less than a year. *Pedorthics Footwear Association: www.pedorthics.org. Board for Certification in Pedorthics: www.cpeds.org.*

 High-Security Driving Instructor. How'd you like to teach police officers how to conduct a high-speed chase? Show a diplomat what to do when a terrorist starts shooting at her car? Show an FBI agent how his car can intercept a moving vehicle? That's what security driving instructors do. Unless you want to take a vow of poverty, forget about being a regular ol' driving instructor — they often earn little more than minimum wage. That isn't enough for the privilege of having a terrified aspiring driver let go of the steering wheel at 30 miles an hour and head straight for a brick wall — yes, it happens. *BSR, Inc. (a security driving school): www.bsr-inc.com.*

 Irrigation System Specialist. Nearly every homeowner, farmer, and golf course owner needs an irrigation system. And if you already have one, chances are it needs to be fixed or upgraded. Irrigation system design is a great career for someone who likes a combination of science and art, indoors and outdoors, business and environmentalism. Environmentalism? Yup, because modern irrigation systems save water, and fertilizing through the irrigation system allows less chemical fertilizer to be used. *The Irrigation Association: www.irrigation.org offers training courses.*

 Musical Instrument Repairperson. Kids aren't known for their tender treatment of anything, let alone school musical instruments. That means plenty of repairs are needed. And, of course, even some older folks' instruments need work. Musical instrument repair is a great career for fix-it types who prefer to avoid things electrical. It's a low-stress job. Working conditions are usually ideal, and you're nearly always assured of pleasing your customer. You should know how to play the instrument. Otherwise, how do you know whether you fixed it? Noted training institutions include Badger State Repair in Wisconsin, Renton Technical College in Washington, and Red Wing Technical Institute in Minnesota. *National Association of Professional Band Instrument Repair Technicians: www.napbirt.org.*

(Neat Niche) **Piano Technician/Tuner.** This is a good niche if you prefer to be out-and-about rather than in your workshop all day. And, if you get bored with just tuning, you can learn piano rebuilding. Despite the presence of electronic aids, piano tuners need a good ear. Unfortunately, the market for piano technicians is poor — synthesizers sound as good as many pianos, are less expensive, can create many more sounds, are portable, and needn't be tuned. *Piano Technicians Guild:* www.ptg.org.

 Sound Engineer. You're the person sitting in the back of a live theater or concert hall with a control board so big it looks like you're running a spaceship. Before the music starts, you set up the right mikes in the right places, and if the performance is for recorded rather than live performance, afterward you use digital tools to manipulate and mix the sounds into perfection. Many sound engineers have a bachelor's degree in sound engineering, but a possible alternative is to start by reading Gary Davis's book, *Sound Reinforcement Handbook,* and learn audio editing software such as ProTools, Reason, Digital Performer, Live, or Logic. Then beg your way into a volunteer apprenticeship at a theater or concert hall. *Wikipedia entry:* en.wikipedia.org/wiki/ Audio_engineering. *Article:* www.wikihow.com/Become-a-Sound-Engineer. *Audio Engineering Society:* www.aes.org.

 Conference Recording Specialist. Tens of thousands of professional meetings take place each year in the United States alone, but only a fraction offer recorded sessions for sale on CD or MP3 to those who missed sessions. This is a simple business. Equipment needs are modest: digital recorders, microphones, a CD duplication machine, and perhaps video equipment for recording keynote addresses. Marketing is straightforward — *Associations Unlimited* (available online through many large libraries) lists most of the world's associations, along with their size and upcoming conferences. Then just call large associations in your local area and make your pitch to the conference coordinator. You may be able to get a yes simply by touting the convenience to the organization's members, but your chances multiply if you offer the association a piece of the action. *Audio-Visual Education Network, a company that has recorded more than 2,000 conferences:* www.aven.com.

 Computer Repairperson. As products become ever-more computerized — from PET scanners to iPhones — ever-more people are needed to repair them. It's a nice job with a pleasant work environment and the chance to use your brains to diagnose problems, and it's in high demand. And when you fix their mission-critical gizmo, they'll love you. *Morris Rosenthal's book: Start Your Own Computer Business.*

(Neat Niche) **Notebook Computer Repairperson.** Because notebook computers are delicate and moved around so much, they break. Training doesn't require a PhD. A few months should do. Start with Morris Rosenthal's book, *Computer Repair with Diagnostic Flowcharts.* Then get certified by one or more manufacturers, such as Apple, Dell, Hewlett-Packard, or Sony.

(Neat Niche) **Hard Disk Repairperson.** People are willing to pay through the nose to retrieve the data they should have been backing up.

(Neat Niche) **Personal Digital Assistant Repairperson.** PDAs such as Treos and BlackBerrys are expensive and so justify repairing. Their portability increases their dropability and, in turn, your employability. *Article: A Cracking Good Repair Guide:* www.computeruser.com/articles/ 2406,5,14,1,0601,05.html.

(Neat Niche) **Biomedical Equipment Repairperson.** This high-tech repair niche pays well because when the machine must be fixed, it must be done perfectly and fast! A patient on a heart-lung machine can't wait long. *Roger Bowles's book: Critical Careers: A Guide to Opportunities in Medical Equipment Service.*

(Neat Niche) **Robotics Technologist.** Does building and fixing robots sound like fun? Until recently, robots mainly welded cars and elevated highway beams. Today, they assist with hip replacement surgery, climbing and painting rusty utility towers, and installing space stations. One perhaps surprising job requirement: the ability to lift 50 pounds. Robots haven't yet been to WeightWatchers. *RoboticsOnline:* www.roboticsonline.com

Computer Forensics Expert. Want to take a byte out of crime? Rev. William Guthrie's wife was found dead of Temazepan poisoning. A computer forensic expert searched the good minister's computer to find that he had visited many Web pages on that very drug. The pastor is now serving a life term. More often, computer forensics experts unearth employees who steal trade secrets and destroy company data. *Information:* www.forensicfocus.com *Amelia Phillips's book: Guide to Computer Forensics and Investigations, Second Edition.*

Telecommunications Specialist. Today's corporate telecom system goes well beyond a switchboard. It likely includes BlackBerries, cellphones, perhaps satellite, videoconferencing, voice over IP (Internet phones), computer networking, and yes, regular ol' phones. The telecom specialist helps a company figure out which combination of gizmos it needs and then supervises the installation. Listening and planning skills are key — a system is only good if it meets a company's current and anticipated needs. *Society of Telecommunications Consultants:* www.stcconsultants.org.

Solar and Wind Energy Technologist/Installer. Few of the many technologist careers nurture the soul of the environmentally conscious like this one does. Not only are you helping to keep the ecosystem clean, but you're also probably working for clients who are similarly minded. And, with today's high energy prices and the need to become energy-independent from the Middle East and Venezuela, demand for alternative energy sources is increasing, although at least in the short-term, the largest demand for solar and wind energy is in third-world countries — they don't have the infrastructure to support conventional power plants. Most solar installers learn on the job, although some community colleges offer programs. *American Solar Energy Society:* www.ases.org.

Millwright. Few high school graduates picture themselves as crucial to the operation of a megacorporation, yet millwrights are. They install and repair heavy industrial equipment. And it can be rewarding work: It can feel great to be called on to figure out what's wrong, and under time pressure, solve a problem that affects an entire plant's operation. You're also called on when a new piece of million-dollar heavy machinery is delivered. You're there to unload, inspect, and move it into position. That can mean deciding which ropes, cables, and hoists to use. It often means constructing special wood or metal foundations and using lasers to get the accuracy down to the millimeter. Fast-growing specialties include robotics and medical diagnostic equipment. Most millwrights learn as apprentices or in community college programs. It's a largely unionized field, so the pay's good. *Information:* www. kwantlen.bc.ca/trades/millwright/careers.html.

  Handyperson. When I tell friends that I have a good handyperson, their eyes light up — they're hard to find. That's largely because ever-more high school students are eschewing the trades for a white-collar career. So, if you have handyperson skills, you'll likely find yourself with plenty of customers grateful to pay you well. Being a handyperson is a fun career because you get to work on a range of projects that are fairly simple. Well, not simple for a klutz like me. *Sarah White's book: Start & Run a Handyman Business.*

(Neat Niche) **Senior Retrofitter.** This is an *Entrepreneur* magazine *Hot Pick.* "The Boomers are getting old but they don't want to see themselves as getting frail," says Jim Lapides of the National Association of Home Builders Remodelers Council. "Making stairs easier to climb or lowering light switches may ease the aging process, but many seniors won't seek out such retrofits." So the NAHB encourages remodelers to suggest retrofitting while doing routine jobs in seniors' homes.

(Neat Niche) **Noise Control Specialist.** Many owners of residences and workplaces near airports, freeways, schools, and factories willingly pay for some peace and quiet. This is a high-value specialty, yet the skills required are often modest. Often, all you're doing is insulating, double-glazing, and weather-stripping windows and doors. *Information:* www. soundproofing.org.

 I don't understand why leaf blowers are legal. They are the noisiest things this side of an atom bomb, and the noise lasts longer. Plus their engines spew out carcinogens. And for what? To blow leaves around? What's wrong with a rake?

   Electrician. I'm shocked that more people aren't becoming electricians. If you'd get a charge out of a career that requires working with your hands and your brain, this career could light up your life. While many electricians plug in via a four- or five-year apprenticeship, others get wired on the job, supplemented with classroom or correspondence courses. According to the federal government's *Occupational Outlook Handbook,* working as an electrician is among the best-paying of careers not requiring a college degree. And surprisingly, electricians are seriously injured by electricity at only half the rate of the general population. Just don't be color-blind: All electrical wires are color-coded! *Elizabeth Lytle's book: Careers as an Electrician. International Brotherhood of Electrical Workers:* `www.ibew.org`.

   Automotive Technician (Car Mechanic). Get that image of a grease-covered dude out of your mind. Today's automotive technician may spend almost as much time with a computer as with a wrench. Cars are heavily computer controlled, as is the equipment used to diagnose problems. If you have the ability to understand a complicated repair manual and a nose for diagnosing what's wrong, this is a better career than it used to be. More good news: Many automotive techs get their first professional job with no training other than having played around with their own car. New opportunities are available for women because the work has become more automated, and physical strength is less important. *Career Voyages:* `www.careervoyages.gov/automotive-service.cfm`

(Neat Niche) **Mobile Auto Repairperson.** Every car needs tune-ups, brake jobs, and so on, and nearly every car owner finds it a hassle to get them: Drop off the car and somehow get to work in the morning, and then somehow get back to the shop after work. Enter the mobile auto repairperson. He does the work right where you park your car for work. What a business: big demand, little competition, and ample markup. Ideal clients: large companies with an employee parking lot. Explain to their human resources director that by allowing you to offer repairs in the lot, employees won't need to take time off work to get their cars serviced. *Google "mobile auto repair" to find examples of such businesses.*

  Mobile Car Detailer. Many people want their cars polished and cleaned inside and out but don't have the time to do it themselves or to take it to a shop where they have to sit around waiting for it to be done. Enter the mobile car detailer. While the customer's car is parked at work or at home, the mobile car detailer does the job. This is another of those low-investment, no-brains, high-markup, easy-to-satisfy-the-customer businesses. One marketing approach is to get local new car dealers, especially luxury brands, to give a coupon for a half-price detailing to each new-car buyer. Luxury car buyers want their babies to keep looking good, and you know they have disposable income. One discounted detailing may yield a customer who'll keep buying your service for years. A variation: Set-up shop in an airport, employee, or shopping mall parking lot. *Eileen Figure Sandlin's book: Start Your Own Automobile Detailing Business.*

  Avionics Technician. In a $20 million airplane, $16 million is avionics (electronic equipment). It's been said that today's airplanes are flying computers. That means plenty of avionics to fix and plenty to upgrade. Electronics are always getting better, so many people are retrofitting — much cheaper than buying a new plane. Avionics technology is a career for tinkerers who read magazines such as *Popular Mechanics,* and of course, who like airplanes. *Professional Aviation Maintenance Association:* `www.pama.org`.

"Dull-normal" Business Owner. Thomas Stanley, author of *The Millionaire Next Door,* found that a disproportionate number of millionaires owned what he calls "dull-normal businesses," such as window manufacture, welding contracting, pest control, transmission repair, mobile home park maintenance, sand blasting, and used truck parts. The book goes on to say that these people, despite their career's lack of status, are generally happy with their worklives. *Thomas Stanley's books: The Millionaire Next Door and Millionaire Women Next Door.*

 I've found that status is often the enemy of contentment. I've seen more happy small business owners than doctors, lawyers, and executives.

  Surveyor. Is that airport runway level? What are a park's legal boundaries? Where does your neighbor's land end? Surveyors figure these things out. They still use the old-fashioned theodolites on tripods, but increasingly use satellite-based Global Positioning Systems (GPS) and Geographic Information Systems (GIS). Surveying is a fine career for someone who doesn't have a college degree but is comfortable around algebra and geometry, likes to learn as an apprentice, and wants an outdoor career with some status. The director of California's state apprenticeship programs told me that of the hundreds of apprenticeable careers, he'd say that surveying was the best. The job market is tight. *American Congress on Surveying and Mapping:* www.survmap.org.

 Geographic Information Specialist. How fast is a forest fire spreading? What's the best location for a highway? Worldwide, which crops will be bumper? (The last is a favorite question of commodities traders.) Geographic information specialists use satellite photos, lasers, and computers to create maps that answer these questions. Sounds like you need a PhD, but only a bachelor's or master's is required. *American Society for Photogrammetry and Remote Sensing:* www.asprs.org.

> (Neat Niche) **Photogrammetry Technician.** You prepare maps of inaccessible regions using aerial photographs. This career requires just two years of education after high school. *Wilfried Linder's book: Digital Photogrammetry: A Practical Course, 2nd Edition.*

> (Neat Niche) **Precision Agriculture.** Instead of blanketing farms with pesticides and fungicides, precision agriculturists use computers and global positioning systems to enable farmers to apply chemicals on an as-needed basis. *Precision Agriculture:* www.precisionag.org.

  Drafter. Can you picture it: sitting at a drafting table with triangles and a T square drawing blueprints? Forget it. Although you still need freehand drawing skills, almost all drafting today is done with a computer-aided design and drafting (CADD) program. Drafters take the designs of an engineer or architect to create blueprints of everything from toys to skyscrapers to rockets. *American Design Drafting Association:* www.adda.org.

Tile Setter. This strikes me as the ideal construction career: Progress on each job is steady and readily apparent, and the results look pretty. Training is short, usually on-the-job, although apprenticeships are available. And here's the kicker — pay is higher than for most construction trades. Perhaps that's because of hours spent on your knees and the toll the chemicals take on your hands. But pay also is higher because half of tile setters are self-employed, which is double the rate in other construction trades and a sign that tile setters find it relatively easy to get work. *National Tile Contractors Association:* `www.tile-assn.com`.

 Locksmith. This is the only career in which you don't get arrested for picking locks. It's one of the best hands-on, physically undemanding occupations: strong need, short training, and many grateful customers. Just think of all those people locked out of their homes or cars, and companies and homeowners who need to keep the bad guys out. As security threats rise, demand for high-tech entry systems grows. *Locksmith profile:* `www.apprenticesearch.com/ fpTrades/locksmith.asp`. *Associated Locksmiths of America:* `www.aloa. org`. *Bill Phillips's book: The Complete Book of Locks and Locksmithing, 6th Edition.*

 Farrier. Horses' hooves grow like your nails do, and when they're over-grown, a farrier must trim them and reshoe the horse. The saying goes: "No hoof, no horse." Pay is excellent — $50,000 to $125,000 a year is typical. Perhaps that's because few farriers can do it after age 45. It's said that every farrier has only so many shoeings in him. Other downsides: You must be careful to ensure you don't cripple the horse and that it doesn't give you a career-ending kick. But if you love the idea of doing physically demanding work with horses, are good with your hands, and don't mind having to face a career change in your 40s, horseshoeing can be a lucky career choice. *American Farriers Association:* `www.americanfarriers.org`.

 Gemologist. A gem of a career: looking at beautiful jewelry all day and decid-ing how much each piece is worth. Even better, after only a few months, you can become one of only 1,000 people to be certified by the Gemological Institute of America. Never again will anyone be able to pawn off a cubic zir-conium as a diamond on you. If you can live with rhinestone pay, you may find this a sparkling career. *Gemological Institute of America:* `www.gia.edu`. *Gerald Wykoff's CD: Analysis Techniques for Gemologists.*

 Arborist. A career in which you start at the top — top of the tree, that is, pruning it, topping it, bracing it, and spraying it. When you climb down, you also advise on which tree to put where, and how to plant and care for it so that — unlike the feeble specimen in front of my house — it thrives. Do a good job and you'll have bolstered Joyce Kilmer's case: "I think that I shall never see a poem lovely as a tree." *Wikipedia entry:* `en.wikipedia.org/ wiki/arborist`.

Specialty Stitcher. Rhonda Webb fits women who have had mastectomies with prosthetic breasts and special lingerie. She markets through surgeons and oncologists and meets clients in their own homes. She says, "People are very appreciative. It's so much more relaxed than walking into a cold department store with everyone hearing what your problem is." Other under-the-radar niches: paraplegics and quadriplegics; ultraorthodox Muslims, Sikhs, and Jews; corporate concierge sewing; and theater curtains, wheelchair accessories, doll clothing, wedding gowns, company banners, sails, and parachutes. *Wikipedia entry:* `en.wikipedia.org/wiki/Seamstress`. *Barbara Sykes's book: The 'Business' of Sewing.*

Personal Chef. The United States Personal Chefs Association estimates that 25,000 personal chefs could find employment in the United States, yet only 5,000 are active in the entire world. This career is better than restaurant cheffing because you cook smaller numbers of meals so you needn't spend long days, nights, and weekends standing over a hot stove. And unlike when starting out in a restaurant, you design all the menus, a veritable executive chef. *United States Personal Chefs Association:* `www.uspca.com`. *American Personal Chef Association:* `www.personalchef.com`.

Dog Trainer. Do you have the patience to teach Rover not to chew up the furniture or pee on the floor when Rover's owner doesn't? Do you like the challenge of convincing a dog to let you walk it rather than have it walk you? Consider a career in dog training. Best way for *you* to train is to visit a few local training centers, watch a few pros work, and ask your favorite for an apprenticeship. Most states don't have licensure requirements. Anyone can claim to be a dog trainer, so choose your mentor carefully to avoid getting bitten. *American Dog Trainer's Network:* `www.inch.com/~dogs`.

(Neat Niche) **Service Dog Trainer.** We all know about guide dogs for the blind, but demand is increasing for dogs for the deaf. Your job is to train the dog to alert its master to specific sounds like a smoke alarm, a ringing phone, and a knock at the door. Because these dogs are generally large, and much of the training requires moving the dog, assistance dog trainers must be physically strong. *National Service Dog Center:* `deltasociety.org`.

(Neat Niche) **Working Dog Trainer.** What sort of work do working dogs do? Typical jobs are sniffing out drugs for the United States Customs Service, sheep herding, and finding injured people in wreckages for local police departments. *Working Dogs Cyberzine:* `www.workingdogs.com`.

Pet Sitter. Americans are nuts about their pets. Forty-three percent of United States households have pets, more than the percentage of households with kids! And pet sitting, which a decade ago was a novelty, today is an established career. Pet sitting can be done three ways. You can open your home to Muffin, live in Muffin's home while her owners are gone, or make daily stops at Muffin's home. Don't think that pet sitting is the same as pet playing. Crises occur. Muffin can be sick or develop a case of separation anxiety when you show up. In such cases, you must instantly become a pet shrink or find yourself with a pooch who refuses to go for a walk or who takes a bite out of your leg. More often, it's a matter of accommodating pet idiosyncrasies, like my cat who likes to roll around in the tub each morning after I shower. To keep the cat happy, the pet sitter moistens the tub and puts the cat in. The more likely way to make a middle-class income from pet sitting is to have a staff of sitters, but that means you don't get to play with Muffin. *National Association of Professional Pet Sitters: www.petsitters.org.*

 Pyrotechnician. Staging pyrospectaculars sounds like a blast, but it's not easy to soar into this field. The problem is that it's dominated by a small number of private, mainly family-run businesses that like to keep their sky shows to themselves. But if this career sounds more exciting than a rocket's red glare, here are some good ways to start. Visit *American Fireworks News: www.fireworksnews.com.* Next, attend training offered by a local fireworks company during the spring or the one-day course offered by the *Pyrotechnics Guild International (www.pgi.org).* Work as an assistant at a July 4th show or two. It's seasonal work for most people in the field, but a small percentage keep busy year-round shooting fireworks for movies, TV, theater, concerts, and sporting events. *American Pyrotechnic Association: www.americanpyro. com. International Pyrotechnics Society: www.intlpyro.org.*

 Product Tester. How'd you like to play with toys for a living? Be a toy tester for Mattel or Hasbro. Michael Ferraro tastes Godiva Chocolate for a living. Jack Brashears's job is tasting Jack Daniels whiskey. Product testers check out everything from software to cars. The field has limitations, though. A rather lazy person contacted the Simmons Mattress Company to ask whether it uses mattress testers. The answer was no.

> (Neat Niche) **Computer Game Tester.** I include this because it somehow had to be in a book called "Cool Careers." But having spoken with some game testers, it's a terrible job. You're put in a room with many other testers, which means the room must be kept cold to keep all the computers from overheating. Most of the time, you're not playing the game, you're trying to break it — for example, you bump against each of the game's 9,000 walls to be sure nothing untoward happens. And because there's always a rush to get the game out, the game company often has you work 12 hours a day. Plus, the pay is abysmal — typically around $10 an hour. Employers can get away with that because ten zillion game fanatics think it's a cool career. Not. *Wikipedia entry: en.wikipedia.org/wiki/game_tester.*

 Diver. I wish I could tell you that the reality matches the stereotype: gliding through glistening tropical waters, harvesting abalone. Fact is, 90 percent of divers are construction workers for whom diving is just a mode of transportation to the job site — except that you have the added challenge of doing it under the sea, so you can't run down to Home Depot for a part. That said,

diving has pluses. Within a few years of deciding to become a diver —
admittedly at low pay and with long hours — diving proves to be one of the
few outdoor careers that doesn't require a college education and that can
earn you $45,000 to $75,000 for a nine-month work year. Engineers can make
more. You get to travel all over the world — often on a moment's notice. And
there are prized neat niches: police divers who look for guys who have been
fitted with cement shoes, research divers who assist marine biologists, and
journalist divers who write articles and take pictures for magazines, books,
and even screenplays. Before you take the plunge (I couldn't resist), remember that a typical job is working in the Gulf of Mexico, repairing oil rigs.
About.com's diving careers portal: `scuba.about.com/od/careersjobs`.

Work with People and Data

Optometrist. "Better with lens A or lens B?" After a while, I can never tell
and feel like a dunce. In any case, optometrists examine, diagnose, and treat
eye conditions, usually by prescribing glasses or contact lenses. In some states,
they're allowed to do some minor surgery. Optometry is among the most
rewarding health careers because it identifies problems that usually have a
ready cure. And because the population is aging, and because optometrists
are a lower-cost alternative to ophthalmologists (medical eye doctors), the
job market for optometrists is good. *Association of Schools and Colleges of
Optometry:* `www.opted.org`. *American Optometric Association:* `www.aoa.org`.

Orthoptist. This is another option for people who want to be a doctor but
don't have the grades or desire to spend that much time in school. Like an
eye doctor (ophthalmologist), but under his general supervision, you check
vision, perform tests for everything from depth perception to eye muscle
problems, and do patient education. Orthoptists more often work with children. A bachelor's degree plus a two-year program enables you to start in a
career that some orthoptists say feels rather like being a physician. *Orthoptics
Online:* `www.orthoptics.org`.

OOH

Pharmacist. You're not just filling prescriptions. You're often a front-line
healthcare provider, teaching diabetics how to inject themselves with insulin,
assisting with blood pressure monitoring, and ensuring that people know
how to take their medications. The latter isn't as easy as it sounds. Many
older people must take many medications, each of which must be taken at a
different time, some of which must be taken on an empty stomach, others
when not drowsy. Perhaps the most important thing a pharmacist does is
ensure that drugs can be taken together. The TV show *Dateline* did a test in
which an obviously pregnant woman walked into ten pharmacies asking
whether two drugs could be taken together. Six of the ten pharmacists said
yes. In fact, when a pregnant woman takes those two drugs together, it's
lethal. Each year, thousands of people are hospitalized because they take
prescription medications improperly. Pharmacists can be lifesavers.

Some of the more interesting pharmacy jobs are in drug companies' research departments and in hospital pharmacies. In the latter, in addition to filling prescriptions, you may attend grand rounds, instruct interns, and assist surgeons in preparing infusions. As in many other fields, the training requirement has been ratcheted up: now a Doctor of Pharmacy degree is standard, which typically requires seven years of post-high-school education. *American Association of Colleges of Pharmacy:* www.aacp.org. *Fred Gable's book: Opportunities in Pharmacy Careers. Accreditation Council for Pharmacy Education:* www.acpe-accredit.org/students/default.asp.

 Genetic Counselor. People are ever-more aware that they're much affected by their genes. The upshot of *Time* and *Newsweek* cover stories is that personality and intelligence are heavily mediated by their biology. What do genetic counselors do? Example: A husband and wife both suffer from severe depression. They're thinking about having a child. A genetic counselor helps them understand the odds that their child will suffer from depression, facilitates their deciding whether to get pregnant, and helps them make peace with their decision. People enter this field from a wide range of disciplines, including biology, psychology, nursing, public health, and social work. *National Society of Genetic Counselors:* www.nsgc.org. *Human Genome Project's profile of genetic counseling:* www.ornl.gov/sci/techresources/Human_Genome/medicine/genecounseling.shtml.

 Dietitian/Nutritionist. They're not just in the hospital basement any more. Now, companies hire dietitians to plan healthy meals for their employee cafeterias and to promote sensible eating habits. (Frankly, I'd rather have an Indian food buffet.) Government uses them to plan such things as school menus. Food manufacturers and supermarket chains use dietitians to evaluate prepared foods and put interesting low-calorie recipes, such as endive salad with radicchio and sun-dried tomatoes (yuck), into their ads.

Health spas, weight-loss clinics, and prisons use dietitians to make sure visitors have a balanced diet. We don't want to lack any of the four basic food groups, now do we? My daughter says that our fridge contains a different four basic food groups: snack foods, jams, condiments, and science experiments.

The previously mentioned dietitian careers are growing, but most dietitians still are kept busy with hypertension, diabetes, and obesity, in hospitals, clinics, and in their own private practices. I'm still hungering for that Indian food buffet, but I'll settle for some chow fun (fat, greasy, delicious Chinese noodles). *American Dietetic Association:* www.eatright.org.

 Patient Advocate. It requires Magellan to navigate the labyrinthine healthcare system. Most people, especially when ill, aren't the best navigators. Enter the patient advocate. You help ensure that the patient gets to see the desired specialist; you do research so the patient is more informed when talking to the doctor; you may monitor the patient in the hospital to ensure the pills really are meant for her; you sort through the mountains of bills and, if necessary, negotiate fees with the healthcare provider, insurance company, or other payer. ("Medicare, how dare you refuse to pay for that surgery!") The confluence of aging Boomers with an ever-more complex healthcare system means unlimited demand for a persuasive, persistent person willing to do the vital work of patient advocacy. Some hospitals and HMOs hire nurses and social workers as patient advocates, but an enormous unmet need remains. *Patient Advocacy Foundation:* `www.patientadvocate.org`.

Manager. Many people like to manage projects and other people, and that's a good thing. Despite all the downsizing, the United States still has millions of managers. What makes a particular management position good? The specific industry or government agency isn't so crucial. Instead, look for the following:

- ✔ An organization with enough money to do things right and pay you reasonably
- ✔ An organizational culture that values excellence *and* its people
- ✔ Compatible co-workers, supervisees, and supervisors
- ✔ A product or service you believe in

Assess those things before accepting a position.

That's what *you're* looking for, but what are employers craving? Kathryn and George Petras, in the book, *Jobs,* describe today's employable manager: "Multilingual, a generalist with technical skills, computer competent, a doer, not a follower, a team player or team leader, a change agent."

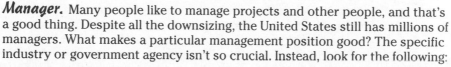

You need to know about some downsides to a career in management. The workplace hierarchy is flatter, so opportunities for promotion are fewer. Indeed, a recent American Management Association survey of middle managers found that only 43 percent thought their job was secure, compared with 72 percent in 1991. And while on the job, managers certainly have their work cut out for them. Their bosses demand ever-more productivity at the same time as new laws make firing incompetents even tougher. And often, you're asked to supervise people who may be halfway around the world. Because of all the downsides, I believe that management can be considered a cool career only if you make the effort to see that the job you accept meets the requirements previously listed. *About.com's management portal:* `management.about.com`. *The Wall Street Journal's Executive Career Site:* `www.careerjournal.com`. *Chapter 11 in this book includes The World's Shortest Management Course.*

(Neat Niche) **College Administrator.** A college campus is a great place to be a manager. Who can resist a beautiful environment, intelligent people, learning opportunities all around you, a pro-social mission, and work hours that tend to be more moderate than in the private sector — not to mention that things really lighten up between terms and all summer? And few organizations hire as many managers: often multiple layers of management for everything from governmental affairs to the physical plant. A downside is that office politics are particularly vicious on many college campuses. And political correctness is epidemic — how ironic that universities, traditionally the clarion callers for free speech, are today among its greatest censors. Not surprisingly, colleges want their managers to have graduate degrees. It doesn't look good if an organization selling degrees doesn't require them of its managers. *Nancy Martin's book: Career Aspirations & Expeditions.*

(Neat Niche) **College Student Affairs Administrator.** This career has nothing to do with steamy dorm room flings. College student affairs administrators coordinate the nonacademic part of student life, from student orientation to graduation. For example, they supervise the fraternities, coordinate residence hall activities and intramural sports, and sponsor antidrug programs. *National Association of Student Personnel Administrators:* `www.naspa.org`.

(Neat Niche) **Government Manager.** Aspiring managers shouldn't overlook government positions. Eighty percent of government jobs are managerial and professional compared with 25 percent in the private sector. In addition to quantity, government jobs often offer higher-quality benefits, stability, offshore resistance, and colleagues dedicated to the public interest. Plus, government agencies are encouraging more customer-service orientation among their employees, so the stereotype of the semicomatose government worker is becoming less accurate. *Links to government job sites:* `www.rileyguide.com/gov.html`.

(Neat Niche) **Court Administrator.** One thing I learned since writing the previous edition of this book is that for many people, a job's setting can be as important as its tasks. Courts tend to be well funded, attractive, peaceful workplaces — unless, of course, two lawyers are screaming at each other or a perpetrator decides to go ballistic in the courtroom. (Oh, that was a TV show. Sorry.) Courts need administrators to do everything from coordinating judges' schedules to figuring out how to get enough jurors and developing more efficient systems for processing traffic tickets. (I have a bachelor's degree in traffic school.) And because these are government jobs, benefits are good, vacations long, and job security maximum. *National Association for Court Management:* `nacm.ncsc.dni.us`.

(Neat Niche) **Manager in a fun business.** Any of these turn you on: toy company (Cranium's and LeapFrog's corporate cultures are well regarded), ice cream making (Ben & Jerry's?), adventure travel company, fashion or cosmetics, country club, sports team, MTV, dance studio, car company (Porsche?), plant nursery, sporting goods firm? In a 2006 *Business Week* survey of large employees, guess which company was rated the #1 best to work for: Disney. (Maybe I should give my assistant a pair of mouse ears.)

(Neat Niche) **Performing Arts Manager.** Many aspiring actors, singers, and dancers, who have realized why the word "starving" so often appears next to the word "artist," move to the back office as a way of staying around the field they love. Today's performing arts managers do more than supervise ticket sales. Indeed, their main job is often to direct fundraising: coordinate galas, e-mail solicitations, and schmooze with potential donors. The coolest such job may be artistic director, who gets to choose what goes onstage and hire the director, crew, and perhaps performers. Performing arts manager salaries generally are low, but many people are willing to live modestly for a life even tangentially related to their creative passion. *North American Performing Arts Managers and Agents:* www.napama.org.

(Neat Niche) **Information Technology Manager.** The term "IT manager" subsumes three kinds of jobs. You can manage an application, such as a database. You can manage a desktop; that is, select, install, and support the organization's computers, including its laptops and PDAs. Or you can manage its infrastructure: for example, its backbone and security system. Beware of becoming too technical and not leaderly enough. According to a Computerworld blue-ribbon panel, by 2010, most programming and similar technical worker-bee work will be offshored to low-cost countries. The successful IT manager of 2010 will need to be a "versatilist": having just enough technology skill to speak with techies and a deeper ability to manage large projects and contribute to the business as a whole.

Of course, whether you're a generalist or specialist, IT is among the world's fastest-changing fields. If you love life on the cutting edge yet have the communication skills to work with mere mortals, IT management gives you the opportunity for money, learning, and advancing the world's ability to communicate and conduct commerce. (See separate profiles in this chapter for Systems Analyst, Network Administrator, Database Administrator, Hardware Engineer, Software Engineer, and Web Developer.) *Computerworld's career section:* www.computerworld.com/taxonomy/000/000/000/ taxonomy_000000010_index.jsp.

(Neat Niche) **Work-Life Manager.** According to *Self* magazine, this job title didn't even exist 15 years ago. Yet today, thousands of companies have hired managers to develop and implement family-friendly work policies, such as flexible work scheduling, dependent care, and family leave. Most such managers have a human resource background. Average salary: $75,000. Work-life managers are overwhelmingly female. *Alliance for Work-Life Progress:* www.awlp.org. *Work-Life and Human Capital Solutions:* www.workfamily.com.

(Neat Niche) **Project Manager.** The project can be a conversion of entertainment content to AppleTV format, an expansion into the Mexican market, or building a satellite. In any case, the project manager's job is to develop a design for the project and then coordinate its completion, usually using scheduling software. This job is good for someone who is second best in many things; for example, a software project manager needs to be good if not tops in programming, managing, art, interface design, and marketing.

Project managers like their job because it has clearly defined milestones. More and more project management jobs will be one-offs: you're hired for a specific project, and when it's done, you have to convince some other employer that your skill set is ideal for the job. *Wikipedia entry: en.wikipedia.org/wiki/project_manager. Scott Berkun's book: The Art of Project Management.*

I find it sad that ever-more workers must work on a project basis. That forces them to spend much of their worklives looking for their next few months of employment. More important, they're denied the extended-family experience of working with the same folks for a long time. I know that just-in-time hiring is efficient, but I have the sense that its net effect on society is negative.

(Neat Niche) **Product Manager.** Being in charge of a product, even if it's toilet paper, is fun. You get to supervise all decisions: how thick and soft it should be, whether it should be embossed with dots or doves, what picture goes on the packaging, how the sales force pitches the product, whether ad dollars are weighted more heavily toward print, TV, Web, or point-of-purchase, and whether the ads should show the product being used. Well, not that. *Wikipedia entry: en.wikipedia.org/wiki/product_management. Donald Lehmann's book: Product Management.*

(Neat Niche) **Facilities Manager.** You run an organization's facilities: deciding where to lease, developing its environmental sustainability plan, hiring the maintenance crew, and continuity management (how to get the facility up and running again after a disaster). My favorite subniche: stadium management. *International Facility Management Association: www.ifma.org. Frank Booty's book: Facilities Management Handbook, Third Edition.*

(Neat Niche) **Association Manager.** Thousands of professional organizations exist, from professional associations to chambers of commerce. Each uses managers. What do they do? Typically they ensure that new members are recruited, the membership list is maintained, dues are collected, the newsletter is sent out, the Web site is optimized, and meetings and conferences are planned and promoted. One way to get a job created for you is to approach organizations that have been volunteer-run and are ready for a step up. Or start your own association. Surprisingly, many fields don't have one. *American Society of Association Executives: www.asaecenter.org.*

(Neat Niche) **City Manager.** You're involved in all aspects of running a city, from distributing the budget to overseeing park renovation to hiring key personnel. City managers are among the more powerful government officials who don't have to run for election. A master's in public administration is usually required. *International City/County Management Association: www.icma.org. Douglas Watson's book: Spending a Lifetime: The Careers of City Managers.*

(Neat Niche) **Environmental Manager.** Government agencies and corporations hire environmental managers to develop plans to minimize pollution to water, air, and soil quality, and to develop remediation plans when things go awry. Corporate environmental managers also draft environmental impact reports before expanding operations. *The WWW Virtual Library: Environmental Management:* www.gdrc.org/uem.

(Neat Niche) **Nonprofit Manager.** It's true that nonprofit management is especially difficult because staff is often largely volunteer and funds are limited, but The Cause is sometimes enough to make it all worthwhile. Oh, and while salaries are generally low, that's not true at the top. According to a 2005 *Chronicle of Philanthropy* survey, the median compensation for the 241 nonprofit chief executives who responded to the survey was $327,575. (See where your charity dollars are going?) *About.com's nonprofit portal:* nonprofit.about.com. *Jobs:* www.idealist.org *and* www.nptimes.com.

(Neat Niche) **Public Affairs Manager.** For altruistic and selfish reasons, many companies, TV and radio stations, nonprofits, universities, and hospitals work hard at being good community citizens. Your job is to direct those efforts. You may set up a community blood pressure screening, a Christmas toy giveaway, or sponsor a neighborhood dispute resolution service. Larger corporations often set up foundations to donate money to local charities. The usual point of entry is a college internship or volunteer position. *Public Affairs Council:* www.pac.org. *Nicholas Henry's book: Public Administration and Public Affairs, 10th Edition.*

(Neat Niche) **Foundation Program Manager.** How'd you like to supervise the giving away of money to worthy causes? Corporations, government entities such as school districts, and wealthy individuals set up foundations to distribute money to nonprofit causes. Foundations hire program managers, often called grantmakers, to write and solicit grant proposals from potential recipients of foundation money and, after money is granted, to supervise the spending of that money to ensure it isn't squandered. *Foundation Center:* foundationcenter.org/grantmakers. *Joel Orosz's book: The Insider's Guide to Grantmaking.*

(Neat Niche) **Healthcare Administrator.** What's a healthcare system to do? Technology is advancing, healthcare laws are changing, HMOs are squeezing, population is aging, hospitals are closing, stand-alone clinics are opening, home healthcare is burgeoning, regulations are increasing, and nationalizing the healthcare system looms. The answer: Hire more administrators to make sense of the madness. A typical challenge: An emergency room administrator tries to balance the budget in the face of increasing nonpaying patients and ever-more parsimonious insurers. *American College of Health Care Administrators:* www.achca.org.

(Neat Niche) **Public Health Administrator.** Working for a government agency, you may coordinate healthcare programs for the poor, direct a safe-sex campaign, or administer vaccination programs. *Association of Schools of Public Health:* www.asph.org.

(Neat Niche) **Human Resources Manager.** HR managers usually wear one of three hats. You can be a hiring specialist, for example, trying to recruit those tough-to-find scientists. You can be a benefits expert, for example, helping employees best use their benefits. Finally, you can be an organizational developer. In that role, you may develop programs to prevent communication problems, workplace violence, drugs, or racial enmity, and serve as mediator when problems arise. An ever-larger part of an HR manager's work deals with issues of race, gender, and disabilities. Alas, diversity training sessions often devolve into angry affairs, and lawsuits and other legal hassles are taking up ever-more of the job. The good news is that organizational developers generally get to be the good guy. While other managers' main job is to make workers do more, better, and faster, your job often, at least ostensibly, is to keep things human. Yes, you're also trying to build the bottom line, but your efforts generally have a more compassionate quality. *About.com's human resources portal:* humanresources. about.com. *Society for Human Resources Management:* www.shrm.org. *Shawn Smith's book: The HR Answer Book.* (Also see the Personnel Recruiter profile in the earlier section "Bringing people together.")

(Neat Niche) **Construction Manager.** Imagine being able to look at an office building, arena, freeway cloverleaf, school, or biotech lab, and say, "I directed the construction of that." Construction managers have the challenging job of helping owners clarify their desires, bidding the job, hiring subcontractors, planning the project's timeline, directing the project's execution, and coming up with solutions to the myriad problems that occur. Increasingly, a bachelor's degree in construction management is important because the jobs are getting ever-more complex and computer-centric. Downside: You're on-call 24/7 to deal with delays, weather, and job-site emergencies. But demand is strong, pay is good, and you get to see the fruits of your labors for the rest of your life. *Construction Management Association of America:* www.cmaanet.org.

 School Administrator. You wouldn't think that turnover is high among school principals. It's a prestigious job with an important mission. Yet turnover *is* high, and here's why: Principals report that it typically takes two years of time-consuming, highly stressful, union-scrutinized effort to have even a chance of getting rid of an incompetent teacher. Thus, most principals feel forced to look the other way, and instead, take the flak from complaining parents and students. Another source of principals' stress is that they often must take on more tasks than in the past. For example, they may be charged with establishing school-based drug, alcohol, and violence prevention programs. Your supervisees, teachers, have ever-tougher jobs, with more limited-English-proficient immigrant students, and orders from on-high requiring teachers to serve ever-more severely learning-disabled and emotionally disturbed students in the regular classroom. And not just serve them, but achieve the new mantra, "No child left behind: All students can learn to high standards." Principals must manage to keep teacher morale high under these trying circumstances. Yet another demoralizer is salary. The strong teachers' unions have gotten solid salary increases for teachers but administrators' salaries haven't kept pace. The result is that teacher salaries often approach those of the principals.

The silver lining in all this is that the job market for aspiring principals has never been better. And a principalship is a launchpad for often more-rewarding jobs as a district or county school administrator. *American Association of School Administrators: www.aasa.org. Ronald Thorpe's book: The First Year as Principal: Real World Stories from America's Principals.*

(Neat Niche) **Private School Founder.** The public schools, especially in mixed-socioeconomic areas, are increasingly prioritizing the needs of low-achieving children over those of other children. Many parents of average and high achievers are becoming convinced that these schools are inhibiting their children from achieving their potential. Even liberal parents committed to the concept of public education are sending their children to private schools lest they sacrifice their children in the name of a political philosophy. Even the nation's leading public school cheerleaders, the Clintons, wouldn't send their child to public schools.

If you're willing to take on the challenge of starting and running a private school, you may well find strong demand. Your school needn't be expensive. Many parents don't care much about fancy facilities — better good teachers in wooden buildings than wooden teachers in good buildings. I know of a school that operates in a large tent, yet there's a waiting list for admission. Parents care that their schools have good teachers, good kids, and a fascinating curriculum. Provide those and you'll always have a waiting list, and you may even change the lives of children in ways that few other people do. *Donald Leisey's book: The Educational Entrepreneur: Making a Difference. National Association of Independent Schools: www.nais.org.*

Labor Relations Specialist. Whether employed by a union or by management, most of your work is done before you ever sit down at the negotiating table. Through the year, your job is to learn the needs of labor and management and to resolve disputes as they arise. If you're employed by a union, you may also try to unionize workplaces. Come contract time, the bulk of your work is still away from the negotiating table. At that point, your main job is to do the research needed to bolster your side's position. And then, of course, during negotiations, you get to play hardball, poker, or win-win. *Wikipedia entry: en.wikipedia.org/wiki/labor_relations. Arthur Sloane's book: Labor Relations, 12th Edition.*

Political Campaign Manager. Everyone who runs for office, from school board member in Lost Gulch to president of the United States, needs a campaign manager. The campaign manager researches the opinions and voting patterns in the jurisdiction; helps develop the candidate's themes; plans fundraisers; coordinates the Web site, e-mail, and snail mail attack; hires staff; trains phone bank workers; coordinates the door-to-door campaign; excites the media with a nonstop barrage of "news"; coordinates damage control; and even helps design the campaign button. It's an exciting job: You're in charge of a winner-take-all contest that can make a difference in society. Start out by volunteering to assist in running the campaign for a local politician. *Information:* www.completecampaigns.com. *Catherine Shaw's book: The Campaign Manager, Third Edition.*

In the crazy U.S. system, leaders get elected largely on who presses the most flesh, buys the best database of undecided voters, makes the speech with the most focus-group-approved soundbites, and more important, extracts the most dollars from special interest groups. If I had my way, elections would be just two weeks long and funded completely with a modest amount of tax dollars. Each registered voter would receive an e-mail or booklet with each candidate's voting record and personal statement. During those two weeks, the candidate could use the tax dollars to campaign as he or she saw fit and would be required to participate in at least one televised debate in which candidates could not dictate the terms. That's it. Substance, not fluff, and much less chance of politicians landing in the hip pockets of special interest groups. Perhaps more important, because of the brief, honorable campaign, outstanding candidates, daunted or disgusted by what it currently takes to get elected, would be more likely to come forward.

Administrative Assistant/Secretary. Many of my clients crave being the right-hand person — and this career affords that opportunity. Ignore Hollywood portrayals of the overworked, abused secretary; this can be a fine career. Trusted administrative assistants may have quite a varied workday: draft a letter, appease a client, conduct research on the Internet, plan a luncheon, create a PowerPoint presentation, organize the boss's file system, prepare a spreadsheet, screen mail and calls, and enjoy a close (sometimes, very close) relationship with the boss. And unlike the boss, admins are usually out the door at 5:00, with little or no work to take home. And increasingly, bosses allow their admins to work at home at least one day a week. *International Association of Administrative Professionals:* www.iaap-hq.org. *Brenda Bailey-Hughes's book: The Administrative Assistant.*

Succession Planning Consultant. A tough time for family businesses is when one generation realizes that it must allow the next generation to take over. Family members are often too emotionally involved to develop a wise succession plan on their own. Enter the consultant, a combination psychologist and businessperson. *Links:* humanresources.about.com/od/succession planning. *Craig Aronoff's book: Family Business Succession, 2nd Edition.*

Fee-only Financial Planner. This is an especially good field for the older career-seeker. Most people with money are older and tend to trust people their own age. Especially as Boomers age and worry about how in the world they're going to save the zillion dollars the experts say they'll need for retirement, the need for financial planners is accelerating. Social Security is unlikely to help. A survey found that more 20-somethings believe in UFOs than believe they'll ever see a penny of Social Security. And with an ever-wider range of investment and insurance options, many confused people want help.

The good financial planner is as much a financial therapist as number cruncher or mutual fund picker. Unfortunately, the traditional financial planner has a conflict of interest: She makes more money if you buy high-commission investments and insurance, and makes even more if you buy and sell often. Enter the fee-only financial planner. These professionals get paid a flat fee, so their only motivation is to please the client. How to get clients? Develop relationships with estate-planning attorneys and accountants, and make presentations at employee workplaces. Some say that the best financial planner training is the one you get if a brokerage house hires you. Others recommend the two-year, $2,000 self-study course offered by the *College for Financial Planning:* www.cfp.net/become. *Financial Planning Association:* www.fpanet.org. *National Association of Personal Financial Advisors (for fee-only financial planners):* www.napfa.org.

Debt Collection Specialist. If you don't mind representing a business against a debtor, this is a good career. It's one-on-one problem solving — the sort of work many people like. And if the debtor can't pay, the world doesn't end. There's always another debtor to call on. That's the key to success in this business — staying pleasant and solution-oriented. It's a great home business. You can sit at home in your comfies with your feet up, with no overhead, and earn 25 percent to 50 percent of every dollar you retrieve for your client businesses. And there are plenty of dollars to retrieve. Consumer debt is two *trillion* dollars. *The Association of Credit and Collections Professionals:* www.acainternational.org. *Robert Bills's book: How to Start a Home-Based Collection Agency.*

> (Neat Niche) **Commercial Debt Negotiator.** Many businesses accumulate too much debt. They hire you to negotiate with banks, collection agencies, and other creditors to accept a discount in exchange for immediate payment. You get clients by cold-calling businesses, or from bankers or collection agencies. Check to be sure that it's legal in your state to represent debtors in this way.

Business Broker. As small-business-owning Boomers retire, they'll be looking to unload their companies. Meanwhile, many people starting out will likely find the job market tight and so will look to own their own business. Your job is to bring them together. *Business Brokerage Press:* www.bbpinc.com. *Ira Nottonson's book: Entrepreneur Magazine's Ultimate Guide to Buying or Selling a Business. VR Business Brokers:* www.vrbusinessbrokers.com.

College Financial Aid Counselor. Guess the sticker price of sending two kids to a brand-name private college for their bachelor's and master's degrees. $600,000! So, it's no surprise that frantic parents are flocking to financial aid counselors. These counselors function like tax accountants, helping you figure out how to plan and fill out the college and government forms to maximize your financial aid. *The Financial Aid Page:* www.finaid.org. *Anna Leider's book: Don't Miss Out.*

Corporate Intelligence Officer. An article in *Working Woman* reassures you, "No need for a cloak or dagger. Corporate intelligence staffers comb through perfectly legitimate sources of information — newspapers, competitors' sales materials, speeches, credit reports, databases, and interviews — for the goods on competitors. You really have to be good at getting information, which means getting people to trust you." *Society of Competitive Intelligence Professionals: www.scip.org. The Competitive Intelligence Index:* www.bidigital.com/ci. *Craig Fleisher's book: Strategic and Competitive Analysis.*

Military Officer. This job title is a catchall for hundreds of occupations, from manager to doctor, accountant to engineer. A military career offers many pluses: fine free training, extensive benefits, and esprit de corps unmatched in most civilian jobs. Of course, you have to accept a life of uniforms, the bureaucracy to end all bureaucracies, and transfers to places you'd otherwise never choose. (The Middle East, anyone?) And, oh yes, you can get your head blown off. Among the many routes in are ROTC, enlistment, Officers Candidate Schools, and the prestigious service academies, such as West Point (Army), the Naval Academy, the Air Force Academy, and the Coast Guard Academy. Those schools offer small classes taught by unusually dedicated instructors. When I visited the Air Force Academy, the cadets were more enthusiastic about their college experience than students at any of the 100-plus colleges I've visited, including Harvard and Stanford. If you think you may like to "be all you can be," start by checking out the clearinghouse for military-related careers: *www.todaysmilitary.com* But also read the downsides presented in the military diaries at *www.objector.org.*

Work with People and Words

Public speaking

OOH

Radio/TV News Reporter. This is one of those long-shot glamour professions that may be worth the risk. You get to investigate fast-breaking stories, sometimes in dangerous environments, and report your findings live. Even in non-emergency situations, you usually have just an hour or two to gather your information before making your report. With the thousands of local news broadcasts, you may be able to land a job, at least if you're willing to start out in Podunk and work nights and weekends. Musts are the ability to write concisely and quickly, a good memory, and an authoritative on-air presence. News reporting is a launchpad for a news anchor position, which, in addition to offering fame, pays awfully well for a job that mainly consists of reading aloud. *Center for Investigative Reporting:* www.muckraker.org. *Society of Professional Journalists:* www.spj.org. *Investigative Reporters and Editors, Inc.:* www.ire.org. *William Jaspersohn's book: A Day in the Life of a Television News Reporter.*

Sports Announcer. Sports continues to be a passion for millions of Americans. That's good news and bad news. The good news is there's plenty of demand for sports announcers: on radio and TV, before the game, during the game (play-by-play and color), and after the game. The bad news is that half the sports fans would give their eyeteeth to make a living as a sports broadcaster. Who does make a living at it? People with the ability to analyze what's going on beneath the surface and who are a goldmine of interesting trivia to fill the large spaces of time in which nothing's going on in the game. Pluses are a commanding voice, a quick wit, being a well-known former athlete, and a degree from a top broadcast journalism program, such as Northwestern, Syracuse, or Missouri. Even then, your first job is likely to sound like this: "We're in the top of the 5th. Jasper High School's up 1-0." *American Sportscasters Association: www.americansportscastersonline.com.*

 Talk Show Host. I excluded this career from this book's first edition because the odds of making a living at it are small. But so many people see it as their dream career or as a marketing tool for their business that I decided to include it and simply tell you how to maximize your chances of defying the odds. Start by thinking about what your unique style would be. Are you a particularly tough interviewer? Someone from the political far right or far left? Someone with encyclopedic knowledge and a palpable passion about something? An unusually self-revealing person? You'll probably increase your chances of success by incorporating your unusual characteristics into your talk show. For me, it's that I have the ability to answer practical questions quickly. So my show is heavily call-in and about a practical topic: work. I also like doing interviews in which I don't just ask the questions, I also participate in a conversation/debate — I often contribute almost as much content as the guest does. I'm also constitutionally fast. I talk fast; I interrupt. Rather than homogenizing myself into being just another mid-speed-talking host, I allow myself to be my regular, fast self. Finally, I'm willing to be very honest on the air. So, I do issue tough love and say politically incorrect things.

So, what are *your* unique attributes and interests? Make those the centerpiece of your radio persona and structure for your talk show. Practice interviewing people and taking call-ins using that style. Do it at home and record the interviews. Critique yourself. Have friends and family critique you mericilessly. When you record an interview you're proud of, edit it down to the best three to five minutes of excerpts and hand-deliver it to the program director of appropriate local radio and TV stations. Any station that won't let you see the program director gets a mailed copy and a follow-up phone call two days later. That's how I got to host my first talk show, and now I'm in my 18th year as producer and host of *Work with Marty Nemko* on a National Public Radio affiliate in San Francisco. Even if you can't make a living as a talk show host, you can get yourself on the air. Build up your chops on a local cable access TV station, by buying airtime on a station, or by webcasting or podcasting your show. *Talker's Magazine: www.talkers.com. Podcasting resource: www.podcasting-tools.com. Tee Morris's book: Podcasting For Dummies.*

Professional Speaker. This is another fantasy career with reasonable prospects. Despite the plethora of electronic alternatives, people still want to hear live speakers. Quite a few people, including some no-names, make a living spreading their gospel at conventions, college campuses, corporate headquarters, and general public forums. Even cruise ships have added speakers to their menu of entertainment. Find an in-demand topic on which you are or could become an expert. Then read books such as Dottie Walters's *Speak and Grow Rich,* study DVDs of great speakers, craft a solid outline of your speech, build in something experiential so they're not just listening to a talking head, and practice, practice, practice until you're able to convey something of real substance while making a powerful connection with your audience. Consider joining a local chapter of Toastmasters, where you learn public speaking principles and get to give talks to fellow members, a sympathetic audience. When you have a knock-your-socks-off sample DVD, send it to conference program chairs and lecture bureaus. The latter can help market you. *National Speakers Association:* www.nsaspeaker.org. *Toastmasters International:* www.toastmasters.org. *The Princeton Language Institute's book: 10 Days to More Confident Public Speaking.*

(Neat Niche) **Speaking Coach.** Most people are called on to "say a few words," whether at a staff meeting, a professional conference, a venture capitalist pitch session, or a toast at their child's wedding. If you're a good public speaker, why not teach others what you've learned? Acquire clients by giving talks on how to give a speech at conferences or at local companies. Don't forget about law firms — many attorneys earn their living as smooth talkers. *Enter google "speaking coach."*

Training and teaching

OOH

Employee Trainer. The need for training has never been greater. More students graduate from high school and even college without basic skills at the same time today's workplace requires them to be communication whizzes and technomavens. Even those who graduated from college with enough skills soon find they need to upgrade. Older workers feel they must stay up-to-the-minute lest they be permanently put out to pasture. Trainers are needed in so many areas: from basic reading to advanced Oracle, peak performance to retirement planning, database management to diversity management. A current challenge for trainers is how to help American workers adapt to globalization. Online training will grow more popular as people, ever-busier, would rather watch their training from a computer, when they feel like it, than to show up in a seminar room at a specified time. And the quality of online training is getting better thanks to improved conferencing software and wider use of full-motion video. *American Society for Training and Development:* www.astd.org. *Howard Stolovitch's book: Telling Ain't Training.*

(Neat Niche) **Software Trainer.** New software and new versions of old software continue to be released. Heaven forbid you should be saddled with

Version 7.0 when Version 8.0 is available. As a trainer, it's a plus if you're certified by the software's manufacturer. Trainers are hired by large organizations, training schools, community colleges, and adult schools. *Linda Johnson's e-book, How to Get Started as a Software Trainer:* `dreamjobstogo.com/titles/djtg0036.html?10456`.

(Neat Niche) **Dream-Career Trainer.** Train clients for those difficult-to-get-into fields to which many people aspire: rock star, talk show host, athlete, comedian, artist, screen writer, voiceover artist, film director, or Web site developer, for example. The trainers usually end up making more money than the dream-career aspirants.

 Health Educator. HMOs know that an ounce of prevention is not only better than a pound of cure, but it also costs less. HMOs' ounce of prevention is to hire health educators to teach people such things as how to lose weight, fit exercise into a busy day, or lower their cholesterol (as though people don't know that broccoli is good and cheeseburgers are bad). Nonetheless, a job conducting health seminars is, as jobs go, pretty salubrious. *American College of Healthcare Executives:* `www.ache.org`.

OOH

Teacher. On its face, teaching would seem like a wonderful career. The workday and work year are short, benefits are tops, job security is unsurpassed, and average pay has risen above $60,000 in many metropolitan areas. So why would one-third of all new teachers leave the profession within five years? Here's how the *Princeton Review* Web site describes teaching: "Usually beginning at 8 a.m., teachers must begin the difficult task of generating interest in their often sleepy students. A good sense of humor and the ability to think like their students helps." Don't get seduced by 3 p.m. dismissal bells and summers off. Especially in gritty urban schools, where the most hiring is occurring, teaching today is no cushy gig. Schools now put everyone from the mentally challenged to the mentally gifted in the same class. It takes exceptional talent and long hours to develop no-snooze lessons for that wide a range of students, often including immigrants who may speak Spanish, Chinese, or Tagalog, but little English. Teachers also have far less power to remove children who chronically disrupt the class — and it takes only one. Students with severe behavior problems used to be placed in special classes. Now, except in the most extreme cases, they're mainstreamed. And new teachers, despite having the least experience, are often given the toughest classes. Now add the many hours after school preparing interesting yet valuable lessons for that wide range of students, correcting papers, the pressures of high-stakes No-Child-Left-Behind testing, and dealing with parents who complain that Johnny's individual needs aren't being met. Finally, remember that teachers are with kids all day, so they don't get much intellectual stimulation. You need a special mentality to do that.

I paint this stark picture because I believe that teaching is among the more important professions. That's the main reason it's on the list of cool careers. Because most public school teachers, after just two years, receive tenure for life, a bad teacher, saddled by the golden handcuffs of job security, can be tempted to stay in the profession forever, damaging 30 kids at a time, year in and year out. So I want to encourage teachers to enter the profession with full knowledge of its realities. Too often, people decide to become teachers based on their own years as a student or on a rewarding experience as a one-to-one tutor. The experience of many of today's classroom teachers is quite different. *About.com's elementary education portal:* `k-6educators.about.com` *Pearl Rock Kane's book: The First Year of Teaching.*

(Neat Niche) **Retreat Leader.** So many people would enjoy getting away for an inspiring, reinvigorating, and fun weekend. On what topic could you captivate people for a weekend? Relationships? Salesmanship? Quilting? Parenting? Procrastination? Libertarian politics? People will often pay a good few hundred bucks for a weekend retreat, so this could be more lucrative than you may think. As always, the keys are good product and good marketing. Mention it on online groups, place an ad for it on a specialty site or `craigslist.org`, put flyers in the right places (including retreat centers), and of course, tell everyone you know. I personally love retreats, so if I were looking for more to do (I'm not), I'd lead a "Find Your Next Career" retreat. *Merianne Litemen's book: Retreats That Work.*

(Neat Niche) **Distance-Learning Teacher.** According to a 2006 *U.S. News* cover story, three million Americans are now pursuing their degrees online. And the trend is spreading into traditional college education. For example, at U.C. Berkeley, students can, 24/7, crank up any part of an interactive Intro to Chemistry course from their dorm room. And rural high schools are now able to offer a wide array of courses even if no local teacher is available to teach them. It takes special skills to teach via distance learning, so if you can make that your specialty, you should be in demand, especially now that — thanks to high-speed connections — full-motion video can be incorporated into online classes. *Distance Education Clearinghouse:* `www.uwex.edu/disted` *S. Joseph Levine's book: Making Distance Education Work.*

(Neat Niche) **English-Language-Learners Teacher.** Immigration continues to jump, and so does the need for teachers of English as a second language. They are hired by K-12 schools, community colleges, adult schools, and by companies for their immigrant employees. This career is often gratifying because most students are motivated to learn the subject — unlike some other school subjects. *Dave's ESL Cafe:* `www.eslcafe.com` *Suzanne Peregoy's book: Reading, Writing and Learning in ESL.*

(Neat Niche) **Adult Education Teacher.** Here's another niche with motivated students. At a community college or school district's adult school, you help students get their General Education Development (GED) diploma, and teach English-as-a-Second Language and other subjects. *Wikipedia entry:* `en.wikipedia.org/wiki/adult_education.`

(Neat Niche) **Program Specialist.** Elementary schools often use specialists to visit classrooms to teach art, music, technology, or special ed. This tends to be a rewarding job because you're the breath of fresh air in a student's humdrum day, and because you're able to focus on your specialty.

(Neat Niche) **Music or Art Teacher.** After years of decline, schools are starting to hire more music and art teachers. *National Association for Music Education:* www.menc.org. *Links:* www.artmuseums.com

Something's wrong when the National Endowment for the Arts gives millions of dollars to a relative handful of artists who produce work that much of the public finds unappealing or even disgusting, while millions of schoolchildren receive little or no art instruction, something that can so enrich the lives even of non-artistic kids.

(Neat Niche) **Vocational/Technical Teacher.** Community colleges and post-secondary career colleges, and some high schools, hire teachers in fields such as technology repair, business education, agriculture, plumbing, and protective services. *Links:* dragon.ep.usm.edu/~yuen/votech.htm

Athletic Coach. I coached an Oakland (CA) Boys Club basketball team. I went in with visions of using hoops to help kids triumph over their life circumstances, but that proved overly ambitious. Just getting them to pay attention took everything I had. It was fun though, and the games were a rush, constantly figuring out what to do to give your team an edge while trying to be a good role model.

The usual starting job is a high school coaching position, but you only start to earn a decent income at the college level. There, you have additional responsibilities, such as meeting with the media and big-time donors. And you must make recruiting trips to convince high school athletes that even though they have a C average at a low-rigor high school, they can succeed in college classes. Because of Title IX regulations, the number of female sports teams is increasing, so job opportunities are good for women and not so good for men. If I were trying to break in, I'd write a letter to every top college coach in my field and see whether I could get any sort of assistant job working for him or her. *Comprehensive Online Access to Coaching Help:* www.coachhelp.com *Jim Thompson's book: The Double-Goal Coach.*

Clergy. A clergyperson told me that the thing I thought was most important in a cleric turns out not to be a requirement at all: She said that many clergy have serious doubts about the existence of God. They are, however, strongly committed to helping people live richer lives using religion as a foundation. Sometimes this help is direct: sermons, religion classes, and ministering to people at high and low points of their lives — birth, marriage, crisis, and death — but clergypersons also spend a surprising amount of time in indirect service, such as fundraising and administrative work. Except for the long hours and having to be on-call at all hours, the clergy is a rewarding profession with high status, unmitigated do-gooding, and a good job market except for Protestant ministers (because their churches are merging). The situation is better for rabbis and *cantors* (they lead singing during services) and excellent for

Catholic priests — lifetime celibacy is increasingly unpopular, and their reputation as abusers of boys doesn't help. Indeed, the Catholic Church has run full-page ads attempting to "collar" future priests. The job market is especially good for aspiring priests who speak Spanish. After checking out the resources here, investigate a career in the clergy by speaking with a clergyperson you respect, and then contacting the ordination organization for your denomination. *Wikipedia entry:* `en.wikipedia.org/wiki/clergy`. *Oye Magazine:* `oyemagazine.claretians.org`. *Barbara Brown Taylor's book: Leaving Church. Charles Foster's book: Educating Clergy. Howard Bleichner's book: View from the Altar. Tel Aviv Cantorial Institute:* `www.taci.org.il`.

Celebrant. Without having to be an ordained cleric or justice of the peace, you can help create and preside over weddings, funerals, and other occasions. *Information:* `www.celebrantusa.com`.

On the creative side

Actor. Like many creative pursuits, acting is one of the world's best hobbies and worst careers. Expressing creativity is a primal need — so primal, in fact, that the competition even for volunteer work in the creative arts is intense. Last year, for example, I auditioned for a part in a community theater production of *Death of a Salesman.* Nobody would get paid a dime, yet more than 100 actors, many with degrees in acting and extensive stage experience, tried out. (I wasn't even invited to the callbacks, let alone offered a role.)

OOH

The good news is that the job market may be improving a bit. With the proliferation of Internet video for commercials, training, and entertainment, increased cable viewership, and more foreign demand for American productions, the need for actors is increasing. But there's plenty of bad news. For example, 80 percent of actors in the Screen Actors Guild (those who have already acted in a union job) earn less than $5,000 a year from their acting! Even the term *actor* is misleading. It implies you're acting, doing something. For the most part, actors wait. They wait to be hired. After they're hired, on the set, they wait for their turn; for the weather to clear; for the tech people to set things up; for the producer, director, and minions to make up their minds. Casting Director Lisa Pirriolli, in the book *Gig,* adds, "It's a horrible life . . . it's all about getting the job and about rejection. If you do get the job, it's all about doing it correctly and getting the next one, and the next one, just trying to become famous. And if you do become famous, it's all about being famous. And then it's about when your star is going to fall."

Okay. Despite it all, you decide to try to make a living as an actor. Here are some keys to making it: First choose a niche. Are you the insecure villain type? A singing airhead? Be sure your headshot, sample reel, and resume capture your niche, and send the package to local acting agencies. It may be smarter to start in a large city other than Los Angeles or New York, perhaps Toronto

("Hollywood North") or Wilmington, North Carolina ("Hollywood East"). To get leads on gigs, contact each city's film commission. Or start out in *industrials* — training and promotional videos. It's much easier to obtain credits and develop a sample reel. To avoid starving in the meantime, rather than or in addition to waiting tables, consider interim jobs that help polish your craft: mock trial participant, mock patient (used in medical school training), role-player in employee training seminars or police crisis simulations, traffic school instructor, and Santa Claus. (Don't let your little kid read that.) *Robert Cohen's book: Acting Professionally.*

Musician. Nothing inspires or heals like music. It can lift a depression, tame an angry soul, move one to gyrate with joy — even if you're alone in your kitchen. How terrific to have a career in which music is your main activity. But how do you fight the odds against making a living at it? First, you gotta find out if you really have enough talent. Don't count on your teachers to be candid. They have too much vested interest in encouraging you. Besides, it's hard for someone who knows you to tell you that you're probably not good enough. How do you discover the truth about your talent? Play for (or send a recording to) people who *don't* know you but are in a position to pay you for your work: orchestra conductors, studio gig contractors, wedding band leaders, nightclub owners, and so on. If you audition 20 times and receive little encouragement, cut your losses. Make music your after-work passion. For example, join a community orchestra. If you get sincere encouragement but not a full-time paying gig, you may have to be entrepreneurial to make a middle-class living. Find great musicians to join your musical group. Then seriously market it. For example, convince local government or corporate leaders to hire you to play at their events, play host to a party for wedding planners, or invite event planners via direct mail to visit your Web site, which contains audio clips of your music. *Sheila Anderson's book: How to Grow as a Musician. Classical Music directory: www.musicalonline.com.*

(Neat Niche) **Background Vocalist.** Ooh, wah. Ooh, wah. Yeah, yeah. No, this isn't the sound of sex. It's the sound of a background singer. This is an under-the-radar, sometimes well-paying career for talented singers who can walk in, read the music, and crank out those "yeahs" and "oohs" so they give you goose bumps. Don't think you can do this job if you're a second-rate singer. Unless the lead singer is a Norah Jones, background singers are often better singers.

Composer. Increasingly, soundtracks, especially for computer games, are created as much by computer cut-and-pasters as by musical wizards. Instead of standing in the orchestra pit, this conductor sits at a computer with a library of sounds, special effects, and music clips, and creates the mood of a computer game, commercial, or film trailer. Of course, traditional songwriters are still out there, but the job market is *molto largo* (very slow). *American Society of Composers, Authors, and Publishers: www.ascap.com. Article: mixonline.com/mag/audio_preps_pros_sound.*

Getting political

Politician. Yes, they always have to have their hands out, and their reputation isn't sparkling, but most politicians I've met try to be fine leaders. And although the wheels of government turn slowly and inefficiently, at least its goal is benevolent. No specific training is required to be a politician, although you must be instantly likeable, a compelling speaker, and have a thick skin. The biggest downsides are loss of privacy and job instability. But if after a couple of losses you decide to switch careers, the connections you've made will likely help you land a job. *Wikipedia entry:* `en.wikipedia.org/wiki/politician`. *William Endicott's book: An Insider's Guide to Political Jobs in Washington, DC. Richard Benedetto's book: Politicians are People, Too.*

OOH

Political Aide. Most politicians have paid aides. They research problems, draft legislation, and sub for the pol at rubber chicken dinners. This is a satisfying job. You actually have some power, and the work is varied and fast-paced. The usual route in is to start as an intern or campaign volunteer. Ask for more responsibility, and prove yourself. *Vault.com profile:* `www.vault.com/nr/occ_profiles.jsp?product_id=524&p=1&ht_type=11`.

Lobbyist. You're a lobbyist for the National Abortion Rights League. A law you want to pass would solidify teens' right to have an abortion without parental permission. You may actually have drafted the legislation, and you certainly dug up research that proves its benefits; for example, the legislation would result in fewer teen moms and avoid unsafe abortions. You play host to a cocktail party for key legislators and just enough other folks to make your goal less obvious. You write press releases and try to get on TV and radio or into the blogosphere to expound your position. That's the life of a *lobbyist,* a professional persuader of politicians. A law degree is a plus, but not essential. Lobbyist jobs are similar to the sought-after positions working for a legislator but may be easier to land. *American League of Lobbyists*: `www.alldc.org`. *Anthony Nownes's book: Total Lobbying.*

If political campaigns were publicly funded, legislators would listen more to the public than to lobbyists who throw big bucks at politicians to gain influence.

One-on-one

Speech-Language Therapist. Think of how you feel when you listen to someone who stutters. Imagine how he feels. The speech-language therapist treats stuttering and other voice and speaking problems, from cleft palate to limited vocabulary to stroke victims trying to recover their speech. For many patients, progress is slow. Patience is a must. Speech therapists who work in schools have relatively short workdays, with ample time off. They may also work in hospitals, clinics, and in private practice. Many speech therapists

OOH

choose a combination. *American Speech-Language-Hearing Association:* `www.asha.org`. *Stuttering Foundation of America:* `www.stutteringhelp.org`.

(Neat Niche) **Accent Neutralization Specialist.** When you call tech support, it's reassuring to hear someone whose accent you can understand. To that end, companies hire accent reduction specialists. Too, many immigrants to the United States, especially those in professional jobs, are eager to improve their accents. In either case, to find clients, contact human resource departments at high-tech corporations. They often recruit from abroad to fill programmer, engineer, and scientist positions. *Articles:* `healthcare.monster.com/therapy/articles/accent` and `esl.about.com/od/speakingenglish/a/accent_reduce.htm`

College Admission Counselor. "Which college should I go to?" "How do I get in?" "How do I find the money?" In high schools, college counselors typically help students answer these questions with individual counseling and group presentations. In private practice, the work is one-on-one. As usual, specializing is wise. You can specialize, for example, in students with learning problems or those aiming for designer-label colleges. *National Association for College Admission Counseling:* `www.nacacnet.org`. *Independent Educational Consultants Association:* `www.educationalconsulting.org`.

(Neat Niche) **College-Bound Athlete Consultant.** Many high school students are pulled kicking and screaming into doing their college applications. Not so with college athletes. They may not care any more than their peers about the joys of learning, but they do care about playing ball. These motivated clients make your job fun. You help Bruiser figure out which colleges will let him play a lot and satisfy him academically and socially. You're a bit like a junior Jerry Maguire: "Show me the scholarship!" *Guide for the College-Bound Student-Athlete:* `www.ncaa.org/library/general/cbsa/2006-07/2006-07_cbsa.pdf`. *Michael Koehler's book: Advising Student Athletes through the College Recruitment Process. Chris Lincoln's book: Playing the Game.*

Troubled Teen Consultant. Few things are more frustrating to parents than an out-of-control teen: School and parents are ignored, and sex, drugs, and rock-and-roll are extolled. What's a parent to do? They increasingly hire consultants to find after-school programs, tough-love camps, and therapeutic boarding schools to help Junior — or at least to get the troubled teen out of Mom and Dad's frazzled hair. *Independent Educational Consultants Association:* `www.educationalconsulting.org`.

Tutor. Many tutors love their jobs. They gush about the close one-on-one relationships, the visible progress, and the fact that you can earn money with minimal startup costs and without endless training. How do you make a decent living as a tutor? Let local public school teachers know that, unlike chains such as Sylvan Learning, you make house calls. It also helps if you carve out a niche, working with, for example, students with attention deficit disorder, or math for girls. I often give just one word of advice to people with patience and the ability to explain things clearly, motivate others, and self-promote: tutor. *Clever Apple:* `www.cleverapple.com`. *Eileen Shapiro's book: Tutoring as a Successful Business.*

(Neat Niche) **Computer Tutor.** Get referrals from employers, computer retailers, or local Internet service providers. Or emulate the guerrilla marketer who got plenty of clients just by standing in front of a computer store and giving his pitch to everyone walking out with a new computer. He often made an appointment on the spot. *Google "computer tutoring."*

(Neat Niche) **SAT/ACT Tutor.** Because students (or at least their parents) are motivated, this type of tutoring can be pleasurable. And done right, SAT/ACT tutoring not only prepares the student for the test, but can also provide skills that can last a lifetime. In studying for the SAT, I learned hundreds of important words. I mean, can one survive without knowing *sanctimonious, hubristic,* and *bloviating?* After all, how else could I accurately describe what I'm sounding like here? I know: *blowhard. Google "SAT tutoring."*

Home Schooling Consultant. As disenchantment with public schooling rises, and the media reports the high SAT scores and top college admission rates of home-schooled kids, it isn't surprising that two million children are now home-schooled. But home schooling is no easy feat. As a consultant, you help parents and kids design learning programs and iron out problems. *American Homeschool Association:* `www.americanhomeschoolassociation.org`. *California Homeschool Association:* `www.hsc.org`.

Work with People and Things

Polygraph Operator. Would you find it fun figuring out whether people are lying? That's what polygraph (lie detector) operators do. Hook up your subject to a machine that monitors heart rate and brain waves. If things start spiking when you ask, "Did you murder your husband?" your subject may be a step closer to Ol' Sparky. Most polygraph operators work for law enforcement agencies, but polygraph tests also are used by attorneys to prove that their clients are upstanding citizens, and in pre-employment testing in sensitive industries such as day-care centers. You don't want a pedophile caring for your child. *American Polygraph Association:* `www.polygraph.org`.

Funeral Director. Many people cringe at this profession, but funeral directors are proud of their work. When a death occurs, a funeral director who helps family members make arrangements that feel right can be a real benefit in a time of need. Alas, too many funeral directors take that opportunity to push $5,000 caskets when a $500 one would do: "You wouldn't want to be cheap with your mother, now would you?" Training is moderate in length, pay is substantial, and demand is growing thanks to the aging U.S. population and because many funeral directors are about to retire. Not a bad combination.

Do me a favor, though. Be sure to spend some time at a funeral home — other than when Granny Fern's lying in state — before deciding on this career. Despite projected fast growth in this field, landing a job isn't easy. Because the career is desirable, many people keep this business in the family. It may take a while to convince an employer that you're, pardon the expression, dying for the job. *Funeral Consumers Alliance:* www.funerals.org. *National Funeral Directors Association:* www.nfda.org. *FuneralNet:* www.funeralnet.com.

Occupational Therapist. You help a stroke patient relearn how to drive. You find an alternative for an arthritis patient who can no longer button a shirt. Using a combination of psychology, computers, braces, and a healthy dose of common sense, the occupational therapist is the practical soul who tries to put it all together. The Department of Labor projects fast growth through 2014. *American Occupational Therapy Association:* www.aota.org.

Electro-Neurodiagnostic Technician (formerly EEG Technician). END techs monitor brain waves. Why would you want to do that? In surgery, brain waves indicate how well the anesthesia is working. In a sleep clinic, brain waves help figure out what's causing a person's insomnia. Doctors use them to determine how well a medication is helping an epileptic. This is a cool career because, despite its important healthcare role, it can be learned on the job or with a short training program, and employment prospects are good. *American Society of Electroneurodiagnostic Technologists:* www.aset.org.

Diagnostic Medical Sonographer. Commonly known as ultrasound technologists, you perform sonograms to, for example, noninvasively diagnose a heart problem or to determine how a pregnant mom and baby are doing. *Society of Diagnostic Medical Sonography:* www.sdms.org.

Low-Investment Food Operations Owner. Simple, no-seating food operations can be relatively low-risk routes to high income.

(Neat Niche) **Pizza-by-the-Slice Business Owner.** Pizza never goes out of style, has a large markup, and is a relatively simple business. One secret to success is to open your shop within smelling distance of a busy walk-in entrance to a college campus. Remember, the pizza has to be to-die-for. Find an ever-crowded pizzeria that serves delicious pizza and is located far enough from your proposed location that the owner won't fear your competition. Ask the head pizza maker to teach you how to make it. If necessary, pay for your lessons. *Google "pizza by the slice."*

(Neat Niche) **Food Carts.** The most important thing about a food outlet is location. Subject to zoning restrictions, carts enable you to move around so you can be in front of a busy office building at lunch time, at the main exit of the local high school during the afternoon, in front of a busy movie theater in the evening, and near the stadium on game days. Carts not only make good locations possible, they also keep rent low — an unbeatable combination. Good candidates for cart-based businesses: sandwiches, burritos, soup, espresso, and pastries. Espresso is my favorite cart business, not only because Americans consume 400 million cups of coffee a day, but also because the profit margin is so high — that $3 latte costs 10 cents to make. That sort of margin would impress even Joey the Loan Shark.

As with all businesses, there are things to watch out for. For example, if the landlord sees you getting rich just by pouring coffee, he can toss you and install his intellectually challenged cousin. So, after you prove to yourself that you can make one profitable, on subsequent carts, get a long lease. Worried about status? Remember, you're not selling coffee; you're president of the Continental Cappuccino Company with stores throughout the region. *Links*: `www.espressotop50.com`

Parking Lot Oil Change Business Operator. Every car needs oil changes, and nearly every car owner finds getting them inconvenient. At best, you sit around at a while-you-wait oil-change service. Otherwise, it's drop off the car, somehow get to work, and somehow get back to the shop. Instead, imagine that when you pull into a parking lot at work, a shopping center, or the airport, you can request an oil change while your car is parked. Isn't that more convenient? What a business: big demand, large income potential, small investment, no extraordinary skills required, and little legitimate competition. *The Automotive Oil Change Association:* `www.aoca.org`.

Work with Data and People

Technically speaking

Technical Support Specialist. I love these people. When I can't get my software to work, or worse, when I get an error message such as, "General Failure, Drive C," I reach for the phone and get a tech support person, who almost always straightens me out. Tech support can be a launchpad to other high-tech careers because you get to understand products and their warts from the customers' perspective. Standout tech support people graduate not only to supervisor but also to sales, marketing, and even product development positions. But you may first have to pay your dues. Unless your employer has outsourced after-hours tech support to India, newbie help-deskers may have to work the graveyard shift. "Help, I'm on the phone with Beijing and my Treo won't sync!" Also, you need the patience of a saint — people are often frantic when they call (or at least I am). *Help Desk Institute:* `www.helpdeskinst.com`. *Association of Support Professionals:* `www.asponline.com`.

Software Designer/Architect. This is what you can do when you've been a programmer for a while and you're ready for a less coding-intensive job. As a software designer, you talk with your bosses, customers, and other stakeholders, figuring out what they want the software to do. Then, you design its architecture and supervise programmers who produce the actual software.

When the problem's too tough for the programmers, you code it. The Department of Labor projects software engineering to be one of the fastest-growing jobs through 2014. *Information:* `www.developers.net`.

Web Developer/Webmaster. Countless organizations and individuals want to build or upgrade their sites. Web developers start by trying to understand the client's needs and then create a site using an ever-cooler software toolkit. Sure, demand for developers is declining as create-your-own-site software is getting ever easier and more powerful. For example, see the sitebuilder at `homestead.com` or *Website Tonight* at `godaddy.com`. But demand for human site builders who can create sophisticated sites that are search-engine optimized will continue. Jobs will also be available for people who can maintain and troubleshoot sites. Site development is a fascinating career because it offers a combination of creativity, art, and business. *International Webmasters Association:* `www.iwanet.org`. *Web Developer resources:* `www.webdeveloper.com`. *About.com's Web design portal:* `webdesign.about.com`. *Top advice on search engine marketing:* `www.searchenginewatch.com`. *Jennifer Niederst Robbins's book: Web Design in a Nutshell, 3rd Edition.*

> (Neat Niche) **Politician's Site Developer.** Designing and upgrading politicians' Web sites is a good niche because during campaigns, politicians prioritize creating a great site. Also, you get to work for a cause you believe in — unless you decide to develop both sides' sites. *Information:* `www.completecampaigns.com`.

Database Administrator. Among an e-commerce site's greatest treasures are its databases. Databases, for example, enable customers to see whether a product is in stock, and provides the site owner with its customers' preferences so it can custom-market. So, no surprise, companies need database administrators, especially those with expertise in Oracle/SQL. The U.S. Department of Labor projects this career to be among the fastest-growing through 2014. *About.com's portal to database careers:* `databases.about.com/od/careers`. *Craig Mullins's book: Database Administration.*

Systems Analyst. What's the best way to enable a traveling salesperson to connect with his company's databases? How can a computer system enable all the employees, suppliers, and vendors to know each order's status? How can three different computer systems talk with each other? The systems analyst, working with programmers and managers, develops the blueprint for system-wide solutions to problems like these. You may not be a hard-core programmer, but you need some skills in programming, networking hardware, software, and data modeling to do what-if projections. Another key skill is the ability to translate between geek-speak and plain English. The more senior version of this position is systems architect. The Department of Labor projects systems analysis to be among the fastest-growing careers through 2014. *Bureau of Labor Statistics profile:* `www.bls.gov/k12/computers06.htm`. *Alan Dennis's book: Systems Analysis and Design, 3rd Edition.*

Operations Research Analyst. One way the U.S. manages to stay competitive in this global economy is its ability to create efficient production systems. The operations research analyst, a practically oriented math whiz, is one of the brains behind it all. He may, for example, help the Green Giant figure out how much corn to plant and when to plant it. He may shorten the time it takes to cash a paycheck. He may even develop a system to ensure an adequate AIDS-free blood supply in the nation's hospitals. *Operations Research Society of America:* `www.informs.org`.

  Purchasing Specialist/Supply Chain Manager/Logistics Manager. How'd you like to get paid for shopping? Well, it's not quite like at the mall. Purchasing specialists do the shopping for companies and government agencies. Of course, it doesn't hurt to have a good instinct for when it is and isn't worth going after a bargain, but this job has rapidly gone technological. Supply-chain software helps ensure that you get what you need when you need it instead of the old way, which meant lots of costly inventory doing nothing in a warehouse. Demand is great for people graduating from supply chain management programs, such as the ones at Arizona State or Michigan State Universities, but any bachelor's degree plus enthusiastic interest in purchasing may be enough to get you in the door. *About.com's purchasing specialist portal:* `purchasing.about.com`. *Institute for Supply Management:* `www.ism.ws`.

 Gerontologist. Unlike the geriatrics expert, who focuses on the *science* of aging, gerontologists are multidisciplinary, melding science, psychology, social work, and public policy perspectives. What can you do with a gerontology degree? Run a social services agency for the elderly, help an assisted-living facility develop its program, or, with a doctorate, conduct research on how to improve the quality of people's aging while controlling societal costs. *Exploring Careers in Aging:* `businessandaging.blogs.com/ecg/2005/05/miscellaneous_g.html`.

Crunching numbers

 College Financial Aid Officer. At most colleges, more than half the students apply for financial aid. With only so much money available, your job is to distribute it equitably and to mollify or negotiate with students who get less than they had hoped for — and after filling out all that paperwork, some *are* unhappy. It's a nice job because it feels good to allocate money, breathing periods between crunch times are sizeable, you need only a bachelor's degree, and you get to work on a college campus — a pleasant work environment. *National Association of Student Financial Aid Administrators:* `www.nasfaa.org`. *Smart Student Guide to Financial Aid:* `www.finaid.org`.

 Accountant. Even if you're the stereotypical accountant — a mumbling recluse — you'll probably find employment. The job market is terrific for bean counters. But higher-level positions require an accountant to be a good communicator, often imparting bad news: "No, you can't deduct that. No, you calculated that incorrectly. No, that's inadequate documentation." That naysayer role is one of the field's biggest downsides. But cheer up — for good accountants who are Certified Public Accountants (CPAs), there's light at the end of the green-eye-shade tunnel. Companies promote good accountants to positions such as comptroller and chief financial officer, where they function more like financial physicians than bean-counting bookkeepers. They're involved in decisions about developing and marketing new products, how to best use existing capital and raise more, and even how to structure the company. Accountants and their closely related finance specialists are a company's antidote to decision making based on gut feelings.

The Big Four firms (KPMG, PricewaterhouseCoopers, Deloitte, and Ernst & Young) offer terrific training, great pay, and challenging assignments. Problem is, it's tough to get them to hire you. If they won't, not to worry: There are plenty of other accounting firms, most mid-to-large-size corporations and nonprofits use in-house accountants, and the government — and not just the IRS — is full of them. To boot, the federal government-imposed Sarbanes-Oxley reporting requirements are essentially a full-employment act for accountants. In short, if you're a halfway decent accountant, the world is your oyster. CPAs (especially with Sarbanes-Oxley experience), experienced cost accountants, junior-level financial and business analysts, and degreed senior accountants are all in demand. And if you want to help people with their taxes or straighten out small business financial messes, you can simply hang out a shingle. *American Accounting Association:* www.aaahq.org. *American Institute of Certified Public Accountants:* www.aicpa.org. *Jason Alba's book: Vault Career Guide to Accounting, Second Edition. Tax preparation franchise:* www.jackson hewitt.com.

(Neat Niche) **Forensic Accountant.** Crooks are ever-more creative. For example, they used those cheapie, tiny USB drives to steal account information from credit union computers. That reminds me of the person who stole one penny from every account in a large bank, so small an amount that no one noticed for years, until a forensic accountant did. The corporate accounting scandals of the mid-2000s, from Enron to Apple, have made forensic accounting a hot career. It's a cross between an accountant and a detective. According to *U.S. News,* these fraud fighters are often called in by law firms, government agencies, and corporations to sniff out such indiscretions as secret CEO compensation, phony insurance claims, improper securities trading, and to testify in court. The Big Four firms alone hire hundreds of forensic accountants each year, and so does the FBI. Who knows? You may be asked to follow the money as it moves from Islamic charities to terrorist organizations or to investigate the finances of Tommy the Blade's cement business. *Association of Certified Fraud Examiners:* www.acfe.org. *Wikipedia entry:* en.wikipedia.org/wiki/forensic_accounting.

(Neat Niche) **Business Valuator.** Every day, companies merge or are acquired. Maybe someday, a grand total of one company will exist. Every merger and acquisition requires someone to figure out the value of the company being merged or acquired. Those high stakes mean big bucks for you. Business valuators are also used when wealthy people divorce or die, determining the value of a spouse's business. *National Association of Certified Valuation Analysts:* `nacva.com` *American Institute of Certified Public Accountants' business valuation section:* `bvfls.aicpa.org`.

(Neat Niche) **International Accountant.** With business ever-more globalizing, companies are crying, "Find me an international accountant!" For example, an American company does business in China. Which accounting and tax laws and principles apply? It sure helps if you speak the language. *Links:* `www.taxsites.com/international2.html`.

(Neat Niche) **Healthcare Accountant.** When you have an operation, its cost depends on the answers to these questions: Are you on Medicare? Medicaid? Do you have private insurance? Which company? Are you a low-income patient? Are you paying your own way? (You may pay more.) Not only is there rarely one set price, there usually isn't just one payer — a single surgery often gets paid for by the government, an insurance company, the patient, and sometimes after all that, the hospital eats some of the costs. A healthcare accountant keeps track of the entire mess. *Links:* `www.pohly.com` *Louis Gapenski's book: Healthcare Finance.*

(Neat Niche) **Environmental Accountant.** Environmentalism has become religion, so government agencies and nonprofits are using more environmental accountants to argue that the environmental damages caused by a company outweigh the benefits. And many companies — especially utilities, manufacturers, and chemical companies — hire other environmental accountants to prove the opposite, or simply to comply with the regulations. CPAs who also are engineers are in particularly great demand. *Article:* `finance.monster.com/articles/environmentalaccounting`. *Environmental Management Accounting:* `www.emawebsite.org/about_ema.htm`.

(Neat Niche) **Consulting Accountant.** CPAs are often called in on a consulting basis, perhaps to computerize a company's accounting function, facilitate a merger or acquisition, figure out how to reduce fraud or comply with Sarbanes-Oxley regulations, or provide advice on how to improve operating procedures. The Big Four accounting firms do a lot of this. *Google "consulting accountant."*

(Neat Niche) **Executor.** Some wills name a bank or trust company as executor, but often, an heir is selected. And the latter often gets overwhelmed by the paperwork and legalese, thus creating a self-employment opportunity for you. Get clients by contacting estate planning attorneys or individuals who are advertising estate sales. *Google "professional executor."*

 Commercial Banker. Banks no longer are limited to offering just loans, checking accounts, and savings accounts. They can sell stocks, bonds, insurance, estate and trust products, and video games. (Well, not video games.) And all those new profit centers require managers. Other new sources of banking jobs are the online banks such as Capital One (www.capitalone.com) and e*trade (www.etrade.com). T's-crossed/i's-dotted types with a business degree, who crave prestige, may find a banking career a wise investment. *Vault.com profile:* www.vault.com/hubs/501/channelhome_501. jsp?ch_id=271.

 Investment Banker. Business's growth hormone is money. A typical I-banker's assignment is to get money on the best terms. Are you willing to work into the wee hours and do lots of traveling to get a company the best deal on the money? You don't raise the dough by calling a few banks and saying, "Hi, will you lend us some money?" Here's how investment bankers work: A growing private company needs more money. Should it go public? Get private equity funding? Spin off a division? Get bought out? You do complex calculations to help the company come up with an answer. Say the company decides to go public and issue stock. You attempt to price it right. Then you hand off the project to a different kind of I-banker — the salesperson — who attempts to convince banks, mutual fund managers, and pension fund managers to buy your stock or bond offering. To sell requires more than a slick tongue, but that helps.

Most I-bankers are first hired with just a bachelor's degree (in any field, as long as it's from a designer-label college at which you got good grades). Your first job is an analyst, a number cruncher. You usually need an MBA before making the big bucks. A couple of years as an I-banking analyst is usually a ticket to top-name MBA programs. But I'm talking full years. In her book *The Fast Track,* Mariam Naficy writes, "The amount you'll work in investment banking cannot be overstated. One analyst reported that he bought 50 pairs of underwear because he had no time to do laundry."

Many people, in part thanks to movies like *The Bonfire of the Vanities* and books like *Liars Poker,* believe that investment bankers do nothing good for the world. In fact, their job often is to help companies raise money so that they can bring a better product to a broader market. Even media-reviled investment banker Michael Milken, by raising money for MCI as an investment banker, was key to making the telecommunications industry more competitive, and in turn, lowering everyone's phone bills. Before deregulation, you were paying 40 cents per long-distance minute. Now, you pay a few pennies. Thank an investment banker. The most sought-after jobs are at "bulge bracket" firms such as Goldman Sachs, but the fastest-growing segment is mid- to large-sized traditional banks, which are now allowed to do investment banking. *Vault.com's investment banking hub:* www.vault.com/hubs/ 501/channelhome_501.jsp?ch_id=240. *Wetfeet.com's book: Careers in Investment Banking. Links:* www.careers-in-finance.com/ib.htm. *Mariam Naficy's book: The Fast Track. John Rolfe's book: Monkey Business.*

(Neat Niche) **Securities Trader.** One floor at an investment bank is called a trading floor. It's filled with rows of computers and intense 20-somethings.

Sales types are on the phones convincing institutional clients, such as pension fund managers, to invest in some stock or bond. Traders execute the buy or sell on the best terms — using quantitative analysis and plenty of guesswork. This is a career for people who are adrenaline-addicted, charismatic, and have thick skins. Not all traders have Ivy League degrees. This is the niche within investment banking in which street smarts, aggressiveness, a winning personality, and quantitative instincts can be enough to yield a salary far in excess of their contribution to the world. *Alexander Elder's book: Entries and Exits: Visits to 16 Trading Rooms.*

 Venture Capitalist. On behalf of a pension fund, foundation, bank, insurance company, or individuals, a VC looks for businesses to invest in, most often small, fast-growing software or biotech firms, but occasionally low-tech ventures such as retail or restaurants. Many proposals come in unsolicited or at cattle calls, in which fund seekers pitch to an audience of VCs. But some of the best investment ideas are discussed at a bar or on the golf course, so it doesn't hurt to be a schmoozer. After you find a prospect, you need MBA-level quantitative skills to estimate the business's future value. Just as important, you need a nose for judging people because a business succeeds or fails as much on its people as on its product. After you're convinced that a business is worth investing in, you need the ability to convince investors. You may, after investing, take a role in guiding the business's development.

A few VCs work on their own, the so-called angel investors. But most work for a VC firm or join one of the banks or companies, such as Cisco Systems and Sony, that have in-house VC shops. Because the salaries can be astronomical, most jobs at top VC firms (for example, Kleiner Perkins and Sequoia Partners) go to graduates of Harvard or Stanford MBA programs, which have specific tracks for aspiring VCs. *National Venture Capital Association:* www.nvca.org. *Venture Capital Resource Library:* www.vfinance.com. *Udayan Gupta's book: Done Deals. Inside the Minds' book*: *Leading Deal Makers.*

Work with Data, People, and Words

 Sports Information Director. The public is mad for information about its teams, and you're happy to give it to them. After all, it helps fill the seats. Your job is to create and distribute information to the media and to field their questions. Your working environment is excellent and you're closer to the team than anyone except the coaches. Oh, and you get great seats to the big game. *Job Profile, Sports Information Director:* www.jobprofiles.org/eduunisports.htm *College Sports Information Directors of America:* www.cosida.com

 Professor. A professorship has many upsides: the joy of creating knowledge and helping others acquire it through your classes, advising, writings, and conference presentations. You have intelligent, civilized (usually) colleagues, and after a few years, tenure for life. Plus, you get to work in one of the more appealing work environments: a college campus.

The professoriate also has its downsides. As a former faculty member at four universities and consultant to 15 college presidents, I'm in a position to know. More and more students are grossly unqualified to do college work and unwilling to work hard, yet routinely complain about too-tough grading if they get a C. (See the eye-opening book *Generation X Goes to College,* by Pulitzer Prize nominee Peter Sacks.) Despite many students' lack of even basic skills, professors, except at two-year colleges, usually need a doctorate, which, depending on the field, takes an average of 6 to 12 post-bachelor's degree years to complete. Does tenure sound good? Be aware that colleges increasingly hire part-timers and temp faculty. Prospects for permanent jobs are best in engineering, business, and computer science, and for Blacks, Hispanics, and Native Americans. Office politics can be intense — in few workplaces is there as much conniving over so few resources. Too, there's often pressure to publish journal articles when you'd rather be teaching. Ernest Boyer, the late vice president of the Carnegie Foundation for the Advancement of Teaching, wrote, "Winning the campus teaching award is often the kiss of death for promotion and tenure."

A final minus: On many campuses, there is the pressure to be politically correct — to assign liberal readings, espouse liberal views, and even to pass students of certain races even though you believe the student's work doesn't justify a passing grade. Harvard president Lawrence Summers nearly got fired when he suggested, in a private brainstorming session, that genetic predisposition may help explain why there are so few female scientists. He thought he survived after promising to spend $50 million to increase the number of women scientists, but no. Soon after, he was forced to step down. *American Association of University Professors:* www.aaup.org. *John Goldsmith's book: The Chicago Guide to Your Academic Career: A Portable Mentor for Scholars from Graduate School through Tenure.*

College classes stress the importance of treating labor fairly, yet colleges are notorious for hiring part-timers to avoid paying for benefits. Do colleges know what the word "hypocrisy" means? Colleges also pay many instructors piece-work, often at very low pay per piece (per course). And don't make the mistake of thinking that if you take a part-time teaching position, you have a reasonable chance of converting it into a full-time, benefited, tenure track professorship. That rarely happens.

Thesis Completion Consultant. Many graduate students get close to finishing their degrees but drop out because they have trouble doing their thesis. You can help. You may guide the student to develop the questions to be addressed, plan the thesis's structure and analysis, and review a draft. *Association for Support of Graduate Students:* www.asgs.org.

Proposal Writer. Every year, state and federal governments issue thousands of requests for proposals for every imaginable product and service. They may request proposals for a state-of-the-art English-as-a-Second-Language program, 300 desks for IRS offices, or 50,000 Navy uniforms. The 35,000 private and corporate foundations issue even more requests for proposals. Organizations that want to win these contracts often hire proposal writers to maximize their chances. To become a self-employed proposal writer, try reading the *Commerce Business Daily* (cbdnet.gpo.gov) and the *Foundation Directory Online* (www.foundationcenter.org) to find proposals you'd like to write, and contact organizations that may want to bid on the proposals. *The Grantsmanship Center:* www.tgci.com. *Jim Burke's book: I'll Grant You That.*

Program Evaluator. "You're judgmental!" That's usually a criticism, but in this profession, you're paid to be judgmental. Typical scenario: You're hired to evaluate a school district's new reading program. You interview students and teachers, compare test scores with a control group, and write a report of your findings. Being an evaluator is fun because you get to check out lots of innovative programs, see what works and what doesn't, and make recommendations for improvement. The bad part is that many program sponsors don't really want your input; they hire you mainly to meet a government requirement. After all, few people like to be evaluated, especially negatively. A master's or doctorate degree filled with statistics courses is usually the admission ticket to the profession, but program evaluators frequently use only the statistics they learn in their intro to stats class. *American Evaluation Association:* www.eval.org. *John Boulmetis's book: The ABCs of Evaluation, 2nd Edition.*

OOH

Marketer. Your company wants to introduce a product — maybe a game that can be played on a cellphone. You review the competition to identify a gap in the market; for example, perhaps no good game exists for intellectual teenage girls. Then, with that general product in mind, you review demographic and psychographic data to find the market segments most likely to buy it. You conduct surveys and focus groups to see what features would attract your target market. You help select packaging and a marketing message, and last, figure out how best to advertise it: A well-linked blog? Ads on cellphones? Print ads in high school newspapers? Demand is great for marketers with technical backgrounds — developing a marketing plan for a circuit board is easier if you're an engineer. If you want to be a self-employed marketing consultant, the key, as usual, is to carve out a tiny but in-demand niche — for example, showing shopping malls how to set up promotions to bring customers to the mall. (A lost cause, in the long run, I'm betting.) *About.com's marketing portal:* marketing.about.com. *American Marketing Association:* www.ama.org. *Jay Levinson's book: Guerrilla Marketing.*

> (Neat Niche) **Online Marketer.** Every Web site wants traffic. Your job is to get it there. Submit the site in the right way to search engines, conduct e-mail marketing campaigns, arrange link exchanges ("I'll link to your site if you link to mine"), create affiliate marketing deals, make submissions to newsgroups, and advertise on related sites and in traditional media. *Web Marketing Today:* www.webmarketingtoday.com. *Bruce Brown's book: How to Use the Internet to Advertise, Promote and Market Your Business or Website with Little or No Money.*

(Neat Niche) **Trend Spotter.** Trend spotters visit clubs, cafes, and malls to see what new things people are buying. They develop the next "in" thing. In addition to retailers, trend spotters are hired by department store chains, e-commerce sites, high-tech equipment manufacturers, ad agencies, and even the government. For example, when a city wants to see what's in store for it, it may send a trend spotter to Berkeley, California. *Trend Hunter magazine:* www.trendhunter.com

(Neat Niche) **Focus Group Leader.** A key step in developing a product is to ask a group of people about it. In today's jargon, that's called a focus group. Often, a focus group is simply a structured discussion, but it can be much more sophisticated. For example, before the president gives a speech, he may read a draft to a private audience of citizens carefully selected to be representative of swing voters. Each guinea pig has a dial that can be turned from 0 (I hate it) to 10 (I love it). They continually adjust the dial as the president speaks. He then uses only the material that gets a high rating. The focus group leader selects the participants, runs the proceedings, and writes up the results. *David Stewart's book: Focus Groups: Theory and Practice (Applied Social Research Methods), 2nd Edition.*

(Neat Niche) **Social Marketer.** The same techniques that Madison Avenue uses to convince you to buy a brand of cigarettes, social marketers use to get you to live more wisely. For example, the U.S. government now spends $200 million each year on prime-time commercials, mainly to spread antidrug or anticigarette messages. It's the flip side of product marketing: You're trying to build market share of *non*use. *Social Marketing Institute:* www.social-marketing.org. *Information:* www.social-marketing.com *Philip Kotler's book: Social Marketing.*

(Neat Niche) **Film Marketer.** There's plenty to market: getting domestic movie houses to rent films and getting the filmgoers to see them. Then you have overseas, airlines, cable and network TV, DVD, and now, video-on-demand markets. I'm not done yet. Don't forget about the T-shirts and baseball caps. *Independent Film & Television Alliance:* www.ifta-online.org.

(Neat Niche) **Marketing Researcher.** You design surveys to collect needed information. In addition to in-house corporate or nonprofit marketing departments, you can work for independent polling organizations. Biggies include Gallup, Field, Harris, and Roper. Pollsters have enormous power. A subtle change of wording can dramatically change a poll's results. The question "Would you eat corn that came from seeds specially bred to produce sweeter corn?" will yield a very different result than "Are you concerned about eating genetically engineered corn?" *Marketing Research Association:* www.mra-net.org.

 Business Developer. Most businesses need someone to ask, "What alliances could I create that would build the business? Would it be to license our cool technology? Co-brand? Merge with someone?" *Business developer* is today's term for the old and crucial job of dealmaker. Surprisingly, for this key position, small companies often hire young, smart, silver tongues not long out of college. Business developer is one of the more responsible and heart-pumping jobs a newbie can get. *David Aaker's book: Developing Business Strategies.*

Management Consultant. Your job is to solve problems too tough for an organization to solve by itself. Examples: A firm wants to start selling in Asia. A nonprofit needs a better system for managing the information flow. A startup has a great idea, but now what? Yes, to address such problems, you need top analytical skills, but you also must be persuasive and tactful — even though you're a 20-something with no real work experience, you're telling a veteran what to do. You also must be willing to work long hours. The typical management consultant for a major firm works 50 to 80 hours a week and travels half the time. Management consulting is a great career for learning about the business world, to have major impact on a company while you're still in your 20s, and to hang around with really smart (and well-paid) people. However, for a decent shot at being hired by a top consulting firm, such as Accenture or McKinsey, you must have good grades from a designer-label college and make a great impression in tough interviews. Small management consulting firms and self-employment are alternate possibilities. One self-marketing tack is to write a proposal to the ten small firms you think you can best help. *Wikipedia entry: en.wikipedia.org/wiki/management_consulting. Vault.com profile: vault.com/hubs/502/channelhome_502.jsp?ch_id=252. Wetfeet.com's book: Careers in Management Consulting. Mariam Naficy's book: The Fast Track. These books are critical of the profession: James O'Shea's book: Dangerous Company, and Martin Kihn's book: House of Lies.*

Organizational Identity Consultant. Large companies and nonprofits hire consultants to create logos and slogans that capture their essence. That sells more product and encourages employees to feel good about the company. Although this may not be the most socially redeeming job, it pays well and, to me, sounds fun. *Wikipedia entry: en.wikipedia.org/wiki/corporate_identity. David Carter's book: American Corporate Identity 2007.*

Organizational Developer. Organizational developers figure out how to make workgroups more effective, often with trainings, sometimes by restructuring. They may also be involved in team building and diversity training. Some insiders, however, report that many ODers approach the latter two activities with trepidation because of past failures. When I recently suggested that a client, an organizational developer with 20 years of experience, may want to do more team building and diversity training, he grimaced, put his hands over his face and moaned, "Noooo! Anything but that!" *Wikipedia entry: en.wikipedia.org/wiki/organizational_development. Organizational Development Network: www.odnetwork.org.*

Small Business Consultant. Many of the 600,000 people who start a business each year are scared of failing. Many small businesses can use help with marketing, accounting, finance, or technology. *Alan Weiss's book: Getting Starting in Consulting, Second Edition.*

(Neat Niche) **Business Plan Writer.** Many business owners know they need a business plan but don't know how to create one. Inexpensive software packages, such as *BizPlan Builder,* can help you make business plans look professional, but the key to being a good business plan writer is understanding what it takes to identify and market a winning product or service, and raise money for and operate the business. This seems like a fun career, helping come up with the business idea and implementation plan without incurring any financial risk or dealing with the headaches of running the business. A way to find clients: Teach a class at a public library or college's extension school on how to write a business plan. *About.com's business plan writing portal:* sbinformation.about.com/od/businessplans/ Business_Plan_Writing.htm.

(Neat Niche) **Client Prospecting Specialist.** Train business owners in sales tactics and in using tools such as prospect lists and customer management software (like salesforce) to find and close customers. *Wikipedia entry:* en.wikipedia.org/wiki/customer_relationship_management.

(Neat Niche) **Private-Practice Consultant.** Many doctors are running scared. So are many dentists, podiatrists, psychotherapists, orthodontists, veterinarians, chiropractors, lawyers, and CPAs. They're scared because they increasingly realize that being good practitioners doesn't make them good businesspersons. So they're turning to consultants to help recruit new customers and develop better systems for billing and collections, payroll, records management, and personnel. Demand is strong, and you work with educated people with the money and motivation to pay you well. *National Society of Certified Healthcare Business Consultants:* www.smdmc.org.

(Neat Niche) **Security System Consultant.** Only one-fourth of homes and businesses have security systems, but many more people are thinking about installing one. The expertise required to become a consultant in this specialty is less than for most fields, but the stakes are high. Thus, customers may be willing to pay for a consultant. *Michael Khairallah's book: Physical Security Systems Handbook.*

Work with Data and Things

OOH

Archivist. What part of the National Park Service's enormous collection of information should be permanently maintained? Which of those items should be exhibited in national parks? How can the rest of the information be stored for easy access? Archivists answer such questions. Best background: a major in history and a master's in library science from a school that offers a specialty in archival management. *Society of American Archivists:* www.archivists.org.

Acoustics Specialist. You probably know that acoustics specialists ensure good sound in a concert hall, but they also keep offices quiet so you can concentrate, and homes quiet so you can sleep. In addition, acoustics specialists help design loudspeakers and microphones, and recording and film studios. *Acousticians* also are the folks who created sonograms — safer alternatives to X-rays and invasive diagnostic tests. *Acoustical Society of America:* `asa.aip.org.`

 Coroner/Medical Examiner. Did Professor Plum do it with the candlestick in the conservatory? Or did the victim die of natural causes? Medical examiners, who, in many jurisdictions, don't need to be MDs, answer such questions. It isn't the sort of medical career that makes a great first impression: you cure no one and you spend your life mucking around with dead people. Fortunately, after a period of desensitization, playing around with corpses begins to feel normal. And it is rewarding work: One medical examiner described it as "the only career in which you enable dead people to save lives." *National Association of Medical Examiners:* `www.thename.org.`

 Microscopist. Imagine being able to look at something at 500,000 times magnification, in three dimensions. That's what today's microscopists can do. Why would you want to magnify something so greatly? To examine what happens to diseased cancer cells at the molecular level, to assess the quality of the ceramic coating on a rocket's heat shield, or to determine whether the DNA of skin underneath a suspect's fingernails matches that of the person who was strangled. *Microscopy Society of America:* `www.microscopy.org.`

 Oceanographer. You see them on TV, diving off a spacious boat on a perfect day, exploring a coral reef in pursuit of new ways to preserve the ecosystem. Those types of oceanographers still are around but increasingly they help restore shorelines, build offshore oil rigs, and rehab bridges. No matter the specialty, a career in oceanography has downsides that don't make it onto the *National Geographic* special. Many oceanographers spend months far from home, much of that time freezing in cramped quarters. Something else those TV specials don't highlight are the many hours oceanographers spend far from the sea: in cubicles, crunching numbers. A master's or PhD in marine science is standard, but people familiar with boats, electronics, or dive apparatus can get onto oceanographic expeditions without a college degree. *Oceanography Society:* `www.tos.org.`

 Geographer. Michael Jordan was a geography major. Can't you just imagine him debating: "Hmm, should I be a geographer or a pro basketball player?" Well, assuming you don't have pro basketball potential, geography offers some pretty cool careers. Don't think that geographers mainly make maps. Only a small percentage does. (Mapmakers are covered under the separate "Cartographer" entry in the later section "Work with Things and Data.") Geographers are often experts on such matters as global warming, where to do economic development, and Afghani terrain. If you decide to become a geographer, you'll be in good company: Mother Teresa started out as a geography teacher. *About.com's geography portal:* `geography.about.com.`

(Neat Niche) **Location Expert.** Everyone knows that the three keys to a business's success are location, location, and location. Because geographers know about demographics, transportation, availability of labor, shopping patterns, and how cities expand, geographers are good candidates for helping organizations figure out where to open up shop. *Zvi Drezner's book: Facility Location.*

(Neat Niche) **Area Specialist.** The government or a company wants to understand a country so its plans are on target. So, area specialists brief their bosses based on information from the media, government documents, aerial photos, and intelligence reports.

 Silviculturist. Silviculturists are forest builders. You create, restore, or maintain a forest or tree nursery. Your job is to pick the right tree varieties and supervise planting, pruning, and harvesting. Also, you may conduct research on topics such as the best way to ensure rapid tree growth, or the effects of animal grazing on the forest. Although most silviculturists live in isolated locations, urban forestry is a possibility as cities look to provide islands of respite amid the maelstrom. *Wikipedia entry:* `en.wikipedia.org/wiki/silviculture`. *Society of American Foresters:* `www.safnet.org`.

 Viticulturist. In plain English, this is a grape grower, and often a vineyard manager. Typically, you work for a winery and direct its field operations. With an *enologist* (wine expert; see the profile in the later section "Work with Things and Data"), you decide which grape varieties to plant and how to grow them for best flavor. Because you're a manager, it helps if you know accounting. Although you aren't the farmer, you'll find yourself doing a lot of bending. But don't worry, there's free wine to dull any aches. *American Society for Enology and Viticulture:* `www.asev.org`. *Lon Rombough's book: The Grape Grower.*

  Pilot. I've often wondered whether this career was boring. After all, it seems you're basically just a bus driver whose bus has wings. Yet many people aspire to be pilots. I guess it's the takeoff, aerial views, and landing, the prestige and good pay, and perhaps, all those motel nights with flight attendants. Most pilots like their careers. But how to land a job? Those plum commercial airline jobs generally go to former military pilots and to others with thousands of air hours and certifications from an FAA-certified training school. The good news is that many under-the-radar pilot jobs exist. And they may be more interesting than long-distance commercial flights on which you spend hours staring at instruments that are actually flying the plane, and as a reward for all that staring, you get jet lag. Under-the-radar pilot jobs: rescuing injured people, aerial advertising, fish spotting, flight instructor, tracking criminals, burial-at-sea, dropping aerodynamically packaged seedlings for reforestation, helicopter-based radio/TV traffic reports, emergency parts delivery, and patrol — oil and electric companies have pilots fly over pipelines and electrical lines to check for leaks. *Aviation Communication:* `www.flightinfo.com`. *Be a Pilot:* `www.beapilot.com`.

Railroad Engineer. Were you the kid who always liked to play with model trains? After short training and probably a stint in the railyard, you can be driving a locomotive, transporting people and the nation's goods. During your railyard work, you're paying your dues: You must labor in all sorts of weather and all hours of the day, and after you're an engineer, you're away from home a lot. But for the person who loves trains, what could be better than living on one? *Association of American Railroads:* www.aar.org. *Modoc Railroad Academy:* modocrailroadacademy.com.

Work with Data, People, and Things

Healthcare

  Registered Nurse. Today, whether the patient gets well depends at least as much on the nurse as on the doctor. As cost-cutting pressures increase, registered nurses are doing more and more substantive medical care, and medical assistants now mainly handle bedpan cleaning. RN pay is solid, in some metropolitan areas, reaching $100,000. A two-year degree is all that's required, although a bachelor's and especially a master's will open additional interesting doors. According to the Health Resources Services Administration, 400,000 nurses with master's degrees are needed for such positions as nursing supervisor, nurse practitioner, nurse educator, midwife, and anesthetist. Yet, only 140,000 nurses have a master's. Here's a field in which a master's makes sense.

 I keep hearing of nurses who ignore patients' call bells and of nurse errors that endanger or kill patients. Please, only consider nursing if you are, even when stressed, a caring, detail-oriented person. *Information:* www.discover nursing.com. *About.com's nursing portal:* nursing.about.com. *American Association of Colleges of Nursing:* www.aacn.nche.edu. *Suzanne Gordon's book: Life Support: Three Nurses on the Front Lines.*

(Neat Niche) **Nurse Practitioner.** You derive most of the benefits of being a physician with few of the liabilities. You get to do the fun parts of doctoring: exams, health education, and treating treatable conditions like that sore throat. And if things get too tough, you refer your patient to a physician. And you needn't subject yourself to four expensive, exhausting years of medical school, an even more exhausting year of internship, and two to four years of residency. A two-year training program following your bachelor's in nursing, and you're in, and with a good salary to boot. *American College of Nurse Practitioners:* www.acnpweb.org.

(Neat Niche) **Nurse Anesthetist.** Anesthesiologists earn $250,000-plus a year and HMOs don't like that one little bit. So HMOs increasingly prefer nurse anesthetists because they can pay them half that — good money for a nurse — and still save a bundle. Some general nursing experience plus a two- or three-year program after the bachelor's degree opens the door to this prestigious, important, but stressful position. Fully half of nurse anesthetists are men, compared with just nine percent among nurses overall. *American Association of Nurse Anesthetists:* www.aana.com *About.com's portal to info on anesthesiology:* anesthesiology.about.com

(Neat Niche) **Nurse Midwife.** More and more moms-to-be and healthcare bean counters are attracted to midwifery's combination of lower costs and more human touch. And midwifery can be a gratifying career. Not only do you deliver babies, but you also provide pre- and postnatal care such as teaching moms to breast feed. Registered nurses must complete a year of additional training for nurse-midwife certification. *American College of Nurse-Midwives:* www.acnm.org. *Juliana van Olphen-Fehr's book: Diary of a Midwife.*

(Neat Niche) **Obstetric-Gynecological Nurse.** Experience the miracle of childbirth on a daily basis. This can be a stressful job, and not just in a problem birth. A writhing mom in labor can raise the stress level of a stone. OB-GYN nurses need a calm demeanor. *Information:* www.obgyn.net.

(Neat Niche) **Transplant Coordinator.** You've drunk yourself into a stupor once too often, so your liver is kaput. Doc says you need a transplant. The transplant coordinator decides where you belong on the waiting list. (Too far back, in your soused opinion.) When someone dies whose liver is the right size and blood type, the transplant coordinator schedules the team for surgery, and gives you your pre- and postsurgery education. *Center for Organ Recovery & Education:* www.core.org.

(Neat Niche) **Wellness Coordinator.** Large employers, hospitals, and occasionally cities hire wellness coordinators to arrange health fairs, conduct blood pressure and lipid screenings, coordinate noon aerobics and stop-smoking classes, and, of course, encourage employees to eat more broccoli and less Häagen-Dazs. *American Association for Health Education:* www.aahperd.org/aahe.

(Neat Niche) **Patient Discharge Planner.** As hospitals release patients more quickly, discharge planners help patients transition to in-home care. A planner decides whether Mrs. McGillicuddy needs a home-health aide, trains her or her family on how to self-administer injections and other treatments, and helps the family solve problems as they arise. The work is generally less stressful than direct patient care. *Jackie Birmingham's book: Discharge Planning Guide.*

(Neat Niche) **Case Manager.** A 90-year-old woman has been battling cancer for five years. Her cancer has now spread to her liver, and she's in pain. Should she receive another operation? How about painful physical therapy for her atrophying leg? Should she be in the hospital? At home? In a hospice? What should and shouldn't the insurer pay for? The case manager coordinates this decision-making process and has one of the more interesting roles in the managed care system. After reviewing the record, speaking with the patient, family, healthcare providers, and insurance company, and leading rounds, the case manager makes recommendations that balance the interests of everyone involved: the payer, the hospital, the family, and, of course, the patient. *Catherine Mullahy's book: The Case Manager's Handbook, Third Edition.*

(Neat Niche) **Clinical Trials Coordinator.** A pharmaceutical company develops a new treatment that works on the computer and with rats, so it's time for human subjects. Nurses are hired to examine potential patients, administer the treatment, ensure that patients are complying, and write reports. This is a neat niche because it's little known, in demand, and a different experience for the nurse burned out on patient care who would enjoy being part of a research team. *Information: www.clinicaltrials.gov.*

(Neat Niche) **Menopause Counselor.** Menopause has come out of the closet, if the number of T-shirts proclaiming, "I'm out of estrogen and I have a gun," are any indication. As they enter the "change of life," some women seek support beyond what their gynecologist can provide during the quickie annual exams that HMOs usually pay for. *Google "menopause counseling."*

(Neat Niche) **Nurse Informatician.** Nurses need to access lots of data: patient records, drug contraindications, disease ins-and-outs, and insurance gobbledygook. The nurse informatician works with the computer programmer to develop systems that are nurse-friendly and is on call to help nurses having trouble extracting information. The pay's good, the job's rewarding, and there's no blood and gore. *American Nursing Informatics Association: www.ania.org.*

(Neat Niche) **Nurse Legal Consultant.** Law firms are inundated with people who want to sue their doctors or hospitals for medical malpractice. To evaluate those claims' legitimacy, lawyers hire nurse legal consultants to review the medical records, and if the case seems meritorious and involves nursing malpractice, to research the nursing literature to develop the case's foundation. Nurse legal consultants also testify in trials as expert witnesses. *American Association of Legal Nurse Consultants: www.aalnc.org.*

 Exercise Physiologist. Athletes are learning to perform better, not just with a coach's help, but with the help of an exercise physiologist. The latter may, for example, show an athlete how to improve by using slow-motion, computer-analyzed video of exactly what his muscles are doing. In addition to consulting with teams, exercise physiologists get jobs in sports medicine, cardiac rehab clinics, and corporate fitness centers. *American Society of Exercise Physiologists: www.asep.org. William McArdle's book: Exercise Physiology.*

 Respiratory Therapist. Humans can live for days without food or water, but without air, we're dead in nine minutes. A respiratory therapist's job is to keep patients breathing — often not just the very old, but also the very young. Newborns must often be placed on sophisticated ventilators. Your job is to

OOH

monitor the ventilators to ensure proper oxygen, CO2, and pH levels. You also administer aerosol medications and perform chest therapy to drain mucus from the lungs. Respiratory therapists are among the first people called to work with doctors to treat acute asthma attacks, head injuries, and drug poisonings. *American Association for Respiratory Care:* www.aarc.org.

Other specialties

Network Administrator. "The network is down. What the heck happened?" "I don't believe it! I lost my data!" Network administrators install and repair those oh-so-complicated systems. You're a combination mega-Tinkertoys assembler, electrician, programmer, and fix-it person. The job's tough, but, for the right person, it's fun because you get to see how all the pieces fit together, and there's variety, including needs assessment with actual human beings and hands-on computer diagnostic brainwork. Plus, you're crucial to everyone who uses the network — you receive heartfelt thank-yous when you get people back up and running. This is no 9-to-5 job; you work until it's fixed. You are well paid, though. The Department of Labor projects great demand. *Network Professional Association:* www.npa.org. *About.com's portal to networking info:* compnetworking.about.com. *The Network Administrator:* www.thenetworkadministrator.com.

(Neat Niche) **Computer Security Administrator.** Your job is to configure and run an organization's firewall, authorization system, and antivirus program. You may also develop and administer policy. This is a complicated field, and specialists are raking it in. To get started, take courses and certifications in security (see www.sans.org) and monitor the Computer Emergency Response Team site (www.cert.org) to learn about the latest threats. *The Federal Computer Security Division:* csrc.nist.gov. *Rick Lehtinen's book: Computer Security Basics.*

Quality Assurance Specialist. If you'd get a kick out of checking out products to see whether they're up to snuff, this job may be for you. And actually, you often get to do more than just try to make the software crash or sniff around the production line. QA people are often brought into meetings with higher-ups and taken on sales calls — you, more than anyone, can describe all the steps taken to ensure that the product works as advertised. The downside: You're the person who's telling everyone to improve — not likely to make you popular at work. With the rush to get products to market before a competitor does, it isn't surprising that software testers don't catch every bug. For example, syndicated columnist Bob Weinstein reports that Microsoft employs 3,000 testers, yet upon release, MS Word reportedly had 60,000 bugs. *American Society for Quality:* www.asq.org.

Risk Management Specialist. The insurance industry is an attractive employer because of good salaries, but for many people, it's a turnoff because of the nature of the product. One of the more rewarding insurance careers is in loss prevention, or as it's increasingly called, risk management. Rather than, for example, being an adjuster, whose job is to give loss victims as little as possible, the risk manager has the more pleasant role of helping a business develop a strategy to prevent losses. *Wikipedia entry:* `en.wikipedia.org/wiki/risk_management`.

 Employment Tester. To avoid costly hiring mistakes and charges of discrimination in hiring, employers increasingly are supplementing interviews with formal testing. Consultants select off-the-shelf instruments and develop customized tests, notably simulations, to predict which candidate is likely to do the job best. *Society for Industrial and Organizational Psychology:* `www.siop.org`.

 School Computer Coordinator. Schools are filling with computers, but after planting, many groves of Apples are gathering dust. The main problem is teachers who don't know how to use them effectively. Enter the school computer coordinator — combination network administrator, teacher trainer, and troubleshooter with a knack for figuring out how to help Johnny with whatever seems not to be working. *International Society for Technology in Education:* `www.iste.org`. *George Lucas Educational Foundation:* `www.edutopia.org`.

OOH
Planner. Should Wal-Mart be allowed to open a store in your city? What's the wisest plan for revitalizing downtown? How can you make the county environmentally sustainable without destroying the economy or greatly impeding people's quality of life? To address such questions, you, the planner, review copious data, conduct studies and public hearings, and before making a recommendation, probably wear many hats, including that of an engineer, economist, architect, sociologist, and politician. A silver tongue is essential if you expect even vestiges of your plan to survive irate community groups. Many planners specialize in urban or rural land use, transportation, housing, air quality, water quality, health and human services, historic preservation, or hazardous materials. *American Planning Association:* `www.planning.org`. *John Levy's book: Contemporary Urban Planning, 7th Edition.*

 FBI Special Agent. Are you an aspiring James or Jane Bond? The reality is usually less exotic, investigating such mundane dalliances as your basic fraudulent bankruptcy, but FBI special agents do search out terrorists, corrupt officials, kidnappers, people spying on the U.S., hackers, drug traffickers, identity thieves, mobsters, and bank robbers. Downsides are that you travel a lot and are alone most of the time. The FBI employs more than 10,000 special agents, and prefers a graduate degree in law or accounting or fluency in a foreign language. No surprise, Middle Eastern languages are in particular demand. Are you 37 or older? Forget it; the FBI wants to hire young. So do most employers, but age discrimination laws prevent it. The FBI is above all that. Entry-level job title: clandestine service trainee. *Federal Bureau of Investigation:* `www.fbi.gov`. *Joseph Koletar's book: The FBI Career Guide.*

 Private Investigator. You're worried that your husband is fooling around. Or that one of your employees is collecting disability but is, in fact, on the golf course. Or that your nanny is abusing your darling daughter. Who you gonna call? Your friendly private investigator. He'll hang out in the neighborhood, talk with some folks (hopefully without arousing suspicions), dig through online public information, and use that time-honored PI technique: dumpster diving. PIs must be able to read people and persuade them to give you information. Remember Columbo?

 Some danger exists here. For example, a wife has a husband followed. If hubby catches you, the private investigator, he may want to redecorate your face. The good news is that such mishaps are rare, especially nowadays, when many more cases are solved by a computer search than by stakeout. This is a cool career if you're clever and have a knack for not getting caught. Best training: apprentice with a pro. *Private Investigator Network:* www.pimall.com. *National Association of Legal Investigators:* www.nalionline.org. *Sam Brown's book: Private Eyes.*

Work with Data, Things, and People

 Physician. With Boomers aging, elder treatments improving, and demand for cosmetic surgery growing, there is a shortage of physicians. Plus, health maintenance organizations hire many doctors at good salaries while relieving them of much insurance paperwork. And of course, this career is prestigious and well paying. But practicing medicine today does have downsides. Getting into medical school is difficult, and after you're in, it's usually an exhausting, expensive ordeal. It can cost $200,000 and is usually followed by a few years of low-paying, 100-hour weeks of internship and residency. Insurers constrain how physicians can practice medicine: Patient visits are shorter, and evermore treatments are subject to insurer scrutiny. Meanwhile, malpractice suits climb. In many specialties, the physician's life is very stressful. Consider the typically six to eight years after college that it takes to prepare to be a physician, the enormous cost of medical school, the fraternity-like hazing called internship, the strain of high-stakes decision making, having to inform unsuspecting patients of severe illnesses, and the now usually prohibitive costs of starting your own practice.

And there's more. Medicine is changing so rapidly that it's impossible to keep up; so many physicians feel guilty that because of their own lack of knowledge and insurer constraints, they may not be providing optimal care. Meanwhile, some patients, armed with Internet printouts, feel they know more than the doc — and sometimes they do. Because physicians have ready access to mind-altering drugs, many docs turn to them for stress relief. *American Medical Association:* www.ama-assn.org. *Jennifer Danek's book: Becoming a Physician. Audrey Young's book: What Patients Taught Me: A Medical Student's Journey. Robert Marion's book: Learning to Play God. Laurence Savett's book: The Human Side of Medicine. The American Medical Association's book: Leaving the Bedside: The Search for a Nonclinical Medical Career.*

For some aspiring physicians, physician assistant (which I cover later in this section) and nurse practitioner (see the profile in the earlier section "Work with Data, People, and Things") may be wiser career choices even though they have less prestige and lower income potential.

If, however, you want to consider the MD route, there are neat niches. They're notable not only because they're relatively pleasurable compared with other niches, but also because they typically offer reasonable work hours.

If you have a bachelor's degree but not the science prerequisites for medical school, many colleges now offer a one-year post-bachelor's program that medical schools will consider.

(Neat Niche) **Infectious Disease Specialist.** As you're reading this, terrorist groups and governments may well be developing one-of-a-kind mutated viruses to use as bioweapons. The chances of that affecting you remain small, but that's not true of this: Natural selection is creating superbacteria that are resistant to even the most powerful antibacterials. Too, the odds of contracting infectious diseases is growing because of easier worldwide travel and continued migration to crowded, urban areas. I'm not just talking about newly discovered pathogens such as the West Nile or Avian flu viruses. Cases of the formerly thought-of-as-cured tuberculosis are increasing in the United States because of uncontrolled immigration. And then there's AIDS: the virus itself and the myriad opportunistic infections that its victims contract. Infectious disease researchers and practitioners do some of humankind's most important and challenging work. *Infectious Diseases Society of America:* www.idsociety.org.

(Neat Niche) **College-Based Physician.** College student health problems are usually curable, you have no overhead, and you work in a beautiful, stimulating setting: a college campus.

(Neat Niche) **Sports Medicine.** How'd you like to be the team physician for a college football team and/or treat weekend warriors' sprains and concussions? Here's another physician specialty in which you succeed with a large percentage of your patients. The difference between sports medicine and orthopedics? Only the latter does surgery. *American Medical Society for Sports Medicine:* www.amssm.org.

(Neat Niche) **Occupational Medicine.** This niche offers many advantages: need, good compensation, variety, and a high success rate. On-the-job accidents and job-related illnesses are frequent, with a relative shortage of occupational medicine docs. Employers and insurers know that your efforts to prevent on-the-job illnesses and accidents will save them lots of money, so compensation is good. Internal medicine, psychiatry, surgery, epidemiology, toxicology, forensic medicine, administration, preventive medicine — occupational medicine encompasses them all. You help a high percentage of your patients. *American College of Occupational and Environmental Medicine:* www.acoem.org.

(Neat Niche) **Radiologist.** Few medical fields have advanced more in recent decades. *Diagnostic* radiologists used to rely mainly on X-rays, which produce crude images while exposing patients to significant radiation. Today, ultrasound, and especially CT (CAT and PET) and MRI scans, enable far more useful images with lower risk to the patient. *Interventional* radiologists now are involved in, for example, cutting-edge (pardon the pun) procedures such as opening blood vessels and inserting stents in diseased arteries. *Radiology Info:* `www.radiologyinfo.org/en/careers/index.cfm?pg=diagcareer`. *Wikipedia entry:* `en.wikipedia.org/wiki/radiologist`.

(Neat Niche) **Dermatologist.** After med school, you first choose a specialty, and dermatology is among the most competitive because it's so desirable: You help most of your patients look better than ever. Patients treated by other medical specialists usually feel fortunate to just get back to where they were. Some dermatologists specialize, for example, in excising cancers, or more often, in doing cosmetic surgery. And newly available techniques make it more likely you'll delight your patients, and with ever-shorter recovery times. (Botox, anyone?) *Wikipedia entry:* `en.wikipedia.org/wiki/dermatology`.

Don't overlook this cool career just because society tends to denigrate cosmetic surgery as a narcissistic luxury, one that objectifies the body rather than focusing on a person's substance. I used to think that way myself. But I've seen a number of people's lives improve as a result of the surgery — they feel better about themselves every minute of every day and are even more productive at work. So, I've become a bit of a fan. I wonder whether cosmetic surgery has done more to improve people's sense of well-being than years on the psychologist's couch.

(Neat Niche) **Infertility Specialist.** Ever-more women are deferring parenthood until getting pregnant isn't so easy. Enter the infertility doctor, with an ever-growing array of fixes, including in-vitro fertilization, with ever-better egg screening to help ensure normalcy. Today, fertility docs even allow you to pick your baby's sex. Most people know couples who had a boy or two and were eager for a girl, only to have another boy. Today's in-vitro fertilization methods allow you to have a child with the gender of your choice. What's next: ensuring that your child isn't ugly? Has a high IQ? *American Society for Reproductive Medicine:* `www.asrm.org`.

(Neat Niche) **Hospital Research Director.** Many hospitals, even those unaffiliated with universities, conduct research. Research director is a great job for a burned-out doc who wants to improve the quality of medical care rather than just implementing the status quo. Grant proposal writing skills are key.

Physician Assistant. This career is similar to nurse practitioner. See that profile in the earlier section "Work with Data, People, and Things." For most doctors, the fun part is doctoring — diagnosing patients, treating them, doing patient education. The dreary parts are the paperwork, managing the office, and dealing with insurance companies. Physician assistants enjoy many of the benefits of being a physician with few of its liabilities. Under a doctor's supervision, physician assistants do diagnosis, treatment, and patient education, but training takes just two to three years — much fewer than doctors put in. And paperwork and management responsibilities are few. According to the Bureau of Labor Statistics, this career is among the fastest growing, as healthcare organizations cut costs by using physician assistants more and doctors less. Salaries aren't doctor-level, but they're respectable — about $80,000 on average. To enter this field, you need a bachelor's degree in a science/health field and a few years of experience as a nurse, EMT, or paramedic. *American Academy of Physician Assistants:* www.aapa.org. *Terence Sacks's book: Opportunities in Physician Assistant Careers. Andrew Rodican's book: Getting Into the Physician Assistant School of Your Choice.*

Audiologist. As Boomers age, their hearing fades, so demand should be strong. Plus, you're ever-more likely to satisfy customers because hearing aids are getting better. For the self-conscious, some new hearing aids are so tiny that everything fits into your ear canal except the gizmo you pull it out with — the nation's most famous user is Bill Clinton. Many audiologists get out of the office and spend part of each week in hospitals, rehab centers, and special schools. Alas, increasingly, a doctoral degree is required. *Audiology Net:* www.audiologynet.com/audiologist.html. *Frederick Martin's book: Introduction to Audiology, 9th Edition.*

Veterinarian. A vet is like a doctor except you need to know a half-dozen species, none of which can describe their symptoms to you. Veterinary medicine offers advantages over being a physician. You get to perform a wider range of procedures because, in many specialties, board certification isn't required. Plus, most veterinary medicine is fee-for-service, so you aren't bogged down with labyrinthine regulations and paperwork. One downside is that veterinary offices tend to be loud: lots of barking. *American Veterinary Medical Association:* www.avma.org. *About.com's veterinary portal:* vetmedicine.about.com. *Gene Witiak's book: True Confessions of a Veterinarian.*

(Neat Niche) **Laboratory Animals Vet.** It's a relatively easy specialty: working hours are 9 to 5, no weekends, and you get to work in a medical school or drug company setting. There are ample jobs because most animal research must be supervised by a laboratory animal vet.

(Neat Niche) **Veterinary Cardiologist.** Demand is growing, treatments are improving, and earnings are excellent for these heart specialists. *About.com's portal to Veterinary Cardiology sites:* vetmedicine.about.com/od/cardiology/Cardiology.htm. *Veterinary Clinical Cardiology:* www.vetgo.com/cardio.

Veterinary Technologist. Much shorter training than for veterinarians, yet veterinary techs get to do much of what vets do. Say that poor Fifi isn't feeling well. You, the vet tech, may take her medical history (if you can speak dog), give her an exam, and take her blood (poor Fifi). The vet diagnoses the problem as a bladder infection and prescribes an injection that you administer. Next, even poorer Bowser comes in — he was run over by a car. The vet decides to operate. You administer the anesthetic and assist in surgery. You're even allowed to stitch Bowser up. Bowser also has a broken leg. You take the X-rays, the vet sets the leg, and you apply the cast. Finally, you educate Bowser's mommy or daddy about how to take care of Bowser during his recovery. You needn't be dogged to land a job because there are four job openings for every vet tech graduate in the United States. The problem is that salaries are poopy. *North American Veterinary Technologists Association:* www.avma.org/navta.

Paramedic. A person is having a heart attack. Or three teens are down after a gang war. Or there's a bad car accident and bleeding passengers are tangled in the wreckage. The paramedic is first on the scene to try to save the day. If you thrive on adrenaline but can stay calm and be gratified by your saves but not burned out by your losses, this can be a rewarding career. Training is short. Initial certification as an emergency medical technician (EMT) is short (just 100 to 120 hours!). Full paramedic status requires 750 to 2,000 hours and certifies you to do the stuff they do on *ER*. This is a burnout profession, so after a few years, figure on going for an RN or physician assistant degree. Demand continues to grow as Boomers age and the number of illegal immigrants (unscreened for violent criminal records) grows. *National Association of Emergency Medical Technicians:* www.naemt.org.

Physical Therapist. An executive with BlackBerry thumb (from checking e-mail too often), an older person recovering from a stroke, an infant with a birth defect — each of these is a typical physical therapy patient. The physical therapist's job is to develop programs to relieve pain and restore function. Many people think of a physical therapist as the person who coaches the patient through exercises, but in many cases, that's done mainly by less expensive physical therapy assistants. Increasingly, the physical therapist is primarily the patient's plan maker and instructor. Aging Boomers will create strong demand for physical therapists. Admission to PT school has become difficult, only a notch easier than medical school. This is another of those fields in which a doctoral degree is becoming required. *American Physical Therapy Association:* www.apta.org.

(Neat Niche) **Sports Physical Therapy.** Helping people who hurt themselves trying to stay in shape tends to be a more rewarding, less burnout-prone niche than traditional physical therapy, which more often deals with cases in which progress is slow. *Sports Physical Therapy Section:* www.spts.org.

Acupuncturist. Insert needles, manipulate carefully, restore balance in so-called "energy fields," and possibly help everything from weight loss to pain control, and from arthritis to upper respiratory infections. Not only is the public willing to try, but some insurance companies are also paying. *Quackwatch.com casts doubt on acupuncture's efficacy:* www.quackwatch.com/01Quackery RelatedTopics/acu.html. *A pro-acupuncture site:* www.acupuncture.com.

Work with Words and People

OOH

Attorney. You're lousy at science and like to argue, so you go to law school, right? Catch this: Three-fourths of lawyers wish they were doing something else. A similar percentage wouldn't recommend that their children become lawyers. That's because the job is often contentious and filled with temptations to be unethical. Yet, armies of college graduates run off to law school seeking money, status, an opportunity to change the world, and/or a TV lawyer wardrobe. It's a myth that law is an easy route to a six-figure income. Assuming you can land a lucrative gig, you'll probably work 60-plus-hour weeks — some law firms buy futons for their offices so the lawyers can sleep there. And many attorneys don't make big money. Indeed, many lawyers are forced to work as paralegals who may make no more than garbage collectors.

Another myth is that lawyers spend most of their time in a courtroom. Even litigators spend only a small fraction of their time before a judge, and transactional attorneys, who draft agreements, rarely see the inside of a courtroom. For most law jobs, the ability to make airtight arguments is key, but another essential is being detail-oriented. Law is about preparation, which often means reading through the sheaves of dry material you can't pawn off on your paralegal.

Final myth: The law is a good option for people who want to cure social ills. Many students enter law school with that hope. The reality is that only a tiny percentage of lawyers end up with public interest jobs. I know one Yale Law School graduate who clerked for a U.S Circuit Court of Appeals judge, yet was turned down for a low-paying job at the National Abortion Rights League.

The good news is that the following neat niches offer a reasonable chance of having it all: the prestige, the money, and a more pleasant life than experienced by the typical corporate or insurance defense attorney.

No profile of attorneys is complete without a lawyer joke. My current favorite: What do you call a lawyer gone bad? Senator. *American Bar Association:* www. abanet.org. *Vault.com links:* www.vault.com/hubs/507/hubhome_507.

jsp?ch_id=507. Article: www.constitution.org/lrev/rodell/woe_ unto_you_lawyers.htm. Deborah Schneider's book: Should You Really Be a Lawyer?

There's money to be made in them thar hills. Most lawyers choose to live in or near big cities, but lawyers are also needed (well, desired) in rural areas.

(Neat Niche) **Computer Law.** My name is McDonald. I register my food business on the Web as www.McDonald#1.com (fictitious). Can the folks from the Golden Arches sue me? My employer lends me a computer to use at home during the days I telecommute. One evening, on that computer, I write a love letter to my wife. The employer screens it and says it's unauthorized use of a company computer. Is the company right? My company outsources to China the development of a peer-to-peer videopodcasting program. A year later, an awfully similar program appears on a Chinese government-sponsored site. Now what? Welcome to the world of computer law, a field that allows you to immerse yourself in the cutting edge issues of our time: intellectual property, privacy, e-commerce, outsourcing, globalization, and telecommunications. *International Technology Law Association: www.itechlaw.org.*

(Neat Niche) **Sports Agent.** Ever since Cuba Gooding yelled, "Show me the money!" sports agents have gained a higher profile. Today, they help with everything from product endorsements to estate planning. *Sports Lawyers Association: www.sportslaw.org. Kenneth Shropshire's book: The Business of Sports Agents. Sports Law Blog: sports-law.blogspot.com.*

(Neat Niche) **Adoption Attorney.** How different this is from traditional adversarial lawyering — helping to match a child needing parents with parents wanting to adopt a child. It's a far cry from the other sort of family law: divorcing couples ready to kill each other over an armoire. *Links: family-law.freeadvice.com/adoption_law/. American Academy of Adoption Attorneys: www.adoptionattorneys.org. Randi Barrow's book: Somebody's Child: Stories from the Private Files of an Adoption Attorney.*

(Neat Niche) **Bankruptcy Lawyer.** An attorney told me that bankruptcy law is among the easiest types of law to practice — the procedures are straightforward and minimally adversarial. *Links: bankruptcy-law. freeadvice.com. Stephen Elias's book: The New Bankruptcy. Vault.com links: www.vault.com/nr/hottopiclist.jsp?ch_id=242&nr_page= 13&cat_id=2812.*

(Neat Niche) **Employment Lawyer.** This is among the law's fastest-growing specialties. Legal employment remedies have been expanded for minorities, the disabled, and homosexuals who believe they have been discriminated against in the workplace. Employers must be increasingly careful to ensure that they comply with all laws and are prudently responsive to the ever-growing number of lawsuits. Employment lawyers are key to all this. Of course, on the other side, claimants need lawyers to handle their cases. Bottom line: lots of work for employment lawyers. *Vault.com links:* `www. vault.com/nr/hottopiclist.jsp?ch_id=242&nr_page=13&cat_ id=2814`. *Fred Steingold's book: The Employer's Legal Handbook.*

(Neat Niche) **Mediator/Arbitrator.** See the mediator profile in the earlier section "Caretaking and coaching."

(Neat Niche) **Education Lawyer.** Johnny has gone through 12 years of schooling and still can't read. Who's responsible? Many parents are claiming that the schools should be, and they're hiring lawyers to file big-dollar lawsuits against school districts. Education lawyers, of course, also defend school districts against these and other claims. Other cases may, for example, involve a teacher who was fired for incompetence and claims that due process was violated, a group of Black parents suing a school district because a disproportionate number of student suspensions are African-Americans, or a child who falls off a schoolyard play structure whose parent claims inadequate supervision. *Education Law Association:* `www. educationlaw.org`.

(Neat Niche) **Intellectual Property/Patent Lawyer.** When you think of patents, contraptions may come to mind, but today, patents often are awarded for such things as genes, computer chips, and genetically engineered mice. The intellectual property lawyer obtains that patent. She must understand both the science and the law to convince the United States Patent and Trademark Office that the new product truly is different from existing products. So it's no surprise that most intellectual property lawyers have a science or engineering background in addition to a law degree. Robert Benson, a patent attorney for Human Genome Sciences, loves his job: "In the lab, you can only do so much research work, but as a patent attorney you get to experience literally hundreds of lifetimes of research work." *National Association of Patent Practitioners:* `napp.org`. *American Intellectual Property Law Association:* `www.aipla.org`.

(Neat Niche) **Space Lawyer.** As more and more government and commercial satellites orbit Earth, disputes arise. Does a country have the right to launch a surveillance satellite that circles the globe? Who owns which rights to the moon? They're already selling tickets for commercial space flights. What sorts of contracts are needed to protect the spacelines and their passengers? Space law is, as they used to say in the 1960s, a new frontier. *Information:* `www.spacelawstation.com`.

(Neat Niche) **Elder Lawyer.** Family members or nursing home staff, exhausted from caring for senile, incontinent patients, often commit elder abuse, leaving old people unturned so they develop bedsores, or tied down with restraints for the staff's convenience. Lawyers specializing in elder law argue whether there's legal liability. *Elder Law Answers:* `www.elderlawanswers.com`. *National Academy of Elder Law Attorneys:* `www.naela.org`. *Steve Weisman's book: A Guide to Elder Planning.*

(Neat Niche) **Environmental Lawyer.** No one wants to despoil the earth, but companies and government regulators have different ideas of how much despoiling is cost-effective to avoid. Even within the government, there's confusion as federal, state, and local regulations often contradict each other, providing plenty of fodder for environmental lawyers. *Links:* `www.findlaw.com/01topics/13environmental/index.html`. *Environmental Law Institute:* `www.eli.org`.

(Neat Niche) **Tax Attorney.** This is among law's highest-paid specialties, and it's easy to understand why. A corporation is structuring a deal — do it right and the company can save millions in taxes. Individuals, too, are willing to pay big bucks to a tax attorney — for example, when being audited for deducting that trip to Bora Bora. *Shannon Nash's book: Vault Guide to Tax Law Careers.*

(Neat Niche) **Estate Attorney.** After a lifetime of work, you've accumulated quite a nest egg. Although you've already been taxed on that income, the government wants to tax it again when you die — nice way for the government to offer its condolences. The estate attorney's job is to write wills and trusts to minimize this double taxation. As the Boomers age, this specialty continues to grow. *Introduction to Estate Law:* `www.mylawyer.com/guide.asp?level=1&id=623`.

 Paralegal. To cut costs, paralegals are doing much of the work that lawyers used to do: researching cases, interviewing witnesses and clients, writing reports and legal documents — just about everything but appearing in court. You get to do that without needing a bachelor's degree plus three expensive years of law school. The most you'll have to do is a four-year program, and many firms hire graduates of one- or two-year programs. Job-market dampener: An excess of lawyers is resulting in their being hired as paralegals. *National Association of Legal Assistants:* `www.nala.org`.

 Administrative Law Judge/Hearing Officer. This is a *relatively* easy way to become a judge, but you still usually must be a well-connected attorney. The difference from the more familiar kind of judge is that administrative law judges rule on the laws and regulations of public agencies, and the process is more informal. Typical role: A school district offers a child with learning difficulties a special class, but the parents want the district to pay for a special private school. An administrative law judge decides. *Virginia's Career Guide, Administrative Law Judge:* `jobs.virginia.gov/careerguides/ALJ.htm` *Federal Reports Handbook: An Insiders Guide to Becoming a Federal Administrative Law Judge.*

OOH

Public Relations/Communications Specialist. I held the stereotypical view of public relations people — sleazebags — until I wrote my first book. In my heart, I believed it deserved to be read, but how was I to get it noticed among the 60,000 other books that were published *that year?* That made me realize that publicists can serve an honorable purpose. *Publicist* is actually only one specialization within the public relations field. Public relations types also develop corporate images consonant with community values, promote anyone from rock star to seminar leader, and of course, do damage control. I recall that when the Oakland (CA) Unified School District school board decided to mandate Ebonics (Black English dialect) for its students, a national firestorm erupted. Then the district hired a public relations firm, and its message was clarified (some say sanitized), and the storm blew over. That's the bad part of PR. You're often a spin doctor, and you're perceived that way.

If you want to be a self-employed PR person, specialize — for example, in books, arts nonprofits, toy companies, or shareholder communications. Key skills include the ability to come up with clever ideas quickly and in quantity and pitch them compellingly — verbally and in writing — to the media. Bonus: Many PR people get to go to cool parties attended by the media and glitterati. My vote for the most effective publicity stunt ever? When IBM pitted its Big Blue computer against chess superstar Garry Kasparov. *Public Relations Society of America:* `www.prsa.org`. *Morris Rotman's book: Opportunities in Public Relations Careers.*

(Neat Niche) **Public Relations for Travel and Tourism.** Paul Plawin, in *Careers for Travel Buffs,* writes, "In order to write about the delights of the Doral Beach Spa in Miami Beach, a Royal Caribbean Cruise, the beaches of the Bahamas, the fun and frivolity of Southern California, or the fjords of Alaska, public relations people must visit those destinations." Definitely a neat niche. *Public Relations Society of America's Travel PR section:* `www.prsa.org/_Networking/travel/index.asp?ident=trav1`. *Dennis Deuschl's book: Travel and Tourism Public Relations.*

(Neat Niche) **Public Relations for High-Tech and Biotech Companies.** Such companies are often flush with cash and recognize the importance of public relations. *The Public Relations Society of America's technology section:* `www.prsa.org/_Networking/Technology/index.asp?ident=tech`

(Neat Niche) **Investor Relations Specialist.** You may write a mutual fund sales brochure, a company's annual report, or articles for a corporation's shareholder magazine. The best-paying and highest-stakes jobs involve running dog-and-pony shows to convince large investors, such as mutual fund managers, to invest in your company. *National Investor Relations Institute:* www.niri.org.

Awards Entrepreneur. Tiffany Schlain decided to give out awards for the best Web sites and turned it into a big business, the Webbys, with money earned from contestant entry fees and awards ceremony ticket fees. She even charges honorees for their award statues and framed certificates! There are contests and awards in countless fields: from blogs and vlogs (the Bloggies and Vloggies, of course) to new car quality (JD Power) to screenwriting (dozens of those contests — screenwriters are desperate to put "award winner" on their resume). Yet, the market for awards isn't saturated. For example, you may set up local analogs to the Tony Awards for your region's best community theater actors, directors, and plays. If you don't make enough money from one such enterprise, do a few. *The Webby Awards:* www.webbyawards.com.

Personal Historian/Biographer. So many parents ask their college student, "What in the world are you going to do with a degree in history?" Well, tell your parents about Ellie Kahn. Her firm, Living Legacies, produces custom-ordered histories of individuals, families, and historical buildings. She's compiled 80 histories in book, video, or audio format. I'm not surprised that she's successful. Most people are egocentric. Deep down, most people would love to have a book written about them, but how do you turn that into a business? You can contact famous people who are in need of a boost. Offer to write their biography. When they agree, write a book proposal and find a literary agent to peddle it for you. Just plain folks may also want their stories recorded as personal legacies for future generations. Or someone may want a biography of his aging parent or a volume that tells his family history. Market through genealogy societies, senior centers, reunion planners, or by placing ads in upscale community newspapers. To avoid putting in too many hours for too little money, I recommend this model: Create the video by doing an hour's interview with each of one to four protagonists and editing it into a 15-minute DVD, with professional-looking titles, dissolves, and background music. *Association of Personal Historians:* www.personalhistorians.org.

Foreign Service Officer. Imagine working in the United States embassy or consulate in one of 250 foreign countries (the government's choice — Afghanistan or Zimbabwe, perchance?). Your first job may include helping poor souls who lost their passports, but things usually get more interesting. Your job may include keeping abreast of political and economic conditions so that you can brief American policymakers. Or you may arrange cocktail parties for business and political leaders of your host country. A cool career, but here's the rub: Eight thousand people apply for the 200 openings each year. Better be a good reader and writer, and have a knack for learning a foreign language in six months — and another language two years later. Urdu, anyone? *Wikipedia entry:* en.wikipedia.org/wiki/United_States_Foreign_Service.

Foreign Language Interpreter/Translator. Millions of hours of Al-Qaeda conversations had been intercepted but weren't translated until after 9/11 because of the shortage of translators and interpreters. (Translators work with the written word; interpreters translate speech.) But you needn't speak Arabic to have good career prospects. Ever-more immigrants are entering the medical and court systems while U.S. firms are importing or outsourcing to ever-more Asian scientists, engineers, and computer programmers. The most in-demand languages are Spanish, Arabic, Chinese, Russian, Japanese, French, and German. Good money is possible if you specialize. Security, medical, legal, and engineering interpreting are good bets.

No matter what your niche, it helps if you're both bilingual and bicultural — understanding both cultures enables you to translate the nuances. The largest employer of interpreters and translators: the federal government, the United Nations, and the Organization of American States. Perk: lots of all-expense-paid travel, but often on a moment's notice. Risk: Instant translation software is getting better and better (for example, try the free demo at `www.systransoft.com`). Within five years, software may be good enough to put many if not most human translators and even interpreters out of a job. *American Translators Association:* `www.atanet.org`.

> (Neat Niche) **Translation.** Translating written material is less stressful than language interpreting on the fly because you have time to think or, heaven forbid, look up a word in the dictionary. Plus, the work hours are more normal. Unlike translators, interpreters must attend events wherever or whenever they occur. Favorite subniches: translating film scripts, Web sites, and software.

OOH

Court Reporter. Picture a court reporter. Chances are, you're envisioning someone in a courtroom pressing keys on a stenotype machine. In fact, only one-fourth of court reporters do that. Most work for attorneys, creating transcripts of out-of-court depositions. Others record the proceedings of government hearings. Still others provide the captioning now required for much live TV. Too, the Americans with Disabilities Act now mandates that all hearing-impaired college students, at no-cost, are entitled to be accompanied to all classes by a court reporter to provide real-time translation. Thanks to voice-recognition software, many court reporters can forgo the stenotype machine in favor of simply talking into a computer. That enables them to be hired with less than a year of training, or even by learning on the job. However, recording 225 words per minute using stenotype machines (mandated for hiring by the federal government and still preferred in many courts) requires an average of 33 months of training. Besides training, the good court reporter must have excellent listening skills and good vocabulary, grammar, and punctuation. They must also be perfectionists; for example, judicial appeals often depend on the court reporter's transcript. *National Court Reporters Association:* `www.ncraonline.org`.

Regulation Compliance Consultant. When a law or regulation changes, it can mean an opportunity for entrepreneurs. For example, a few years back, North Carolina decided to require all high school students to take an earth science course. Well, many of the state's teachers had never taught earth science, so an enterprising woman contacted the state's education department and got to provide earth science training workshops for teachers all across North Carolina. Every time you hear of a new law or regulation, ask yourself, "Does that create an opportunity for me?" Quiz: The U.S. Postal Service recently announced that in 2010, it plans to remove thousands of those blue mailboxes on the street. Does that offer a business opportunity? Here's one: Bid as a contractor that removes the mailboxes. Then sell them on eBay as, for example, childproof garbage cans or even just as "future antiques."

Work with Things and People

Interior Designer. What fun! Helping people figure out how to make their homes or offices beautiful and functional. And you get to go on shopping sprees. Trouble is, if you expect to make a living, the job usually requires much more than shopping: reading blueprints, creating estimates for commercial and residential projects, developing mockups using computer-aided design (CAD) systems, and knowing whether you can knock down a wall without the building collapsing. In short, you're somewhere between a decorator and an architect. Interior *decorators* often practice without credentials, but interior *designers* must have a bachelor's degree, and to get the respected American Society of Interior Designers certification, must know building codes and space planning. The ivillage.com site explained the latter: "If a person enters a building's lobby and can't easily figure out how to get to the bathroom or the elevator, then back to the lobby, you've got a problem." Side benefit: You have to have a cool-looking office. *American Society of Interior Designers: www.asid.org. Mary Knackstedt's book: The Interior Design Business Handbook.*

> (Neat Niche) **Housing for the Elderly and Disabled.** To meet the needs of the elderly and disabled and to comply with the Americans with Disabilities Act, housing developers are turning to interior designers with expertise in these areas. *Victor Regnier's book: Design for Assisted Living.*

> (Neat Niche) **Elective Medical Care Clinics.** Fat thighs? Thinning hair? Varicose veins? Age-ravaged face? Recent advances have made these treatable in non-hospital settings. So, free-standing clinics are popping up. These must have environments that inspire confidence and comfort. Enter the interior designer.

Home Stager. This is a well-paying career for artistic types without much artistic talent. When a homeowner decides to sell, he's willing to invest some bucks to make the house look its best. Stagers come to the house to recommend moving and removing furniture and decorations. ("That stuffed moose head simply must go!") They also suggest low-cost improvements, such as painting one wall a dramatic color to enliven a nondescript room. Because the home seller stands to make big bucks, these one-day decorators can earn good money, and although it's an artistic career, staging doesn't require a Rembrandt. *Information:* www.stagedhomes.com *HGTV's book: Designed to Sell.*

Landscape Architect. A landscape architect's projects can be mundane, like designing the spaces between buildings in an industrial park or building an artificial pond in a homeowner's backyard. Or they can be exotic like designing the landscapes of resorts, golf courses, zoos, urban plazas, colleges, cemeteries, landmark monuments, wetlands, or scenic highways. For example, landscape architects designed the U.S. Capitol grounds, preserved Yosemite Park, and created Boston's "Emerald Necklace" of green spaces tying the city to the suburbs. Because most landscape architecture projects don't have as many components as designing a building, young landscape architects, unlike building architects, may more quickly get to design entire projects. Also, the training is shorter: You typically can get a job with just a bachelor's degree and an internship of a year or less. One downside: Landscape architects are subject to an ever-growing thicket of environmental regulations — you're more likely to stay calm if you're an ardent environmentalist. *American Society of Landscape Architects:* www.asla.org. *Nicholas Dines's book, Landscape Architect's Portable Handbook.*

Garden Designer. Many people allow their yards to decline into the too-natural look. Sure, you can hire a garden-variety gardener, but she doesn't have design skills. Landscape architects have design skills, but you may need a second mortgage to afford one. Enter what I call the Garden Doctor. She makes house calls and performs transplants. Armed with a laptop and software like *Better Homes and Gardens Home Designer Pro 7.0,* the Garden Doctor and client can design the perfect Eden right there onscreen without lifting a shovel. When the design is just right, the homeowner can do the job or contract with the Garden Doctor. *Association of Professional Landscape Designers:* www.apld.com. *About.com's landscape portal:* landscaping.about.com. *Gordon Hayward's book: Your House, Your Garden: A Foolproof Approach to Garden Design.*

> (Neat Niche) **Green Gardener.** His specialty is gardens that require little water (xeriscaping) and little use of pesticides and fungicides.

> (Neat Niche) **Quick-Thumb Gardener.** She creates gardens that require minimal effort to stay looking good.

(Neat Niche) **Interiorscaper.** Hotels, hospitals, restaurants, atriums, malls, universities, and corporate headquarters are potential clients. My favorite company name: Plant Parenthood. *About.com's interiorscaping portal:* `landscaping.about.com/cs/indoorlandscaping/a/interiorscaping.htm`

Home Inspector. Buying a home can be love at first sight, but love is often blind. Enter the home inspector, whose job is to help the blind to see. No surprise, you'll need to know how to assess the soundness of a home's wiring, plumbing, heating, building materials, and so on. Market your service to local real estate agents, perhaps by giving lectures at local Board of Realtor meetings titled "How to Keep an Inspection from Killing the Deal." *American Society of Home Inspectors:* `www.ashi.com`. *National Association of Certified Home Inspectors:* `www.nachi.org`.

Home Remodeling Contractor. This is one of the construction industry's most rewarding jobs. Typically, you help design the project, bid the job, hire the workers, and keep a nice percentage of what you charge, without ever getting your hands dirty. Neat niches: green remodeling, converting buildings for use by computer-intensive tenants, upgrading biotech labs, home offices, greenhouses, and additions for elder relatives. *National Association of the Remodeling Industry:* `www.nari.org`. *Building Online:* `www.buildingonline.com`.

Athletic Team Trainer. Suddenly a player goes down. You race out onto the field and must make an instant evaluation: How bad? Do we need the stretcher? A doctor? You don't want to overreact — the player, the team, and the fans want to see her play again, or at least walk off the field, but of course, better safe than sorry. The athletic trainer's key skill is decision making. He also has important decisions to make before and after the game. For example, an injured athlete is dying to play again. The doctor has given the okay, but as you tape up the player, you notice him wincing. What should you do? Other interesting parts of the job: developing conditioning programs for the team and rehab regimens for injured athletes and motivating them to implement those programs. And there's more. Michael O'Shea, a trainer at the University of Louisville, explains, "The trainer is a 24-hour father confessor." Training jobs for sports teams are tough to land, but there's growth at corporate fitness centers. *National Athletic Trainers' Association:* `www.nata.org`.

Dentist. It's a myth that you must be excellent with your hands to be a good dentist. Studies find that an average person can develop the hands-on skills. You do, however, need a good back. Many dentists develop back problems from constantly leaning over patients. And dentistry is stressful. It's no fun to see patients flinch (hopefully, not writhe) in response to your gentle touch. A major upside compared with other medical professions is that you cure most patients' problems. Plus, it's one of the few medical professions left in which self-employment remains a viable option. And there are neat niches. *American Dental Association:* www.ada.org. *Jeffrey May's book: The Art and Science of Being a Dentist.*

(Neat Niche) **Cosmetic Dentist.** Help turn yellowed, cracking teeth into movie-star whites. Much more pleasant than having to tell unsuspecting patients, "I'm sorry, we have to do a root canal." Bonus: Only minimal extra training is required. *American Academy of Cosmetic Dentistry:* www.aacd.com

(Neat Niche) **Veterinary Dentist.** You knock Fido out before starting, so there's no flinching (or biting) to stress you out. Also, it's a nonimpacted (pun intended) field. *Academy of Veterinary Dentistry:* www.avdonline.org.

 Dental Hygienist. More than just cleaning your teeth, a dental hygienist takes and develops X-rays and administers anesthesia. In some states, hygienists even examine patients who are unable to come to the dentist's office. And, of course, part of their job is to show you ugly pictures of diseased gums to guilt-trip you into flossing more and rinsing with Listerine. Dental hygienists must take precautions to avoid repetitive strain injuries and back pain. *American Dental Hygienists' Association:* www.adha.org.

 Surgical Technologist. Just a bachelor's degree, sometimes quite a bit less, and you can play a role in the life-and-death drama of the operating room. The surgical technologist preps the patient (I remember having my chest shaved before my appendectomy. Not fun!), provides emotional support (I definitely needed that), and gets the surgical tools and machines ready in the operating room. During the operation, when the surgeon calls, "Sutures! Clamp! Retractor!" or any of those things they yell for on *ER,* the surgical technologist is the one being yelled at. According to the Department of Labor, surgical technology is a fast-growing field. *Association of Surgical Technologists:* www.ast.org.

 Cardiovascular Technologist. Heart disease is the number one cause of death in the United States and is the leading reason that men die six years earlier than women. The cardiology technologist plays a key role in diagnosing the problem before it's too late. The range of diagnostic tools has advanced well beyond the traditional electrocardiogram. Cardiovascular techs have a stressful job, especially if they're assisting in heart catheterization — an invasive but accurate test for heart blockages. It helps to have a knack for calming people down. *Alliance of Cardiovascular Professionals:* www.acp-online.org.

 Dispensing Optician. This job is a nice blend: part technical, part people. You help customers pick out the frames that make them look sexy, intellectual, whatever. You then take some measurements — for example, the distance between the patient's pupils so the lenses can be made the correct distance from each other. Then you make the actual glasses, grinding over-sized lenses until they fit. In states where opticians are licensed, you can make a reasonable living. The growth is in the chains like Wal-Mart. Most opticians are trained on the job or by apprenticeship. *Optician Career:* *www.careeroverview.com/optician-career.html.*

Massage Therapist. This is one of the few careers in which nearly every customer is extremely satisfied. The best massage therapists are not only wonderful with their hands but also demonstrate a sense of caring. Training is short, typically 500 hours, but be sure to enroll in a program accredited by the Commission on Massage Therapy Accreditation (www.comta.org). Downsides: You're on your feet all day doing physical work, and there is risk of repetitive strain injury. *American Massage Therapy Association: www.amta massage.org. Martin Ashley's Book: Massage, A Career at Your Fingertips.*

> (Neat Niche) **Corporate Massage.** A corporate massage therapist is a stress buster who gives in-chair (or on a massage table in the conference room) massages to employees. Massage has been called the new coffee break. How do you convince tightwad employers to hire you? You might say, "No perk costs less and increases morale more. And your company is seen as benevolent, which can boost sales and make it easier to attract quality employees." Some employers are going halfsies: they pay half, the employee pays half. Sounds like a deal to me, but at least one employer isn't at ease with on-site massage. The IRS office in San Jose offered on-site massage to its employees (ah, our tax dollars at work), but there was a problem: the sound. The IRS's Morgan Banks explains, "You can't have taxpayers coming into an audit hearing 'oohs' and 'ahhs.' Now we're looking for a room with thicker walls." *Infinite Massage: www.infinitemassage.com*

Barber/Hairstylist. There's no way to avoid an occasional bad hair day, but hairstylist keep them to a minimum. Your job is to consult with your client on style — perhaps urging that cool new look you saw at the latest trade show Then, you cut, color, perm, and otherwise torture the person's hair into beauty — natural looking, of course. If beauty ain't gonna happen, there's always a hairpiece. And in any case, you can offer a bit of pampering — for example, a facial or shave. You do all of this while chatting away. Don't like chitchat? This career isn't for you. At the end of each session, you may want to push some of those mousses, gels, and sprays because a big part of your income comes from selling product. Almost half of hairstylists own their own salon, but increasing numbers rent space in others' salons, day spas, resort spas, department stores, or residential care homes. Downsides to this career: You're on your feet eight hours a day and often work evenings and weekends. Too, there's a risk of repetitive strain injury and tight shoulder muscles. One thing you needn't worry about: that your job will be offshored. They would need awfully long scissors to cut your hair from Mumbai. *J. Elaine Spear's book: Haircutting For Dummies.*

Cosmetologist/Makeup Artist. A fun job, making people look attractive while chatting with them. And training is short. Although most cosmetologists don't get rich, some, like my sister, do just fine. Sandy always loved putting makeup on others, so she learned everything she could about it, and went to a manufacturer who put Sandy's brand name on ready-made cosmetics. Then, Sandy opened a store called *Let's Make Up.* There, she did free makeovers and showed people how to do it themselves. When the women saw how good they looked, they usually bought fistfuls of the stuff. Within two years, Sandy was making fistfuls of money. *National Cosmetology Association:* www.ncacares.org. *Kevyn Aucoin's book: Making Faces. Debbie Purvis's book: The Business of Beauty.*

(Neat Niche) **Special Effects Makeup Artist.** How'd you like a career making up puppets and creature masks? According to the *Hollywood Reporter,* "Since 1992, membership in the Los Angeles Makeup Artists and Hairstylists Union has increased by more than 50 percent. There are 720 people working in this field and their handiwork is in demand like never before. . . . " Michael Westmore, makeup supervisor at Paramount for the *Star Trek* series, says that he's never seen anything like the latest bull market: "I've hired over 80 people myself." But not everyone's a bull. One insider warned that computer technology is replacing a lot of what special effects makeup artists do. *Janus Vinther's book: Special Effects Make-Up.*

(Neat Niche) **FBI/CIA Theatrical Effects Specialist.** The CIA Web site says, "We are seeking candidates with three years in cosmetology, theatrical makeup, costuming, art/graphics." *Antonio Mendez's book: The Master of Disguise: My Secret Life in the CIA.*

(Neat Niche) **Wedding Makeup Artist.** Many brides hire a pro to ensure the bridal party looks luminous, not just for the ceremony, but for the zillion photographs that immortalize that one-of-a-kind (hopefully) day. The camera often requires that you wear special makeup to avoid looking washed out. To get clients, hold a mixer for wedding consultants and photographers. *Article:* www.favorideas.com/learn-about/bridal-beauty/ choosing-a-wedding-makeup-artist.

Fashion Designer. "Next year, I think our line of children's swimsuits should use more tricot in earth tones. Parents are tired of cutesy. For a change, we might also try a loose fit. Here's a sketch of a couple of designs. If you like any of them, I'll cut a few samples. Maybe we could try them out at our sales meeting or at a fashion show." That's the life of the fashion designer. This is another of those careers in which there are few jobs, but colleges admit zillions of students. Most people often think of designers focusing on haute couture, but they may have a better chance of landing a job if they pick an under-the-radar niche such as uniforms, children's swimwear, or hospital garb. (Wanna try to bring style to the patient gown?) *State of Virginia's profile of fashion design careers:* www3.ccps.virginia.edu/career_prospects/briefs/ E-J/Fashion.shtml.

(Neat Niche) **Accessory Design.** Designs for shoes and handbags change almost as often as clothing designs, yet many aspiring clothing designers don't think of this niche, so it isn't quite as crowded. *Jennie Bev's e-book, Breaking Into and Succeeding as a Handbag Designer:* www.stylecareer. com/handbag_designer.shtml.

Photographer. As with most artistic careers, to be successful, you must be both talented and a willing and able marketer. Photographer Dennis Miller says, "Photography is 75 percent sales — *if* you're very talented; 95 percent if you're not." To be competitive, a photographer must be expert at using Photoshop to edit digital images and at using the Web for sales and marketing. *About.com's photography portal:* photography.about.com. *Professional Photographers of America:* www.ppa.com. *Rohn Engh's books: How to Sell & Resell Your Photos, and SellPhotos.com. Donna Poehner's book: Photographer's Market.*

(Neat Niche) **Newborn Photographer.** It amazes me that life's most awe-inspiring event, childbirth and the day after, is rarely photographed professionally. Try to get a hospital director to grant you the exclusive right to offer photographic services to expectant parents who will be giving birth at the hospital. *A birth photographer's Web site:* www.mother-birth. com/Birth%20Photography.htm.

(Neat Niche) **Government Photographer.** Government work can be an island of security in the photographer's tempestuous sea, infamous for irregular employment and low pay. The feds may hire you to take aerial photographs. Law enforcement agencies hire forensic photographers: "Did that piece of headlight come from a suspect's car?" Enhanced photographs of evidence can tell the tale.

(Neat Niche) **Industrial Photographer.** This is another photography job that's potentially stable. Plus, you get to work with top-of-the-line equipment. A downside is that the work is unlikely to quench your thirst for artistic expression. A typical project: taking photos of a prototype at each stage in its development. *An industrial photographer's site:* www.proshooter.com

(Neat Niche) **Photojournalist.** As periodicals try to stay competitive, they use more photos. The job market is still tight, but if you have expertise in digital photography and postproduction, this rewarding job may be a bit easier to land than in years past. A relatively easy entry point: small-market or specialty publications, such as a local sports monthly. *National Press Photographers Association:* www.nppa.org.

(Neat Niche) **Lithograph Cameraperson.** You use computers and cameras to lay out magazines and mail-order catalogs. With so much media moving to the Web, it's easy to ignore such publications, but they're still large businesses and, because of the higher quality possible in print, are excellent places to showcase fine photography.

(Neat Niche) **School Photographer.** Taking headshots of 100 kids a day isn't the most creative work in the world, but plenty of customers are out there. At many schools, picture taking is an annual event. One of my clients takes a more creative approach to school photography: She takes close-up action photos of varsity team members and sells them to the proud parents. Another plus for school photography is that, unlike most photography niches, your evenings and weekends are free. *Professional School Photographers Association International:* `www.pmai.org/sections/pspa.htm`

(Neat Niche) **Pet Photographer.** People love their pets, sometimes as much as their kids. I really enjoy looking at the photo of my dog's head lying in a teddy bear's lap. I recommend taking a very low-cost approach to marketing a pet photography biz: Create an 8½-x-11-inch ad filled with your best pet photos. To it, attach a pad of tear-off discount coupons. Mount the ads on stand-up cardboard easels. Place them near the cash register in vet's offices, pet supply stores, pet stores, and pet adoption facilities. Or rent a booth at dog shows. Owners of purebred show animals are especially proud of their pets. (I prefer to get my pets from the pound or rescue organization: hybrid vigor, plus I feel I'm saving a life.) *Portal to articles on pet photography:* `www.animalpetsandfriends.com/Category/Pet-Photography/68.` *Pet Pix:* `www.petpix.com`

(Neat Niche) **Real Estate Photographer.** Increasingly, properties for sale — from home to factory — are in full view on the Net, with a 24/7 virtual open house, full of photographs. Someone's gotta take those pictures. Could it be you? The cutting edge: a full-motion video house tour. *Example:* `www.surroundpix.com.au.`

(Neat Niche) **Annual Report Photographer.** Every public company, mutual fund, and investment company is required to produce an annual report. The successful firms usually opt for spartan reports, but the ones hungry for business make a glitzy full-color magazine filled with, you guessed it, photographs. How to get gigs? Two-thirds of the work comes out of New York. Send your portfolio to each company's investor relations director.

Accident Reconstructor. "It was his fault. He ran right into me!" It's the job of the accident reconstructor to find out whether he's lying through his teeth. Using photographs of the crime scene, statements from drivers and witnesses, knowledge of the physics of what is and isn't possible, and computer simulations, accident reconstructors learn the truth. *Accident Reconstruction Network: www.accidentreconstruction.com*

 Business Equipment Broker/Lessor. More people are starting businesses, and because new businesses often fail, more people will be ending their businesses. Business equipment brokers profit from both. They lease to new businesses and buy used equipment from companies going bust. And of course, they handle upgrades. As technology advances ever faster, rather than buy, many businesses prefer to lease the latest model, and in two years, lease the next-generation one. *Equipment Leasing Association: www.elaonline.com*

 Firefighter. All the firefighters I've met like their jobs. Disadvantages such as irregular hours and living in a firehouse are usually outweighed by the exciting, rewarding work of responding to emergencies and helping people. Plus, typically, only a high school diploma or perhaps a two-year fire science degree is required. According to the U.S. Department of Labor, firefighting ranks 14th in likelihood of dying on the job. That seems daunting, but numbers 1 and 2 are truck driver and farm worker, careers most people don't think of as inordinately death-inducing. *International Association of Fire Fighters: www.iaff.org. Steve Delsohn's book: The Fire Inside: Firefighters Talk About Their Lives.*

OOH

 Golf Course Superintendent. Where do we put that new bunker? How do we schedule the groundskeepers? What's the best way to keep those greens perfect without using too much water or chemicals? To answer those questions, every golf course has a superintendent. This is another cool career that doesn't require a bachelor's degree: A two-year degree in turfgrass management will do. *Golf Course Superintendents Association of America: www.gcsaa.org.*

 Park Ranger. People think this is the career for shy souls who spend their lives alone, searching through binoculars for forest fires. Granted a few of those are around, but most park rangers spend lots of time with people — preaching the environmentalist gospel or pestering park patrons, "Do you have a fishing license?" "No dogs allowed," and "I'm going to have to ask you (drunken fool) to leave the campground." A park ranger's first job is usually filled with physically demanding tasks, such as shoring up eroding paths. Jobs, albeit low-paying ones to start, are available in national, and especially in state and regional, parks. Insider's secret: Job seekers overlook jobs on federal lands other than parks. Check out national forests, wilderness areas, wildlife refuges, and scenic rivers. Good-paying administrative park jobs are rare. For those cut out for this career, however, it doesn't really matter what the job is — nothing is better than a life in the wilderness. *Park Ranger Career Site:* www.angelfire.com/realm2/parkrangers/home.html.

   Sports Referee/Umpire. I loved being an umpire. It was fun making a decision every few seconds that was respected — usually. Somehow, even getting booed wasn't so bad — when I was able to remind myself that in the larger scheme of things, it didn't matter whether it was a ball or a strike. And as a sports fan, umpiring was a way to be a part of the game even if I wasn't a great ballplayer. Don't count on making full-time money as an ump. Sure, Major League Baseball umpires and National Basketball Association referees make six figures, but for most high school and college refs, officiating is a sideline, as much for the fun as for the money. There are perks, though. You get to travel and, in sports such as basketball or soccer, it's a fun way to stay in shape. And demand is high. You, however, need skills: competent decision making under pressure and the ability to stay cool when coaches and fans yell in your face. *Referee/Umpire Homepage:* www.gmcgriff.com/refonline. *Harry Wendelstedt School for Umpires:* www.umpireschool.com. *National Association of Sports Officials:* www.naso.org. *Jerry Grunska's book:* Successful Sports Officiating.

  Stunt Person. Ready to dive from a cruise ship into a frigid ocean? How about getting set on fire? Leaping from a tall building? If so, maybe you'd like to be a stunt person. Be sure your health insurance is in place. Most of the "gags" that pay well don't just look dangerous, they are. The risk doesn't deter aspirants; competition is fierce for stunt jobs. You usually need to be quite an athlete and well trained. *One training school, Stunts Are Us, is located in, of all places, Kenosha, Wisconsin:* www.stuntsareus.org. *Another school is the United Stuntsmen's Association Stunt School:* www.stuntschool.com. *First step, though, for a career in which you swing from nooses and tumble down stairs is to read Jack Bucklin's book:* Stuntman.

Work with Things and Data

  Engineer. This is a career for math and science junkies who like to solve practical problems, usually by designing an object. Perhaps it's a snowboard that turns better, a way for diabetics to take insulin without injections, or a hydrogen-powered car. Turnover is low, although twice as many women leave the profession. The engineering major is long, grueling, and often irrelevant. One engineer I met, who works for General Dynamics, told me that 95 percent of what he learned in college — a prestigious one — was irrelevant to his work. Engineering is among the highest-paid, most in-demand, bachelor's level careers, but more companies are offshoring engineering work to low-cost countries like India and China, which have thousands of skilled engineers willing to work for much less than their U.S. counterparts. Some of the more offshore-resistant engineering jobs will be in the government. *National Society of Professional Engineering: www.nspe.org. Junior Engineering Technical Society: www.jets.org. Susan Echaore-McDavid's book: Career Opportunities in Engineering.*

(Neat Niche) **Hardware Engineer.** Your job is to design and produce electronic devices. You may, for example, design the wireless module for the next-generation iPhone, a computer chip for a robot that enables a world-class surgeon to do brain surgery on a patient halfway around the globe, or the procedure for mass producing that chip. No way around it, you have to be smart for this career, know a lot of science and math, and have the knack of solving hard problems thrown at you left and right. For example, when you're designing a new chip, a million unexpected problems come up — after all, you're charting new territory. Through it all, you have to communicate well, orally and in writing, to tease out what your bosses really want, fight with them if you think they're nuts, and coordinate with your teammates. After you develop your widget, you help create documentation and training that ensures that users can actually use it. *Institute of Electrical and Electronics Engineers: www.ieee.org.*

(Neat Niche) **Biomedical Engineer.** You may design a better artificial heart, a device that will cure disease at the subcellular — or even nano — level, a noninvasive alternative to biopsy, an implantable device to address depression, or a vital-signs monitor for patients, astronauts, or deep-sea divers. In writing this book's 500-plus career profiles, I find myself more excited about this career than any other. (Too bad I have lousy spatial ability.) *Biomedical Engineering Society: www.bmes.org.*

(Neat Niche) **Nuclear Engineer.** The demand for energy independence from the Middle East and Venezuela combined with concern about global warming is motivating development of a new generation of nuclear plants. The market for nuclear engineers is already strong and likely to improve further. *Wikipedia entry: en.wikipedia.org/wiki/nuclear_engineering.*

(Neat Niche) **Packaging Engineer.** How should a small toy be packaged so it's theft- and tamper-resistant yet allows the shopper to play with it so he can plead, "Mommy, can I have it?" How should a drug be packaged so it's childproof yet accessible to an arthritic adult? What's the least expensive packaging that keeps frozen shrimp from smelling fishy after its journey from a Thailand aquafarm to a U.S. supermarket? *Packaging Engineering Forum: www.eng-tips.com/threadminder.cfm?pid=793.*

(Neat Niche) **Telecommunications Engineer.** The Olympics are seen instantly around the world. A paralyzed person talks, and a computer types his words as fast as he can speak. You check your e-mail while on the toilet. The hero? Telecommunications engineers. What's next? Soon, your cellphone will respond to your voice commands to send to your friends (and CNN?) the high-definition video you just took with your phone's built-in camcorder. When telecommunications engineers tire of working on the bench, they have opportunities in sales, marketing, and management. *Steve Winder's book: Newnes Telecommunication Engineer's Pocket Book, 3rd Edition.*

(Neat Niche) **Robotic Engineer.** You're leading a troop in war. Can you safely move over the hill? A robot will tell you. Thousands of Cambodians lost limbs to land mines. Many such mines still remain. How can they be removed without more loss of life and limb? A robot. Robots are now used, not just for welding cars, but also for everything from battlefield surveillance to crop picking, long-distance surgery to nuclear plant maintenance. And soon, a robot may vacuum your house — but then again, they've been predicting that for 20 years and I'm still pushing my Hoover around. *Robotics Online:* www.roboticsonline.com. *American Association for Artificial Intelligence:* www.aaai.org. *iRobot:* www.irobot.com.

(Neat Niche) **Sales Engineer.** It often takes an engineer to convince an engineer that his company needs to buy a high-tech widget. The engineer who can do that often commands a six-figure salary. This is one of 39 fields in which, according to a Bureau of Labor Statistics report, women earn significantly more than men: $89,908 versus $66,660 as of 2003, the last year studied.

(Neat Niche) **Environmental Engineer.** Companies are spending big to prevent and cure environmental messes. The pollution prevention industry in the United States is already $1 billion a year and skyrocketing. Job opportunities should also be strong in Eastern Europe and Asia as they begin environmental cleanups. *Wikipedia entry:* en.wikipedia.org/wiki/environmental_engineering. *American Academy of Environmental Engineers:* www.aaee.net.

(Neat Niche) **Spacecraft Engineer.** More passenger spacecrafts will come, but for the next decade, more growth will be in designing and building unmanned vehicles. Typical applications: broadcasting TV shows across the earth, monitoring rogue nations' nuclear activities, predicting the weather, documenting worldwide pollution changes. Lockheed Martin (www.lockheed.com) has already built 1,000 spacecrafts and clocked 1,500 years of on-orbit performance. Many people think that spacecraft engineering mainly involves designing the vehicle itself. Actually, the main work is designing the thousands of computer programs needed to drive the vehicle's many systems. Don't worry. You can still say you're a rocket scientist. *American Institute of Aeronautics and Astronautics:* `www.aiaa.org`. *Peter Fortescue's book: Spacecraft Systems Engineering 3rd Edition.*

(Neat Niche) **Flying Car Developer.** It's absurd that the best idea transportation planners have for coping with gridlock is to simply stop building roads, thereby forcing people into mass transit that no matter how expanded, will greatly inhibit their freedom of movement. A solution: a flying car. Don't laugh. It vastly increases the area on which people can drive — without spending a dime on freeway construction. Think it's science fiction? At least one flying car already exists (see `www.moller.com`). And it's radar-controlled to help ensure that vehicles don't hit anything. *60 Minutes,* the *Wall Street Journal,* and *ABC News* have done features on it.

(Neat Niche) **Nonpolluting Car Developer.** Whether or not you're a high-powered engineer, working to develop an environmentally clean car, probably using hydrogen fuel cells, may involve you in an effort that could save the planet. *EVWorld:* `www.evworld.com`.

Engineering Technician. Your job is to assist an engineer in designing and developing products. For example, you may test and troubleshoot electrical and computer systems or work on a survey party, calculating land areas, estimating costs, and inspecting construction projects. A two-year degree in engineering technology is the norm. In choosing to be an engineering technologist rather than a full-fledged engineer, you trade some prestige for a shorter training, and still often end up with an interesting job. *American Society of Certified Engineering Technicians:* `www.ascet.org`.

Patent Agent. You get to do everything a patent lawyer does except appear in court. Sam invented a gadget that opens jars more easily and wants to patent it. Your job is first to assess whether it's really new enough to justify a patent. If so, you draft a patent application to the U.S. Patent and Trademark Office. It describes, in words and pictures, how the new invention is different from anything that preceded it. People will always want to patent their innovations to protect their rights, and the position can't be automated, so there should always be a need for patent agents. A background in science or engineering is almost a requirement. *How to Become a Patent Agent:* `inventors.` `about.com/od/patentattorneys/ht/patent_agent.htm`.

Inventor. Sixty thousand kids a year are treated in hospitals for trampoline-related injuries. So Mark Publicover invented JumpSport (`www.jumpsport.` `com`), which provides 360-degree protection around standard-sized trampolines. JumpSport is now sold in thousands of outlets. How does an invention get invented? It can start by asking yourself: "What's annoying?" and "What could I invent that would solve the problem?" Inventors, mostly engineering types, usually develop their prototypes as an after-work spice to their corporate or government day jobs. How to do it successfully? You needn't build the prototype yourself. Find a model maker (www.modelmakers.org has a directory). Then test your prototype on potential customers and retailers. If it passes muster, find out what it would cost to manufacture — use the Thomas Manufacturing Register of 160,000 manufacturers to find a manufacturer (www.thomasregister.com). Is it cheap enough to allow ample profit? Have them make a small run and distribute it through trade shows, a Web site, or wholesale to retailers. Or try to get a corporation to buy (and not steal) your invention. (See an intellectual property lawyer first.) Avoid services that promise to take your idea and turn it into a moneymaker. They usually aren't worth it. *Inventors' Digest: www.inventorsdigest.com. Robert Merrick's book: Stand Alone, Inventor! Maurice Kanbar's book: Secrets from an Inventor's Notebook. Harvey Reese's book: How to License Your Million-Dollar Idea, 2nd Edition.*

Industrial Designer. Your alarm clock goes off. You flail to find the snooze button, to no avail. Industrial designers try to design better ones. Your cellphone can do all sorts of things, but you can't figure out how to make it work. An industrial designer is trying to make it idiot-proof. Your Prius looks cool. Thank an industrial designer. Good news: To be an industrial designer, you needn't be an engineer or an excellent artist. Industrial designers aren't the engineers; they work with engineers. And although it helps if you can draw, it's as important that you care deeply about how products are made, look, and feel. The rest can usually be taught. Top training institutions: Carnegie Mellon, Rhode Island School of Design, and Art Center College of Design (CA). *Industrial Designers Society of America: www.idsa.org.*

(Neat Niche) **Packaging Designer.** Your company wants to introduce a new shampoo. Dozens of brands already are on supermarket shelves. Your job is to design the bottle so shoppers are compelled to pick yours. Working with graphic artists, marketers, and accountants, you design the most compelling packaging possible within budget. *Packaging Design Magazine: www.packagedesignmag.com. Marianne Klimchuk's book: Packaging Design.*

(Neat Niche) **Toy Designer/Inventor.** Sounds simple, but toy design, more than most careers, requires you to have expertise in many fields. You have to be enough of a developmental psychologist to know what sorts of activities will stimulate a 7-year-old. You must be enough of an artist to create something beautiful. You must be imaginative enough to think of all the ways a toy can break or be unsafe. You must be enough of an engineer to design a product that is both cool and that will work — even if Junior drops it. Next time you pick up a toy, have a little more respect for its designer. *About.com's toy design and invention portal:*

inventors.about.com/od/toydesigning. *Toy Industry Association:* www.toy-tia.org. *My favorite toy and game company:* www.cranium.com.

Broadcast Technician/Broadcast Engineer. This is a back door into a field whose front entrance is mobbed. And you don't even need performing talent. Broadcast technologists operate and maintain the recording equipment in radio stations, TV studios, and on remotes. An utterly nonrandom example is going to Hawaii to cover the Aloha Bowl. The bad news is that you must often work nights and weekends, and the pay can stink. Training is less than a year at a private technical school or a bit longer at a community college. But there's an alternative. The broadcast engineer at my radio station told me that in decades past, techie teens would, like groupies, hang out at radio stations to learn broadcast engineering. Now, few do, perhaps because most teens view radio as passé. That leaves an opportunity for you. *Society of Broadcast Engineers:* www.sbe.org. *About.com's radio portal:* radio.about.com. *Radio Online:* www.radioonline.com.

(Neat Niche) **Webcasting Technician.** It's already happening. Hundreds of radio stations make their shows available live or archived on the Net. This cool career will likely expand, and by the time you're reading this, video-compression technology and fatter-piped Internet access should mean that you'll be able to — on your computer or even cellphone — watch your favorite TV shows, movies, even that rare footage of Albert Einstein holding forth in his lab, whenever you want. There should be great demand for technicians who know how to make it all happen. *International Webcasters Association:* www.webcasters.org. *Streaming Media World:* www.streamingmediaworld.com.

Cartographer. That's the fancy word for mapmaker. Although you still need some drawing skills, this is yet another field that's been revolutionized by the computer. New maps are often of remote areas, only now accurately mappable thanks to computer interpretation of aerial or satellite data. Rendering, too, is done on computer, using, for example, AutoCAD. Cartographers may also map seascapes to identify coral reefs, or create drainage maps to help farmers plan irrigation. They even develop video games — you know, the ones with 37 labyrinthine floors filled with dungeons and monsters. *American Congress of Surveying and Mapping:* www.survmap.org. *GoogleEarth:* www.earth.google.com.

Enologist. Want to make wine for a living? A bachelor's degree and internships during crush time in wineries provide the preparation. Alas, only a few colleges offer a major in enology. The best-known program is at the University of California, Davis. *American Society of Enology and Viticulture:* www.asev.org. *Pascal Ribéreau-Gayon's book: Handbook of Enology.*

Brewer. Don't like wine? How about beer? Although I'm not sure the craft brewing fad will last, beer drinking will. Don't think the job is mainly tasting. It's part chemistry, part management, and okay, part tasting. *About.com's portal to information on beer:* `beer.about.com`. *Master Brewers Association:* `www.mbaa.com`.

 Criminalist. He's lying dead. Near the corpse lies a tiny white hair. The criminalist picks it up. Under the microscope, it's clear that it's a pet hair. A visit to three suspects' homes finds that one of them has a pet whose hair matches exactly. No, it's not just a CSI episode. Real-life criminalists search crime scenes to unearth physical evidence — a weapon, fingerprints, a clothing fiber, blood, drugs, even vapors — and then perform tests to see whether they link the suspect and the victim. It's safer than a detective job because you usually show up after the danger is over. Entry-level criminalists may need only a certificate or associate degree in forensics/criminalistics; biology or chemistry is often an acceptable substitute. When you get bored with picking up stuff at crime scenes, get a bachelor's or master's degree and you may get to do more interesting work, like analyzing ballistics, fingerprints, arson, forgeries, and crime patterns, to help the cops plan their strategy. *American Society of Criminology:* `www.asc41.com`.

 Historic Preservationist. America has hundreds of thousands of buildings under the protection of the Landmarks Preservation Commission — 21,000 in New York City alone. In many of these buildings, continuing efforts are made to restore the property to its original state. That means hiring people who can do research to find out what the building looked like way back when, and who have the management skills and/or artistic ability to re-create it. Much of this work is done on a volunteer basis, but a few jobs are available for the eager and well trained. *National Trust for Historic Preservation:* `www.national trust.org`.

Work with Things, People, and Words

   Filmmaker/Director. What could sound cooler: "Hi, I'm a feature filmmaker"? Beyond sounding cool, directing feature films *is* cool. You get to orchestrate the telling of a story that you put in front of millions of viewers. And the process is the ultimate in creativity and camaraderie, with you leading your film crew, working intensely for months, and then it's done — you can sit back and watch your masterpiece and see the money roll in. What a dream! Unfortunately, for 99.99 percent of aspiring filmmakers, it *is* only a dream. Even many graduates of the top film schools (UCLA, USC, and NYU) end up never earning enough even to pay back their student loans, let alone make a subsistence living as a filmmaker. Nevertheless, if my daughter said, "Dad, I want to be a filmmaker," I wouldn't discourage her — the prospect is just too exciting. I'd feel that if she couldn't make it as a filmmaker in Hollywood, she could somehow make a living in some lesser Hollywood role or by directing training videos. As important, she'd have acquired skills transferable to many other careers. Worst case, in a few years, she'd have to read the next edition of this book. *The filmmaking portal:* `www.filmmaking.com`

Restaurant Menu Creator. There are countless restaurants, and each of them needs a menu, many of which need to be changed periodically. Because the menu is what the customer reads at the moment of truth — when deciding how much to spend — an appealing menu design can mean big bucks to the owner. So if you become an expert in menu design, you may be able to charge amply for your services. Start by studying restaurant menus. Compendia are available at hotel concierge desks, in the *Entertainment Guide,* and online. *Lora Arduser's book: The Food Service Professionals Guide to Food Service Menus. Menumaking software:* `www.themenumaker.com` *Agile Rabbit's book and CD: Menu Designs.*

OOH

Curator. A museum exhibition begins with your idea. You then choose the objects that best convey the idea and create an innovative way to install the exhibit. Then you work to publicize it. In between exhibitions, you try to acquire interesting stuff. You do all this in one of the more peaceful work environments imaginable. Most curators major in an academic field, such as art, history, archeology, or computer science, and then join a museum, zoo, or college or government library in that field. To advance, you usually need a master's in library science. Museums are expensive to maintain, so to land a good museum job, you usually must have business expertise (translation: an MBA). *American Association of Museums:* `www.aam-us.org.` *The Exhibitionists:* `www.liverpoolmuseums.org.uk/nof/maths.`

OOH

Architect. When a filmmaker wants to create a character worthy of respect, he often makes the person an architect. After all, architecture is an ideal blend of art and science, creativity and logic. An architecture career also seems exciting: designing a building and seeing it become a reality. Alas, most architects spend many years before designing a building that actually gets built. First, you have a five-year bachelor's degree or a master's. Then you have a three-year internship. After that, many architects in firms must spend years designing building components, like ensuring that the wiring meets the requirements of Section 13.02.05 of the Springfield County Building Code. A good architect must be an excellent communicator; someone who can tease out what the client really wants and convince the Springfield County Building Department that the wiring deserves a variance to Section 13.02.05. He must also be a good project manager — a building is comprised of a thousand headaches. Patience is beyond a virtue; it's a necessity — the client or the city is always changing something. One thing you needn't be good at is drawing, thanks to CAD programs, which are dominant in architecture.

An increasing amount of architecture is being offshored. So, moving forward, successful architects need offshore-resistant skills: client relations, sales, and macro project planning. *About.com's portal to info on architecture:* `architecture.about.com` *Lee Waldrep's book: Becoming an Architect. Roger Lewis's book: Architect? For an authoritative ranking of architecture schools, DesignIntelligence:* `www.di.net`.

(Neat Niche) **Green Architect.** Some evidence suggests that inhabitants are healthier in green buildings. Because those buildings make extensive use of natural light, people in them feel better, and with careful material choices for carpets and drapes, and good ventilation, people don't cough or scratch their eyes because of poor air quality. People feel better in green buildings, not only because the materials are safer, but also because they're largely recyclable and energy efficient, so they feel like they're doing their part for the environment. *About.com's Green Architectural portal:* `architecture.about.com/od/greenarchitecture`. *Alanna Stang's book: The Green House.*

(Neat Niche) **Senior Housing.** Aging Boomers will require housing to meet their physical needs.

(Neat Niche) **Entertainment Architect.** Design movie sets, theme parks, resorts, venues, and museums.

Corporate Security Consultant. Corporations have always had a problem with security, and not just with customers. Employee theft is an even greater problem — for example, stealing client lists or proprietary technology. Now with corporate property ever-shrinking (genes, microcircuits, formulas) and surveillance technology ever-more sophisticated (such as software that cracks encryption codes), the field of corporate security is, well, exploding. To succeed, specialize — in museums, hotels, or e-commerce sites, for example. *American Society for Industrial Security:* `www.asisonline.org`. *International Association of Professional Security Consultants:* `www.iapsc.org`.

(Neat Niche) **Violence Prevention/Resolution.** Workplace violence is epidemic. More than 500,000 incidents of workplace violence occur each year. Courts increasingly find that the lack of a thorough violence prevention/intervention plan is evidence of liability if a worker assaults another worker. This creates a job market for you. *National Institute for the Prevention of Workplace Violence:* `www.workplaceviolence911.com`

Business Home Economist. For years, women have been ridiculed for going into home economics, so few do anymore. Finally, the need has exceeded supply. Business home economists are used by manufacturers of large appliances to do demonstrations and by large department stores to suggest what to buy and how to display it. Supermarket chains, food manufacturers, and trade boards employ business home economists to prepare and present information to consumers. The Egg Board, for example, may ask a business home economist to develop a Web page showing how to prepare eggs without unduly clogging your arteries. *American Association of Family and Consumer Sciences:* `www.aafcs.org`.

A Guide to the Future

Being ahead of the curve can be key to your success. Think, for example, of the people who got in on the ground floor of the automobile age, television, rock 'n' roll, or the Internet. What's next?

Consider the megatrends in the following sections in choosing your career or a business you want to start. These trends may also help you strategize within your current career — for example, helping you or your employer decide which directions to take. In addition, the 15 minutes it takes to read this guide to the future should make you a more interesting conversationalist and a more thoughtful observer of our ever-faster-changing society.

Of course, he who lives by the crystal ball eats broken glass, so, to mix metaphors, take these predictions, indeed any predictions, with a grain or two of salt.

Computers and technology

Personalization Nation. The latest Web applications (often dubbed Web 2.0) will yield an ever-more personalized approach to many things.

Some career implications:

- Marketing will be ever-more customized. As ever-more people shop on the Net, data about individuals' buying and voting tendencies will be captured, and custom e-mail ads and commercials created. Experts in personalized marketing will be in demand.

- Mass customization of clothing. We take for granted the ability to get Dell to build us a computer with the precise specifications and options we want. Clothing is next. Most people have experienced the frustration of trying to find a piece of clothing they like, in the color and size they want, that's in stock. Soon, they'll be able to go to an e-store, search the styles to pick precisely what they want, enter their body's measurements, and in a few days, the customized garment will be at their front door. Lands' End already offers a first-generation version: see its Custom Clothing section at `www.landsend.com/custom`. For more on mass customization, see `www.mass-customization.de`.

✔ Networking will, more and more, move online because improved matching paradigms will do a better job of hooking up compatible people. I believe that companies such as match.com, MySpace, orkut, YouTube, and LinkedIn will continue to grow, and therefore provide good opportunities for employment. Activist organization moveon.org uses what I believe will become a dominant approach to marketing: merging online personalized marketing with online and in-person networking. For more on online networking, see `entrepreneurs.about.com/od/online networking/Online_Business_Networking.htm`.

✔ Medicine. By the end of the decade, you'll start to see diagnoses and treatment based on information about a person's individual physiology. This will cause an increase in biotech jobs. (See the later section "Health and science" for more on biotech. For more on personalized medicine, see `www.personalizedmedicinecoalition.org`.)

E-Populism. Until recently, corporate publishers almost completely controlled what people bought: They hired editors to decide what topics to cover and pick the person to write each piece. After publication, corporate-owned periodical publishers chose one person to review each of what they guessed were the top $\frac{1}{1000}$ of new works. With contributions and judgments made by so few people, it's not surprising that publications too often didn't satisfy — haven't we all paid for books, movies, and videogames that we ended up disliking?

Things are changing. Using tools such as digital video cameras, video cellphones, blogs, videopodcasts, and improved editing software, ever-more people can easily create and publish their radio show, illustrated article or e-book, news report, sitcom, film, or training video on the Net, thereby making it available to the entire world. Then, the public's collective wisdom evaluates it: If your video gets high public ratings, it will get a zillion viewers on GoogleVideo/`youtube.com`. If the public loves your article, it will be prominently placed on `digg.com` and in the blogosphere. Today, the public can rate everything from doctors (at, for example, `healthgrades.com`) to cars (`edmunds.com`) to spas (`yelp.com`) to books (`amazon.com`) and other consumer products (`epinion.com`).

Some career implications:

✔ Marketing professionals must become experts at figuring out how to get consumers to rate products on those citizen-rating sites.

✔ Use mass collaboration. The most famous example is Wikipedia, the online encyclopedia created and constantly upgraded by the public with minimal editing. It turns out its quality is better than one may have expected. A study reported in *Nature* magazine found that Wikipedia's science articles were about as accurate as those in the Encyclopedia Britannica, the gold standard of reference books. So it's not surprising that corporate America is jumping on board the mass collaboration bandwagon. For example, Procter and Gamble solicits public (paid) help in developing 60 percent of its new products. GoldCorp paid $575,000 to members of the public who helped figure out where to mine for gold. Even federal intelligence agencies have created *wikis* (sites designed for mass collaboration) to gather intelligence information from among their employees. So, if you have expertise to share, search the Net for companies who want it. If you need expertise, solicit it on the Net. Sometimes, you won't even have to pay — many people love to solve challenges, just for the heck of it. Why else would people climb Everest? As a job seeker, the ability to start and maintain a wiki may put you ahead of the competition. I believe mass collaboration and wikis will become a huge aspect of Web 2.0.

✔ As ever-more people look to the Web for buying guidance, opportunities will continue to grow at online rating services. Work for such companies as Epinion, Digg, and Amazon, or create a site that offers ratings in a niche likely to be ignored by those major players. Examples: medical imaging machines, management training tools, political candidates, eldercare services.

✔ The de-monetization of entertainment. Entertainment choices continue to grow. For example, you can find the following:

- Ever-more appealing Web sites, such as `youtube.com` and `myspace.com`

- Free or cheap downloads of every imaginable piece of music at places like `apple.com/itunes`

- An attempt to make most of the world's books available for free at `books.google.com`

- Dozens of cable TV channels

- Video on demand (which will soon replace NetFlix and, of course, the video rental store)

- Custom, RSS-fed, online "newspapers," amalgamating content from multiple sources

- Ever-more immersive video games (for example, the next generation of games will replace those hand-cramping game controllers with eye-movement control)

All those entertainment choices mean that the public will be willing to pay ever-less for them, and, in turn, cause a decline in salaries and the number of jobs in the entertainment industry. Avoid this field. More than ever, creative pursuits such as writing, filmmaking, and so on, should be thought of as hobbies and not relied on for income, because now, anyone can easily publish his article, artwork, book, or movie, and users can easily find and access those works for free using `google.com`, `youtube.com`, and so on. The odds of your making a living in such creative endeavors are smaller than ever.

E-commerce finally triumphs. Web-based stores have long offered unbeatable advantages both to customers and store owners. The customer can shop from the convenience of home, 24/7. With price search engines such as `shopzilla.com` and `pricegrabber.com`, he can, in just a few minutes, find the best-rated products and which vendor has them in stock and at the best price (including shipping). The online store owner loves that she has no need to pay the enormous costs of renting and building out a bricks-and-mortar store. In addition, she doesn't have to worry about shoplifting or inventory — she can simply have the manufacturer or wholesaler ship the product directly to the customer. Plus, online store owners earn money while they sleep.

But in its early years, e-commerce was slow to catch on. Customers found site navigation and checkout difficult and too often were disappointed by shipping delays and poor customer service. Too, store owners found it difficult and expensive to create a workable e-commerce site. Now, those problems have largely been resolved. For example, in an hour, you can create a good e-commerce site using templates from `ebay.com`, `yahoo.com`, `godaddy.com`, or `homestead.com`. As a result, even late-adopter shoppers and retailers are jumping on the e-commerce bandwagon. Increasingly, shoppers use bricks-and-mortar stores only for inexpensive or heavy items, or as a place to see the merchandise, after which they go home and buy it on the Net.

Some career implications:

- Employment opportunities in the retail sector should be available at price search-engine and review sites: for example, `pricegrabber.com`, `froogle.com`, and `shopzilla.com`, the latter of which attracts 20 million visitors a month!

- Avoid working for retailers, even the big ones, such as Wal-Mart and Target, and even for online retailers. Ever-more customers will buy from the lowest-priced provider, which often is one of a zillion tiny Web sites run by one person willing to sell on just a few percent margin. Few good jobs or even self-employment opportunities will be available. The best option in this space may be a Web site selling very niched products: advanced magic tricks, stud peacocks, or parts for high-powered lasers.

For more info, check out `www.ecommercetimes.com` and `www.ecommerce-guide.com`.

Online education and training. The word "webinar" didn't even exist when I wrote this book's previous edition. Now, it's standard training fare. And online education has exploded. A 2006 *U.S. News* cover story reports that three million students are now pursuing an entire degree online. Although traditional education and training will long endure, I predict the online numbers will grow much larger still because Web-based training and education will soon combine these five powerful features:

✔ Full-motion video, on-demand

✔ Interactivity with simulations

✔ Human interactions via e-mail and chats

✔ Ease of course development using new online tools

✔ Portability, thanks to such devices as iPhones and video iPods

Combine all five, and online education becomes vastly superior to in-person instruction. Instead of having to commute and find a parking spot to listen to some instructor — good, bad, or indifferent — drone on, you get a hand-picked instructor, augmented by simulations and discussions that any student (even a homebound disabled person) can access on demand, 24/7.

Additional pressure to move to specialized online training will come from the ever-faster pace at which knowledge grows — impossible for the average university instructor to keep up with. (See, for example, the video tutorials on cutting-edge topics at www.tubetorial.com.)

Perhaps the most compelling application of online education will be K–12 education. Political exigencies (which I think are absurd, but that's another book) are forcing students of all abilities — from developmentally disabled to gifted — to be placed in the same teacher's class. Without computers, it's virtually impossible to provide all the students with appropriate-leveled instruction. Simulation-based, individualized online teaching modules will someday — if the teachers' union relents — revolutionize instruction. At that point, the teacher's role will primarily be to get kids unstuck and to preside over socialization activities.

Some career implications:

✔ Consider working for an online training firm or an organization's in-house training department. Learn the art of creating and leading a webinar.

✔ In your own education and training, before signing up for a bricks-and-mortar course, let alone for a degree program, evaluate online options.

Some resources to check out include Association for the Advancement of Computing in Education (`www.aace.org/pubs/webnet`) and Ruth Colvin Clark and Richard E. Mayer's book, *E-Learning and the Science of Instruction.*

Wireless videofication. Today, text and audio are wireless in the form of e-mail and downloaded music, for example. Even *still* video is wireless. For example, an iPhone enables you to wirelessly e-mail that photo you just took on the beach in Hawaii to your grandparents in Chicago. Soon, you'll be able to use your cellphone for full-motion video. Imagine you're on that Hawaiian beach and feel like watching that Adam Sandler movie *50 First Dates,* about falling in love in Hawaii. Just click and you can watch it. No wires required. Or feel like a video chat with a friend in Maine so you can rub in her face that you're strolling along the beach while she's huddled in the frozen tundra? Soon that will be possible. (First-generation versions exist. For example, see Yahoo! Messenger's "View my Webcam" feature at `messenger.yahoo.com/superwebcam.php`.) Or instead of sitting at your desk and using kludgy Web-conferencing software for that regional meeting (or actually flying to one), you'll soon be able to attend while sitting on that beach, wirelessly seeing each other in full-motion, non-jerky video. (See `WebEx.com`.) Ads, especially for big-ticket items such as cars and real estate, will have migrated from text in newspapers, and more recently, `craigslist.org`, to full-motion video commercials that — based on your interests — are e-mailed to you. Or imagine taking that boring class, not in Stern Hall Room 3101, or even chained to your home computer, but on that beach, or at least under the tree near your favorite lake.

Some career implications:

- ✔ Job hunting will become videocentric. Using such software as Videocaster (`videocaster.com`), winning resumes will include a video presentation of the candidate, ideally demonstrating himself at work. For example, a manager may include a video of himself running a meeting. A teacher may include a demonstration lesson. They will post their position-wanted video resumes on Web sites from `monster.com` to `youtube.com`.

- ✔ Advice-givers, such as lawyers, counselors, and even doctors, should consider offering online video consulting.

- ✔ Become a salesperson for a company that provides targeted e-mail commercials.

- ✔ Work for a company that develops wireless video infrastructure — for example, Bluetooth.

✔ Work in the wireless distribution departments of content development companies — for example, major film studios or top providers of online training.

✔ Developing nations lack the infrastructure for wired telecommunication and therefore make heavy use of cellphones. So demand for cellphone-based video should be strong, thus creating employment opportunities.

Health and science

Biotech Decade. This field is about to reach the tipping point, at which its long-standing promise will be realized. It's taking ever-less time to conduct experiments to determine the functions of the 23,000 genes in the human genome, which proteins affect which gene function, and, in turn, what can be done genetically to prevent and cure disease. For example, the day I wrote this section, scientists announced that they can create cows that are immune to mad cow disease. The next few years will likely see a breakthrough in the treatment of a major human disease, and in turn, an increase in biotech research and investment budgets, and, of course, patient demand for those new treatments.

Some career implications:

✔ Biotech companies will be employers of choice, not just for scientists, but also for all the support people required: from accountants to administrative assistants, manufacturers to marketers, risk managers to regulatory affairs specialists.

✔ Fertility clinics will expand into reproductive choice clinics, in which prospective parents will be able to use in-vitro fertilization not just to get pregnant (while selecting their child's sex, which is now possible) but also to ensure the child is born without serious disease. They may even ensure characteristics such as high intelligence. Demand for reproductive choice services will grow, creating significant employment opportunities.

✔ Bioethics will become a more prominent career, as ever-thornier questions become issues: A new cancer cure costs $500,000. What should determine who gets it: Ability to pay? Worthiness of the candidate to society? A lottery? We allow parents to choose the sex of their babies. Is it ethical to allow them to ensure their baby has a pleasant personality?

For more information, check out en.wikipedia.org/wiki/human_enhancement. Also see Ramez Naam's book, *More Than Human: Embracing the Promise of Biological Enhancement.*

Nanotechnology. In nanotechnology, matter is manipulated, molecule by molecule. This will enable the creation of molecule-sized machines. Why would anyone want such a small machine? Well obviously, you'll be able to wear a heckuva powerful computer on your wrist. But more intriguing applications may include cleansers that can remove any stain, insulation that can keep homes at a constant temperature, and true medical miracles. Back in 2000, *Time* magazine was already touting nanotechnology's potential: "A diagnosis of pancreatic cancer would be devastating to any of us, bringing with it the horrors of debilitating chemotherapy and a slim chance of surviving the next five years. Fifteen years from now, however, you might not even bat an eye at the news. Your doctor will simply hand you a capsule packed with millions of nanosensors, each programmed to seek out and kill the cancer cells in your body . . . And that's not all. One day, autonomous 'Nanobots' far smaller than motes of dust will patrol the body, repairing aging organs and fixing genetic damage before it can turn into disease."

Nanotechnology is already used in a variety of products: next-generation water-filters, sunscreens, automotive polishes, recording tapes, and stain-resistant fabrics, and soon, superior tires and solar cells. The U.S. government now funds a nanotechnology initiative involving 20 federal agencies and a budget of $1.3 billion — see www.nano.gov. That site also contains links to other nanotechnology information. See also, www.smalltimes.com.

Some career implications: The National Science Foundation predicts that within 15 years, two million people will be employed in nanotech. Already, there are 20,000 nanotech researchers. Although most jobs will be for engineers, physicists, and mathematicians, their work will be supported by people in a wide range of backgrounds. For training opportunities, see: www.nano.gov/html/edu/eduunder.html.

Aging. Today, just 12 percent of the U.S. population is 65-plus. By 2030, it will jump to 30 percent.

Some career implications:

✔ Demand for preventive products and services will grow. Boomers are all too aware that the healthcare system is creaky and, even at its best, doesn't yet have good answers for aging's major diseases. So Boomers are exercising more, eating healthier foods, and trying to control stress. As a result, employment prospects should be good in such areas as organic food, exercise facilities aimed at older adults (e.g., Curves and yoga studios), and weight-loss programs such as Weight Watchers.

✔ I predict that national healthcare is coming, so experts in transitioning from the private to a public system will be in demand. But whether the U.S. goes single-payer or not, healthcare providers such as HMOs are realizing that computerizing medical records, prescriptions, and diagnoses is a cost-effective way to improve quality while lowering cost. So, experts in computerizing healthcare, public health, and health delivery quality control will be in demand.

✔ Few Boomers have saved enough to last the longer lives they're expected to live. And most people believe Social Security is unlikely to help much. So the market for financial planners and estate planners should be strong. Alas, financial planners can do only so much, so there will be many impoverished elders. As a result, government programs for seniors will burgeon, with accompanying opportunities for employment.

✔ Many Boomers have accumulated significant equity in their homes and will sell them to finance their future. Generally, they'll move to smaller residences, often in retirement communities. More such facilities will need to be built and run, creating significant job opportunities.

✔ Many Boomers have aged parents to care for, often at a distance. So, demand for geriatric care managers will grow. Too, many Boomers will decide to move their aged parent nearby. As a result, demand for in-law units will increase. Real estate investors and developers should consider properties with such units attached.

Environmentalism is America's fastest-growing religion. Not withstanding Al Gore's film and the media's froth, a dispassionate look at the science suggests that scientists remain unsure whether global warming is man-made and, more important, whether realistic-to-implement efforts can significantly forestall it. A recent major British study hailed by environmentalists argues that global warming can be forestalled, but a surprising number of experts disagree. For example, the Copenhagen Consensus, a group of Nobel Prize–winning scientists and economists that, in 2006, attempted to identify the optimal ways to spend a hypothetical $50 billion to benefit mankind, rated global warming as a bad use of money. A 2006 *San Francisco Chronicle* article by senior editor Andrew Ross summarized expert judgments this way: "It is already too late, according to an emerging consensus of opinion." Sixty Canadian scientists who wrote to Prime Minister Stephen Harper asserted the same thing: There is "no consensus among climate scientists."

Nevertheless, the United States and most Western countries are on the brink of deciding — perhaps heavily for political reasons — to make an all-out effort to control global warming and other environmental degradations — it's hard for leaders to admit it's not worth spending the money. In addition to the billions in dollar costs, governments have decided to impose significant hardships on the citizenry. For example, the San Francisco Bay Area's transportation master plan prohibits building any new freeways for the next 20 years. That's forcing commuters into gridlock, stealing time from an already overpacked day.

Some career implications:

- ✔ Green building will become mainstream building. This will create opportunities in such industries as recyclable lumber, solar cells, and organic insulation, paints, and carpeting, and even straw-bale construction.

- ✔ "Sustainability" will become hot, creating opportunities in such areas as recycling, locally and organically grown produce, and population control.

- ✔ America's desire to reduce use of fossil fuels will continue to grow for environmental reasons and to become energy-independent from the anti-American Venezuela and Middle Eastern countries. So, employment in both the research and production sides of the nuclear, solar, clean coal, and wind energy fields should grow.

- ✔ Employment in pollution control industries should be strong.

- ✔ Research efforts will increase to develop no-emission vehicles. For the latest trends, see the Institute of Transportation Studies (www.its.ucdavis.edu).

- ✔ Employment in regulatory agencies should increase, especially with the increase in elected Democrats that I project will continue.

For more info on this megatrend, see Andres R. Edwards's book, *The Sustainability Revolution: Portrait of a Paradigm Shift.*

Politics, culture, and economics

Terrorism is coming. As extremist groups continue to grow and the availability of hard-to-detect miniaturized weapons such as dirty nukes and bioviruses increases, the probability grows that terrorist attacks will occur on U.S. soil. Most experts believe that such an attack will come sooner rather than later. The 9/11 attack hit merely three buildings yet profoundly affected the nation's economy. A nuclear or biological attack, or a hack into banking systems' computers, will have far greater effects.

Some career implications:

- ✔ Employment in federal, state, and local Homeland Security and disaster preparedness will continue to grow.

- ✔ Employment in private sector firms specializing in terrorism prevention and remediation will grow.

For more information, see Stephen Flynn's book, *America the Vulnerable.*

America turns inward. Losses in Vietnam and Iraq are a one-two punch that will knock out America's belief that it can be the world's policeman. The new isolationism will, of course, save a fortune. Alas, the money won't be returned to the taxpayer. It will just be redirected to domestic government spending.

Some career implications:

- Increased hiring in federal social service agencies — for example, Education, Environmental Protection, and Health and Human Services.

- Increased hiring by contractors who serve these federal agencies.

- National healthcare (socialized medicine) will be adopted, especially if, as I predict, Hillary Rodham Clinton or Barack Obama wins the presidency in 2008.

- Decreased hiring in the military and by defense contractors.

The atheism era. Society's mind molders — schools, colleges, and the media — continue to increase their ridiculing of religion, especially Christianity. An example: College classes emphasize religion's role in causing violence rather than its benefits to individuals and society. The news media typically portrays religious people as airheads in rapture or highlights the worst in religion — for example, Pat Robertson's indefensible statements and Ted Haggard's, Jim Bakker's, and Jimmy Swaggart's sex scandals. The media rarely reports the views of religious moderates or liberals; for example, the media makes one think that mainstream Christians consider gay people to be sick sinners. CNN founder Ted Turner said, "Christianity is a religion for losers." Movies usually portray religious people as stupid, evil, or both. I recently rented Stephen King's thriller movie *Misery.* It's about a woman who breaks the legs of her favorite author so she can control him. Even though the movie has nothing to do with religion, throughout it she's wearing a large cross, with the cinematographer shining a bright light on it at all times, lest we forget she's religious. Of late, major book publishers have focused on books advocating atheism. As I write this, *The God Delusion,* a book ridiculing religion and advocating atheism, is number six on *The New York Times* bestseller list. And, of course, the terrorist acts and threats of radical Muslims haven't helped religion's image. In light of all this, with the exception of Muslims and Latino Catholics, I predict a decline in religiosity in America.

Some career implications:

- While the first years of the 21st century saw an increase in attempts to bring spirituality into the workplace, moving forward, employees in many workplaces need to be more cautious before discussing religion at work, especially among higher-level employees, where antireligion bias is likely to be greatest. Job seekers should, more than ever, avoid bringing up religion in interviews.

✔ Advertisements in the 1990s and early 21st century often displayed religious symbols, notably the Christian sign of the fish. Such approaches will be increasingly risky.

✔ A decline in religiosity won't mean a decline in the need for sources of inspiration or for emotional support in tough times. Therefore, secular organizations offering such support should flourish. An example is what I call *secular religious nonprofits,* such as environmental advocacy groups and bereavement, illness, and divorce-support organizations. Job seekers may find these fertile grounds for finding employment. Too, entrepreneurs may consider serving this market.

Islam is in. Islam will buck the U.S.'s atheism trend. The Muslim birthrate is very high and more people, especially African-Americans, are signing on. This trend is abetted by the media's increasing positive attention to Islam — for example, the extraordinary coverage of the sitcom *Little Mosque on the Prairie.* Another example: Today, as I write this, the cover story of the Sunday *San Francisco Chronicle*'s travel section, spanning three full pages, urges Americans to vacation in Iran.

Career implications: Both in the U.S. and Europe, experts in Islamic cultures and languages will be in great demand by corporate marketing departments and by government agencies and nonprofits attempting to incorporate Muslims into Western societies.

The Latinization of America. According to a 2006 *Time* magazine cover story, Latinos in the United States have a 60 percent higher birth rate than Whites. In addition, more than one million new Latinos — legal and illegal — immigrate to the United States every year. More than half the growth in the U.S. population is now Hispanic. By 2050, the United States will be less than half White, with Hispanics becoming, by far, the largest ethnic group. Earlier waves of immigration were largely from European countries, nations that had high levels of socioeconomic development. This wave of immigration is largely from countries with low levels. In addition, this wave, because more than 50 percent arrive illegally, is largely unscreened for diseases and criminal records.

Some career implications: Bilingualism in Spanish and understanding of Latino culture will become an increasingly important qualification for employment, especially in these areas:

✔ **Marketing.** Latinos have, on average, distinctive product and service preferences. Companies will be eager to tap this market.

✔ **Healthcare.** Latino immigrants come to the United States with greater-than-average healthcare needs. For example, communicable, multiple-drug-resistant tuberculosis is a growing problem. Doctors and nurses, in healthcare facilities and in outreach efforts, must be able to speak Spanish. Public health departments will also require more bilingual/bicultural personnel.

✔ **Education.** Previous waves of immigration were controlled, so schools could handle the numbers of children who didn't speak English. Today, it appears that American society has decided not to heavily control immigration. As a result, many schools are already overwhelmed by limited-English-proficient students. Therefore, the demand for bilingual/bicultural teachers, aides, and administrators will continue to climb.

✔ **Social services.** The average Latino immigrant's income is low, and so their demand for government-provided services is high. Examples of these services include cash welfare payments, food stamps, Medicare, and subsidized housing. Advocates are working hard to ensure that immigrants get those social services, so the government will continue to hire more social workers and other professionals to meet the demand.

✔ **Criminal justice.** Illegal immigrants commit disproportionate numbers of violent felonies. According to the California Department of Corrections, 25 percent of all incarcerated felons in California are illegal immigrants from Mexico. This creates a great need for bilingual/bicultural lawyers, judges, court administrators, and so on.

✔ **Border security.** Securing the 2,000-mile border between the U.S. and Mexico will require significant new hiring by the government and by government contractors. Both human and technological solutions will be adopted. Thousands of people are required just to build that 700-mile fence.

For more on the Latinization of America, see the Web sites of the Pew Hispanic Center (www.pewhispanic.org) and the Center for Immigration Studies (www.cis.org).

Declining America. Fed Chair Ben Bernanke has warned that America's economy is at risk of serious decline. Corporate earnings (and in turn, tax payments and job openings) are likely to decline for many reasons:

✔ Americans will spend less as fewer of them will be able to afford a materialistic lifestyle as more well-paying jobs are offshored and remaining ones will require technical expertise that few Americans have the ability, time, and money to acquire.

✔ Brain drain: Top Asian employees are increasingly leaving the United States to work in Asia for Asian companies, especially those in China.

✔ Ever-increasing environmental (for example, California's strict new global warming law) and financial (for example, Sarbanes-Oxley) regulations are decreasing earnings, while companies in other countries, such as China, have far fewer restrictions.

✔ Shopping price engines now enable both business and consumer customers to price-shop better than ever before. That lowers profit margins.

✔ The current wave of immigrants, unlike previous ones, spends less money in the U.S. Instead, they send money back to their family in their home country. For example, in 2005, Mexicans living in the U.S. sent $45 billion back to Mexico.

✔ Corporations have a growing desire or pressure to give away profits. Last year, American businesses donated to nonprofits an all-time high $4.1 billion. They make additional large noncash donations. For example, Home Depot contributed 50,000 employees and two million hours to community service. In previous generations, much of that money would have been fed back to shareholders to pump into the U.S. economy, or reinvested in research and development, which would ultimately result in improved products, increased sales, and in turn, more job growth. Now, those funds are spent on causes less likely to have such multiplicative effects — for example, a donation to the symphony or art museum. Meanwhile, government tax revenues, thus decreased because of likely-to-decline corporate earnings, will be less able to keep up with social spending for the rapidly increasing numbers of needy aged and immigrants.

Also contributing to America's decline is its descending social norms: For example, integrity among its residents appears to be declining. Examples: corporate leaders' financial fraud, athletes cheating by taking performance-enhancing drugs, escalating student cheating on exams and adult cheating on taxes, increased "creative writing" on resumes, and clerics' having sex with children parishioners. Also straining the social fabric are society's mindmolders — the schools, colleges, and media — who are encouraging people to identify more with people of their race or ethnic group than with people in general, which is straining life in and outside the workplace. That model has led to devastating violence in many societies around the world, past and present (Sunnis and Shiites, Serbs and Croats, Hutus and Tutsis, Israelis and Palestinians, Irish Catholics and Protestants) and portends to do the same in the U.S.

America needs less pluribus and more unum.

Some career implications:

✔ The retraining business will boom. As Boomers retire and as technology demands increase, employers will be forced to provide or subsidize community-college-based retraining. Employees will see it as the only way to earn more than subsistence wages.

✔ This is China's and India's century. Americans may most easily capitalize by working for U.S. companies with current or intended interests in those countries. Entrepreneurs beware, however. It isn't easy to do business in those countries without deep in-country connections. Eastern

Europe, only now fully embracing capitalism, may offer better entrepreneurial opportunities. For example, a client of mine set up a medical journal publishing company in Poland. Another conducts corporate training in Hungary. Both of those fields are fairly saturated in the United States but less so in Eastern Europe. Both clients are now millionaires.

✔ Pressures to offshore jobs will increase, and in turn, the need for U.S. employees expert at finding quality employees overseas and in training them to work well with American co-workers and customers will also increase.

✔ Hiring and salaries will decline in most sectors, but mostly in the private sector. The last bastion of reasonable job security will be in government employment. Exception: Public sentiment and decreased tax revenues will usher in a new era of U.S. isolationism, so employment in the military-industrial complex will decline.

✔ A small number of interesting jobs may exist in corporate foundations — the entities that companies create to give away money to nonprofit causes.

✔ Public schools will, in ever-more locales, become unacceptable to middle-class families. This will increase demand for private schools and home-schooling consultants. In just the last 20 years, the number of home-schooled children has grown from 300,000 to two million!

✔ People will cocoon more. Traffic and crime will likely increase. So, as home-based entertainment gets more impressive, people will choose to spend more discretionary time at home. Careers involved in making home environments more pleasant (for example, home remodeling) should benefit.

✔ The middle class will shrink and the lower class will expand. This will give rise to government policies to redistribute wealth downward and/or increased social unrest, such as youth riots like those seen in France in 2006. Thus, government careers assisting (or resisting) the poor should increase.

✔ Increasing numbers of middle-class and wealthy Americans will relocate to Asia, and to less volatile English-speaking countries, such as Canada, Australia, and New Zealand. Specialists in helping people to relocate will be needed.

✔ More people will need to learn to find happiness without materialism. They will need to come to realize that the life well led comes far more from good work and good relationships than from expensive jewelry, a luxury car, a fancy house, or five-star vacations. With that realization, you'll be able to consider a far wider and perhaps more rewarding range of careers than you otherwise may have.

Chapter 3

The 35 Most Revealing Questions About You

- -

In This Chapter

▶ Assessing values, abilities, and passions

▶ Gauging your potential for self-employment

▶ Taking in the big picture

▶ Working with your *virtual career coach*

- -

*Y*ou meet. Your heart starts pounding. You fall madly in lust. You don't stop to think that he's married to his work. Or that her earning potential is worse than an aspiring artist's.

Or the opposite, you meet the logical choice: intelligent, employed, no vices. Rationally, it's right, but the chemistry's not.

As in finding a mate, choosing a career should involve both your head and your heart. You've already used your heart: You picked out the careers from the *Cool Careers Yellow Pages* in Chapter 2 that make your heart beat faster. Now it's time to use your head. Which of those careers (or perhaps another career) logically makes sense? If you're like most career searchers, you're not sure.

That's where the 35 questions in this chapter come in. Over the years, with my clients and callers to my career radio show, I've tried every approach imaginable to tease out people's *career musts:* the things that people really want and need in a career. I've found these 35 questions to be the most helpful to most people.

Making the Process Easier

When a doctor takes your medical history, she knows that only a few of your answers to her many questions will reveal anything significant. She still asks all the questions because she can't know in advance which ones are significant for *you*. The same is true of these 35 questions. Only a few will reveal your true career musts.

Questions that yield a career must usually elicit an immediate "Aha!" So if you have any trouble answering a question, skip it and go on — that question is unlikely to be significant for you.

After you answer these questions, I tell you how to make use of your career musts in the later section "The Virtual Career Coach: Integrating Head and Heart."

Examining Your Values

Each night, when people put their heads on their pillows, they feel good if they worked and lived in accordance with their values. But what are *your* values? These questions will help you unearth them.

1. **Are any of the following crucial, almost nonnegotiable, in your next career? If not, leave this item blank.**

   A minimum salary of _____

   A prestigious job title

   The opportunity for self-expression/creativity

   Variety in your workday

   A specific location, such as at home, in a particular city, on a college campus, in a big city, in the country, in an office building, or near water If so, specify: _____

   A fast- (or slow-) paced job

   Short training time

   Being self-employed

   Working on a team

   Working by yourself

   Working for a for-profit organization

   Working for a nonprofit organization

Working for the government

Working in a particular industry, field, or for a specific cause: _____

2. **Write your worklife mission statement:**

In one sentence, describe what you most want to accomplish. If that suggests a career or a career must, write it here:

_____

_____

_____

Taking Stock of Your Abilities and Skills

It's all well and good to want a career that's consistent with your values, but your success or failure in that career will depend on your abilities and skills. This section will help you tease out yours.

3. **To be successful and satisfied at work, do you want to spend the bulk of your workday on one or two of these? (If none pop out at you, leave this question blank.)**

Speaking one-on-one

Speaking to groups

Reading

Writing

Working with data, numbers, or computers

Supervising people

Being entrepreneurial

Helping people

Doing office work

Working by yourself

Convincing people

Making something artistic with your hands

Making or fixing something

Perhaps most important, other: _____

4. **Do you have specific expertise that you know you want to use in your career? Write it here.**

   For example, a degree in molecular biology, the ability to program in Java, or three years of import-export experience.

   _____

   _____

   _____

5. **What do you find easy that many other people find hard?**

   Many people aren't sure what their best skills are. The government-sponsored Skills Profiler may help. It's free at www.careerinfonet.org/acinet/skills/default.aspx.

   _____

   _____

   _____

6. **What have people complimented you on that may have career implications?**

   For example, they may say, "How can you stay so calm in that situation?!" or "You wrote all that in an hour?!" or "You could sell ice cubes to Eskimos."

   _____

   _____

   _____

Eyeing Your Interests

Some people can get interested in almost any field — well, maybe not sewage treatment. But for other people, choosing a career in an area of personal interest is key to their finding career passion.

7. **If you wrote a book, what would it be about?**

   Does that topic suggest a possible career for you?

   _____

   _____

   _____

8. What do you most enjoy talking about?

Pick something that may suggest a career for you — your darling daughter, probably not; fashion, maybe; health, even more likely. I encourage you to come up with unusual, even weird topics. If you come up with something that everyone seems to be interested in (say, pop culture), you may have a tough time landing a well-paying job in that field. If you come up with something unusual — for example, improving school curriculum or hydrogen-cell-powered cars — your chances are better.

_____

_____

_____

9. What is/was your favorite subject in school?

_____

_____

_____

10. Can you think of a type of organization that you'd love to work for?

Here are some that my clients picked: TV news show, shopping Web site, filmmaking company, guitar manufacturer, educational software company, snowboard factory, American Association of Retired Persons, biotech company, cosmetics firm, National Institutes of Health.

You have much less competition for good jobs and then advancement in fields that few people aspire to work in. Examples of these fields include the scrap metal industry, database administration, and heavy equipment manufacturing.

_____

_____

_____

11. Have you or someone you love faced an adversity that suggests a career that excites you?

Having undergone a mastectomy, Rhonda now fits other women who have had mastectomies with prosthetic breasts and special lingerie, meeting clients in their own homes. She says, "People are very appreciative. It's so much more relaxed than walking into a cold department store with everyone hearing what your problem is."

_____

_____

_____

12. **Write the last two or three times you felt a surge of energy at work. Does that suggest a career?**

   _____

   _____

   _____

13. **What are you angry about? Do you want a career that addresses that anger?**

   For example, a client was angry about reverse discrimination hurting White males. He became a career counselor specializing in White males.

   _____

   _____

   _____

14. **What are you passionate about? If you see a passion or two on this list that you'd love to have as part of your next career, circle it/them.**

Accounting/taxes	Film	Politics
Aerospace	Fitness	Public policy
Aging	Food	Public speaking
Animals	Foreign languages	Real estate
Architecture	Getting a good deal	Relationships
Artificial intelligence	Healthcare	Religion/spirituality
Aviation	Health planning	Research
Biotechnology/genetics	History	Science
Books or periodicals	Human rights	Selling
Cars	Information systems	Sex
Computer games	Insects	Sports
Computer hardware	International affairs	Telecommunications
Computer software	Investments	Television/radio
Construction	Labor-employee relations	Terrorism
Consumer advocacy	Landscaping	Theater
Cooking	Law	Transportation
Counseling	Machines	Travel
Creating beauty	Management	Urban/regional planning

Drug abuse	Music	Web sites
Educating/training	Nanotechnology	Writing
Electronic equipment	Offshoring	Other: _____
Energy	Outdoor recreation	
Environmental issues	Plants	

15. **Is there a certain type of person you definitely want to work with? If so, circle the type in this list; otherwise, leave this item blank.**

   Adults

   Alone

   Arty people

   Children

   Entrepreneurs

   Happy people

   Nerds

   Older adults

   People of a particular race, gender, or sexual orientation:
   _____

   People who build or fix things

   People with a specific problem: _____

   Teens

   The highly intelligent

   The mentally troubled

   The physically sick

   Those of average intelligence

   Those of low intelligence

   Perhaps most important, other: _____

Considering Self-Employment

You live in an era in which highly paid, secure employee jobs are increasingly reserved for superstars. For everyone else, self-employment may be a more likely route. But not everyone has what it takes. What about you? These questions can help you decide.

If you can't honestly answer yes to the following questions but are still eager to consider self-employment, you may want to work as an assistant to a successfully self-employed person. You'll either acquire the skills and mindset you need or realize that you're wiser to be employed by someone else.

16. Do any of these self-employment categories excite you?

- Distributing the work of creative people: Examples include being an agent for performers or artists, being a film distributor, or owning an online art gallery.

- Replicating a successful business in a different geographic area: For example, opening a New York–style pizza place in the South or selling previously best-selling computer equipment in developing countries.

- Being self-employed in a high-profit-margin, niche field that has little competition: For example, selling used parts for 18-wheel trucks.

- Paying $10,000 to $100,000-plus to be shown how to run a particular business, step by step (buying an existing business or franchise)

- Turning people's complaints into a business that you can start

- Converting a hobby or personal interest into a business

- Finding a product or service that you want to sell

- Creating a template for a difficult-to-stage event and replicating it for different customers: An example is staging fundraising auctions for nonprofit organizations.

- Starting a grungy business, which means you have few competitors: Examples include commercial bathroom maintenance, hazardous waste disposal, and high-voltage electrical work. (Those aren't exactly cool careers, but sometimes making big money in a mundane career feels cooler than making chickenfeed in a cool career.)

17. Do you like being in charge?

Do you love running the show and hate having someone tell you what you can and can't do? When you're your own boss, you make all the decisions — from which computer to buy to whether to take on a lucrative but risky project. Staying motivated when you're on your own is easier when you crave one of the main benefits of being self-employed: control.

18. Are you flexible?

Planning is valuable when you're on your own, but often, you have to throw out your plan and reinvent. If you're looking for a relatively fixed job description, you'll do better in a salaried job. But if you like the idea of continually reshaping what you do, self-employment feels good.

19. Can you get things done?

Are you unusually productive? Ideas and dreams are a dime a dozen. The key to turning them into reality is implementation. As they say, success is 5 percent inspiration and 95 percent perspiration. If you're easily distracted from work, you'll have problems being self-employed.

20. Are you good at solving real-world problems quickly?

Think of stumbling blocks you've faced at work and at home. Did you overcome most of them quickly, or did you stay bogged down? When you're your own boss, there's always a thorny issue to address. The successfully self-employed solve problems quickly, by themselves or with some affordable help.

21. Are you persistent?

Even the successfully self-employed face many setbacks, but they don't sulk. They quickly move to develop a new strategy. (Of course, that doesn't preclude an occasional private cry.)

22. Do you communicate well?

As the front person, you must make a good first impression, orally and in writing.

Today, much of the world's communication occurs by computer. To succeed in most businesses, you must be able to quickly draft e-mails, find information on the Internet, and continually update your Web site. The latter has become easier with do-it-yourself Web site-creation software such as store.yahoo.com or www.homestead.com.

23. Are you willing and able to market and sell?

No matter how much you enjoy doing your work, you won't get the chance to do it as your own boss unless you can find a way to let others know what you can do for them.

Answering Big-Picture Questions

Often, career searchers get bogged down trying to figure out their career building blocks: skills, interests, and values. Yet sometimes, the wisest career choice is more organic — think bigger-picture. These questions may help you see the forest through the trees.

24. What are your peak accomplishments?

You had plenty of drive to complete these achievements, and they gave you a strong sense of accomplishment. If you can't think of at least two from adulthood, go back to your younger days. Does looking at your peak accomplishments suggest a career must or a career?

_____

_____

25. Describe your dream workday, from the moment you get up until the moment you go to sleep. Does that suggest a career must or even a career?

_____

_____

26. What career do your parents, partner, or close friends think that you should pursue?

If you don't know, ask them. But don't too quickly accept or reject their advice because of the source. Make an open-minded choice.

_____

_____

27. If you didn't care what your family and friends thought, what career would you pursue?

_____

_____

28. What would your twin tell you to do?

_____

_____

29. If you're a person of faith, what would God tell you to do?

_____

_____

30. Do you know of a wealthy, well-connected, eminent, or highly skilled person who can help you get hired for a better job than you can get on the open market? If so, what work could you do for that person?

_____

_____

31. If you acted like a true grownup, what would you do?

_____

_____

32. What do you want your life to look like ten years from now? Does that suggest the sort of career you should pursue?

_____

_____

33. **Sometimes, what you need more than anything is a change. What career appeals to you that represents a dramatic change from what you're currently doing?**

   _____

   _____

34. **If you're thinking about a career change, what makes you think that seeking a new career is wiser than finding a new job in your same career or doing more to make the most of your current job? For example, can you seek out new assignments or a new boss, or work on your personal demons without changing careers?**

   _____

   _____

35. **Deep down, some people know what they want to do. They simply need to be asked point-blank. Richard Bolles asks, "What job would you love to do more than any other in the world?"**

   _____

   _____

TIP

Want more good questions, with links to specific careers? Take the Eureka Career Inventory (www.eureka.org). A year's access costs $29.95. The inventory is worth the money even if you use it only once. If you do that, here, write any new career musts you derive, so you have all your career musts in one place.

   _____

   _____

The Virtual Career Coach: Integrating Head and Heart

Great! You used your heart to pick out careers that feel good from the *Cool Careers Yellow Pages* (see Chapter 2). You used your head to answer the *35 Most Revealing Questions* earlier in this chapter. Now, I show you how to integrate head and heart so you end up choosing a career that satisfies you both rationally and emotionally.

I'm going to be straight with you. Despite my best efforts, the remaining few pages of this chapter can be, frankly . . . well . . . let me just say it . . . hard.

They require you to do some careful thinking about your career. However, these pages are also important. Otherwise, I would have simply pressed the delete key. Stay with me. Most of you will find this section worth the effort.

Step 1: List your career musts

Look at your answers to the *35 Most Revealing Questions* and circle the answers that you consider most significant. These are your career musts.

If you circled more than five career musts, see whether you can whittle them down to the five most important without feeling like you're cutting off your right arm. *Hint:* You can often cheat by combining two musts into one.

Step 2: See whether the careers you picked satisfy your career musts

Look at how well each career you picked from the *Cool Careers Yellow Pages* satisfies your career musts. Do your career musts make you want to eliminate any of those careers?

Step 3: Note other careers suggested by your career musts

Look at your career musts. Do any other careers come to mind that are at least as interesting as those you picked from the *Cool Careers Yellow Pages?*

Want more ideas? Show your career musts to your friends — a decent party game. Here are some examples:

- ✔ When Jacque saw "sales," "romance," and "aesthetic" among her career musts, she added wedding planner to her list of possible careers.
- ✔ When Luther saw "writing," "travel," "high-income," and "fluent in Spanish," he added "marketing communications writer for a fast-growing company that does business with Central America" to his list of possible careers.

Many people's career musts are quite general — for example, "I like managing adults." Beyond that, in their heart of hearts, they don't really have any career musts. As long as the job pays well, they're cool. If that sounds like you, you have two choices: sally forth with that general career goal, or force yourself to narrow. Most job seekers find that their search goes more smoothly if they do the latter. For example, if you like managing adults, here are ways to narrow:

- ✔ Focus on one industry — for example, biotech or fashion.

- ✔ Decide where you want to manage, perhaps in a hospital, in a home-based business, or on a cruise ship to Bora Bora.

- ✔ Think about whom you want to manage. Arty types? Business people? Techies? Highly intelligent people?

A wise client once said, "Managing is managing, so why not pick an uncrowded industry, one that most people wouldn't think of?" He looked through the index of the Yellow Pages (the phone book, not this book's *Yellow Pages*) and stopped at "acid manufacturers." He read up on the acid industry, e-mailed all the local firms, and soon got a management job with a minimum of competition.

Step 4: Add careers from the 35 Most Revealing Questions

One or more of the 35 earlier questions may have elicited not only a career must, but also an actual career that intrigues you. If so, do you like that career at least as well as the careers you picked from the *Cool Careers Yellow Pages?* If so, add it (or them) to your list of possible careers.

Step 5: Pick one or more careers that may actually work

Look at all your possible careers:

- ✔ Careers you identified in Steps 3 and 4
- ✔ Careers you picked from the *Cool Careers Yellow Pages* in Chapter 2
- ✔ Other careers you're considering — like going into your uncle's widget business

And now, ta-dah, the moment of truth: Which career seems most intriguing? Don't expect to feel orgasmic about it yet. Intrigued is good enough for now.

Step 6: Find out more

Before making your final career choice, you want to learn more about that top-choice career(s) of yours. Chapter 4 shows you how to do just that.

Chapter 4

Making Your Career Choice

In This Chapter

▶ Reviewing what's published

▶ Getting the scoop from people in the field

▶ Paying a visit to a workplace

▶ Addressing your career fears

▶ Making a final check on your choice

*Y*ou've found a career (or three) that sounds good. But what if you picked wrong? What if you fail in that career? Or what if you succeed but are totally miserable?

This chapter boosts your chances of picking well. It shows how to find out what a career is really like — before taking the plunge. And it's not complicated. Reading, contacting, and visiting are the three approaches. Read about the career, and if it still sounds good, contact a few people in the field, and if it still feels right, visit a few people at their workplaces. This chapter shows you how to make the most of all three approaches.

A side benefit of all that digging is that you have insider information about the career, which should make you impressive in job interviews. (I give you the full scoop on interviews in Chapter 10.)

Despite all that sleuthing, some people will be afraid to commit to a career. (They're probably the same people who are afraid to commit to a relationship.) Not to worry: This chapter concludes with a smorgasbord of strategies that can help even the most commitment-phobic person choose a career.

Reading about a Career

Articles and books are among the most underrated products. (And a college education may be the most overrated, but that's another book.) If you're willing to do only one thing to check out a career, read. A good article or book constitutes access to the best, most thorough, and most carefully organized ideas. And they're available to you 24/7 online or at the library for free, or worst case, for the cost of a large pizza.

By reading a career-related article or skimming a book, you usually discover things that one or more experts took years to figure out. Take, for example, the *Occupational Outlook Handbook*. It includes authoritative profiles of 270 of the most popular careers, based on interviews with many people in those fields. What a treasure! Reading the OOH is like discovering what thousands of people have to say about their careers. Plus, the information is distilled for you and available whenever or wherever you want it. To me, that's cool.

In this section, I explain the benefits of reading before contacting or visiting people in a field, and I give you tips on the best reading material out there.

Why read before phoning or visiting?

Okay, so why read about a career before contacting someone in that field? Simple: You don't want to sound like a dodo. Read about the career and you're more likely to impress your contacts as being worth their time. Who knows? One of them may then be willing to take you under wing, reveal inside secrets, and maybe even help you get hired.

Also, boning up in advance means you make the most of your contact — you need to ask only about the things you couldn't discover on your own.

What's the best stuff to read?

"All right, so you've guilt-tripped me into reading stuff. What should I read?" I tell you in the following sections.

Getting help from the library

Try this elegantly simple approach recommended by Mary-Ellen Mort, career librarian and founder of jobstar.org, a leading career site.

1. **Call your area's central library and ask which branch (or local college or high school) has the best career collection.**

   If no career collection is available, ask for the business collection.

2. **Visit or call the librarian in charge of that collection and describe the career you want to learn more about.**

   That's all you need to do. The librarian is likely to help you find the right information. It's that simple.

In addition to books and periodicals, many of today's libraries subscribe to powerful online services — too expensive for home users — that can search enormous databases for information about your target career. So, even if you live hours away from a decent library, you may be able to access their databases from your home computer or even get the librarian to do a little searching for you and e-mail you the results.

Brushing up on other reading materials

If you're a do-it-yourselfer who'd rather I hand you some cool references, here they are. No need to consult them all. Just pick any that jump out at you.

- ✔ *The Occupational Outlook Handbook* ($17.95 as a paperback book, free online at www.bls.gov/oco). Its strength is its authoritativeness. Its weakness is that it avoids any subjectivity. So it's great on the facts, lousy on the feel. For the latter, use the guides in the next bullet.

- ✔ **Vault.com's guides and WetFeet.com's Insider Guides** are filled with insider information on popular fields. They do a particularly thorough job on investment banking, attorney, and management careers in a variety of industries. Also, they provide insider-written profiles of large companies.

- ✔ **University of California, Berkeley Career Site** (www.uhs.berkeley.edu/Students/CareerLibrary/Links/ occup.cfm). I'm touting this not because it's from my alma mater but because it offers an amazing amount of well-organized information on hundreds of careers. Not surprising for a university site, the focus is on careers requiring a degree.

- ✔ **Career Voyages** (www.careervoyages.gov/students-links.cfm). Compliments of the Feds, this site offers text and video information on 100+ careers, with an emphasis on the cutting edge.

- ✔ **America's CareerInfoNet** (www.acinet.org). This site is also a federal freebie and offers links to some of the Net's best career information sites.

- ✔ **Google.com.** Use your prospective career as the search term. Rely not only on Google's Web search, but also click on its "groups" tab, and you can search thousands of online discussion groups — often a source of scuttlebutt. There, you can also post a query such as, "I'm thinking about a career in X. What should I know about it that might not appear in print?"

- ✔ **Amazon.com.** Simply enter your career into Amazon's search feature and out pops book titles with your career in the title. Bonus: The listings include descriptions and usually reviews of the books.

- ✔ **Professional association publications.** A professional association's Web site often contains a gold mine of information about the field assembled by the field's leaders. I provide Web addresses of associations for most of the 500+ careers in this book's *Cool Careers Yellow Pages* (see Chapter 2).

✔ **The Riley Guide** (`www.rileyguide.com`). This site links to other sites for hundreds of specific occupations.

Contacting People in the Field

You can't find out everything by reading. As you find out in the following sections, talking to people lets you ask the questions that your reading didn't answer. It's also a way to start building your professional network.

Many career seekers are reluctant to call people in the field. The two main reasons are "I don't want to impose" and "I'm afraid I'll sound stupid." Remember that most people like to talk about their careers. And if they don't, they're adults — they can say no. And if you do sound stupid, so what! How important is that in the larger scheme of things? Besides, with that advance reading you've done, you probably will sound brilliant.

Need more prodding to pick up the phone or send that e-mail? Chapter 12 offers cures for *procrastitis*.

"Okay, okay, but whom do I contact?"

This list should yield you more contacts than you can stomach:

✔ If you have a friend or relative in your target career, you can start there. At the end of the conversation, ask for the names of colleagues you could speak with.

✔ Your college's Web site or career center may maintain a list of alumni, including their line of work. Some may be willing to tell their career tales.

✔ Attend a local meeting of your prospective career's professional association or an on-campus professional club.

✔ Get the phone numbers of members of the professional association by checking its Web site.

✔ Find names in the professional association's magazine or newsletter. Authors and cited experts are often more accessible than you may think.

✔ If you have chutzpah, just open your Yellow Pages and start dialing. Use your printed Yellow Pages for locals, and use `anywho.com` for out-of-towners. If you're considering an entrepreneurial career, out-of-towners are more likely to talk with you because they're less afraid you'll become a competitor.

Each person's viewpoint is idiosyncratic. One dentist may gush that business is booming while the next dentist moans that attracting new patients is like pulling teeth. (I couldn't resist.) So don't get too swayed by one person's opinion. Speak with at least two or three folks.

"What should I say?"

Nearly everyone gets nervous when asking something of another person. The antidote is preparation. In the following sections, I do much of that preparation for you: a model script for how to open your conversation followed by a smorgasbord of questions to choose from.

Getting through to your target and introducing yourself

Count on getting turned down often in your quest for information, but the following approach works often enough, and, unlike oft-recommended ruses, it's honest.

When you phone, you'll rarely get your target person. The key to getting through a gatekeeper or voicemail jail is to briefly tell your true human story. Here's a gatekeeper example:

> Hello, my name is *(insert your name).* This may be one of the weirder *(trust me, that word works)* calls you've gotten today, but I really need your help. I'm trying to choose my career and I think I may want to be a *(insert career),* but I'm not sure yet. I've read about the career but feel I should talk with someone in the field. Can I ask you to see whether your boss may be willing to answer just a few questions about what it's like to be a *(insert career)?*

If the gatekeeper can't or won't put you through, ask for your target's e-mail address. But for now, assume you have your target person on the phone. This approach works well:

> Hello, I'm *(insert your name).* I'd really appreciate your help. I'm considering becoming a *(insert career).* I've read a lot about the field but would like to talk with someone who's actually in that career. I wonder if I could ask you just a few questions about your experience as a *(insert career).*

If the person says that now isn't a good time, ask when you can call back or whether you can meet in person. Read on to find out what to do if the person agrees to answer your questions right away.

Asking useful questions

Next, ask your questions. You may have your own, but these questions are likely to elicit useful information. There are more here than you need; pick your favorites.

✔ How'd you get into this career?

✔ Can you walk me through a typical day?

✔ What do you find to be the best and worst things about your career?

✔ Can you think of anything I should know about this field that is unlikely to find its way into print? (My favorite question.)

✔ What skills have you found crucial to succeeding in your career?

✔ Can you think of anything you know now that you wish you'd known when you were deciding to enter this field?

✔ *Describe your background and interests. Then ask:* Do you think I should consider this field? Any other fields I should consider?

✔ Are there any particularly interesting specialties within your field?

✔ Any advice about the smartest way to prepare for this career?

✔ Are there entry-level jobs in this field that provide particularly good learning experiences?

✔ In this field, where are good job openings listed?

✔ What kind of salary can I expect?

✔ How is the field changing?

✔ Why might someone leave this field?

✔ Do you know someone else you think I should talk with or something else I should read before deciding whether to pursue this career? Any event I should attend? Any organization I should join?

✔ Any other advice you'd give someone entering this field?

If the conversation goes well, ask whether you can spend an hour watching that person at work.

Visiting a Workplace

Why visit? Because, like sex, some things you just have to experience to fully appreciate. Watching someone at work is the next best thing to trying it yourself.

Craig, for example, thought he might want to be an arborist (tree surgeon), but after spending an hour on-site with a professional, realized that having to spend that much time on high branches, often in bad weather, outweighed the joy of artfully shaping trees.

In the following sections, I explain what to do during a workplace visit and give you the scoop on virtual visits.

At the risk of stating the obvious, send a thank-you letter or e-mail to your contact after you visit a workplace. For secrets to writing a winning letter, check out Chapter 10.

Knowing what to do during a visit

Okay, so you're on-site. What now? Just ask the person to show you around and to let you watch tasks that are central to the job. (Sometimes an hour will give you all you need; other times, you may want to spend an entire day or even longer.) If possible, get introduced to others in that career at the worksite.

Use your head and your heart. Rationally, can you see yourself doing this work, day in and day out? Emotionally, do you sense that you'd feel good in such a career?

Taking a virtual visit

If you live on an isolated farm, visiting an urban planner may not be easy. That's why videos can be valuable. In some ways, career videos are better than in-person visits because they usually round up a variety of people in the profession, ask good questions, and give you the full tour. And a virtual visit is perfect for those shy souls who simply can't make themselves set up an in-person visit, let alone ask lots of good questions. Large libraries, especially those in a high school or college career center, often have a collection of career videos. Videos on hundreds of careers can be viewed at `www.careervoyages.gov/careervideos-main.cfm` and `www.acinet.org/videos.asp?id=27,1&nodeid=27`.

Getting Serious about a Career

By now, you should have identified a top-choice career, but it's worth a little more digging to ensure your choice is a wise one. Here are some methods:

- ✔ **A seminar or short course in your chosen field:** The professional association for that career may offer live, recorded, or online versions. Also check your local college's extension catalog. Taking a short course helps you assess both your aptitude for and interest in the field.

- ✔ **Conferences and trade shows:** Here you find hundreds of practitioners plus their suppliers and customers all in one place. Exhibit areas sell tools of the trade, and ongoing workshops teach you the field's basics and cutting edges. Plus, the many meals, breaks, and parties are designed to facilitate discussion. These events often are listed on a career's professional association Web site. *Associations Unlimited,* an online database available through many large libraries, also lists upcoming major meetings for most professional and trade associations.

✔ **Volunteering, interning, or project work:** Nothing takes the place of an actual tryout. A brief one is often enough to show you what you need to know about a career. For instance, before deciding to become a high school teacher, Derrick volunteered as a classroom aide. After a week, he began to feel the draining effect of trying to keep 30 students — a different 30 every 50 minutes — motivated, let alone educated. He also quickly tired of the conversations in the teachers' lounge. Teaching wasn't right for him. Two weeks of volunteering saved him two years of training plus many more years of unhappiness in a career he didn't like.

Think of a short-term volunteer or low-pay stint as a tuition-free education. Working for little or nothing gives you power — the power to ensure you get to do meaningful work. So, before signing on, negotiate your role. Licking envelopes for an oceanographer won't give you a good idea of what the job is like. Accompanying the oceanographer on a dive in a bathyscaph followed by a day entering data into a computer will.

Good internships can often be created simply by asking a desired mentor whether you could be her slave in exchange for some mentorship. The advantage of that approach is that you get to pick your supervisor. Or to find existing internships, see www.rileyguide.com/intern.html.

Finding the Courage to Commit

No matter how much analysis you do, saying, "Yes, this is the career I want!" can be hard to do. People hesitate to commit to a career for three reasons: you don't know enough about your prospective career, one career doesn't stand out, and fear. The courage builders in this section address all three.

When you don't know enough about a prospective career

What's making you nervous about your proposed career? Sometimes, getting more information can reassure you. Could reading something, talking to someone, or observing a workplace help you decide whether your prospective career is a wise choice? (I cover all these tasks earlier in this chapter.) Examples:

✔ **"Am I good enough in math to be an economist?"** Possible solution: Ask economists how much math they use and whether niches exist that require less. Can you do that much math?

> ✔ **The cost and time of training.** Possible solution: Keep asking around. Often, you can find shortcut training.
>
> ✔ **"Does a market really exist for the product I'm thinking of selling?"** Possible solution: Ask potential customers.

When no career seems attractive enough

Sure, maybe you just need more options. But often, you can scour every career collection in the world and still have a hard time committing. Often, that's because you're holding out for a career that feels clearly superior to your other options.

True, some people know, early on, that they were meant to be a doctor, ballet dancer, or whatever, but those folks rarely use career guides. If that uniquely perfect career was going to hit you like a lightning bolt, it probably would've done so long before now.

If I filled a room with 100 people who love their careers, most of them would say that before entering the career, they weren't sure they'd love it. Most of them could easily have chosen another career. What brought them to career contentment was getting started, choosing something. They got to the point where they just bit the bullet: "I'm just going to choose something, dammit!" That enabled them to turn their attention toward the things that make a career wonderful: getting good training, finding a good job or self-employment opportunity within that field, and then tailoring their job to fit their strengths, weaknesses, and preferences. Not surprisingly, after all that, they started to experience success in the career. Only then could they say, "I love my career."

So, follow these steps to be like most of those 100 people:

1. **Pick your favorite careers from the *Cool Careers Yellow Pages* in Chapter 2 and from the *35 Most Revealing Questions* in Chapter 3.**

2. **Distill that input using *the virtual career coach* in Chapter 3.**

3. **Take a moderate amount of time to check out a prospective career(s) using the approaches I tell you about earlier in this chapter.**

4. **Select your top-choice career, even if it doesn't generate career ecstasy. *As long as that top-choice career feels likely to be better than the status quo, choose it.***

Until you get into the career, you can't really know for sure whether it can make you happy. But taking steps down one career path is more likely to help you figure that out than additional thinking at the trailhead.

Be passionate in pursuing the career, even if you're ambivalent. That's key to ensuring your success. Focus on

✔ **Getting the best training possible.** Good training makes you feel and become competent. You can often find the best training at a student-oriented college rather than at a prestigious, research-oriented one. Even more practical training options include mentors, workshops, tapes, and articles. Part II covers your training options.

✔ **Doing a thorough job search.** If you can get multiple job offers, you maximize your chances of finding a job with good co-workers, learning opportunities, an organization you feel good about, and one that offers annual paid training in Hawaii. Part III shows you how to land a great job.

✔ **Molding your job to fit your strengths.** Revise your job description to make use of your assets. Propose projects you'd find fun. You may even be able to incorporate some advantages of other careers you considered. For example, if you choose interior design over photography, make before-and-after photos a part of your service. Head to Chapter 11 for more on making the most of any job.

✔ **Recognizing that your career contentment depends not just on a well-suited career and job, but on other factors as well:**

   • **Accepting that work is work.** Even those who have worklives that many people envy usually think that work is still work. Work isn't often as pleasurable as going out to eat, walking in nature, or being with someone you love. I can gratefully accept that work is work, mainly because I value being productive, feeling needed, having structure, and earning a living, even when it isn't fun. If you make this mindset permeate your workday, you can feel good about your worklife in almost any career.

   • **Maintaining an accepting attitude.** Resenting work's many moments that are too hard, too easy, too stressful, or too boring is easy to do. Or you can view those moments with a Zen-like acceptance and a commitment to handle each moment with grace, reminding yourself of the good in your life. For me, this is the key to happiness, not just in a career, but in life.

At minimum, starting down a career path helps you discover that you made a wrong choice. Millions of people change careers. If your next career choice bombs, you'll learn about yourself and make a better choice next time. You'll certainly make a wiser choice than if you had attempted to divine the perfect career while sitting on the sidelines.

When you're afraid that you'll fail

Fear of failure is sometimes legitimate — in your gut, you know your chances of success are small. But sometimes, even if your rational mind believes you have a reasonable chance of success, your fear of failure makes you too scared to give it a try. The following courage builders may help.

Know that it's usually worth risking failure

Many successful people have failed a lot. In my first after-school job, I was an office clerk — and got fired for making too many careless errors. My first professional job was as a school psychologist. My contract wasn't renewed because I wasn't supportive enough of teachers' efforts. My first book was rejected by 18 publishers before one publisher offered me the grand sum of $5,000 for it. Yet if you look at my bio in the front of this book, I daresay you'd call me a success. To maximize your chances of success, try difficult, exciting things, and when you fail, ask what you can learn from it.

Failing usually is better than not trying at all. Not trying is the one way to guarantee you fail. You'd be surprised how often trying something difficult works out: Your adrenaline is pumping, you scramble awhile, and eventually you do okay. And that feels great.

Yeah I know, your shrink told you that your fear of risk taking stems from your childhood: Your mother taught you not to take risks, or your father yelled at you when you made a mistake. I also know that the kindly shrink probably inadvertently supported your inertia: "I know how hard it must be when your parents were so tough on you." Bottom line, you gotta make yourself get over it. If the benefits of trying something exceed the risks, feel the fear and do it anyway. Force yourself to stay focused on taking small steps and getting help when you're stuck. After working with 2,600 clients, many who have had therapy, I believe that many people are helped more by the previous sentence than by years on the therapist's couch.

All your ducks needn't be in a row

Many people think that before starting their career, they must start with a crystal clear idea of their ultimate career goal and *know* they have the potential to succeed. It rarely works that way.

Many successful people get their first jobs with only a general idea of their career direction. Many are unsure whether they'll succeed in that career. They simply sallied forth. Kumar, a new college graduate, had the sense he wanted to work in high-tech but couldn't be more precise than that. He got a quickie certification in Java and Oracle and stuck those on his resume to see what that bait would yield. He got a job as a Web site programmer. Who knows whether he'll end up happy in that career, but I'd sooner bet on him than on someone who waited for crystal clarity before acting.

The chief resident at a New York medical school greets each year's interns by saying, "Each of you is entitled to one clean kill. You can't become a good doctor without lots of practice and inevitably that means you'll kill someone. Accept it. Over your lifetime, your worth as a doctor will be determined not by your early errors but by the sum of what you do." If that's true for doctors, it's probably even truer for you — I suspect that your errors won't kill anyone. Remember, every newbie scrambles. Key to success then is to stop stewing and start acting.

Compare your options against the status quo

Instead of judging your candidate career(s) against some abstract ideal, write the advantages and disadvantages of your candidate career versus the status quo. The right choice often comes clear.

The Judge Judy technique

Pretend you're a lawyer and give all the reasons why Career A is better. Then pretend you're the opposing attorney and give the reasons why Career B is better. Finally, be Judge Judy and render a decision.

Try out your new career as a sideline

Unsure whether your new career will work? Charlie liked the idea of producing videos of playful interviews with employees for showing at company parties. Charlie started his video business as a sideline, not wanting to quit his job until he was sure he could make money at his new pursuit. He wins either way: If he's successful, he can, with confidence, quit his job and go full time; if not, he still has his job.

Give yourself a trial period

Can you make it as a singer? Will that pizza-by-the-slice business be worthwhile? Reduce your risk by giving your new venture a fixed amount of time. On your calendar, circle a date, perhaps a year from now. If, by then, you don't see signs you'll succeed in your new endeavor, drop it. Limiting your risk can give you the courage to give it a shot.

How I made a career decision

I was teaching graduate students at Berkeley when I realized I'd never be happy as a professor. I am practical at heart. I wouldn't be content in a career in which my primary task was to publish esoteric articles in the *Journal of Educational Psychology,* but I couldn't think of a career that really excited me. The best I could come up with was career counseling, but that felt just okay.

I nonetheless took the plunge. In the beginning I was unhappy and asked myself why. The job was too passive; I was sitting and listening most of the time. So I adopted a more active style, but the job still needed more spice, so I volunteered to host a weekly radio show on careers and education. That opened the door to the other cool things I now get to do.

Molding my career to fit me converted a so-so career into a happy one. I truly am eager to get up each weekday morning — well, most weekday mornings. If I had remained a professor until I found a career that excited me right off the bat, I might still be waiting.

Choose more than one career

Can't decide? Choose more than one (for example, a part-time tutor, copy-writer, actor, and bartender). Having multiple careers can be exciting, but you'd better be a quick study and enjoy long hours. For some people, that doesn't work. It's hard enough to succeed in one career.

Choose a less radical option

Not sure it's worth tackling a totally new career? Choose a less radical option:

- **Tweak your current job.** (See Chapter 11.) Many people who think they need a new career can solve their problem by changing bosses, renegotiating their responsibilities, or improving their skills.

- **Find a new job in your current career.** Maybe a different organization's culture can cure your workplace woes.

- **Find a different niche within your current career.** Sick of being a biologist in a lab? Try field-based biology. The *Cool Careers Yellow Pages* in Chapter 2 lists neat niches in many careers.

- **Stay in the same industry but change job titles.** Or change industries but keep the same job title.

- **Find more meaning outside of work.** Pursue a hobby that allows for self-expression; do volunteer work; fall in love.

A Final Check: Is Your Choice Right for You?

It's time. You've reviewed lots of careers and picked the one that feels best. Now it's time for a final check: Does your career have all five signs of being right for you?

1. **Can you, within an acceptable amount of time, acquire the knowledge and skills to succeed in this career?**

   If you're unsure, ask someone in the field to review your previous efforts. Or try to understand an introductory textbook, or find someone to teach you a bit of the field's essentials. Are you getting it?

2. **Can you get the time and money to train for this career?**

   Before rejecting a career on this basis, read Chapters 5 and 6, which describe cost- and time-effective ways to get the training you need. And if you're thinking of starting a business, Chapter 13 shows ways to get the cash flowing quickly.

3. **Will this career likely sustain your interest?**

   Picture yourself in this career for five years. Are you likely to feel good about having chosen it?

4. **Are you likely to enjoy working in this career's environment?**

   For example, at home? Outdoors? In an office?

5. **Are you likely to enjoy the typical people interactions in this career?**

   If so, congratulations. Sounds like you've found a cool career!

Part II
Training for That Cool Career

The 5th Wave   By Rich Tennant

"...faster than a speeding bullet...more powerful than a locomotive...hmm. Oh good, you type!"

In this part . . .

Competence: It's one of life's great feelings. Getting up in the morning knowing you're a pro, confident that you'll be a star at work. This part shows you how to maximize your chances of becoming competent. You can go degree-free or head back to school; I tell you about both options in this part.

Chapter 5

Degree-Free Career Preparation

· ·

In This Chapter

▶ Deciding whether you should pursue a degree

▶ Discovering the benefits of You U.

▶ Getting an employer to hire you over someone with more degrees

▶ Mastering the art of keeping current

· ·

> *Everyone may tell you the rule is "To do this work, you need a master's degree . . ." But you want to find out about the exceptions.*
>
> — Richard Bolles, *What Color Is Your Parachute?*

*I*magine how you'd feel knowing you're an expert who can be counted on to do the job wonderfully. Nothing is more central to career satisfaction.

Of course, key to becoming an expert is good training. This chapter helps you figure out whether you need a degree at all. More often than you may suspect, you can find wiser ways to prepare for your career. This chapter even shows you how to convince an employer to hire you over someone with more degrees. But as good as non-degree training can be, it's certainly not right for everyone. Ready for a back-for-a-degree stint? Chapter 6 can help.

The Bad and the Good about Pursuing a Degree

Today, many people view a degree as a magic pill. Sometimes it is, and sometimes it isn't. The following sections will help you decide whether you should take that pill.

Lousy reasons to get a degree

If you have a good reason, going back for a degree can be a fine idea. Alas, many people don't have a good reason. Here are some classic lousy reasons:

- ✔ **To help decide what career to pursue:** Mistake. Most degree programs expose you to only a fraction of the career options. Far better to choose your career using the approach in Part I of this book.

- ✔ **To postpone looking for a job:** Part III of this book shows you how to land a rewarding job without undue pain. No need to spend years and megabucks to postpone that.

- ✔ **Because you think it will lead to a good job:** Find out whether a degree is absolutely necessary. By informational interviewing, you can find out whether there's more than one way to reach your goal.

- ✔ **To impress friends and family:** Can't you think of less costly and time-consuming ways to do that? How about landing a good job years sooner than if you had gone for a degree?

- ✔ **To feel legitimate:** In many fields, you can more legitimately prepare for your career away from the halls of academe, at what I call *You U.:* a self- and mentor-selected combination of articles, seminars, professional conferences, the Internet, and on-the-job training. Don't commit years of your life and lots of money just to create the illusion of legitimacy — sometimes what a degree mainly provides.

- ✔ **To dazzle employers:** In many fields, your boss is likely to be more impressed with a well-designed You U. education than with a diploma that both of you know doesn't mean that you're career competent. Later in this chapter, I show you how to dazzle employers more legitimately.

Good reasons to get a degree

Of course, there are good reasons to pursue a degree:

- ✔ **For your enlightenment.** A degree program can help you become an informed citizen and to experience life more richly.

- ✔ **Some fields absolutely, positively require a degree.** For example, if you want to be a physician, the state isn't going to let you treat patients just because you had a mentor. In fields like engineering, management consulting, investment banking, and at top law firms, employers generally ignore applicants who aren't waving a prestigious diploma.

- ✔ **Your efforts to effect a career change without going back to school have failed.** You hate your current career, so before springing for the big bucks and time for a degree, you've taken seminars and networked in your target field's professional association, sought out mentorships, read relevant stuff, redone your resume to emphasize your transferable skills, and cold-contacted dozens of potential employers in your target career, yet everyone's telling you that you need a degree.

✔ **You need the structure of school.** To design and follow through on a You U. education, you must be a real self-starter, even if you have a mentor. (I show you how to find one later in this chapter.) Many people need the structure of school: Be there from 7 to 9 p.m. on Tuesdays and Thursdays; read pages 246 through 384 by next Monday; write a term paper as follows; take the final on December 20, from 2 to 4 p.m.

✔ **You want the consistent social contact that comes from meeting from 7 to 9 every Tuesday and Thursday night.**

More reasons to save your tuition money

Many people recognize the drawbacks of getting a degree, yet they insist it's worth the time and money because of what the piece of paper, the diploma, can do for them. Will that be true for you?

When I think about my 2,000+ degree-holding clients, despite their spending all that time and money on degrees, many feel like imposters in their careers. That's far more psychologically damaging than having acquired competence while lacking only a piece of paper that attests to it. Higher education may be a reasonable way to become a connoisseur of life, but if your goal is to advance your career, in many fields, I've become convinced that higher education is among the most overrated, overpriced products of all.

Yes, people with degrees earn more than people without degrees, but that doesn't mean the degree is the main reason. They earn more mainly because degree seekers, on average, are more able and motivated to begin with. If you locked degree seekers in a closet for four years, they'd likely earn more than people who don't pursue degrees.

True, many employers place want ads that specify a degree. But if you write an application letter like the one I recommend in the later section "Convincing Employers to Hire You without That Degree," many employers will consider you, just as they may consider a candidate who lacks some other job requirement stated in the want ad. Mightn't it be worth trying to land that job without the degree? If it doesn't work, you can go back to school with greater confidence that you really do need that degree.

In her book, *Success Without College, New York Times* editor Linda Lee cites a *Newsweek* article by Robert Samuelson that says, even "going to Harvard or Duke won't automatically produce a better job and higher pay. Graduates of these schools generally do well. But they do well because they are talented." The article was titled, "The Worthless Ivy League."

Some bad news

The *Phi Delta Kappan,* a prestigious education periodical, provided this discouraging information:

A Rand Corporation report concluded that new doctoral degrees in science and engineering average 25 percent *above* appropriate employment opportunities. A National Science Foundation study found a 41 percent oversupply of PhDs in the supposedly in-demand electrical engineering field and a 33 percent oversupply in civil engineering. Rand charged that universities are oblivious to the job market. . . .

Thousands from other professions face the same situation. Even graduates from America's most prestigious business schools are finding no guarantee of a job. An amazing 16 percent of newly minted MBA graduates of Stanford University were unable to find jobs. Less prestigious business schools fared even worse: 40 percent of the graduates of Ohio State's business school could not find jobs; the figure for the University of Georgia was 30 percent; for the University of Texas at Austin 24 percent; and for Tulane University 24 percent. Experts project that of the millions of university graduates, only a mere 20 percent will find the well-paying, challenging jobs for which they were trained.

That article was written in 1997. Now, graduate schools admit even more students at the same time as companies are offshoring ever more high-level jobs.

What do you think the following people have in common? Malcolm X, Rush Limbaugh, Barbra Streisand, PBS *NewsHour*'s Nina Totenberg, Tom Hanks, Maya Angelou, Ted Turner, Ellen DeGeneres, former Governor Jesse Ventura, IBM founder Thomas Watson, architect Frank Lloyd Wright, former Israeli president David Ben Gurion, Dell Computer founder Michael Dell, Woody Allen, Warren Beatty, Domino's pizza chain founder Tom Monaghan, folksinger Joan Baez, Bill Gates, director Quentin Tarantino, ABC-TV's Peter Jennings, Wendy's founder Dave Thomas, Thomas Edison, Blockbuster Video founder and owner of the Miami Dolphins Wayne Huizenga, William Faulkner, Jane Austen, McDonald's founder Ray Kroc, Oracle founder Larry Ellison, Henry Ford, cosmetics magnate Helena Rubenstein, Ben Franklin, Alexander Graham Bell, Coco Chanel, Walter Cronkite, Walt Disney, Bob Dylan, seven U.S. presidents from Washington to Truman, Leonardo DiCaprio, cookie maker Debbie Fields, Sally Field, Jane Fonda, Buckminster Fuller, Dreamworks co-founder David Geffen, author Alex Haley, Ernest Hemingway, Dustin Hoffman, famed anthropologist Richard Leakey, airplane inventors Wilbur and Orville Wright, Madonna, satirist H. L. Mencken, Martina Navritalova, Rosie O'Donnell, Nathan Pritikin (Pritikin diet), chef Wolfgang Puck, Robert Redford, oil billionaire John D. Rockefeller, Eleanor Roosevelt, NBC mogul David Sarnoff, Apple Computer founder Steve Jobs, and thousands of computer whizzes?

Not one of them has a college degree.

Of course, these people are exceptions, and it may be that only the brilliant or unintelligent can afford to forgo that diploma.

REMEMBER

But you need to know one of higher education's dirty secrets. Colleges' Web sites usually trumpet the careers possible with a given major. This information misleads readers into thinking that if they spend the years and money, they'll land one of those careers. Here's the truth: In many fields, as you'll now see, nowhere near enough jobs exist for the number of degree holders.

For example, I was sitting in one of the executive suites in the Time-Life Building, meeting with four editors of one of Time-Warner's major magazines. In the course of conversation, someone said, "It's obscene what these schools of journalism are doing. They're accepting millions of students into their journalism programs knowing full well that 90 percent of them will never make more than McWages from journalism." Everyone nodded.

You U. — Often a Better Way

In more fields than you may think, motivated people can use an approach to career preparation that offers a greater payoff than pursuing a degree. I call it *You University*. At You U., you, perhaps with the help of a mentor you select, decide what you want to learn and then design a plan to learn it (see the following section for more details).

One of my clients, Phillip, wanted to learn how to create partnerships between corporations and schools. Instead of going back for a largely misfitting master's in education or business, he did a You U. "master's." How, you ask? He simply followed these steps:

1. Phillip searched the Net for articles on business-education partnerships.

2. He interviewed, by phone, people at companies involved in those partnerships. One person suggested materials he should read and mentioned an upcoming conference on business-education partnerships.

3. At the conference, our hero attended sessions, spoke with experts, visited the vendor booths, and found out about an on-target newsletter and an Internet discussion group. He also visited corporations with model school programs.

Now, imagine you're a corporate employer looking for someone to develop a program with local schools. Would you rather hire someone with a master's in education, or someone like Phillip, who attended You U.? Good choice. Phillip got hired as a school liaison by a large telecommunications company.

Here's another example: When prominent nature recording artist Jonathon Storm decided to switch from pursuing an architecture degree to becoming a recordist, instead of changing majors, he left school to learn directly from a master. He contacted the nation's leading nature recordist and asked to study personally with him. Today, Jonathon is a master.

Just look at these differences between degree programs and You U:

✔ Starting with the basics, in a degree program, you must show up at specified times at that not-so-nearby university — assuming you can get a babysitter and afford the tuition.

In a degree program, you're taught by PhD types, theoreticians often out of touch with the practical knowledge people preparing for a career need most. Worse, you're stuck with whichever professors happen to be at that college.

✔ In contrast, if you attend You U., you're taught by precisely the right sort of people. Whether you're looking to become a graphic designer, a skyscraper developer, or whatever, you can probably find a master practitioner somewhere in the world willing to mentor you for a fraction of the cost of college tuition. (See the following section for ways to find one.) You can take workshops taught by some of your field's leading practitioners. Searchable, online databases offer plenty of these learning opportunities in every imaginable field.

And if you *are* looking for theoretical knowledge to round out your education, books, audiotapes, and videotapes allow you unlimited access, 24/7, to the world's best theorists. For example, The Teaching Company (www.teachco.com) sells CDs and DVDs of hundreds of liberal arts courses taught by some of the best professors at the most prestigious colleges.

Plus, if you want or need the contact of on-campus college courses, at You U., you're not limited to only one campus. You can find the best professor in your locale for each course. In major cities, you have a number of universities to choose from. (There are many ways to find the good professors. For example, most colleges publish a list of their teaching award winners and/or post the student evaluations of faculty.)

You U. is beyond comparison with regular degree programs, but I do it anyway in Table 5-1. Before heading back for a degree at State U. — let alone Big Bucks Private U. — ask yourself whether the smart choice might not be You U.

Table 5-1	Degree Program versus You University
A Degree Program	**You U.**
A massive amount of information all at one time, when you don't have the opportunity to apply it.	Especially if you learn on the job, you learn what you need when you need it.
Many required courses. Sometimes a course is required mainly because a professor likes to teach it.	Study only what you need and want. Often, get what you need in a fraction of the time it takes to earn a degree.

A Degree Program	*You U.*
Get a degree, only to find that you don't remember, let alone use, much of what you were taught. Own a sometimes-valuable piece of paper.	Because you learn what you want, how you want, at the pace you want, often when you have the chance to apply it, you remember much more.
Learn when it's convenient for the professor, like Mondays and Wednesdays from 7 to 10 p.m.	Learn when it's convenient for you.
You are passive. You focus on learning what the professor wants to teach, fearing a low grade if you don't. Many students leave school with poor self-esteem. This is often because of professors who teach material that is of little value outside the classroom yet is difficult, so students feel dumb.	You are empowered. You study what you want, to the level you believe necessary. You U. builds self-reliance and self-confidence. A key part of what makes a career feel good is the sense that you're an expert in your field. In many careers, you're more likely to feel like — and be — an expert with a "degree" from You U.
The material, especially in science or technology, is often obsolete. As long as professors keep cranking out articles in their microniches, many universities care little that they don't update their course material.	You can get up-to-the-minute information: on the Internet, from periodicals, by talking with people in your field, and from seminars offered by your profession's leading practitioners.
Costs range from $10,000 to more than $100,000, not to mention the loss of what you could have earned had you not been in a degree program.	Costs are 50 to 90 percent less than in a degree program.

Planning Your You U. Education

Planning your own education is simpler than you may think, as I show you in the following sections.

Finding a mentor

Start by finding a mentor who is an expert in your field, someone who can suggest resources, ensure you're covering enough of the bases, and answer your questions. Expect to compensate your mentor with money or by volunteering as her assistant. Sometimes though, people, especially older folks, will mentor you for free. Many people 50-plus want to pass on their wisdom to the next generation.

Where to find a mentor:

- Someone in your field whom you already know, like, and respect.

- At a meeting of your field's professional association. Some such associations have formal mentoring programs.

- Posting a request for a coach on your field's Internet discussion group.

- Calling SCORE, the Service Corps of Retired Executives (www.score.org).

- The Yellow Pages. Open the Yellow Pages to the appropriate category and dial until you find the right person.

- Someone who supervises interns. Don't know of anyone? www.riley guide.com/intern.html is a portal to databases of internships.

- That unusual professor with enough practical knowledge to coach you.

- Post a flyer at the local senior center or an ad in its newsletter.

No need to limit yourself to one mentor; different people provide different expertise and opinions. Besides, you don't want to overtax your mentor.

Figuring out what to learn

When talking with a potential mentor, ask this question: "I'm trying to learn X, Y, and Z, using books, articles, the Internet, CDs, DVDs, and seminars. Any titles you'd particularly recommend?" In addition to asking your mentor(s), you can pose this question to other professionals in the field. Additional ideas can come from

- A respected member of your professional association

- Your association's Web site

- Public, college, or corporate libraries and their librarians

Surveying sources of courses

Consider local colleges' extension programs and regular colleges that focus more on students than on research.

Some people are more satisfied with online classes. As long as you're a self-starter (and not tempted to cheat), they're fast, at-home convenient, and less expensive. They also offer other advantages:

✔ With tens of thousands of choices from one-hour quickies to semester-long comprehensives, you can pick an online class on the right topic and in the right length for you. With online classes, you choose what you want instead of what your local university is selling that semester.

✔ Before signing up, you can check out an online class's quality more easily than with a live course — many such courses offer a demo. You can check out five courses in an hour without leaving home. The quality of online classes is especially variable. Do check out a course carefully before paying your money.

✔ Online classes usually allow you to set your own pace. (That's an advantage and a disadvantage. Procrastinators beware!)

✔ Increasingly, online classes are more interactive, often including simulations, demonstrations, and e-mail discussion groups. (You'll want a high-speed Internet connection for video-centric classes.)

✔ When a question is asked, *you* get to answer it, without embarrassment, unlike in a live class where only the called-upon student does.

✔ You can replay (and fast forward!) video-based classes as often as you like. Try fast-forwarding a live instructor!

✔ You can attend class in your slippers.

These resources offer a treasure trove of distance- and in-person learning opportunities:

✔ **Peterson's Online Learning** (www.lifelonglearning.com): A database of credit-bearing distance learning courses offered through universities.

✔ **Globewide Network Academy** (www.gnacademy.org): A database of 32,000 courses and 6,000 programs.

✔ **Distance Education Clearinghouse** (www.uwex.edu/disted/catalogs.cfm): A portal to directories of distance learning courses and programs.

✔ **The Small Business Administration** (www.sba.gov): This federal agency offers many courses for current and aspiring businesspeople.

How'd you like to put a prestigious college's name on your resume after attending class for just a few days and without undergoing a rigorous admissions process? Most designer-label and other colleges allow the public to take in-person or online seminars, workshops, and often, full courses. It's the easiest, fastest route to getting Harvard onto your resume.

I'll bet the house on this: The decline of in-person college for adult students

I'm convinced that the bricks-and-mortar college's heyday for adult students is over. Increasingly, online learning — getting your knowledge on a just-in-time basis with at-home convenience — puts that 7 to 9 p.m. Tuesday and Thursday, campus-based class to shame. And high-speed Internet brings to your home videos of top teachers augmented by interactive simulations.

I'm even more certain that online classes featuring video lectures from national-star professors will largely replace that backbone of traditional college education: the large lecture class. I'll bet the house that, within a decade, the large in-person lecture class will be as obsolete as the cigar-smoking fad.

Scoping out other learning tools

Here are additional effective learning techniques you can use in You U.:

- ✔ The book and the article are among the most underrated learning tools. You can often find on-target readings simply by visiting your professional association's Web site, googling for articles, and checking out amazon.com for books. Using those tools, in just a few minutes, you will have searched millions of books and articles to find the right ones for you. Now tell me that's not cool.

- ✔ Another time-effective learning method is the tutor. For example, rather than taking a course in Java, get a study manual and have a tutor start you off. Then keep a list of questions and problems, and use that as the basis for the next tutoring session. Sources of tutors: your workplace, your professional association or discussion group, community college instructors, and tutor.com.

- ✔ Another practical approach to career training is to buy it as part of a franchise. Look for companies that have a proven system, have been in business at least five years before franchising, have been franchising for at least five years, and have at least ten franchisees. For a searchable database of franchises, see www.entrepreneur.com/franzone.

Convincing Employers to Hire You without That Degree

Imagine that you're an employer. Do you consider the candidate who wrote the letter in Figure 5-1?

Dear Ms. Hirer,

When you're inundated with applications, it's tempting to weed out those without a prestigious MBA, but I believe I'm worth a look precisely because I don't have any MBA.

I considered getting an MBA, but after talking with a number of MBA holders and examining the courses I would have to take and their relevance (or, too often, lack thereof) to becoming a fine software marketing manager, I concluded that the two full-time years could be more profitably spent.

I contacted directors of marketing at leading Silicon Valley software companies and offered to work for them for no pay in exchange for their mentoring. I figured that was cheap tuition for the on-target learning I would receive. A marketing manager at HP took me on. After three months, I felt I had learned about as much from him as I could, whereupon I made a similar arrangement with a director of marketing at Cisco Systems.

In these apprenticeships, I was deeply involved in a number of projects similar to those mentioned in your ad, specifically Internet marketing and managing a national consumer branding campaign. In addition, I attend American Marketing Association conferences, read the best articles and books recommended by the AMA, and spend much of my commute time listening to relevant books on CD. To get the bigger picture, I even read a couple of books by leading academics.

But now comes the moment of truth. In choosing a self-directed education over a traditional one, I believe I prioritized substance over form. Now the question is: Will you interview me?

I hope that you'll appreciate my having developed an outside-the-box learning plan, that I was assertive enough to make it happen, and persistent enough to see it through to completion without a professor and deadlines forcing me to do so. Perhaps more important, in working at the elbow of top hardware marketing executives, I learned a tremendous amount about how to do the job well.

I recently discussed my You U. education with an MBA holder from Stanford, and he said that I probably learned more of real-world value than he did.

I'm hoping you will call me for an interview, but as any good employee, I won't just passively wait. If I haven't heard from you in a week, I will take the liberty of phoning to follow up.

I enclose samples of the deliverables I produced during my work at HP and Cisco. Thank you for your consideration.

Sincerely,

Christopher Wah

Figure 5-1:
A letter like this can convince an employer to hire you without a specific degree.

Two cool compromises

A certificate program is often a good compromise between You U. and a degree program. For a master list, see `certificates.gradschools.com`.

For blue-collar professions, formal apprenticeships sponsored by a union or state government represent another good option. Lots of supervised hands-on learning, punctuated by practical, low-cost community college classes — and you earn while you learn. Interested? Check out the federal government's clearinghouse of apprenticeship information: `www.doleta.gov/OA/eta_default.cfm`.

This letter makes clear that the candidate both learned more of practical value than in most graduate programs and, perhaps more important, was a take-charge person — precisely what many employers look for in an employee with an advanced degree.

Would you interview Christopher? Even if other applicants had Ivy League degrees? During a speech, I asked the 300-person audience that question. Almost everyone raised his or her hand. On my radio show, I asked the same question of the associate dean of the U.C. Berkeley Business School, and even he agreed that he'd interview Christopher.

Engaging in Lifelong Learning

Lifelong learning has become a cliché, and it can sound exhausting — forever upgrading yourself until you retire. But there's an upside. In past generations, after years on the job, many people felt bored — like they had been there, done that. There always have been new things you *can* learn, but now to survive, you probably *must* learn them. Consider staying permanently enrolled in You U. That can mean one or more of the following:

- ✔ Join or form a group of your peers that connects live or electronically, to discuss problems and solutions.

- ✔ Don't let the monthly issues of the magazine from your professional association stack up.

- ✔ Attend at least one professional conference a year.

- ✔ Find one or more mentors. Times have changed. A mentor/protégé relationship used to be a one-at-a-time, time-intensive deal. Today, such a relationship is likely to be more fluid. You call with a question, exchange e-mails on a new development, and occasionally commiserate over a cup of coffee. Ideally, you'll have a few mentor relationships, some in which you're the mentor, others in which you're the protégé.

Chapter 6

Degree-Based Career Preparation

. . . .

In This Chapter

▶ Finding the right program

▶ Getting into a hard-to-get-into college or grad school

▶ Paying for your education

▶ Making the most of your back-to-school stint

. . . .

*A*t its best, a back-for-a-degree stint in school can be a blast: Taking time out from the real world, learning stuff you're really interested in, meeting lots of interesting fellow students, and mentoring with a wise professor who takes you under wing and lines up a cool job for you after graduation. That ideal is too rarely realized, but this chapter shows you how to maximize your chances.

You may be able to land a cool job without going to school; in fact, I recommend trying this option before you opt for a college or grad school stint. Check out Chapter 5 for more details on degree-free career preparation.

Choosing the Right Program

When going back to school, finding the right program is usually more important than finding the right college. Here's how to do just that.

Identify your career niche

Don't make the mistake of thinking to yourself, "I'll choose my career niche in school." That rarely happens, or if it does, you're usually choosing based on unimportant criteria such as "that professor's course was interesting."

So please choose a career niche before choosing the institutions to apply to. The *Cool Careers Yellow Pages* in Chapter 2 describe neat niches for hundreds of careers. Need more help? Read, and talk with people in your field. Chapter 4 gives you guidance on doing research and contacting people.

Identify programs in your niche

Here are some ways to find the right program for you:

- Massive searchable databases of degree programs are offered through Web sites like `Petersons.com`, `gradschools.com`, and `www.usnews.com/usnews/edu/college/tools/search.php`. The latter has a separate database of all the nation's community colleges. A community college can often be a smart choice for career preparation — even if you already have a bachelor's or graduate degree.
- Compare offerings at your local colleges by visiting their Web sites.
- Your field's professional association may list relevant programs.
- The military offers top training for a wide range of careers. And not only is it free, but you also get paid to learn. See `www.militarycareers.com`.

That should take care of your initial screening, but how do you find a great program and one that's right for you? Read on.

Assess the program's quality

Talk with graduating students or with recent graduates. Talking with its customers is a great way to assess a program's quality.

How can you do this? If the college is far away, you may be able to e-mail students through the college's Web site. If it's nearby, sit in on an advanced class that includes students who have almost finished the program. At the end of class, go up to a group of students and ask, "Do you like the program?" and "What are the best and worst things about it?"

How do you get to sit in on a class? Just phone or e-mail the instructor and ask permission.

When you contact the instructor, ask questions such as, "What should I know about the program that might not be in the official program description?" or "What's this program's actual average time to completion?" Some programs report the "expected" time to completion, but not the time it takes the average student, which can be years longer.

Also, find recent graduates of the program in the alumni directory, which is often available on the college's Web site. If it's not there, ask the department's administrative assistant to persuade a few recent graduates to phone you. Recent grads are in a great position to assess their degree program's value.

Read through the official materials

Although a college's Web site is the electronic equivalent of a sales brochure, you can usually find much of value there. For instance:

- ✔ Find out whether a program's emphasis matches your interests. You don't want a psychology master's program that focuses on Freudian theory when you think it's a bunch of hooey.

- ✔ How many full-time professors teach in the program? A small department can mean too few choices.

- ✔ Do the required courses sound interesting? How about the assignments? Will the workload allow time for respiration? To find out, check syllabi. They're often on the college's Web site or available from the department administrative assistant.

Calculate the program's true cost

The listed tuition may be irrelevant. As on an airplane, passengers pay different amounts. To find out how much you'll pay, *before applying,* describe your situation to a financial aid officer at the college, and get a written estimate of how much aid you're likely to get that is cash, not a loan. Don't like the answer? Contact the head of the program to which you're applying. See "Finding the Money," later in this chapter, for more about paying for school.

Finding the Right College or Grad School

Many people choose a car more carefully than a college. Would you buy a car without a good test drive or reading *Consumer Reports?* Colleges seem so difficult to judge that many college shoppers shrug their shoulders and rely mainly on the institution's brand name: "Harvard has a great name, so it must be good," or "The Harvard name on my diploma will get me a good job."

Not necessarily.

Before I explain, I feel the need to establish my bona fides here as an expert in higher education. After all, this is a career guide, not a college guide. What I'm about to say is so contrary to what you've been led to believe that if I don't establish credibility upfront, I fear you'll dismiss my advice out of hand. My PhD from Berkeley specialized in the evaluation of education programs, and Berkeley subsequently went on to hire me to teach education evaluation in its Graduate School of Education. I have written three well-reviewed books on higher education and have been a consultant to 15 college presidents. ABC-TV, in its summit on education, introduced me as being "among the nation's leading education consumer advocates, the Ralph Nader of Education."

Okay, enough of that. Now, onto why you may well want to turn down Harvard, even if you can get in.

The problem is that most brand-name colleges derive their prestige from their research, not the quality of education they provide. They hire and promote faculty based mainly on how much research they can publish (usually in a tiny, arcane area), with little regard to how well they teach. Such professors are ideal if you want to become a professor, but not otherwise.

I can hear you now — "But the brand name on my diploma will open career doors!" Yes, a designer label on a diploma is a plus in the job market. But top students may get an at-least-equal advantage by attending a less prestigious college because they're more likely to get practical rather than theoretical instruction, top grades, personal attention, leadership opportunities, and top letters of recommendation.

My own daughter was admitted to Williams College, one of the nation's hardest-to-get-into colleges. Instead, she opted for a less selective (and less expensive) one. Because she was able to excel there, she was noticed by her professors, one of whom gave her a tip on a job in the White House. She ended up working for almost a year in Hillary Clinton's research office. (We have a cool picture of her with Hillary on our living room wall.) Bonus: She got a scholarship she wouldn't have received at a more prestigious college.

Lest you think my daughter is an exception, more than half of the CEOs of America's 50 largest corporations received their college degrees at public universities. Although making career connections is easier at a prestigious college, and one does grow from spending four years around the best and brightest, as you'll see, many, many students, having mortgaged their financial security and that of their parents by attending expensive private colleges or graduate schools, end up feeling disillusioned, even ripped off.

You may protest: "But look at the most successful people! So many came from places like Harvard and Yale." Yes, Ivy graduates are disproportionately represented in top positions, but that doesn't mean the institution caused that. On average, Ivy-caliber students are smarter, come from better schools, and have brighter, better-connected parents. You could lock top students in a closet for those college or grad-school years, and on average, they'll end up with better careers than other people.

A study reported in the *American Economic Review* concluded that *even in terms of earnings,* "What matters most is not which college you attend, but what you did while you were there. . . . Measured college effects are small, explaining just 1 to 2 percent of the variance in earnings." Important things to do while you're in school include selecting a major such as engineering or computer science, choosing professors carefully, getting to know them, making the most of classes and assignments, and finding leadership opportunities. More on all these topics in the section "Making the Most of the School You Choose," later in the chapter.

Loren Pope, in *Colleges That Change Lives,* wrote that 35 years after graduation, "*The New York Times* reported that a quarter of Harvard's class of 1958 had lost their jobs, were looking for work, or on welfare, just when their careers should have been cresting. . . . Many in the class of '58 thought their degrees ensured career success. They were wrong. 'The autobiographical sketches written for the 35th reunion did not radiate with expressions of success and optimism,' said author and Yale professor Erich Segal. 'Quite the contrary, they seemed like a litany of loss and disillusion.' And Harvard was not alone. Alumni groups at other Ivy League schools, the author added, 'are reporting that their members in growing numbers are suffering from the upheavals in corporate America.' If there is a lesson in all this it is that a degree from a college like Harvard is no longer the lifetime guarantee of success in careers that it used to be."

Despite the fact that you can get a good education at non-brand-name colleges, many people choose the most renowned college they can get into. It's understandable. Designer-label colleges attract smart students, so chances are, something will rub off. And some employers — investment banking firms, for instance — tend to round-file resumes from applicants without a "Top 25" diploma. Even with other employers, you may ask, "If I go to Who Knows U., how will I compete in the job market against graduates of Brand-Name U.?" Fact is, the job search strategies in Part III, which most people don't use, can fully compensate for the advantage of a brand-name diploma.

The easiest way into a prestigious degree program

Many prestigious colleges offer a program that makes gaining admission to a bachelor's degree program far easier for people with nontraditional backgrounds (working adults, child geniuses, and so on). These special programs aren't well publicized, so knowing their specific names is helpful. Harvard: Extension School. Yale: the Special Studies Program. Penn and Columbia: School of General Studies. Georgetown: Liberal Studies Program.

Getting in

Only a small percentage of undergraduate programs are difficult to get into. Fact is, most are 98.6 schools — all you need to get in is normal body temperature. (I'm exaggerating only somewhat.) Too, admission to many graduate programs is easier than you might think.

As I've been stressing, just because a college is difficult to get into, doesn't mean that it's better. I liken a designer-label school to a Mercedes. It has a prestigious name and costs a fortune, but ironically, it's more of a hassle (requires more maintenance and has more frequent breakdowns) than inexpensive cars with less exotic names. I must admit to feeling a certain pleasure driving along in my Toyota and seeing some fru-fru fussmobile broken down along the side of the road.

The hassles with selective colleges start with getting in but don't stop there. Professors at selective colleges are likely to care more about their research than about their students. The high concentration of star students also instills fear, inhibiting many students from speaking up in class and turning them into studyholics. Harvard's student health center reported that the second most common student complaint is stress and burnout.

When you were a teenager, you may have been more likely to fall in love with someone because he or she played hard to get. By now, you realize that's foolish. Please apply that mature thinking when choosing a college or grad school. Many people aspire to be admitted to hard-to-get-into colleges mainly because they're hard to get into. Far better to fall in love with a college because of what it is, not how hard-to-get it plays.

My favorite place for adults to earn a credible degree quickly

Thomas Edison State College (phone: 609-984-1150; www.tesc.edu): Called "one of the brighter stars in higher education" by *The New York Times,* the fully accredited TESC grants extensive credit for prior learning, including learning acquired through life experience. You can complete your additional units through any combination of exams, live courses, or distance courses offered anywhere in the United States, including TESC's many self-study courses. To its 11,000 students, it offers associate, bachelor's, and master's degrees. A TESC degree is well regarded. For example, 90 percent of its bachelor's graduates gain admission to their first choice graduate school. The kicker is that TESC is a public college, so the price is right.

It's a buyer's market. Because college selection is often name-driven rather than quality-driven, many non-designer-label colleges and graduate schools, including high-quality ones, can't fill their classrooms — largely because their diplomas don't bear a brand name. The message to you is: Be picky. Most colleges — perhaps even those that will do you the most good — may want you more than you want them.

Getting into killer colleges

Despite all my warnings, suppose you do want into one of the most selective colleges, like Harvard or Yale. For starters, of course, you need top numbers. An A-average or better and being in the 90th percentile or higher on The Test (ACT, SAT, GRE, MCAT, LSAT, or so on) put you in the running. Most applicants to designer-label institutions have numbers in that range, yet only a fraction are admitted. Usually, it's those who *benefit* the institution more. You say: "Me, benefit a college?" Yes, you. Benefits fall into the following categories:

- **The student has potential to do big things.** Those institutions select only the nation's top applicants. Do your accomplishments suggest potential to do big things, like invent something, become a CEO, or be elected to high office? Does your admission essay convey ambition? Are you so well connected (Daddy's on the Ways and Means committee?) that you're likely to have a big impact? Your application, especially your essay, must make a convincing case.

- **The student is likely to particularly enrich the campus community.**

  - A true intellectual can invigorate classroom discussions.

  - A person of color may lend a different perspective to discussions. Some sorts of diversity, however, count less: An Appalachian, a Chinese immigrant, or the child of a brilliant scientist is usually viewed less enthusiastically than "underrepresented" minorities.

  - A person (especially an undergrad) with the ability to play on varsity sports teams or to perform in campus music and drama offerings improves the quality of the college's offerings.

  - An iconoclastic thinker is likely to present unconventional but intelligent ideas in and outside of class. But be careful: Political correctness is rampant on college campuses. Writing an application essay advocating conservative ideas is risky.

- **A professor wants the student.** Here's how you might make that happen: You phone a professor who specializes in a topic of interest. At the end of the conversation, you agree it would be great if you were the professor's advisee and research slave. That professor — usually in response to your request — writes a note about you to the admissions team. No surprise, that boosts your chances of admission.

- ✔ **The student's family has given a bunch of money to the college.** Those students usually receive an edge in admission proportional to the size of the bunch. Generally, this works better at private than at public colleges.

- ✔ **The student is a fine fit for the program to which he's applying.** How do those students benefit the college? If you choose a program because its unusual aspects are just right for you, you're likely to be satisfied and thus more likely to donate money to the college. So if you're applying to Duke's PhD program in biomedical engineering, explain the specific reasons why you prefer it over its major competitor, Johns Hopkins.

Finding the Money

Adults, particularly applicants to graduate schools, have a tough time finding financial aid because government formulas penalize working adults. It's still worth applying because you'll probably get a government-guaranteed loan, and you may use a lifelong learning tax credit, but unless you're a real star or underrepresented minority, don't count on significant cash aid.

Get the financial aid applications early. Some colleges' deadlines are almost a year before the enrollment date. These deadlines are firm. Meet them.

Sometimes worth the effort is applying for a private scholarship — you know, like the David Letterman Scholarship, which is reserved for students just like Dave: C students at Ball State University in Muncie, Indiana. To find private scholarships you may qualify for, use `Fastweb.com`, a database of 1.3 million scholarships. Searching it will likely generate dozens of good fits, but it's usually only worth applying for your few best shots. The odds of winning are tiny, so applying for too many is usually a waste of time. If, however, you're Black, Latino, Native American, or a superstar, applying to 10 or 20 is worthwhile.

Some test-prep advice: Choose a CD, not a course

A note about preparing for The Test (SAT, ACT, GRE, GMAT, LSAT, or MCAT): If you're self-motivated, instead of taking a course, use a CD such as *How to Prepare for the GRE*. Not only is it $20 versus $1,000, but you also don't waste time getting to the test center, and you can have a lesson whenever you want, 24/7. The CD individualizes instruction so you don't waste time on stuff that's too easy or too hard. In a course, that's particularly likely if you're a non-average scorer: below the 40th percentile or above the 90th percentile on a practice exam.

If you're applying to graduate school, don't just contact the institution's financial aid office; contact your specific department's office. Often, it has special funds.

A great source of info and links on financial aid is `www.finaid.org`.

Comparing the Deals

If you apply to more than one institution, before saying yes to one, carefully compare financial aid offers:

- ✔ How much cash will you have to come up with?

- ✔ How big a loan will you have to pay back?

- ✔ If your income stays the same, will your *cash* award be renewed each year, or after they have you, how likely is it that they'll pull the plug?

If your award from your top-choice college seems too low, try to negotiate a better deal. The key is to provide new data that can justify a new decision. For example, can you say that other colleges have offered you better deals? Or, point out that your financial picture isn't as rosy as the financial aid form makes it appear — you have big medical expenses, or your home needs major repairs? Sometimes, sending an itemized budget can make your situation clearer.

Why is college so darn expensive, anyway?

Colleges keep raising tuition. When you count all expenses, four years at a brand-name private college costs $200,000! The government's response: urging us to start saving when Junior is a fetus. Plus the government offers students even more aid, which simply allows colleges to raise tuition even higher — at taxpayer expense.

Why is no one asking colleges to be more efficient? For example, should professors really be earning a nice salary and full benefits for teaching two or three classes a semester and working on research that's useless in the real world? Why aren't interactive video-based online courses, taught by the nation's best professors, used instead of large lecture classes? That would raise quality while lowering cost. For more, see my article, Utopia College, at `www.martynemko.com`.

Making the Most of the School You Choose

Two identical twins could enroll in the same program, yet one twin could have a far better experience. Here's how to make the most of yours.

Find good teachers

A good instructor can make medieval linguistics come alive, while a bad one can turn Rock 'n' Roll 101 into a snooze. When you enroll, be a savvy consumer:

- **Pick the campus's teaching award winners.** The list is usually on the college's Web site or available through its office of academic affairs.

- **Check student ratings of professors.** Some colleges publish the results. Check on the college's Web site, but you may have to dig — some colleges aren't that proud of the evaluations. Can't find them? Call the office of the campus's student newspaper or student government.

- **Ask the department's administrative assistant.** These assistants see the faculty evaluations, and some may even give you an answer other than, "All the professors are good."

- **Check out syllabi.** Often they're on the Web, or the department administrative assistant has them.

- **Look at the required books in the bookstore.** A great way to avoid spending big bucks on textbooks you won't read anyway.

- **Get picks from students or TAs who've been around awhile.** As with any key purchase, it's wise to talk with people who have bought it.

- **Over-enroll.** Plan to take three courses? Sign up for four, attend the first session of each, and drop the worst one. Don't put up with a professor who sounds as bored as a class reciting the Pledge of Allegiance.

- **Choose courses that help prepare you for your profession.** Sure, take that course in Sanskrit linguistics if (for some unimaginable reason) it fascinates you, but in general, keep your eyes on the prize.

- **When in doubt, choose the teacher rather than the course title.** European Epistemology taught by a great teacher is usually better than Human Sexuality taught by a dud.

Read first

If you do the assigned reading, you're more likely to stay awake in class. You're also more likely to participate, which also helps you stay awake. Do I sound like your mother or what?

In class, stay active

If you just sit there, your chances of remembering much after the course is over are about as good as your chances of swatting a fly with a hammer. So ask a question, make a comment. Of course, you'll be hated if your hand is up all the time, so the next best way to be active is to ask *yourself* a question every minute or so. For example, "What's the real-world relevance of this?" or "How might I use this in my career?"

Choose your advisor well

A good advisor can help you find good professors, sign you on as an assistant, become your career coach, line up job leads, ponder the meaning of life with you, and make sure you don't find out three days before you expect to graduate that you're missing Statistics 101. Before settling on an advisor, chat with a couple of candidates whose specialization sounds interesting to you.

Look for one-on-one opportunities

Most people learn best in one-on-one situations. Beyond your advisor, look for opportunities for one-on-ones — even on a one-time basis. See a prof during an office hour, a peer advisor when you have a problem, or a student who said something that aroused your interest.

Adapt assignments to fit you

Where possible, tie term papers and fieldwork assignments into your career plans. If an assignment doesn't turn you on, propose an alternative. You'll be surprised how often the prof says yes.

Build relationships with potential employers

The key to landing a good job after graduation is to develop relationships with potential hirers while still in school. So, get fieldwork and internship assignments at places you may want to be employed. And work hard to impress the person there with the power to hire you.

Network at professional association meetings — they tend to be especially welcoming of student members.

Also, while still in school, e-mail 10 or 20 potential employers, explaining that you would love some advice on how to best prepare so that employers are more likely to want to hire you after graduation.

Don't take crap

A member of the orientation committee at Harvard gave the following advice to incoming students. She advised, "Fix it. If you can't, ask. If someone says no, ask someone else." If you think of this every time a problem arises, you're on the path to college happiness.

Succeeding in school after 40

Many older people contemplating a back-to-school stint worry:

- **"I won't be able to learn stuff as quickly as when I was younger."** For some people, that's true, for others not, but most older students have a secret weapon: maturity. They're more likely to put in the study time and be efficient at it. That usually trumps any decline in learning speed. And if you need help, professors and teaching assistants love when students come in. In addition, many colleges offer special tutoring and workshops for returning students. Another plus for you: Older students are more likely to make wise contributions to class discussion, which makes you a valued class member, and likely to get a good grade.

- **"I'll be the outsider among all those young people."** It's true, at many of the nation's 100 designer-label colleges, most students are 17–22 and some tend, foolishly, to look askance at older students. But most of the nation's 3,500 colleges enroll many adult students. In addition, to help you find kindred spirits, many colleges offer special get-togethers for adult students.

Part III
Landing That Cool Job

The 5th Wave   By Rich Tennant

"My sense is that you're personalizing
your resume too much."

In this part . . .

"Most of us hate to look for work. Period. We want the great job to knock on our front door and say, 'I'm here.' . . . It's the Job Charming fantasy. . . . Most of us also hate to market ourselves. . . . It feels sleazy."

— Cheryl Gilman, *Doing Work You Love*

Good! You've picked out a career. Now you need to find someone good to hire you. This part shows you a proven better way to do just that. It's generally easier and faster than traditional methods, and it doesn't require sleaze.

Chapter 7

Creating the Right Mindset for Job Seeking

In This Chapter
▶ Keeping your spirits up
▶ Beating a fear of failure
▶ Letting go of your anger

A good mindset makes your job search more successful, maybe even borderline fun. In this chapter, I discuss some ways to think about your job search. The keys are learning how to stay upbeat, beat your fears, and get all chips off your shoulder. Read on to find out how to do that.

Staying Upbeat

A job search is a medium-distance race. Get despondent after the first 100 yards, and you're not going to win. This section shows you how to go the distance.

Pretend that you're going to the mall

When you shop, you stroll the mall in search of treasure, asking salespeople for tips. You try stuff on, most of which looks worse on you than on the rack, but it's still fun, like a costume party.

A job search is similar. You're exploring a "mall": your target career's milieu. You look around (by reading, searching the Net, phoning people in likely workplaces, and visiting work sites — as I explain in Chapter 4), ask people for directions to the areas within the "mall" that are most likely to have the job you're looking for, and sooner or later, you find something good.

Thinking of your job search as a mall visit helps create the right mindset: only moderate preparation, plenty of exploration, meeting people, trying stuff on, and enjoying the process, even if you don't end up buying anything (accepting a job offer) for a while.

Picture the benefit

How would your life be better if you got a job? List all the ways. Keep that list on your desk. Look at it all the time. It'll keep you going when those inevitable rejections roll in.

Be playful yet persistent

Some of my most successful clients treat their job search like a game. The motto: "Playful yet persistent." Some experiences, such as a rejection by a dream employer, are unavoidable energy drains, but most experiences are, at least partly, under your control. For example, trying to make a cold call interesting, even playful, can keep you upbeat, even if the call leads nowhere. When the receptionist answers the phone, instead of saying, "Hello, ma'am. I am seeking information about a possible position at your firm," try this: "This may be one of the weirder calls you've gotten in a while." (The receptionist usually laughs and/or says something like, "You wouldn't believe the calls I get." If she says the latter, ask, "What's the weirdest?") Next, say, "Okay. Let me tell you why I'm calling. I've heard great things about your company and I think I would *love* to work there. Can you think of a nice person who might be willing to talk with me?"

For more examples of making your job search interesting, even playful, see Chapter 8.

Fake it 'til you make it

Sometimes, the key to feeling upbeat is to act the way you do when you're *not* ready to pull your hair out. In psychologist's lingo, "Often, behavior change precedes and causes attitude change." In plain English: Fake it 'til you make it. To do so while still being honest, pretend that you're your best self: Think of the hour in your life when you were most confident, most together. Especially at key moments in your job search, pretend you're that best self.

Be real

Being real may seem inconsistent with "fake it 'til you make it," but it's not. It just means not overselling yourself. If you're just a basic, good, hard worker, describe yourself as just that.

If you're not a star, don't try to pass yourself off as one. The thought of having to do all that B.S.ing will stress you out and make you more likely to procrastinate in your search for work. You'll probably sound unnatural and therefore won't be successful. And if, against all odds, you manage to bamboozle someone into thinking you're more capable than you're likely to be, you risk failing on that job and making you and your boss miserable.

So don't make a false impression. Sell who you really are. You'll enjoy your search for work more and be more likely to end up with work you'll do well. Besides — although increasingly this quality is seen to be unimportant — it's honest.

Be in the moment

The following phrase is key to contentment, even during your job search. The phrase: Be in the moment. Stop thinking or looking back or ahead so much. Instead, try to fully immerse yourself in every little task — whether it's the puzzle of deciding what to say in your resume or the challenge of convincing a gatekeeper to let you talk with a prospective employer. At this moment, I'm trying to enjoy the challenge of how to phrase this paragraph so it's helpful but not preachy. (I'm not sure I solved the preachy problem.) Taking life one moment at a time — at least in my opinion — is key to a successful career and a contented life.

Have six balls in the air

When you have a hot job lead, you may be tempted to stop your job search. Fact is, the odds of a hot lead turning into a job are small. So, here's a useful rule of thumb: Have at least six balls in the air at all times. If one falls, find another. Keep six balls in the air for a while and you'll soon be able to stop juggling.

Breathe

Whenever you feel stress, take one to ten deep breaths. Nothing so simple is so potent. A breath

✔ Increases oxygenation to your brain, thereby improving your thinking power

✔ Relaxes your neck and torso muscles

✔ Gives you a break while requiring almost no time

Breathe. Do it now.

Get support

Sometimes, all the strategies in the world can't generate enough fire in your belly. Often, the answer is to gain energy from the support of others, ideally fellow job seekers. Find job-search support groups through your state unemployment department, chambers of commerce, or job search ministries at churches. Here are some Web sites to start you off:

✔ For a nationwide database of support groups, see www.job-hunt.org/ job-search-networking/job-search-networking.shtml.

✔ A number of large cities have branches of the 5 O'Clock Club (fiveoclockclub.com), which offers, for a moderate fee, by-phone or in-person support groups led by a professional trained in a job search methodology similar to what I advocate in this book.

✔ Have a few wrinkles? You may prefer a support group with fellow experienced folks. If so, consider 40 Plus (40plus.org/links). Many state unemployment offices offer similar groups.

Shrugging Off Fear of Rejection and Failure

Do you dread making contacts because you fear rejection and failure? See whether adopting any of the following mindsets helps.

Make a solid effort, and you won't be a loser

Are you afraid you seem like a loser if you ask people for job leads? The key is how you think of it: You're not desperate; you're simply exploring to see whether you can find a more satisfying worklife. People can respect you for that. Many of them wish they had the guts to do the same.

Afraid you seem like a loser if you apply for a bunch of jobs and don't get one? All that means is that you're applying for the wrong jobs — jobs in too tight a market or for which you aren't that qualified. There truly is a job for almost everyone in the world — as long as you don't give up before having made a solid effort. The only thing that makes you a loser is giving up before you really try.

Also, remember that your worth as a human being isn't defined solely by how successful you are in the work world. For whom do you have more respect: a successful lawyer who's sleazy at work and callous outside of work, or a dishwasher who's ethical at work and kind to everyone?

Recognize that you have skills

Sure, the want ads make it seem like every job requires you to be a techno-geek, but the fact is that most jobs, especially nontechnical ones, aren't advertised. Many, many good jobs require mainly those generic skills we take for granted: intelligence, people skills, organization, communication, and reliability. Want two examples?

- ✔ David Wolper, who was the producer of *Roots,* the *1984 LA Summer Olympic Games,* and *LA Confidential,* and who brought Jacques Cousteau to TV, admitted to me that his main skill was talking to people on the phone.
- ✔ Recently, my wife, Dr. Barbara Nemko, was named her region's Schools Superintendent of the Year, beating out 100 competitors, and she insists the key to her success is just plain common sense.

These examples aren't exceptions. Thirty-eight million managerial positions exist in the U.S., and most of them don't require the ability to program in Java, perform chemical assays, or create a blueprint using *AutoCAD.* They mainly require some combination of people skills, organization, communication, reliability, integrity, and the ability to learn quickly. Don't you have at least some of those skills? So, go forth and show prospective employers that you do.

Ask yourself "What would God think?"

Ask yourself, would God — or if you're an atheist, your higher self — think you should contact that potential employer? Knowing that even God would urge you to go after that job can give you the strength to shrug off fear of rejection.

Think of your contacts as library books

When you're at the library looking for information, you pick a book off the shelf, glance through it, and if it isn't helpful, you simply move on to the next book. Try to think of each person you contact in your job search like a book in the library. If one person isn't helpful, simply go on to the next one, with no more emotion spent than if that person were an unhelpful library book.

Know that batting .050 is good enough

The good news about a job search is that you need to find only one good job. It's not like baseball, in which you need a good batting average. I like Tom Jackson's description of a job search in *Guerrilla Tactics in the Job Market:*

NO. NO. NO. NO. NO. NO. NO. NO. NO. NO. NO. NO. NO. NO. NO. NO. NO. NO. NO. NO. NO. NO. NO. NO. NO. NO. NO. NO. NO. NO. NO. NO. NO. NO. NO. NO. NO. NO. NO. NO. NO. NO. NO. NO. NO. NO. NO. NO. NO. NO. **YES**.

Stay cool

Imagine two gold miners. Each time the first miner tries a vein that turns out to contain nothing but rock, he gets frustrated. The other miner, knowing he needs to strike gold only once every 50 times to make enough money, stays cool. Is there any question as to which miner ends up making more money? Any question as to who is a happier person?

Pretend that rejection is a blessing

Look at a rejection as a blessing in disguise. It may keep you from a job that is wrong for you. At least think that way.

Envision the worst that could happen

Picture the worst cases: embarrassing yourself in an interview for a cool job, sending out a bunch of job applications and never hearing from any of the employers, plugging away for six months and still not getting a job. Ask yourself, in the larger scheme of things, even in that worst-case scenario, can you survive? Can you develop a Plan B?

For folks who are 40-plus: Be proud of your experience

Many older workers especially fear rejection and failure, seeing them as confirmation that they're over the hill. They may be insecure because they don't look as good as that 20-something hottie or aren't as techno-savvy as people fresh out of college who've been playing with technology since they were toddlers.

Those fears may be legitimate, but remember that employers hire thousands of older people every day. And that's not because employers are charitable. Employers hire older people because older people have more experience, which is a great teacher. Too, employers know that many older people are more reliable: They may have a stronger work ethic and be less likely to come to work exhausted (or call in sick) because they were up all night partying or calming a crying baby. Yes, some employers may want younger employees, but many others will appreciate you *because* you're older. So, wear your gray hair proudly. (Or dye it.)

Help yourself cure a deep-rooted fear of rejection

How you handle stressful situations, such as those that come up in a job search, may be affected by your family. For example, as a child or spouse, were you considered stupid? Made to feel guilty for speaking up? Expected to live with scarcity? Disliked by your parents? Were your role models inadequate: For example, did you have a lazy or short-tempered spouse?

Solution: Every time you feel uncomfortable during your job search, in a memo pad, write down

- What happened
- What you're saying to yourself
- A family-rooted explanation for your feeling badly (if there is one)
- How you behaved as a result
- What, if anything, you want to do differently next time

Sometimes, fear of rejection is exacerbated by physiologically rooted depression. If, even in the absence of a specific problem, you persistently feel sad, hopeless, guilty, and have a lack of interest in most activities, treatment — brief cognitive therapy, increased exercise, plus a selected-for-you antidepressant — can often be very helpful. For more on depression, check out www.nimh.nih.gov/HealthInformation/depressionmenu.cfm.

Getting That Chip off Your Shoulder

Upon probing, a number of my clients admit resenting having to look for a job:

- Some people are bitter that they were let go from a previous job. They feel that less competent people were kept, yet they were fired. Or they're amazed that the employer had no loyalty despite their faithful service and friendship.

- Other people think that with their qualifications, a job should practically fall into their laps. Or they've had jobs fall into their laps before and somehow expect it to happen again. Yes, jobs do fall into people's laps, but that can take months or even longer, and that random position is unlikely to be as appropriate for you as a career goal you work hard to select for yourself (see Part I of this book to do just that). Placing your hopes on a great job descending on you like manna from heaven is risky.

- Still other people resent looking for a job because they're frustrated that finding something is taking so long. Fact: Even if you follow the 30-Days-to-a-Cool-Job plan in Chapter 8, the average person takes a few months to actually seal the deal. A job hunt, even when done well, is rarely a sprint; it's a medium-distance run. Knowing that upfront is better than starting to sprint and fading after just a few days of hard work.

No matter how legitimate the reason, a chip on your shoulder hurts your chances of landing a job. Even if you don't actually say, "I'm angry!" people know. The best advice I can give may sound unsympathetic and simplistic, but here it is: If you want to land a job quickly, force yourself to get over it. Don't allow yourself even a moment of anger. It tends to build rather than "get out of your system."

If you can't make yourself get over your anger, try this approach before spending a dime on a shrink. Every time you become aware of a chip-on-your-shoulder thought, in that *instant,* force yourself to replace the thought with a constructive one. Ask yourself, "What's the next one-second task I need to do to line up the work I'm seeking?" That simple strategy works for many of my clients. Frankly, I used that strategy every time I felt overwhelmed with the task of writing this book.

Chapter 8

30 Days to a Cool Job

In This Chapter

▶ Making time to look for a job

▶ Knowing what to do, day by day

*O*f course, there are no guarantees. If you're ability-free and personality-impaired, your job search can take years. But after refining the approach in this chapter over the past 20 years and seeing it work so often, I can look you in the eye and tell you that finding a good job in 30 days is a realistic goal for most people — if you spend those 30 days wisely.

Certainly, many employers take their sweet time deciding which candidate to hire, so after the 30-day mark, you may have to undergo additional interviews or wait until funding has been approved, but after 30 days, you'll have set all the balls in motion.

Before getting started, convince a good nag (perhaps a relative or friend) to allow you to give daily progress reports. The fear of having to answer the inevitable question — "Well?!" — will help keep you on the program.

My colleague Libby Pannwitt urged me to add this statement: "Before beginning, you must shut off all internal voices that say, 'I can't do that,' 'It's scary,' 'Eek,' 'Yes but,' and so on."

It's going to be an intense 30 days, but well worth it. Just picture how you'll feel in that cool new job. Onward.

Finding the Time to Search

Most people, especially those working full time, wonder how they'll find the time to do a job search. The good news is that you can do a lot after work: researching fields and employers, writing your resume and cover letters, even interviewing for jobs. Most employers are willing to schedule interviews before or after work, respecting that you don't want to interview on company time.

Many people waste oodles of time on things they agree are less important than finding a job. Examples:

- ✔ Watching TV.
- ✔ Phoning and visiting friends. (Is it really worth the time to go to your cousin's wedding in Topeka?)
- ✔ Time-sucking hobbies, such as golf, quilting, sports watching, or puttering in the workshop or garden.
- ✔ Zoning out or reading a trashy novel on the commuter train or bus instead of writing job-related letters on your laptop.
- ✔ Hanging out with family. Especially in the short-term, quality, not quantity, family time is what's important.

I'm not asking you to give up these activities forever, but landing a good job can make your life so much better. Put in the 30 days and chances are good that you'll have a better life for years. Isn't that a good deal?

I'm not going to lie to you: The first ten days or so (20 if you're currently working full time) will be intense but worth the effort:

- ✔ You'll complete most of a job search's yucky tasks in less than two weeks. Just keep picturing that cool job you'll get.
- ✔ Unlike when doing a job search in drips and drabs, you'll build momentum, finding yourself on a roll.
- ✔ Having made all your contacts in less than two weeks, you'll have maximized the chances of receiving more than one job offer at around the same time. Having that choice of job offers allows you to pick the one with the best combination of good work, wise boss, pleasant environment, and reasonable compensation. Because of that, this short but intense approach is more likely to lead to career contentment than even having picked a cool career.

At first glance, this process may look complicated. But I promise you that if you take it just a baby step at a time, it's not only doable but also effective, and maybe even sort of fun.

Day 1: Craft a Winning Resume and Research Your Field

The Internet will make creating your resume easier than you may think. Too, the Net will help you identify important information about your field that, even if you're a newbie, will give you the patina of an insider.

Creating your resume

Create your resume using resumemaker.com ($29–$39). It walks you through every step. When you use ResumeMaker, creating your resume is a half-day task, one-day tops.

I find that people have only so much energy they'll devote to a job search. Waste more than a day on a resume and you'll probably end up spending less time on more important job-search activities.

When you start your resume, follow these guidelines:

- ✔ **Decide on your job target.** You can choose something specific (for example, entry-level forensic accounting) or something more general (for example, "a position requiring qualitative research skills"). General, however, doesn't mean, "I'm desperate. I'll take anything."

- ✔ **Incorporate two or three brief PAR stories into your resume.** A PAR story includes a **P**roblem you faced, the intelligent way you **A**pproached it, and its positive **R**esolution.

- ✔ **If you're just starting out, fill your resume with relevant accomplishments at school and in after-school jobs.**

- ✔ **Incorporate praise quotes from bosses, peers, supervisees, or customers.**

- ✔ **Don't worry whether it's one or two pages, just fill as much space as you can impressively and legitimately fill.** Some people, usually later in their careers, can even go three or four pages.

- ✔ **Get feedback on a draft, ideally from people you know in your target field.**

Need more resume advice, like how to deal with the fact that you've been unemployed for two years? See Chapter 9.

If you finish your resume before Day 1 is done, start on the task in the next section. If not, start it tomorrow.

Studying your field of interest

Learn about your target industry or profession. It will be helpful in your subsequent contacts with employers. Sources include the following:

✔ A portal to industry information is at `www.careeronestop.org/jobseeker/Jobseekers_info.asp#JobMarketInformation`.

✔ Find professional and trade associations' Web sites at `www.asaecenter.org/Directories/AssociationSearch.cfm` and `dir.yahoo.com/Business_and_Economy/Organizations/Professional`.

✔ The Web sites `www.vault.com` and `www.wetfeet.com` offer insider guides to leading fields and companies.

✔ Google the industry or profession at `google.com`. Use Google's Web tab, News tab, and Groups tab.

✔ Search `amazon.com`'s database of three million books.

Spend just one to four hours on all this research. Like undue resume primping, more research on the profession or industry at this point is usually overkill. (If you need more help with research, check out Chapter 4.)

Day 2: Concoct Your Pitch and Identify Your Target Employers

This is the heart of the matter. Give the right pitch to enough of the right employers, and you're halfway home.

Coming up with a winning pitch

Craft a 10-second and a 45-second pitch. Each must explain why you're looking for a job, what you're looking for, and proof that you're good and will add value for an employer.

✔ For example, a 10-second pitch may be: "The company downsized, I've always gotten great evaluations, but that's the way it goes. So I'm looking for another graphics designer position where my efficiency will be appreciated."

✔ The 45-second pitch adds information about the kind of job you're looking for and provides credible evidence that you bring a lot to the table. For instance: "When my boss had a client who needed something done fast and well, he always gave me the job. For example, I remember the time when United Way had their annual gala but had forgotten to create the printed program. They called the day before the event saying all they had was raw text and could anything be done? I stayed up until midnight. The next morning, we sent it to the printer, and that night, a program sat on everyone's seat."

But what if you're just starting out? I can hear you wondering, "What could I bring to the table?" Emphasize a skill or experience that would impress your contact. Here's an aspiring nurse's 45-second pitch: "I loved nursing school. It really confirmed that I was meant to be a nurse. I especially loved my fieldwork assignment in the emergency room. I remember one time, five people were brought in, the casualties of a gang fight. I saw the doctors and nurses leap into action. I watched them, fascinated. All of a sudden, they asked me to lend a hand. I only got to hand them instruments and hold the patient in position — I wasn't allowed, by law, to do much until I got my license — but afterward, I said to myself, 'This is where I belong.' By the way, all five guys lived."

Have a ready answer for the question(s) you're most afraid you'll be asked; an example is "Why have you job-hopped so much?" For guidance on how to address such questions, see Chapter 10.

Targeting specific employers

Identify 25 employers you'd like to work for, without regard to whether they're currently advertising any openings. Most job seekers should focus on small, growing companies and government agencies in their target industry within reasonable commuting distance.

How to find such employers? Sure, ask friends and colleagues, but also look for want ads with multiple job openings at a company you've never heard of. Those are usually small companies in growth mode — the ones most likely to be hiring for a wide range of positions. Find those ads by entering your locale on `www.simplyhired.com` and `www.indeed.com`, both of which aggregate listings from thousands of employment sites, including `monster.com` and `careerbuilder.com`.

Check out the following Web sites for specific types of jobs:

- ✔ To find federal agencies with job openings, go to `www.usajobs.opm.gov`.

- ✔ For state and local jobs, go to `www.statejobs.com`.

- ✔ For jobs aimed at those just starting out, see `monstertrak.com`.

- ✔ For jobs aimed at people 50+, see `www.yourencore.com` and `www.seniors4hire.com`.

To find the name of the person with the power to hire you, of course, first check the employer's Web site. If it's not listed there, phone each organization's main number and say something like, "Hi, I'm updating my mailing list. What's the correct spelling of your marketing director's *(or whoever you think would be your target boss)* name? And what's his (or her) direct-dial phone number? And e-mail address?" Enter each employer's contact information in

ResumeMaker's Contact Tracker. If you receive only a person's name, you can often find the contact info by googling the name along with the name of the company, the word "e-mail," and perhaps the company's area code. Or ask the switchboard operator for the mailroom. Those folks have the desired information but not gatekeeper responsibility.

Day 3: Research Your Target Employers

Research the 25 employers you identified during Day 2. Take no more than 15 minutes on each. Just look at the company Web site and then google the employer's name, using Google's Web, News, and Groups tabs. Keep notes on each employee in ResumeMaker's contact tracker. You don't want employers to think that you picked them at random. They want to feel loved.

Days 4–5: Contact Your Network

E-mail or phone the 50 people in your network who are most likely to help you get a job, especially a job at one of your 25 target employers. You say you don't know 50 such people? You're wrong. Consider these sources:

- Past and present co-workers and bosses
- Your professors
- Past and current friends, even back to childhood, and lovers (be careful there)
- Family (Don't forget about your second cousin twice removed. Really. I discuss the power of distant ties later in this chapter.)
- Your professionals: your doctor, lawyer, hairstylist, clergyperson, and so on
- Even someone as distant as a fellow student in your statistics study group 20 years ago

The odds are tiny that any one person will give you a lead that results in a good job offer, but if you contact 50 people, chances are good. Truthfully, it's best if you contact not 50 but 100 people. That greatly increases your chances of getting multiple job offers, so you have a choice. But it's okay; I'll settle for 50.

In the following sections, I show how to make your contacts without taking a lot of time, and with less stress than you may think.

During Days 4 and 5, you also spend time getting responses from the people you contacted, making follow-up calls, and writing thank-you notes. (See a sample of a thank-you note in the later section "Following up.")

Knowing how much networking time you need

I can hear a complaint: "You expect me to contact 50 people in one day?!?!" I forgive you if you take two days to do it, but the average person can, indeed, do it in a day. Salespeople, for example, are often expected to make 150(!) dials a day.

Break it down. Assume you're sending 25 e-mails and making 25 phone calls:

- The e-mails are identical except for a couple of lines to personalize each one. So, each should take no more than five minutes: That's a total of two hours.

- Of the 25 phone calls, you probably get voicemail 15 times. At two minutes each, including dialing time, that's a half-hour. Add ten phone calls, say 15 minutes each, and that's two and a half hours.

You wind up with a total of five working hours. Allowing you an hour's worth of breaks, if you start at 9, you're done by 3. No sympathy.

Making 50 contacts, especially for shy people, can be an odious task, and I find that my clients are a lot more likely to get it done if they just cram it into one yucky day than if they space it out.

E-mailing contacts in your network

I can hear you protesting: "Why in the world would my second cousin twice removed, let alone someone in my statistics study group 20 years ago, help me get a job?" I'll show you: Pretend you were in that study group, and out of the blue, 20 years later, you get the e-mail in Figure 8-1.

Can you see how even a distant tie feels, somehow, close enough? If you did know someone, mightn't you tell Henry about it? I routinely ask that question of the attendees of my job seeker workshops and, invariably, most raise their hand to say yes.

Dear *(Name here)*,

I'd imagine I'm the last person on the planet you'd expect to hear from. You and I were in the same statistics class with Professor Marascuilo at Penn State 20 years ago.

I've been a project manager with a video game company and got great evaluations, but they just sent all the work to India.

I've been reading a book on how to find a job and it urges job seekers to call everyone they know, no matter how distant the tie. So, I'm wondering, by any chance, if you might know someone who might need a good software project manager or could lead me to one. And by any chance, might you know someone at one of these employers? *(Insert your list of 25 target employers.)*

Thank you for considering my request. I love my work and am eager to get back to it.

Sincerely,

Henry Mikulski

Figure 8-1:
You may find a promising job lead with an e-mail to a network contact.

Succeeding on the phone

In *Blink,* Malcolm Gladwell reminds readers that they make a hard-to-change impression within the first few seconds of a conversation. Your tone of voice must be friendly and confident without coming on too strong. Yet you must be yourself. Sounds paradoxical, but it isn't. At different times, people use different voices. Avoid your depressed, I-hate-looking-for-a-job voice. Into an audiocassette recorder, record your friendly, confident-sounding voice, listen to that tape, and use that voice. When you pick up the phone, smile — it comes through. Standing up also can help.

If you're phoning, save any chitchat for the end of the conversation. If you chat upfront, your motive for friendliness may be suspect. Also, by saving the small talk for the end, if the person needs to cut short the conversation, you'll have already finished the important part of the call.

Day 6: Contact Leads

Phone (or e-mail if you're better in writing) a hirer or a connection to a hirer you've obtained from your network. Don't, however, contact anyone at your 25 target employers yet. That's for later, when you've seen whether anyone in your network knows someone at those firms. (See the section "Day 9: Contact Your Target Employers" for more information.)

In the following sections, I explain how to ease into making contact, how to reach the people you're seeking as quickly as possible, what to say when you reach them, and how to follow up.

The most important idea to keep in mind with every contact: *Be persistent but likable.* Please remember this phrase. These two words are keys to a successful job search: *Persistent. Likable.*

Making contact when you have cold feet

Before calling a lead (including an actual employer), role-play a call with a friend. Then call your *lowest*-priority potential hirers, your throwaways — you're going to mess up on your first few. After you've had a couple of good phone calls, move up to your top-choice employers.

Afraid you'll stumble on the phone? A few mess-ups may actually make you *more* credible. When I started out on radio, to avoid stumbling, I scripted much of what I said. Boy, did I sound perfect — too perfect. Reading a script stripped away the human connection that's key to a successful interaction. Now, I simply start talking, and only when I get stuck do I look at the few phrases I've written down to remind me of my main points. Now, after many years on the radio, I stumble more than I did when I started, which makes me seem more human, and in turn, actually connects me better with my audience. So relax. Keep your few talking points in front of you to help you when you're stuck, and, when you stumble, know that it probably won't hurt you.

The first call is the hardest, so don't make just one call per sitting. Set a goal, such as, "I'll take a coffee break after I've made ten calls." I can hear you protesting, "Ten calls! That will take all day." Remember, if you make ten calls, you'll probably get through to only a few people. It takes only one minute to leave a full voicemail message, so the coffee break will come sooner than you think.

Getting through

One of job seekers' greatest frustrations is being unable to get through to the right person. They can't get past a gatekeeper or through voicemail jail, and they leave messages that are never returned.

No method always works, so prepare to be turned down much of the time (that's no big deal). But each of the following strategies increases your chances of getting to speak with the Great and Powerful.

Getting out of voicemail (or e-mail) jail

If you get Ms. Hirer's voicemail, don't be disappointed. Voicemail is your friend. Unless the gatekeeper screens his voicemails and deletes yours, the hirer will get to hear your 10- or 45-second pitch (your choice) — of course, told in your natural, pleasant, and not-stuffy voice. Remember, your first few seconds are key. Here's a sample:

> Hi, this is Ellen Neiman. I'm following up on the letter I sent you last week. I'm the Trenton State graduate who's really interested in selling for the cable industry. If you think I might be of help to you or have any words of wisdom on how I might find a job in this field, I know you're probably busy, but I'd love a call back. My phone number is 510-555-2740. *(Say it slowly.)* That's 510-555-2740. The best times to reach me are today until 5 p.m. and tomorrow morning from 8 to 9. Thanks so much.

To help ensure your e-mail is read, choose an intriguing but honest subject line — for example, "Query from an eager, aspiring salesperson."

Getting past a live gatekeeper

Here's a tough scenario. In this case, Ellen didn't write first, so it's a total cold call, and she got the gatekeeper from hell. Here's how she handled it:

> **Gatekeeper:** Mr. Hirer's office.
>
> **Ellen:** Hi. Is he available? *(The brevity and informal tone suggests she's not an interloper and increases the chances that the gatekeeper will put her through without an interrogation.)*
>
> **Gatekeeper:** Who may I say is calling? *(So much for no interrogation.)*
>
> **Ellen:** Ellen Neiman.
>
> **Gatekeeper:** May I ask what this is in reference to? *(The dreaded question.)*
>
> **Ellen:** I could really use your help. *(An opener that has been known to calm even dragon-like gatekeepers.)* I just graduated from college and am very interested in a sales position in the cable industry. I'm sure Mr. Hirer is busy, but could you see if he might speak briefly with me? Even if he can't use someone like me, maybe he might have a few words of wisdom about where I might turn.

Gatekeeper: I'm sorry, Mr. Hirer is unavailable. If you wish, you can leave a message, but there are no positions open.

Ellen: Could you recommend someone else it might be wiser to speak with?

Gatekeeper: No. *Would* you like to leave a message? I really must go now.

Ellen: Does he have voicemail? Perhaps I could leave him a voicemail.

Gatekeeper: No he doesn't. *Would* you like to leave a message?

Ellen: Thank you, no. I'm tough to reach. When's the best time for me to try back? *(Leaving a message, especially with this gatekeeper, is unlikely to bear fruit. Besides, you want to be sure the call happens when you have your notes in front of you. Better to retain control and call back.)*

Gatekeeper: (Sighs) I don't know. He does stay late occasionally. *(Finally, a morsel.)*

Ellen: Thank you very much.

At least half of all gatekeepers are this useless to you — their job is to protect their boss's time. That's okay. Don't let the grinches get you down. Laugh them off as you would a troll in a video game and move on. Sooner rather than later, a guardian angel is likely to descend.

When to phone back? If the gatekeeper doesn't recommend a specific time, try a *prime time:* a time when the hirer is likely to be at the desk, not in meetings, and without a gatekeeper you need to cajole. Prime times are 7:30 to 9 a.m. and 5 to 7 p.m.

If you're self-employed and looking for clients, try making cold calls. Whenever public relations consultant Michael Cahlin needs business, he simply whips out the phone book and starts calling companies he'd like as clients. He asks them whether they're happy with their PR. Often they aren't, and soon he has several new clients.

Walking in when you have the nerve

Have guts? Try walking in. Here's why it works so well. If someone phones you to ask whether you want to find a home for a new baby, chances are good that you say "No." But if that same baby is dropped on your doorstep, you probably take it in and try to get it cared for. The same holds true for walking in to an employer's office. It's much easier for an employer to turn down a phone call or e-mail than a flesh-and-blood human being.

When I'm in a TV studio waiting to go on the air, I often chat with the producer and camera people. I usually ask them how they got their cool jobs.

Frequently, they say that they went door to door, from studio to studio, until someone said yes. Similarly, when my wife and I came to California, we got in the car and drove from school district office to school district office. She got three job offers within a week. Colonel Sanders started his career by going from restaurant to restaurant asking the owners to try his chicken.

Richard Bolles, author of the classic career guide *What Color Is Your Parachute?,* advises that walking in without an introduction works best for entry- to mid-level jobs; and for blue-collar jobs, walking in is *the* most effective job-search method.

So, if you have the guts, walk in, explain that the company is a dream employer, and say that you'd love to talk with someone who may be able to help you figure out how you could get hired. Always start by telling your 10- or 45-second pitch and seeing whether you can make an appointment for an interview or, if you're really lucky, get an interview on the spot.

If the gatekeeper says no and you're really gutsy, sit and wait until the boss walks past you. That can easily result in wasted hours, but it has worked. (Or maybe that was a movie.)

Such direct strategies may work with small companies, but with larger organizations, it's usually more productive to visit their Web site and e-mail a senior person from there. In those cases, try to contact the person who would be your boss or your boss's boss, but an HR person is okay too. Pleasant persistence can help you prevail.

Speaking to a lead

Whether you leave a voicemail or are speaking with your contact, start with your 10-second pitch, enthusiastically delivered. (Smile on the phone.) Example:

> Hello, Mr. XXXX, I'm a high school teacher who's doing well — my principal gives me top evaluations — but I'm ready to move on to a job where I can spend time with adults, not just teenagers. If you might possibly need someone who's able to explain things simply and is well organized, or if you know of someone who may need a teacher like me, I'd love a call. My phone number is 510-555-7457. That's 510-555-7457. The best times to reach me are between 8 and 10 a.m. and 4 and 6 p.m. Thank you.

If you get the person on the phone, after giving your 10-second pitch, listen more than you talk. If you think it would impress that particular contact, tell one or two of your PAR stories (see the earlier section "Creating your resume" for more details about PAR stories).

If the person you're talking to asks more than two questions (questions are signs of interest), say something like, "You know, if you think it might be helpful, I'd be pleased to come in so you can connect a face to the voice." A face-to-face meeting increases your chances of getting good information and/or a job.

Ask questions about the employer's needs so you can better understand how you might be helpful. If you have an idea, tactfully propose it by saying, for example, "In listening to you, it would seem I could help you by doing X. What do you think?" If he likes your proposal, say something like, "Would you like me to draft a one-pager that summarizes it?"

If the employer isn't interested in you, end the conversation by asking, "What would you suggest I do next? Is there someone else you think I should talk with, an event I should attend, or something I should read?"

Following up

After each call, e-mail your resume, cover letter, proposal, paper on a topic of interest, or thank-you note as appropriate.

If your resume is likely to be weak in comparison with likely competitors for a job, don't send it. Just send a thank-you note. Check out the sample in Figure 8-2.

Dear Mr. Johnson,

Thanks for taking my call yesterday.

I am pleased that you think my experiences at college make me marketable. I do think that my job marketing the campus radio station on the Web taught me a lot that would be valuable to an employer.

And, of course, I appreciate your offering to keep your ears open for a position that may be appropriate for me.

I've already followed up on your suggestion that I contact Jamal Washington. I just called and left a voice mail.

Work aside, it was fun hearing about your new sailboat.

Best regards,

Harry Moskowitz

Figure 8-2: Sending a thank-you note to a lead is a smart idea.

The biggest-steak-in-Texas approach

Dan Kennedy, author of the *No BS Marketing Newsletter,* insists that this version of cold contact is a surefire way to land a job:

✔ Target ten successful entrepreneurs or CEOs of small- to mid-sized growing companies in the field you want to work in.

✔ Research their lives and companies, perhaps just using Google (google.com).

✔ Prepare individual letters to each of your targets, selling yourself — and add, "Someone must have given you your first

chance. I'm looking for someone to give me mine." — and offer to work for free.

✔ FedEx those letters.

✔ If you don't hear from them quickly, pursue them with phone calls, e-mails, ideas, or anything else you can think of to secure interviews.

Kennedy says, "I'll bet you the biggest steak in Texas that within 30 days, you'll be working for one of those 10 leaders."

If you're just entering a field, your resume simply documents your lack of experience. So, instead, along with your letter, submit a short white paper — for example, "Thoughts on what it takes to be a great TV news reporter."

Days 7–8: Answer Want Ads the Smart Way

Many career guides and counselors opine that answering ads is a weak approach to landing a job. But in light of the number of jobs posted on the Net, the new easy tools for sifting through them, new laws and policies requiring the public advertising of jobs, and people getting ever sicker of being "networked," answering ads may be a more powerful tool than you think — especially if you use the techniques I show you in this section.

Answering want ads: An underrated job-search method

The want ads are a more powerful job-search tool than you may have been led to believe. Consider these facts:

✔ **With literally millions of easy-to-search online job ads to choose from, you can focus on those that really fit.** The odds are much smaller that a networking contact will lead to a well-suited job.

✔ **It's fast.** Respond to an ad today and you could be hired within weeks or even days. Other job-search methods, such as networking, typically take months or even years.

✔ **Ads are a legal cheat sheet for job applicants.** Unlike with networking or cold calling, you usually know exactly what the employer is looking for — the job requirements are right there in the ad. So you can tailor your resume, cover letter, and interview to the employer's needs.

✔ **Responding to want ads is more psychologically rewarding than networking because:**

   • You know you're probably applying for an actual job opening.

   • Responding to want ads is less stressful than asking people to help you find a job, or trying to convince an employer who hasn't listed a job opening that she should hire you.

   • Networking and cold calling often involve trying to convince someone to buy something they're not looking for. Unless you're a real sales type, that's not fun.

✔ **Using the want ads is an ideal approach for people who work during business hours.** "When will I find the time to network and make cold calls?" is a frequent cry of working stiffs. In contrast, you can search for and respond to want ads at night and on weekends so you don't have to take time off work. And unlike when you're networking, you don't have to worry if you're having a bad hair day.

✔ **Using the want ads is ideal if you're looking for a job out of town.** The Web contains sites with literally millions of instantly searchable job openings all over the world. In fact, want ads should be an especially large part of an out-of-town job search because you probably don't have many faraway networking contacts.

✔ **Responding to want ads is ideal for people who write better than they schmooze.**

✔ **The want ads are a great place to discover employers who are in hiring mode.** Even if their posted ads don't fit you, contact them and they may create a job for you.

✔ **Want ads can even be useful when you're self-employed.** Use them to identify organizations seeking someone to do work that's right up your alley, and then propose doing the job on a project-by-project basis.

> ✔ **Want ads may be better for you than other job-search tools.**
> Networking works if you have a 500-person Rolodex. Cold-calling dream
> employers works if you're a terrific self-promoter. Unfortunately, most
> people, especially those who consult career guides, aren't like that. For
> most people, responding to want ads feels more doable. Career guide-
> books call networking and cold calling the best job-search techniques,
> but they're useless if you're too uptight to use them. Want ads are a job-
> search tool for the rest of us.

Want ads have long been underrated, and networking overrated, but today,
that's truer than ever. More and more job openings are subject to affirmative
action hiring requirements, so fewer jobs are filled from the "inside." To fulfill
legal requirements, they must be advertised.

Meanwhile, thanks to the Internet, answering want ads is a job-search
method on steroids. Millions of job openings are posted on the Web. You
can search through them to find tailor-made jobs from the comfort of your
home. You can even have personal electronic job scouts on `monster.com`
or `federaljobsearch.com` scour the Net for you 24/7, searching through
those millions of job openings and delivering the best fits on a silver platter
right to your electronic door. All free to you! Now tell me that's not cool.

Deciding how much to use the want ads

Other career guidebooks give everyone the same advice: Use want ads spar-
ingly. But one-size-fits-all advice rarely does fit all. So how much should *you*
use want ads? Some people should devote no time to scanning the want ads;
others should devote more than half of their job-search time. To tell what's
right for you, check out the following questions. The more you answer *yes,*
the more you should use want ads:

> ✔ Are you better at writing resumes and letters than at networking?
>
> ✔ Are you more likely to answer ads than to network?
>
> ✔ Do you know only a few people in your field?
>
> ✔ Are you new in town?
>
> ✔ Are you expecting a salary of less than $70,000?
>
> ✔ Is your target job in demand?
>
> ✔ Are you currently employed in or near your target field?

Despite the advantages of want ads, few job seekers should devote all their job-search time to answering ads. More than half the jobs, in all fields and at all levels, are never advertised. So spend some time contacting target employers even if they have no listed openings, and tell people in your personal network what sort of job you're looking for — especially if you're trying to break into a new field. Employers don't have to advertise to find someone without experience. They can get candidates by asking their current employees, friends, or cousin Gomer. (See the earlier section "Days 4–5: Contact Your Network" for more details.)

Not sure whether the want ads will work for you? Craft good responses to perhaps 20 carefully selected ads. If you get no positive responses, you have your answer.

Starting to answer ads

Visit each of your 25 target employers' Web sites and apply for any on-target jobs. Start your cover letter by mentioning your referrer, if you have one. Then — and this is crucial — explain, point-by-point, how you meet the requirements stated in the ad. Include a sentence or two that capitalizes on the knowledge you obtain in Day 3 about that employer. (*Cover Letters For Dummies,* 2nd Edition, by Joyce Lain Kennedy [Wiley] has everything you need to know about cover letters.)

Your goal is, by the end of Day 8, to have applied for ten openly advertised on-target jobs. You probably won't find ten on those 25 target employers' sites. Find the rest on employment Web sites. Particularly look at niche sites aimed at your profession. For a list of those, see www.rileyguide.com/jobs.html. But also consult indeed.com and simplyhired.com, each of which lists millions of openings.

Hunting for job-seeking help with recruiters and agencies

If you're seeking a job for which you have previous experience, contact recruiters, also known as headhunters. Don't consider a recruiter who asks you for money — the employer should pay the fee. To find appropriate recruiters, call the human resources department of a target employer and say, "I'm looking to submit my resume to a recruiter for a *(insert type of job)* position. When you use a recruiter to find that type of employee, who do you use?" You may also consult a directory of recruiters, such as The Directory of Executive Recruiters (`www.selectrecruiters.com/kijs`).

If you're looking for an entry-level position or are changing careers, forget about headhunters. You may, however, contact a few employment agencies. The difference between agencies and headhunters is that agencies generally focus on lower-level positions, especially temporary ones. Look in your Yellow Pages to find on-target agencies. Again, if an agency asks you for money, hang up. The employer should pay the agency.

Unlike other cover letters, when writing to an employment agency or headhunter, include your salary requirement. State it as a range, such as "$58,000 to $68,000, depending on the nature of the position." (*Cover Letters For Dummies,* 2nd Edition, by Joyce Lain Kennedy [Wiley] is a fine resource on writing cover letters.)

Also tell the agency or headhunter that you don't want your resume sent to an employer without your permission. Otherwise the recruiter could blast your resume to ten zillion employers and demand a hefty commission from the one who hires you. That could add $20,000 to the employer's cost of hiring you. That's often enough to make the employer move on to another candidate.

Day 9: Contact Your Target Employers

At each of your 25 target employers' Web sites, look for an on-target job to apply for. If you can't find one, e-mail a person who potentially could hire you or someone one level above that. Try to contact the person who would be your boss or your boss's boss, but a human resources person is okay too.

In the situation in Figure 8-3, the job seeker isn't clear about what kind of work she wants to do. Most career counselors would say, "You're not ready to contact employers. Go back and figure out what you want to do first." But I find that many people, despite all efforts, remain open to lots of jobs. They're better off sallying forth and telling the truth. Figure 8-3 is the kind of letter an open-minded job seeker may write.

Dear Mary,

Tom Hawkins suggested I contact you. I have long been fascinated with fragrances and imagine that working in a perfumery would be wonderful.

I'd guess that I could do more than one thing for you, so I thought I'd share a few things I've done. Perhaps the following will enable you to see how I might help you:

* I helped turn around the shipping department at McFallon's Wholesale Nursery. I developed a new system, hired great people, and created an environment in which everyone — well almost everyone — wanted to work hard.

* I developed the Web site for a little home business — see www.rosefragrances.com.

* I received a grant from Exxon to create a catalog of South Carolina's wildflowers. It was an amazing experience.

Am I deluding myself *(Yes, that phrase works)* into thinking that I might be of help to you even though I lack direct experience in a perfumery?

If you think I might be worth interviewing, or if you simply have a little advice for me, I'd love to hear from you. My number is 510-555-3888, and the best times to reach me are between 8 and 9 a.m. and 5 and 6 p.m.

Sincerely,

Monica Pataki

Figure 8-3:
Be honest when you contact a target employer.

The method in Figure 8-3 works so well because you get to be considered without having to compete with zillions of other applicants. And it can work fast — create good chemistry and show up at the right time, and you can get a job offer pronto. You may balk at the phrase, "Am I deluding myself?" but it actually works. Try it.

Most people are more effective in cold contact if they e-mail first and follow up with a phone call. But if you feel that you'll be more persuasive in a cold call, feel free to phone first and follow up with an e-mail. And if you're really gutsy, especially for low-level positions, walking in can be the most effective approach of all.

For more information about contacting target employers, use the methods that I describe in the earlier section "Day 6: Contact Leads."

Days 10–11: Follow Up

If, within a week, you haven't heard from the people you contacted, call to follow up. Don't hesitate to leave a voicemail. If, for example, you had cold-contacted an employer, say something like this:

> "I'm *(insert your name),* the manager at the Big Whup Widget Company who was just part of a downsizing and phoned you. I'm assuming that not having heard from you, you're too busy to respond. I can understand. But I know that sometimes, things can fall between the cracks, so I'm taking the liberty of calling to follow up. If you or one of your managers is interested in talking with me or have any advice as to where I should turn, I'd appreciate a call. The best times to reach me are *(insert)* and my phone number is *(repeat the number twice).* And my name, again, is *(insert name).* Thank you."

Of course, you won't hear back from most of the people you contact — even from employers whose ads you're responding to — but you're likely to get at least one bite. Often it's from an employer who has been thinking about hiring but hasn't gotten to that laborious process yet. Sometimes, an employer finds it easier to just vet you and be done with it.

Days 12–30: Interview and Land That Cool Job

Congratulations. You set in motion everything you need to do to land a job. During Days 12 through 30, you should be getting responses, leads, and interviews. Hopefully, you'll also start negotiating for a cool job. In this section, I briefly describe the interviewing and negotiation processes.

Here are a few other tasks you can do during Days 12 through 30:

- ✔ Follow up a second time with people who didn't respond to your initial follow-up query. That second follow-up usually is well worth it, because the potential employers are feeling guilty about not having responded despite your persistence.

- ✔ Twice a week, revisit employment sites to find on-target ads. Of course, also apply to on-target jobs e-mailed to you by the electronic job scouts you signed up for. (I cover want ads earlier in this chapter.)

You know your job search is on track if you have at least six live prospects, including, for example, a person who doesn't have a job opening now but asks you to check back in a month.

Interviewing

Tips for job interviews include the following:

- ✔ **Before the interview, reread the research on the firm from Day 3.** Perhaps do some more. You can, for example, call the receptionist, explain that you have an interview scheduled, and ask whether he can direct you to any material about the organization that's not on its Web site but that could help you prepare.

- ✔ **Have ready a few PAR stories.** A **P**roblem you faced at work, how you **A**pproached it, and its positive **R**esolution. Pick those you think would impress that particular employer. (See Chapter 9 for more about PAR stories.)

- ✔ **Early in the job interview, ask a question or two that helps guide your responses throughout the interview.** Examples: "What attributes end up being most crucial on this job?" or "What's an important task I'm likely to be asked to do in the first few weeks on the job?"

- ✔ **Ask whether the job description has been fully mapped out or whether it depends on the candidate.** If it's the latter, you have a golden opportunity: Play consultant and see whether you can identify employer's problems that you could solve. That could encourage the employer to recast the job in your own image.

- ✔ **If possible, demonstrate that you can do a key task.** For example, for a sales position, demonstrate how you'd try to sell the product. If you're applying for a training position, demonstrate how you'd teach a concept. Providing a job sample can convince many employers that you're capable of doing the job even though you have no experience.

Some employers, especially in unionized or government workplaces, require all candidates to receive an identical interview, so you may not be allowed to ask questions or do a demonstration until the end. Don't force it.

- ✔ **Especially if your job history suggests you're underqualified for the job, try to move the discussion away from your past and to the future.** Ask about the job's tasks and explain how you might tackle them.

- ✔ **E-mail a thank-you note the same day.** Sounds obvious, even corny, but many employers see it as a sign of motivation and professionalism. (I give you a sample thank-you letter in the earlier section "Following up.")

- ✔ **Follow up three days later.** Say something like, "I'm quite interested in the job, so I'm calling to follow up. May I ask where I stand?" If you aren't number one, ask whether there's anything that makes the employer hesitant to hire you. Offer to submit additional material, such as a short proposal outlining how you'd address a problem the organization is facing.

For more on interviewing (for example, a list of ways to create chemistry with an interviewer), see Chapter 10.

Negotiating

When you get the call offering you a job, don't negotiate terms on the phone. Make an appointment for a day or two later. That subtly makes clear that you won't accept just any offer.

Prepare for the negotiation by creating a list of comparable salaries for the position. You can often get these from www.rileyguide.com/salary.html, from trade publications, or from local employment agencies that specialize in your field.

In the negotiation, if appropriate, first try to get the job description upgraded to greater responsibility. That can justify a higher salary. And don't settle for a dead-end job at a no-name employer. Hold out for a *launchpad job:* one offering the chance to learn important skills, ideally for a well-known employer. My daughter's first job was in the White House. That was the good news. The bad news was that her job was to answer letters to Socks, the Clintons' cat. Before she got typecast as a low-level employee, she told her boss, "I'm willing to pay my dues, but I'm a pretty good researcher and writer, so I'm wondering if I could be more useful doing something else." Soon, she was working on Hillary's daily briefing.

What If, After 30 Days, You Got Zippo?

If the *30 Days to a Cool Job* method doesn't bear fruit for you, your best bet is to repeat the process with a different job or industry target. Or seek assistance from a private career counselor or government-sponsored "One-Stop." (To find your local One-Stop, go to www.servicelocator.org.) Perhaps some mock interviewing with a pro can help.

But if you follow the plan, you're miles ahead of most job seekers, and I'm betting that you'll land a cool job.

Chapter 9

Crafting the Right Resume in Less Time

In This Chapter

▶ Writing a resume in a few hours, not a few weeks

▶ Putting together a just-right resume in 11 easy steps and 1 hard one

*C*reating a resume is a great first step in your job search. It usually helps you realize that you've accomplished more than you think. Plus, it distills your accomplishments into impressive sound bites you can use in networking (see Chapter 8) and interviews (see Chapter 10). Purists may sniff, but this chapter contains my client-tested, not-too-fussy, not-too-lazy, just-right guide to creating a plenty-good-enough resume. To use this approach to maximum advantage, use it with www.resumemaker.com ($29 for students and entry-level workers, $39 for more senior people).

Despite my efforts to make do-it-yourself resume making straightforward, some people want a human hand holder. The person I refer clients to is Beth Brown (www.susanireland.com/writers/bethbrown.html). If someone wants a resume for a federal government job, I refer them to Kathryn Troutman at www.resume-place.com.

Spending a Limited Amount of Time on Your Resume

Yes, your resume should demonstrate competence and create chemistry. Yes, it should be formatted for easy reading. Yes, it should avoid errors in speling (just kidding). Yes, tweak it a bit for each individual employer. But no, it's not worth taking the time to craft your resume as carefully as a prenuptial agreement. A resume, created efficiently, is a few-hour, not a few-week, activity. Jobs are rarely won because of the tweaking done beyond those first few hours.

Remember, many of today's employers usually use resumes only for a quick screen — average inspection time is 15 seconds. Why? In part because employers know they can't trust resumes: More than one-third of resumes contain inflated credentials, and even the honest ones can't be trusted. Thanks to rev-up-your-resume books, chapters like this one, software, and resume ghostwriters, a resume may better indicate whether a candidate got help on her resume than whether she can do the job.

So put your job search time where it counts — in putting yourself, your letter, work sample, and maybe your resume in front of the right people.

Notice that in the previous sentence I said, "*maybe* your resume." Why? Because unless your work history is likely to be superior to that of most other candidates for your target job, you're better off hitching your prospects on your letter, work sample, and perhaps a bio, which is a brief listing or narrative of your highlights. Yes, some employers will reject you for not submitting your resume, but many others won't look askance, and when the day is done, you'll probably get a good job quicker with no resume than with a mediocre one.

If you're looking for work as a self-employed individual or small business, never use a resume. Use a bio, portfolio, or presentation kit. Why? A resume makes you look like an employee who can't find a job, not a business owner.

Step 1: Write Your Name and Contact Information

Even with something as basic as your name and contact info, there are do's and don'ts:

- ✔ Put your name, address, phone number, and e-mail address on separate lines. Otherwise, computers may read the info as one long string, and, poof, your contact information is lost.

- ✔ List your home address. If possible, list a street address rather than a post office box. It presents a more stable image.

- ✔ Include your home and cellphone numbers. You're probably wise, however, not to include your work phone and e-mail address. Sure, that makes you more accessible, but it also suggests that you're job hunting on company time. (You wouldn't do that, now would you?)

- ✔ Don't have a home e-mail account? Plenty of free ones are available. My favorites: `gmail.com` (Google's e-mail service) and `mail.yahoo.com`.

✔ If you have a Web site or blog, list it. It's a good place to display your work samples and post your resume. Think twice if your site or blog's address is `deathtotheestablishment.com` and features your grunge band photos.

Don't have a site? Maybe this is the time to get one. The free site builder at `www.homestead.com` lets you create a good-looking, functional site in no time. And the site-hosting fee is just $9.99 a month. Setting up a blog is free and even faster, plus there's no hosting fee: go to `www.blogger.com`.

Step 2 (Optional): Write Your Objective

If you'd consider a wide range of jobs and would rather your first impression stand or fall on your Highlights section (see Step 9), then you don't need an objective. Include an objective only if you have a specific job target and would turn down anything else, or if you're tailoring your resume to a specific job opening.

An objective can follow this form: "A position requiring abilities A and perhaps B plus personal attribute Z." For example:

✔ Petroleum geologist position requiring extensive knowledge of computer-based drill site analysis and Alaska field experience, and the ability to work well in isolation.

✔ Psychologist position requiring successful experience with drug abusers and with diverse populations, and the ability to remain calm under stress.

✔ Management position requiring the ability to make good decisions quickly, solid understanding of video signaling technology, and unquestionable integrity.

✔ High school English teacher position requiring successful experience in teaching advanced-placement classes and the willingness to take on extensive after-school responsibilities.

✔ Cushy job requiring a laid-back personality, the desire for a six-figure income, and the willingness to accept it without feeling guilty that it wasn't earned.

Or simply state your target job (for example, high school English teacher), and present your attributes in your resume's body (see the next section).

Step 3: Choose Your Format: Attributes or Chronological

The main headings in an *attributes* resume are — no surprise — your attributes: skills, expertise, or abilities. Figure 9-1 shows an example.

In contrast, a chronological resume's main headings are the jobs you've held, listed in — again, no surprise — chronological order, with your most recent job listed first. (See Figure 9-2.)

Attributes Resume

Maynard G. Krebs
9 Dobie Dr.
Gillis, MN 66696
e-mail: whatmework?@whitehouse.gov

Job Target and/or Summary

Attribute that would most impress the target employer:

Evidence of that attribute #1 and, if available, an accomplishment
Evidence of that attribute #2 and, if available, an accomplishment
Evidence of that attribute #3 and, if available, an accomplishment (optional)

2nd most impressive attribute:

Evidence of that attribute #1 and, if available, an accomplishment
Evidence of that attribute #2 and, if available, an accomplishment
Evidence of that attribute #3 and, if available, an accomplishment (optional)

3rd most impressive attribute:

Evidence of that attribute #1 and, if available, an accomplishment
Evidence of that attribute #2 and, if available, an accomplishment
Evidence of that attribute #3 and, if available, an accomplishment (optional)

Work History

Most recent employer, job title, dates of employment
Next most recent employer, job title, dates of employment
Next most recent employer, job title, dates of employment

Education

Personal Interests

Figure 9-1:
An attributes resume lists your skills and expertise.

Chronological Resume

Maynard G. Krebs
9 Dobie Dr.
Gillis, MN 66696
e-mail: whatmework?@whitehouse.gov

Summary

Professional History

1998-present Title, employer

Accomplishment that would most impress the target employer
2nd most impressive accomplishment
3rd most impressive accomplishment (optional)

1996-1997 Title, employer

Accomplishment that would most impress the target employer
2nd most impressive accomplishment
3rd most impressive accomplishment (optional)

1993-1996 Title, employer

Accomplishment that would most impress the target employer
2nd most impressive accomplishment
3rd most impressive accomplishment (optional)

Education

Personal Interests

Figure 9-2:
A chrono-
logical
resume lists
the jobs
you've held.

Almost all employers prefer a chronological format, so consider an attributes format only if you've never held a job related to your desired position: for example, you've always been a supermarket bagger and now are seeking a job as a physics teacher.

If you're concerned about your boss discovering that you're looking to leave, your resume should indicate that you're employed by, for example, a major consumer products company rather than by, say, Procter & Gamble. That can avoid, for example, getting caught by your human resources department searching the Net for resumes with the words "Procter & Gamble" to see which employees are looking to leave.

Step 4: Select a Specific Resume to Use as a Model

Resumemaker.com contains a large collection of model resumes. Pick one that

- ✔ Uses your chosen structure — attributes or chronological
- ✔ Has content relevant to your target job
- ✔ Uses language and has a feel you like

Use that resume as a template. In addition, keep handy one or two more of your favorite model resumes as sources of phrasing or inspiration.

Step 5: Draft a Resume that Builds on Your Model Resume

This step is the hard one. I do my best to make it as easy as possible.

A survey of 1,133 resumes by ResumeDoctor.com found that 42.7 percent of resumes contained false information. So, it's not surprising that ever-more employers are verifying information. Ninety-six percent of 2,500 HR professionals surveyed by the Society for Human Resources Management said their companies *always* check references, credentials, or both. So, don't exaggerate on your resume. It may well come back to bite you. Besides, do you really want to beat out a more qualified candidate by lying?

In the following sections, I show you how to build the body of your resume with accomplishments, skills, and careful wording.

Listing impressive accomplishments

For each of your past jobs, list two or three of your accomplishments that would most impress your target employers and, importantly, are the kind of work you want to do (or at least wouldn't mind doing) on your next job. Limiting yourself to just two or three accomplishments makes it more likely that the employer actually reads your most important points. It also makes the reader curious to know more. To find out more, he or she has to do precisely what you want — interview you.

Before you send your resume to a particular employer, review it to see whether the accomplishments you listed would most impress that employer. If not, see whether you can come up with more appealing ones.

Plan on keeping your resume to one or maybe two pages. Okay, okay. If you can fill three or even four pages with accomplishments that would impress your potential employer, go for it.

The general rule is to write only about the jobs you've had in the last ten years. But if going back further would make you look better to your target employer, go ahead.

In the following sections, I describe a variety of accomplishments that you can include on your resume.

If your target employer would be more impressed by your school-related accomplishments, focus on those rather than, for example, that summer job driving a beer truck.

Quantitative accomplishments

Quantitative achievements are powerful. Examples:

- ✔ Developed proposal that received $25,000 foundation grant.

- ✔ Spearheaded quality improvement initiative that reduced product defect rate by 15 percent.

- ✔ Only one accident in two years as operations supervisor.

- ✔ Conducted study that resulted in a 20 percent decrease in my employer's phone bills and earned me a cash bonus (which only partly compensated for the personal phone calls you made to your girlfriend in Shanghai).

- ✔ Especially impressive are achievements that compare your performance to a benchmark. For example: Ranked second of 15 salespeople in net profit generated. Of course, you needn't mention that the other 13 were part of the state prison's early-release program.

References and recommendations

Less quantifiable accomplishments in the form of recommendations and compliments are also fine:

- ✔ A quote from your performance evaluation or letter of recommendation: "Tawanda is one of our brightest and easiest-to-get-along-with employees."

- ✔ Successful projects: "I developed a new procedure for assaying immunosuppressants."

- ✔ Increased responsibility: "Within three months, was given sole responsibility for the agency's largest graphic design projects."

- ✔ Compliments you've received from co-workers or satisfied customers. (Don't mention the time you were complimented for finally getting something right.)

Get letters of reference early in your job search. Not only will they be useful as quotes in your resume, but reference letters also are great for sending to prospective employers.

PAR stories

Some accomplishments can be particularly powerfully stated as PAR stories. In a *PAR story,* you describe a **p**roblem you faced, how you **a**pproached it, and the positive **r**esult. Take the accomplishment, "Only one accident in two years as operations supervisor." By itself, it's okay, but here's how it reads as a PAR story:

> When I was hired, three serious accidents had occurred during the previous year. *(Note that this will benchmark the achievement about to be mentioned.)* One man lost part of a finger. I observed and interviewed all the relevant people, and we developed a new plan for reducing accidents. In my two years as supervisor, the company experienced only one accident, a slightly twisted ankle.

My clients have found that anecdotal style effective — it feels real — but some job seekers insist on being more traditional. If that's you, you can write something like, "Collaborated with team members to develop a successful accident-reduction plan, achieving a 20 percent reduction in onsite accidents within first year."

"Soft" accomplishments

To get a job offer, you must prove three things:

- ✔ You can do the job.
- ✔ You will do the job.
- ✔ Your personality fits the organization.

So don't forget about "soft" accomplishments, such as people skills and Boy/Girl Scout attributes like reliability and hard work. If true, include such accomplishments as:

- ✔ Voluntarily worked, on average, a 55-hour workweek. Took only four sick days in three years.
- ✔ Well-liked by co-workers. If they gave an award for employee most likely to be asked out to lunch, it would be me. (Of course, as a result, I now weigh 967 pounds.)

Other accomplishments to list

Still can't think of enough accomplishments? Try these:

- ✔ Think of all the people who benefited from your efforts. What would they say about you? Any statistics you can cite?

> ✔ Sometimes, you can jog your memory by looking at a list of action phrases and verbs. A long list can be found on `resumemaker.com`. In general, use more dynamic verbs such as "spearheaded" and "championed" rather than the bland "managed" or "ran."
>
> ✔ Don't forget about unpaid work or school activities if necessary. If you're including unpaid work, title this section of your resume "Work History" rather than "Employment History."

Including transferable skills

If you're trying to land your first job in a field, your previous experience, by definition, will be less applicable to your target job. The good news is that nearly everyone has accomplishments that use *transferable skills* — those you used in a different context but would also be helpful in your target job.

For example, if you're a new college graduate seeking a job as a TV news reporter, an accomplishment using transferable skills would be that term paper in which you "interviewed 50 students to identify new strategies for an anti-alcohol abuse campaign. Findings were heavily used in the final project design."

Or, say you're tired of being a starving artist and decide you want to become a project manager for an art-related company. Highlight accomplishments as an artist that may be relevant as a content manager; for example, "Curated a student art exhibit, including design, text, and marketing. The event attracted 285 people. A review in the *New Orleans Times-Picayune* called it, 'Bold and fascinating.'"

My favorite example of a transferable skill: A prostitute decided to give it up. What transferable skill did she put on her resume? Excellent customer service. True story.

Compensating for an imperfect work history

Sometimes your work history is less than ideal. But you can present flaws honestly without killing your chances of landing a job. In the following sections, I tell you how.

Unemployment

If you're worried that your current unemployment will hurt you in interviews, consider getting a volunteer or temp job, ideally for a prestigious employer in your desired field. Or set yourself up as a consultant. Before putting consultant on your resume, do have at least one consulting assignment (even if unpaid) so you have an answer when the interviewer asks, "Well, Binky, tell me about one of your consulting assignments."

Job-hopping

If you've job-hopped, give reasons why you left; for example, you were in a temp position, or you had to move because your spouse got a job offer she couldn't refuse.

But sometimes people have more problematic reasons for leaving. If, for example, your boss hated your guts, you might list the reason for leaving as "incompatibility with the company. (My boss insisted on a standardized approach with customers while I found a more individualized approach to be more effective.)" In a case like that, have the objective you create in Step 2 state what sort of employer you want to work for. In this example, you may say, "an employer who encourages employees to innovate."

Little or no work history

You haven't been catatonic all this time (I hope). Even most party-hearty, kickback, down-a-brew types have done enough constructive things to fill a resume, at least a one-pager with lots of white space and wide margins. So, if you don't have a lot of real-world work experience, make a list of your accomplishments: classes you've taken, projects you completed, volunteer work, and so on.

Don't use vague language to hide what you were doing, like the homemaker who wrote: "Operations manager for multi-dimensional enterprise." Such creativity appears deceptive, which is the last thing you want an employer to think.

The late Yana Parker suggested that parents who stopped working to raise their kids be honest, and be sure to include any out-of-home paid or volunteer work. For example:

> 2006–present, Full-time parent. Handled intricate logistics for young children, including other parents' kids, involved in many activities. Plus community work involving fundraising, voter registration, and community service committee work.

A gap in work history

To combat a gap in your work history, list your resume in years rather than months. Fill in the gaps with any education or volunteer work.

That solution, however, doesn't solve David's problem. He worked for a firm that took on too much work with a too small budget, so David burned out and took a yearlong vacation.

My recommendation: Tell the truth. In addition to being honest, the truth can work well. For example:

> April 2006–March 2007, Personal Sabbatical.

> I'd never had a break, and figured while I was still plenty young enough to enjoy it, I'd spend a year on pure pleasure: traveling in Europe for two months, helping my brother remodel his kitchen, taking golf lessons, even cleaning out my basement! And lest you think I was a total slug, I attended a landscape architecture conference, and during a drive through California, visited a half-dozen award-winning landscape architecture projects. I'm now back and eager to get to work.

Are you surprised? A narrative in a resume? And so informally written? Yes and yes. Key to landing a job that you'll be happy and successful in is to tell your *true human story* throughout the process: in resumes, cover letters, cold calls, and interviews. In today's era of the oh-so-sanitized job applicant, a candidate who tells his true human story often stands out as the sort of person the employer wants in her organization. And if the employer doesn't want to hire that sort of person, it's a sign that you don't want to work there.

You may ask, "Shouldn't a story like that go in the cover letter rather than the resume?" Answer: It should go in both. It's wise to repeat crucial material that explains away problems and creates positive feelings about you. Besides, resumes and cover letters have a habit of separating from each other, as when the recipient of your resume and cover letter forwards only your resume to his boss. (Want to know more about cover letters? Check out *Cover Letters For Dummies,* 2nd Edition, by Joyce Lain Kennedy [Wiley].)

Phrasing carefully to get your resume past the computerized gatekeeper

Most large employers electronically scan resumes for words that match their job descriptions. To outsmart the computerized gatekeeper, follow these steps:

1. **Make a list of 20 to 30 words or two-word combinations that you think will most impress your target employer.**

   For example, if you're looking for a job as a biotech scientist, you might list: *protein purification* and *molecular modeling* and such soft skills as *communication.*

   Use nouns rather than verbs: *manager of* rather than *managed* and *programmer* rather than *programmed.* The resume-scanning programs generally look for such nouns.

   Don't know the right keywords for your target jobs? Pick them out of on-target job ads.

2. **Insert into your resume as many of those words as you legitimately can.**

   Don't, however, insert those that don't accurately reflect you. They may get you past the computer screening, but last I checked, companies still use human beings to make actual hiring decisions. And those human beings tend to probe your resume's veracity.

   Also, don't insert keywords that would lead to jobs you don't want. For example, if you have a lot of sales experience, but want to get away from sales, avoid the use of the word *sales* in your resume. Indeed, minimize mention of your sales experience throughout your resume. Your resume should highlight the things you want to do in your next job.

3. **If some keywords don't fit naturally into the body of your resume, list them in a section at the end of your resume entitled, "Additional keywords."**

Step 6: Write the Education Section

Normally, the education section follows the employment section, but list your education first if it's more impressive than your work achievements. This is true of most job seekers just starting out.

Include your grade-point average if it's at least 3.0 in your major or overall. Also include any honors, like Dean's List or cum laude. (No, second prize in your fraternity's belching contest doesn't count.)

If you started but never finished college, simply list your years of attendance and your major. For example:

> 1999–2000, Kegger College, major in sociology.

If you're still working on your degree, write your expected graduation date.

If not obvious from your major, list courses that are particularly relevant to your career goal. Include education outside of school, such as seminars. For example, here's David's education section:

> 2006, Geohydrology issues in shoreline foundations. University of California, Santa Barbara Extension.

> 2005, BS in Landscape Architecture, California State Polytechnic University. San Luis Obispo, 3.3 overall grade-point average, 3.5 landscape architecture grade-point average.

Special career-applicable courses:

Three years of college-level Spanish. (moderate fluency)

Business courses in project management and finance.

If you learned things that may impress an employer, you might add ". . . which taught me X." For example: "BA in political science, which taught me survey methodology, database management, and statistical analysis."

If most of your career-relevant learning occurred outside of school, describe it. Figure 9-3 shows the education section of an aspiring curator with a career-irrelevant major and lots of out-of-school education.

Education

Academic Education

1998, Williams College, BA in political science

Curating-Related Education

1996-1998 Apprenticing/coaching by:

Miriam Weinstein, curator, Williamstown Art Museum

Dave Murphy, curator, Kansas City Museum of Art

Sharon Presley, curator, Chicago Museum of Science and Industry

Professional conferences

American Association of Museums, each annual conference from 1995 to the present

Seminars

The Business Side of Curating: Three-day pre-conference workshop, American Association of Museums, 1996

Exhibit Traffic Planning: Williamstown Museum symposium

1994-present Independent reading: 7 books, 50+ articles (titles on request)

Figure 9-3:
The education section of a resume for a person with plenty of out-of-school education.

Step 7: Decide on Optional Sections

Depending on your situation, add a section for awards, community involvement, publications, computer skills, licenses, or professional affiliations. Only include an affiliation if it's likely to impress your target employers. Fellow of the American Academy of Sciences, yes. Member of Hell's Angels, no.

Step 8: Write the Personal Section

Here, list volunteer activities, personal interests, hobbies, and so on. This section can sometimes be a door opener. Seeing a resume from a fellow backpacker can move an employer to pick up the phone.

Step 9: List Your Highlights at the Top

This is the most important part of your resume. Here, spend time. In the few seconds of attention that your resume may get, this is the only part you can be sure will get read.

You have three options: Most people will choose just one, but if two are more impressive in your case, include them both.

Option 1: A summary of accomplishments

In one line each, list the few accomplishments that will most impress your target employer. Call it a summary.

SUMMARY

Received A.S.L.A. Award as landscape architect on U.S. Highway 1 shoreline restoration project.

Top evaluations from supervisor: "Gets the job done right, plus he's fun to be around!"

Eight completed projects. (See online portfolio at dpwilens.com.)

Excellent customer satisfaction (many references available).

Solid knowledge of AutoCAD 2007 and TrackIt project management software.

Led 12 friends on a trip down the Amazon.

Option 2: A paragraph of attributes

Alternately, you can write a short paragraph describing the things about yourself most likely to impress your target employer. This is a good option if you're a good employee who can't point to specific achievements. The key here is to imagine yourself as the employer. What attributes would he most value that you can honestly claim? Say you're hankering for another general medical-surgical nurse position:

> **SUMMARY:** Four years as general medical-surgical nurse, known for exceptional concern for patients and absolute accuracy in treatment and in providing emotional support. Supervisor wrote, "Jan is thorough and remarkably helpful not just to patients, but to all of us."

Option 3: Your human story

The third option is a short paragraph that quickly tells your human story — what brings you to wanting this job. Weave in the best thing(s) you bring to the table. This is the preferred option if your best shot at the job is making a human connection rather than selling your previous experience.

> **SUMMARY:** I was able to work with a number of patent examiners as an engineer at Loral. As time went on, I became fascinated with what they do. After a year of intensive preparation, I now am eagerly seeking a position as assistant patent examiner.

Often, the most qualified person doesn't get the job. One reason: Another candidate created chemistry. A resume summary and cover letter are excellent ways to give you an edge when your actual qualifications are unlikely to be best-among-the-bunch.

Step 10: Get Feedback

Show your resume to a respected friend and then to a personnel recruiter or potential employer. Make any recommended changes.

John Sullivan, Professor of Management at San Francisco State University, suggests that you have your reviewers circle all the items in the resume that impress them, put an X through all items they don't like, including typos, and a question mark next to all items that confuse them or slow them down.

Step 11: Create an Unformatted Version of Your Resume

The resume you've just created is fully formatted, and in Microsoft Word. You also need to create an unformatted version for pasting directly into an e-mail or posting on an employment site.

You ask, "Why can't I just send the formatted version? Everyone has MS Word." First, not everyone has Word. Also, some employers don't like attachments because they can have viruses and because they take time to open. In addition, many employment Web sites require you to paste elements of your resume into their site's template. It's more likely to look better if it's unformatted.

Don't worry. Creating an unformatted version of your resume is quick and easy. Here's how Margaret Riley Dikel, coauthor of *The Guide to Internet Job Searching,* and resume writer Beth Brown recommend you do it:

1. **Make a copy of your resume in MS Word.**

   Simply open your resume in MS Word, click "Save as," and name the copy something like "unformattedresume.doc."

2. **In that new copy of your resume, put your section headings in caps.**

3. **Use a plus sign to bullet items in a list.**

4. **Surround italicized words with asterisks.**

5. **Use the space bar instead of indents (for example, five spaces for one indent).**

6. **Alter the margins so they're 65 characters wide. To do that:**

   a. Go to the *File* menu, select *Page Setup,* and change the right margin to 2".

   b. Select (shade) what you eyeball to be the longest line on the resume.

   c. Go to the *Tools* menu, select *Word Count,* and check how many characters with spaces are on that line.

   d. If the number is more than 65, make the margin bigger and re-check.

7. **Make sure the unformatted text looks good in an actual e-mail:**

   a. Select (shade) the entire resume and press Control-C.

   b. Go to your e-mail program (for example, Outlook Express or Eudora) and press the key that creates a new e-mail.

   c. Be sure your cursor is in the body of that e-mail. Then press Control-V to insert your resume.

   d. If anything doesn't look right, go back to the unformatted version of your resume you just created in MS Word, make needed changes, and repeat steps a through c again.

8. **As a final check, e-mail it to yourself.**

9. **Finis!**

When you want to e-mail your resume to someone or post it on an employment site, just select (shade) that unformatted resume in MS Word and press Control-C. Then move your cursor to the place in your e-mail or employment site you want to insert your unformatted resume. Press Control-V to insert it.

 In your e-mail cover letter to a prospective employer, write, "To ensure my resume's readability on your system, I enclose it two ways: an unformatted version in this e-mail and a fully formatted version attached as an MS Word file."

Step 12: Stop Obsessing and Start Celebrating

You're done!

Chapter 10

Impressive Interviewing

In This Chapter

▶ Preparing for the interview: Twelve smart things you can do

▶ Eighteen potions for creating chemistry

▶ Proving — right there in the interview — that you can do the job

▶ Winning the job — after the interview

▶ Dealing with job offers and rejections

Many interviews can feel like the Inquisition. This chapter shows how to make it more like a first date: a pleasant discussion in which you're both trying to see whether you should get involved. This chapter also shows you how to be your most impressive self while being honest.

Getting Ready for an Interview

As in most things, preparation is half the battle. Try the tips in the following sections to get set for any job interview.

Study

I know, I know — everyone hates studying. But a little studying will pay big dividends. Don't worry, I'm not asking you to study calculus:

✔ **Study the job description.** Come up with 20-to-60-second anecdotes of problems you've solved that are related to the job description. For example, if you're a new college graduate interviewing for a job as a PR person, tell the tale of how you helped promote your fraternity's successful blood drive. Don't, however, tell how you convinced the university not to close down your fraternity following Bongo Night.

It's always good to have an anecdote that demonstrates how quickly you learned something. That attribute is valuable in nearly all jobs.

✔ **Bone up on the field and the organization.** You want to make clear that you're not just applying for jobs at random. So, brush up on your field's trends, key players, and lingo. Study the employer's Web site and ask the interviewer's admin whether she knows of anything you can read or someone you can talk with in preparation for your interview.

✔ **Try to learn about your interviewer.** Check with your network (see Chapter 8 to find out who's included in a network) or at least google your interviewer. One of my clients thus discovered that her interviewer volunteered in a Montessori school. So did the candidate, which gave her a perfect topic for small talk before the formal interview.

✔ **Bone up on any technical skills or knowledge required for the job.** It can be tempting to try to slide by on soft skills: organization, people skills, and so on. These days, an ever-increasing percentage of jobs want those skills plus technical knowledge. So, be prepared to strut your stuff.

Prepare

Next, get ready for these questions:

✔ **"Why should we hire you over other candidates?"** Technical expertise? Work ethic? People skills? Use those 20-to-60-second anecdotes.

✔ **The question(s) you most fear, such as, "Why did you leave your last job?"** Preparation is the best antidote to fear.

✔ **Behavioral questions.** As job seekers are ever-more prepped to answer stock questions like, "Tell me your greatest weakness," employers are moving to *behavioral questions* in which you're asked to describe what you did in past work situations.

So, a potential employer may say to you, "Tell me about a conflict you had with a boss or co-worker," or "Describe a situation that demonstrates your thinking skills."

✔ **Case questions.** You may well be asked a *case question:* to describe how you'd respond to a situation likely to occur in the new job. Example: "Here's a one-pager on a widget we'll be introducing. Read it and then lead a marketing meeting with the three of us."

To see how well you think on your feet, Microsoft (and I imagine other top employers) ask such questions as

- Why is a manhole round?

- How would you design a better vending machine?

- What's your favorite Web site and how would you improve it?

To prepare for case questions, rehearse the following ritual:

1. Take a deep breath and a few moments to think before you speak. The interviewer knows that case questions are the most challenging.

2. Take 10 or 15 seconds to jot down a couple of ideas. That will structure your thinking.

3. In a calm, measured way, describe your approach. Qualify your statements, saying, for example, "Of course, in the real world I might want to look at some data and talk with some people, but shooting from the hip, here are some thoughts that come to mind."

Answers aren't the only thing you need to prepare. In addition, you should

✔ **Prepare a few questions to ask.** Examples: "What would you hope I'd accomplish in the first few weeks?" and "Where's the best place around here to get a massage?" Well maybe not that one. Want more ideas? Just think of yourself in your first day on the job. What would you want to know from your boss? No, not "Where is the bathroom?"

✔ **Prepare a portfolio of your work.** It's axiomatic in education, screenwriting, and sales: show, don't tell. That also applies to job seekers. Could you bring work samples to the interview? Of course artist types bring portfolios and filmmakers bring sample reels, but other applicants could bring a sample. Teacher? Bring a video of you in action. Computer programmer? Bring a cool program you developed. Manager? Bring thank-you notes from bosses, supervisees, or customers. If you're a sewage treatment worker, don't bring a sample.

Practice

Now, just practice what you've developed earlier:

✔ **Practice your 10- and 45-second pitches.** Those explain what you do, that you're good, and why, if you're so good, you're looking for a new job. Sample 10-second pitch: "I was a therapist at Kaiser, loved my work and they loved me, but when my wife got a job in Florida, I had to move." The 45-second version would add an accomplishment or two that would impress your target employer. If it's your first job, talk about relevant experiences at school. Check out Chapter 8 for more details on coming up with 10- and 45-second pitches.

✔ **Do a mock interview.** Do one with a trusted friend and then pay a professional career counselor or coach to do one with you. Have him record it so you can review it together. Some state employment services offer videotaped mock interviews for free.

> ✔ **Be ready to be quizzed on your resume.** Most interviewers will have your resume in front of them, and sometimes find it easiest to structure the interview around it, even asking about that stupid little job you had 12 years ago.

Eighteen Ways to Create Chemistry in an Interview

Alas, hiring is often based as much on gut feeling as it is on the hard merits. So, you gotta connect chemically with the interviewer. In the following sections, I provide potent ways to ensure you do just that.

Check your body chemistry

Start with the basics. You can't have chemistry with the interviewer if you have bad breath or body odor.

Dress one notch above

Dress the way your future boss might. Don't know what that's like? Call the receptionist or boss's admin: "I'm coming in for an interview for a job working for *(insert potential boss's name)*. Any suggestions for what I should wear?"

Arrive early

Arrive 20 minutes early. Then find the nearest coffee shop to hang out at for a few minutes. Go over your notes, including your 10- and 45-second pitches, why you're looking, why you're interested in this job, a few anecdotes of problems you faced and solved, and answers to the questions you most fear. (See the earlier section "Getting Ready for an Interview" for details on this preparation.)

Walk into the building five minutes early. Get a feel for the place. Like it?

The interview starts the moment you enter the building and ends only when you leave it. Why? Slouch into the building and the person next to you may be the interviewer returning from lunch. After the interviewer says good-bye, many applicants blow it by letting their guard down and saying something stupid. My wife often asks her admin about a job candidate's behavior.

Help yourself relax

Think back to a moment when you were confident. In the interview, pretend you're that self and remind yourself that millions of jobs are out there. If you aren't meant to get this one, it doesn't mean you'll be a bag lady.

If possible, learn something about the interviewer in advance, even if you only ask the receptionist, "What can you tell me about Mr. Crasdale?" Even knowing that Mr. Crasdale just came back from vacation will help you feel more confident, like you have inside information, and in turn, more relaxed.

Try to have a good time from the get-go

A good time and a job interview seem to be mutually exclusive, but not necessarily. Here are some ideas for enjoying an interview from start to finish:

- ✔ Enjoy the décor in the reception area.
- ✔ Try to figure out whether the interviewer is nervous.
- ✔ Check the interviewer's office for clues to what she's like: the family pictures, the golf clubs in the corner, the desk that looks post-tornado.
- ✔ Listen well to the interviewer. Does it sound like she'd rather talk about her upcoming vacation than "What is your greatest weakness?"

- ✔ When you're asked a killer question, answer it quickly and move the conversation to a more pleasant area.
- ✔ Ask the questions you're curious about, the serious and the playful. After you establish some credibility, it may enhance your image as a nice person to ask a human question such as, "What do most people do for lunch?"

Establish the first-date mindset

Many people think of a job interview as an interrogation: you're sitting there under a bare light bulb, bombarded with questions, many of which you can't answer.

As I mention in this chapter's introduction, you can often make an interview more like a first date, in which each of you has a chance to decide whether you're well-matched, logically and chemically. Treat an interview like a first date, and you'll both more wisely decide whether to hook up. A first-date mind-set also discourages you from assuming that too-formal, phony-appearing job-seeker persona: "I believe I am uniquely qualified for the position," or "I'm seeking a position with a dynamic organization."

You also make an interview more like a date by asking a few questions during the interview, not just at the end. Your questions can come from your pre-interview research about the employer or as follow-ups to what the interviewer said, but here are generic questions:

- ✔ What should I know about working here?
- ✔ Can you tell me a bit about the culture in this workgroup?
- ✔ To whom would I be reporting? What sort of person gets along best with him?
- ✔ What do people say they like best and worst about working here?
- ✔ How many people have held this position in the past few years? Why did they leave?

Most interviewers are glad to answer a few questions — indeed, questions show intelligence and that you're interested but not desperate. Too, their answers can guide what you'll say in the rest of the interview.

Make the most of the first ten seconds

Malcolm Gladwell, in *Blink,* asserts that you make a hard-to-change impression in the first few seconds you meet someone. How to make a good first impression? It's a sad commentary on human judgment, but just follow the advice offered by Gary Ripple, author of *Campus Pursuit:* Smile, offer a firm handshake, look the person in the eye (long enough that you know what color they are), and pleasantly and confidently say, "Hi, I'm Joe Blow." Wait to be invited to sit down, then lean slightly forward, keep a pleasant look on your face (I said pleasant, not psychotic), and maintain eye contact most of the time.

End the interview similarly. Smile, look the interviewer in the eye, shake his hand, and, if true, say that you enjoyed the interview. If not, thank him for an interesting experience.

Rehearse the above ritual ten times. It's that important.

Avoid turn-off mannerisms

Richard Bolles, author of *What Color Is Your Parachute,* urges interviewees to beware of trivial mannerisms that can nix you:

- ✔ You slouch in your chair.
- ✔ You fidget in your seat.

- ✔ You play with your hair or hands.

- ✔ You continually avoid eye contact.

- ✔ You're overly negative.

- ✔ You're too self-critical.

- ✔ You speak as quietly as a church mouse or as loud as a wrestling announcer.

- ✔ You constantly interrupt the interviewer.

I add one more no-no: bragging. But you ask, "How can I let the interviewer know good stuff about me without bragging?" Two ways: with those anecdotes demonstrating your abilities (see Chapter 9 for details), and by having someone else brag for you. For example, you can say, "My co-workers always say I'm the go-to guy when there's a thorny problem."

Really try to understand the employer's needs

Suppose you're applying for a position as an accountant. The employer's main priority may be developing a new accounting system, improving employees' reporting practices, or even a desire to avoid an IRS audit. If you understand the employer's needs and show how you can meet them, you'll stand a much better chance of landing the job than if you simply answer the interviewer's questions blind.

Avoiding uncomfortable questions about salary

Standard advice is to never bring up salary until the job is offered, let alone early in the interview. My clients find that conventional wisdom to be wrong. Typically, somewhere in the interview, the interviewer asks, "What is your current salary?" or "What is your salary requirement?" No answer to that question is helpful to you. So, preempt the problem by striking first with a question like, "The position seems to involve *(insert as high-level a description of the tasks as possible)*. What salary range have you budgeted for the position?"

If they respond, "Well, how much are you looking to make?" respond with, "I'm just looking to be paid fairly. What have you budgeted for the position?" If they continue to hedge, that's a sign you don't want to work for them. If forced, offer a wide range like "$65,000 to $85,000 depending on the scope of responsibilities."

When negotiating as a self-employed person or independent contractor, gather information about his needs, describe what you can do to meet them, and then give the cost.

Sometimes you can tease out an employer's needs with questions such as, "What sorts of issues are important for your new hire to address?" or even, "Any problem you're facing these days that is particularly worrisome?" Other times, you simply need to listen well. The interviewer's questions and statements usually reveal her concerns.

In short, think of yourself as a consultant, helping the client to identify his needs and then collaboratively figure out a way you can help solve them. To that end, you may even offer to write a proposal or work on a small project. That can really help you stand out in comparison with the other candidates.

Be yourself, but be your best self

By being your real self, whether it's quiet, jovial, whatever, you're not that sanitized middle-of-the-road person that most job seekers try to be. As a result, you're more likely to end up at the top or at the bottom of the heap than in the middle. Sure, if you're not what they're looking for, they'll turn you down. Fine! Better to show the real you before you commit to each other, rather than after — just like marriage.

Having said that, I recognize that there are many "real yous": The you zoning out in front of the TV isn't the same as the you working on your greatest accomplishment. Be yourself, but be your best self.

Really listen and watch

Especially in an interview, most people listen poorly. You may be so worried about how you're coming across and so busy planning what to say next, that you only half-attend to what the interviewer is saying and revealing with body language. That's a shame because you may miss crucial hidden messages:

- ✔ The interviewer may show what she's mainly looking for in a candidate. Example: She's always talking about getting stuff done fast.

- ✔ The interviewer's reactions may reveal what she likes and dislikes about you. Does she, for example, start getting fidgety as you go on about the latest technology?

- ✔ The interviewer may yield clues to what she or that workplace is really like. Maybe you'll discover you don't want to work there if, for example, an employer stresses the importance of teamwork on this job and you go nuts when having to rely on others to get your work done.

✔ Look out for signs of empathy, such as when an interviewer says, "I've only been here a few months myself." That can relax you.

✔ Look out for signs of nervousness, perhaps because she's afraid that if she makes another bad hire, she could be fired. That too can relax you.

✔ When you're really listening, you're able to ask questions that follow up on what the interviewer is saying — a great way to create chemistry.

Talk the right amount

Most comments should be 20 to 60 seconds long. More than that and you risk sounding egocentric or putting your interviewer to sleep. If the interviewer wants more information, she can ask a follow-up question. If your utterances are generally less than 20 seconds long, especially if they're mainly one-sentence answers, an interviewer may think you're withholding or unknowledgeable.

Keep the Traffic Light Rule in mind: During the first 30 seconds of an utterance, your light is green. During the next 30 seconds, it's yellow — the risk that your listener thinks you're long-winded is increasing. After the 60-second mark, your light is red: Yes, sometimes running a red light is okay (for example, when you're telling a truly fascinating anecdote), but almost always, you should stop, perhaps asking a question.

Beware of interviewers who talk the whole time. You may think that will benefit you, but according to an M.I.T. study cited in the 2007 edition of *What Color Is Your Parachute*, unless you're talking roughly half the time, your chances of getting hired decline. So, if your interviewer won't shut up, at an opportune moment, interrupt and say something that would give you an opportunity to talk, such as "Would you like me to share some thoughts on how I'd handle this job?"

Ask one or more power questions early in the interview

"What would a star be like in this job?" "Anything else?" "What are the most important things you'll want me to work on in the first few weeks on the job?" The sooner you can ask these questions, the sooner you can start tailoring your answers to what's important to the employer. It's like getting the answers to the test in advance.

To avoid sounding like you're simply parroting back what the employer wants, be sure to back up your claims with facts or anecdotes. For example, if the boss says he's most looking for someone with fire in the belly, it's not enough to say that you have drive. You need to back it with evidence that you go the extra mile. This is the time to use one of those PAR stories: A **p**roblem you faced, how you **a**pproached it, and its positive **r**esolution. (See Chapter 9 for more information about PAR stories.)

If you're interviewing with a startup or other fiscally shaky employer, ask a few questions about the company or workgroup, such as, "What's been your net earnings over the last couple of years? What's your burn rate (monthly expenses)? How long will you be able to sustain that rate?" Any ethical startup will understand that you have the right to ask such questions. Indeed, asking them tends to impress employers.

At the end of the interview, think about asking, "Do you have any remaining concerns?" or "Based on what we've talked about today, I sense that I could do this job well. Do you agree?" That gives you a chance to counter any objections.

Stay connected with all your interviewers

A panel may conduct your interview. The regular interview rules apply with the following additions. When responding, mainly look at your questioner but occasionally establish eye contact with the others. When asking a question, look mainly at the person you want to answer it, but if another panelist seems eager to respond, give that person the nod to go ahead.

Bring up one weakness early on

Bringing up a weakness of yours can help you and the interviewer assess whether you're likely to be successful on the job. In bringing it up yourself, not only do you demonstrate candor — unusual in a job candidate — but you also allow an open discussion of how serious a liability the weakness would be. That's good for interviewer and interviewee. Take that team-player example. You may say, "I'm looking for a job where I'll have a lot of autonomy. I find that, when I'm on teams, I tend to dominate or feel too forced to constrain myself, but if you're looking for a self-starter, that is one of my strengths."

Mirror the interviewer

If she's strictly business, you should be too. If he's social and playful, show that side of yourself.

Reveal a bit about your personal life

Talk a little about your family, hobbies, and so on. If you get a good response, reveal a bit more.

Know the secrets to video interviewing

To save travel costs and reduce scheduling hassles, employers increasingly use video interviewing instead of face-to-face. Increasingly, the employer simply mails the candidate a Webcam. You have only a few special things to remember:

- You look shifty if your eyes avert to the side. You look depressed if your head is tilted downward. The solution: When you're talking, keep your head straight and your eyes trained slightly *above* the camera.

- A lag exists between the video and audio transmission, so voices can seem out of sync. Before answering a question, wait until you hear the interviewer finish. Don't rely on the video or you risk interrupting the interviewer.

Other Keys to Wowing Interviewers

Here are more strategies that help make you the winning candidate.

Don't just say you can do it — prove it

Many career guides tell job interviewees to focus on their accomplishments — what they did in the past. I've found that interviewees are even more likely to score by focusing on the present: by demonstrating — during the interview — how they can help the employer.

Imagine you're director of sales for a publishing company and are interviewing two candidates for a sales job. Candidate A discussed his previous sales experience while Candidate B pretended he was on a sales call and sold one of your products to you. Assuming the candidates were otherwise equal, which one would you hire?

Ask something like: "What's a typical problem I might encounter on the job?" After getting an answer, ask: "Can I show you how I might approach it?" Start by asking the interviewer a question or two about the problem to give you the information you need to craft a plan for addressing it. Then say, "In light of what you've said, might this approach make sense? *(Then outline it.)* Of course, I'd know much more if I were actually working on the project, but this gives you a sense of how I might approach things."

Maximize the good part of the interview

Give longer answers to questions you like, shorter answers to questions you don't. Many job seekers do the opposite. They keep trying to dig themselves out of trouble and often just dig themselves deeper, and at minimum, ensure that a larger proportion of the interview is spent on their weaknesses.

Also ask questions to redirect the interview to areas you want to talk about — for example, the new job and how you'd approach its challenges.

Fit the job description to your strengths

Often, the employer knows she needs to hire someone but isn't sure how to best use the person. If, in the interview, you can help clarify that she needs someone with your strengths, you may talk your way into a well-suited job.

Early in the interview, ask, "Is the job description mapped out or does it depend on the candidate?" If there's some play, the interviewer may be grateful for your help. Ask her to tell you about some of the organization's needs. Then gently propose how the position may be structured to meet those needs and how your strengths would be well suited. Example:

> "You've identified two key problems: getting the staff comfortable with the new computer program and reducing the backlog in processing claims. That would be fun to tackle. My software training background will help me in getting the staff comfortable with the computer program, and I know I'll enjoy figuring out how to streamline the claims process."

If the job description is fluid, expect that you won't get a job offer right away. The employer probably won't hire until he's figured out what he wants. So, focus on helping the hirer do just that. Offer to do a little homework that may be helpful — for example, write a short proposal or report. That should put you ahead of the competition.

Success at 40-plus

After 40, many job seekers start to worry about age discrimination. Here are some antidotes:

✓ **Dress your age, but well.** Don't try to look like a teeny bopper, but avoid clothing worn only by the aged — string ties come to mind. Also, be sure your clothes aren't too tight. That accentuates your perhaps no longer lithe body.

✓ **Use good posture.** Helen Gurley Brown was only slightly exaggerating when she said, "After 40, it all comes down to posture." Not sure about yours? Stand naturally in front of a mirror.

✓ **Reassure about your vigor.** If you do have good energy, say so, perhaps even mentioning your hobby as a skier or tennis player. Move purposefully as you stride (not trudge) in, sit down, get up, and walk out. Someone who seems to need a crane to get up from a chair may not create the right impression.

✓ **Sell your age as a plus.** Wisdom (sometimes) comes with age. If true, explain that your experience can help prevent mistakes that others may have to learn on their own skin.

✓ **Talk about new things you've learned over the years, especially those relevant to the job you're applying for.** For example, a teacher may say, "A decade ago, research started to indicate that phonics is — for low-intelligence students — a better approach to teaching reading, so I quickly learned how to incorporate it into my instruction. Now, with a decade of experience with it, my kids' test scores are higher than comparable kids' scores in other teachers' classes."

Employers' revenge

Sick and tired of hearing job interviewees' BS, employers are starting to subject their finalist candidates to a cram-proof, valid final test: the day-long job simulation. The employer hires them for a day and watches them doing the job they're being considered for.

Offer to fill other needs if you sense you're a poor match for the job

Sometimes, you can turn the lemon into lemonade. Try this:

> "In listening to you, it sounds like I'm a poor fit for this position, but I'm wondering if I might be of use to you in another way. What I bring to the table are *(insert your best attributes)*. Might someone with that background be of help to you?"

This is an example of industrial magnate Henry Kaiser's famous advice to job seekers: Find a need and fill it.

 Sometimes, you may think you've done well in the interview but, by the end, you nonetheless get the sense you won't get the job. It's worth asking, "Is there any reason you'd be hesitant to hire me?" You may tease out an objection you can successfully counter.

After the Interview: When the Job Is Often Won or Lost

Right after the interview, while everything's fresh in your mind, grade yourself on the *Interview Report Card* I talk about here, and draft a thank-you note. Then prime your references and make follow-ups.

The Interview Report Card

Grading yourself on this report card helps you in future interviews. Without it, you may be tempted to deceive yourself into thinking that you did better than you did. Ask yourself the following questions to see how well you did:

- ✔ Did your face, voice, and body language convey interest?
- ✔ Did you create a good impression in those crucial first few seconds?
- ✔ Did you share a weakness early? Did it seem to help or hurt you?
- ✔ Did you listen well?
- ✔ Did you describe the accomplishments most likely to impress the interviewer?

✔ Did you not just tell, but also demonstrate, that you could do the job?

✔ Did you ask questions during the interview, not just at the end?

✔ Did your questions help you get clearer about whether you want this job?

✔ Did you talk roughly half of the time?

✔ Did your comments rarely exceed one minute in length?

✔ Did you show caring about the people, asking personal questions as appropriate?

✔ Did you show that you care about the organization's product or service?

✔ Did you reveal an appropriate amount about your personal life?

✔ Did you mirror the interviewer's style?

✔ Were you honest enough?

✔ Were you your best self?

✔ Were you able to have a reasonably good time?

✔ Would you hire yourself for this job?

Ahead-of-the-pack thank-you letters

It's best if you can draft the darn thank-you letter right after the interview. Then let it sit overnight, review it with fresh eyes, and mail or e-mail it.

I'm frequently asked, "Should I send my thank-you note via e-mail, or should I send a handwritten note?" It depends on the recipient. Trust your intuition. Richard Bolles, in *What Color Is Your Parachute,* suggests you do both.

A thank-you letter can do more than say thank you. It enables you to

✔ Remind the interviewer of the things he was most impressed with. "I'm pleased you think my experience managing designers would be valuable."

✔ Give a better answer to a question you flubbed. "I've given further thought to that question you asked about polymerase chain reactions."

✔ Say more about things the interviewer cares about. "There was one more thing I thought you might be interested in."

✔ Reiterate your interest in the position.

Figure 10-1 shows a letter that accomplishes all this.

Dear Nadine,

I really enjoyed the opportunity to interview with you. The dyslexia project is generating some impressive results. I am pleased that you think my background in pathology would be helpful and look forward to the possibility of joining your staff.

You asked a question that got me thinking. You asked what sort of study I think would be the most valuable next step. On reflection, I think we'd get valuable information from doing PET scans of dyslexic children of different ages to better understand how cerebral structure and function change developmentally. That could point us to the best times to provide educational as well as physiological interventions.

I am excited about the prospect of working for you.

Sincerely,

Allan Gold

Figure 10-1: Draft a thank-you note as soon as you can after the interview.

References

Ask potential references whether they're willing to serve. That can avoid surprise bashings. Try this wording: "I was hoping to use you as a reference. Do you feel you're in a position to provide a strong one?"

When a prospective employer is ready to call your references, you call them first. Explain the ways you're well suited to the job and the issues you'd like your reference to address.

If you're employed, ask hirers to defer contacting your references, especially your current employer, until ready to hire you. You don't want your current boss to find out you're looking if you don't actually get a job offer. And even if you're excited about a possible job, don't tell anyone who may tip off your current employer. Hot prospects often turn cold. The career battlefield is littered with people who talked about their next job too soon and got shot down by their current boss who didn't want an employee he couldn't count on. Hold off until you've signed the new job offer. Trust me on this one.

The end game

Often, this is where the game is won and lost. Most employers appreciate polite persistence.

A few days after sending your thank-you letter, call to ask where you stand. If you're not the front-runner, ask, "Is there anything that makes you hesitant to hire me?" If a concern is raised, explain why it's unjustified (if it is), have a reference do so, or offer to provide a work sample — a report, proposal, or one-day trial, for example. End the call by affirming that you're eager and confident you can do the job. If it doesn't feel too pushy, say something like, "Of course, we only scratched the surface. If you might find it useful, I'd be pleased to talk further with you." Send a follow-up note reiterating all this.

If the job is worth using up some of the goodwill of one of your references, ask him to phone the hirer to say how wonderful you are.

Two weeks later, if you haven't heard anything, you can send a letter that says, "You and I discussed *(insert topic)*. I came across this article and thought you might be interested. I'm still interested in the position and hope to hear from you soon."

Dismissing a full-time employee has become extraordinarily difficult, so employers take extra time to make a hiring decision. Expect multiple interviews and possibly employment testing. This is especially likely when the job description is fluid. Keep trying to help the hirer develop the job description and you'll more likely get the job.

Handling Job Offers and Rejections

It's finally over. Unless the employer failed to even give you the courtesy of a rejection letter, the results are in: you got a job offer or not. Here's how to make the most of both situations.

You got the job offer!

Congratulations! Being offered a job is a great feeling, but don't sound too eager. At minimum, it will hurt you when negotiating the terms of your employment. I even know a case in which excess enthusiasm resulted in a retracted job offer. The employee was so ecstatic that he appeared desperate. That motivated the employer to check his references more closely than he otherwise would have, whereupon the employer developed buyer's remorse and offered the position to another candidate.

The right response to a job offer that you'd consider is a moderately enthusiastic, "I'm pleased. Can we set up an appointment in a couple of days to discuss salary and other terms of employment?"

Someone else got the job, but all's not lost

If someone else lands the job and you're in mourning about it, phone the interviewer or, if a group interviewed you, the nicest interviewer. Say something like, "I'm disappointed. I believe I could have done a good job for you. Might I ask what made you hesitant to hire me? Anything else? *(That follow-up question often yields something valuable.)* I want to know if there's something I need to work on." Close with, "If by any chance your situation changes, I hope you'll keep me in mind. Would you mind if I phoned you back in a month to follow up? And is there anyone else you think I should talk with?"

Despite all efforts, even the best candidates get rejected a lot. The successful job seeker sees whether he can learn anything from it, doesn't allow himself to get frustrated, and moves on to the next constructive task.

A rejection after you've revealed your true best self is often a blessing. Wouldn't you rather hold out for someone who wants you for who you are?

Part IV
Making Any Career Cooler

The 5th Wave   By Rich Tennant

FREELANCE PEPPERIER

I just got tired of the 9 to 5 grind. Say when...

SOUP 'N SALAD

In this part . . .

You buy a suit. Off the rack, it probably looks just okay. To really look terrific, you need to tailor and accessorize it to fit your body and tastes. The same is true with your career.

In this part, I show you how to tailor and accessorize an off-the-shelf career so you're maximally likely to be happy and successful. For example, I show you how to get your assigned tasks changed so they match your strengths, how to reduce your job stress, and how to become a beloved employee — or at least a fire-resistant one.

Another way to make your career cooler is to overcome the tendency to procrastinate. In this part, I do my best to light a fire under you.

Yet another way to make your career cooler is to be your own boss. In the final chapter of this part, I show you how to become successfully self-employed, even if you're not a born entrepreneur.

Chapter 11

Making the Most of Any Job

In This Chapter

▶ Tailoring your job to fit your strengths

▶ Becoming a star . . . or at least fire-resistant

▶ Staying fresh

▶ Succeeding when you're just starting out, in mid-career, and a Boomer

▶ Earning your three-minute MBA

▶ Moving up and moving out

*Y*ou've completed the first two of the three steps to a satisfying worklife: You've selected a career and landed a job in that career. Now I turn to what may be the most important step: making the most of that job.

Most people who love their jobs appreciate six things about it:

- A good boss and co-workers
- A moderate workload
- Work that's interesting
- Moderate stress
- Winning at office politics
- Fair compensation

This chapter shows you how to maximize your chances of having the first five. My favorite book on negotiation is Jim Camp's *Start with No* (Crown Business).

Managing Your Boss

Do you change readily? Neither do bosses. So it's best if you can start out with a good boss. How to maximize your chances of that? Job search vigorously so you get multiple job offers and can pick one with a good boss. Other chapters in this book urge you to ask questions during the interview and after being offered the job. That should help you avoid the clinkers.

But assume it's too late for all that. And assume it's the worst case: You've been assigned to the boss from hell. Even if this is your first day on the job, if even a remote possibility for a better option exists, request the transfer right away. Changing bosses before everything is cast in stone is often easier.

No dice? Try the fixes in the following sections for dealing with a bad boss or making the most of a good one.

Tailoring the job to fit you

Give your boss a suggestion or two for tailoring the job to fit you. Can any of these make *your* career cooler?

- ✔ **A revised job description that capitalizes on your strengths and minimizes your weaknesses.** For example, a programmer who's good at troubleshooting but lousy at design may offer to trade roles with another programmer who's the opposite.

- ✔ **A piece of equipment.** An architect's life can be made easier by getting his own CAD terminal.

- ✔ **Alternate work hours.** Working from 7 a.m. to 3 p.m. instead of 9 to 5 avoids traffic jams and allows you to watch your kid's Little League games.

- ✔ **Autonomy.** A manager at a Web 2.0 business got permission to take full charge of a new part of the site, from design to marketing.

- ✔ **A new challenge.** A biotechnician got the okay to use a cutting-edge technique for his next experiment.

- ✔ **More feedback.** Feedback junkies enjoy being kept apprised of how they're doing.

- ✔ **More time in the field or in the office.** A salesperson was supposed to spend most of his time in the field but, on many appointments, felt unprepared. So he requested more time in the office to learn more about his client before the appointment. It was granted.

- ✔ **Changing who you work with.** A manager had worked well with an employee in another unit. She got that person transferred to her department.

- ✔ **Dressing unconventionally.** All the co-workers in my client's workplace wear ties. My client hates ties. He got his boss to make an exception for him.

Developing wonderful communication skills

Are you trying to get something from your boss (or co-worker or lover)? Needing to get out of trouble? Communication skills are key. Most people think they're terrific communicators — but few actually are. These tips may help:

- ✔ **Learn your boss's decision-making style.** It boils down to two questions: Is she fact- or emotion-driven? Fast- or slow-paced? Respond accordingly. If you have a slow-paced, emotion-driven boss, you'd be foolish to barge into his office rapid-firing, "Hi, Joe. If we do A, B, and C, I think we can generate big bucks. Whaddya think?" Yet the same approach can work with a fact-driven, fast-paced boss.

- ✔ **Curious, not convince.** When you're annoyed with your boss (or a co-worker or a loved one), it's tempting to try to convince her of the error of her ways. Alas, that rarely results in future improvement. Think back to the last time you tried that. Did it help?

Here's a better approach. Rather than trying to *convince* the other person that he's screwed up, recognize that there's usually another side to the story. Ask questions demonstrating your *curiosity* about that other side. Remember this mantra: *Curious, not convince.* Try starting your next tough talk with a sentence like, "I'm unhappy because *(insert perceived wrongdoing),* and I'm wondering if there's something I'm not understanding." Then really listen to the other person's perspective. That requires 100 percent of your attention — you have no room for judging or devising solutions. You'll have time later for solutions. When the person stops talking, and you sense more could be said, just wait, say "mm-hmm," or ask a question that encourages him to say more.

- ✔ **When your protagonist makes an accusatory statement, paraphrase it back.** Doing that shows you really hear the statement, forces you to better understand the other person's perspective, and usually serves as a more helpful response than your first instinct: "You idiot!" So when she says, "You've been slacking off," you may respond with, "I can understand why you'd think that. I *have* been taking long lunches." Then, she may be more open to hearing your explanation, which may be something like, "I've been having a hard time working in this room with all the noise. So, from noon to 2, I've been going to a coffee shop to work. I get a lot more done. Can I show you what I've been accomplishing?"

✔ **Get your boss or co-worker to come up with a solution.** How do you feel when someone says, "You should do X"? Chances are, your internal reaction is, "No!" Few people like to be told what to do. The key to getting someone to change is to try to get him to come up with a solution. Ask questions that make that possible, such as: "So it sounds like our inventory database is causing the problem. Any sense of what should be done?" If your counterpart gets stuck, and you want to propose a solution, say, "John, would you mind if I suggest something?" Getting his permission makes him more likely to feel some ownership of the idea.

✔ **Conclude by asking the other person to summarize what's been agreed to.** And then if true, thank her for making a difficult conversation easier.

These tips are just the beginning. In the following sections, I provide additional guidance on some of the personality types you may encounter.

If the boss is a hothead

Don't take it personally. The louder she yells, the sorrier for her you should feel, but don't dismiss everything she says. Just because the tone is off-putting doesn't mean the feedback is invalid. Try to judge what she says on its merits and not its tone. If you want to discuss a criticism with a hothead, be sure to use those excellent communication skills.

It's usually wisest to let the person vent it all out, and then ask whether you might go to the bathroom. When you return, she's likely calmed down and more open to hearing your response.

If, despite trying to make changes to improve, you find yourself continually having to endure tirades or passive-aggressive attacks, get a transfer or quit. You deserve better.

If the boss is a micromanager

Use a Zen approach. Fight back by not resisting. Keep your boss as informed as possible. For example, offer to e-mail him an update each day. There's a decent chance that after your boss sees that you're someone he can trust, he'll redirect his micromanaging to less trustworthy types. And remember, sometimes a supervisor micromanages because you do need a lot of guidance. Before resenting the close supervision, ask yourself whether you might benefit from it.

If the boss is lazy or incompetent

You won't change these tendencies. Work hard at accepting her as she is. Just as you wouldn't be furious at a developmentally disabled child's inability to perform, you must react that way with an incompetent or lazy boss. As you plan, of course, don't count much on her. Ask only for the most crucial things. If you need support, look for it elsewhere.

Maintaining a Moderate Workload

Your perfectly good job can become miserable in a hurry when you have too much work or the work is too hard. The following sections show ways to cut your workload down to size.

Working at home

Of course, many people don't want to work at home. They'd miss the office chitchat, find goofing off too tempting, or discover they live next door to someone who practices the drums all day.

For many others, though, telecommuting, for at least part of the week, is great. I work at home and I love it. I work relaxed — no worry about someone looking over my shoulder. And I'm much more efficient. When I used to work in an office building, I was faced with nonstop meetings and interruptions such as "Let me tell you about my daughter's sweet sixteen." Now, when I want to work, I work. And when I want to socialize, I chat on the phone or invite someone to lunch. Between clients, I get to play the piano or play with my cat. My normal writing attire: underwear. Try that in an office! I don't have to waste time getting dressed for success — unless you call Jockey shorts and uncombed hair dressed for success — and I have a ten-second commute.

Here are keys to keeping your boss and yourself happy as you merrily work at home:

- ✔ **Reassure your boss.** Many bosses are control freaks. They're afraid that if you're out of sight, your work is out of mind. They have visions of you sleeping 'til noon, watching soaps 'til 3, and squeezing in a smidge of work before your kids come home at 3:30. Offer to document how you use your time to stop your boss from losing sleep over that lavish lifestyle she thinks you're living on company time.

  Remind your boss that she's saving on office space and that you'll be a more effective employee now that you can start work each day without hours worth of makeup, hair-styling, and a draining commute. Besides, she has an employee who's happier, and therefore less likely to bolt for a job paying a few pesos more.

- ✔ **Set limits.** Your boss may be at least partly right. Work at home and you have endless temptations: morning tennis, housecleaning, a call to your girlfriend, and, yes, the refrigerator — telecommuting can be a diet killer. And, of course, the biggest impediment to a successful telecommuting day is kids. If you have young children, it may be worth getting childcare so you can work in peace.

✔ **Be your own OSHA inspector.** In most workplaces, especially larger ones, the employer takes steps to ensure an ergonomically reasonable workplace. Telecommuters also are entitled to one. Be sure your chair is adjustable, the keyboard is placed so your wrist needn't strain, and if you use the phone much, you have a headset. Yeah, I know they look dorky, but they feel wonderful.

✔ **Try to get compensation for telecommuting.** If you're working at home, your employer saves office space, furniture, utilities, phone, computer costs, and so on. Why should you have to pay for all that?

✔ **Stay in the loop.** Telecommuters often are passed over for promotions — out of sight, out of mind. Especially if you're telecommuting more than a day a week, be sure to stay in the loop — phone and e-mail colleagues frequently, and don't miss the company picnic.

For a portal to articles about telecommuting, see `telecommuting.about.com`.

Time-efficiency, no matter where you work

Even if you don't work at home, you still have a variety of options for keeping your workload moderate. Why not try the following strategies?

✔ **Make *time-efficiency* your mantra.** Have a little voice always on your shoulder whispering, "Is this the most time-effective way?" Not the fastest, not the best, but the optimum balance of the two — that's what time-effectiveness means.

✔ **Adjust your quality standards to suit the task.** Ask yourself whether you're doing some of your tasks too perfectionistically.

✔ **Use the one-minute struggle.** Rarely does struggling with a problem for more than a minute result in a solution. It usually just results in more frustration. So when you reach a roadblock, struggle for no more than one minute. At that point, decide that your imperfect solution is good enough, that you need help, or that you can complete the project without solving that problem.

✔ **Ask the most efficient person you know to watch you work** for a half-hour and then have her offer suggestions for how you can improve.

✔ **Get your job tasks realigned.** You'll get more done faster if you spend maximum time using your strengths and minimum time using your weaknesses. A lawyer was great at drafting documents, but a paralyzed wimp in the courtroom. He arranged to trade tasks with another of the firm's lawyers who was the opposite.

✔ **Outsource some work.** You're already managing time well: You prioritize, you try to be efficient, you BlackBerry even in the bathroom. Yet you rarely catch up. If you can't offload work onto a co-worker or get permission to hire a temp or consultant, find an intern. After clearing it with your boss, post a position announcement at a local college's internship office.

✔ **Just say no.** Of course, sometimes that's impossible, but often you can say no without hurting your career. One of my clients, insecure by nature, felt that the only way he would be deemed worthy is saying yes to everything. He was known as the designated workhorse and worked an average of 60+ hours a week. He got laid off anyway, in part because he was often exhausted and resentful about his workload. In his next job, we agreed that he would learn to say no. When he was hired again, he asked whether he should put in long hours for the first few weeks to get off to a good start. I urged him not to because it would create the expectation that he'd always work that hard. So, he limited himself to 50 hours a week, and when asked to do tasks that would take him beyond those 50 hours, he would say, "My plate is full. Would you like me to substitute this (the proposed new task) for something else I'm working on?" He's much happier . . . and, six months later, still employed.

Keeping Your Job Interesting

You spend more waking hours at work than any other activity. Don't let yourself get bored. The following sections show you how.

Compose a mission statement

Have a personal mission statement and, where possible, allocate your time accordingly. Mine is: "To use my best skill — the ability to communicate verbally and in writing — in the service of helping people with their work-lives, exposing higher education as America's most overrated product, and advocating for a now-neglected group: boys."

So, for example, if a publisher asked me to write a book on small business marketing, I'd say no. If I were asked to write an exposé of higher education, I'd enthusiastically agree.

Propose a special project

Sometimes, all you need is a special project. During a tour of my friend Pat's house, I noticed a wall of awards she had received from her various employers. I asked her, "What's the secret of your success?" not really expecting an answer. To my surprise, she offered one: "On every job, I propose a special project that I'd find fun and that would please my boss." What project can you propose that would inject some pleasure into that humdrum job of yours?

Perhaps your boss may indulge your do-gooding desires and, for example, let you spearhead an adopt-a-school program, or even give you a half-day-a-week released time to do community service. Brian Kelly, President of Napa's Charter Oak Bank, requires all his employees to do community service.

Develop a mentoring relationship

A mentoring relationship can help keep your job interesting. Have a role model? If so, tell the person that. Ask his advice about something. If that works well, ask something else later. And it shouldn't be a one-way street, so look for an opportunity to do something for him.

Can't think of someone you'd like as a mentor? Perhaps be a mentor to someone else at work. It doesn't need to be someone young. Sometimes, an older worker can use counsel on something, perhaps some new technology that you're whiz-bang at.

Or form an online or in-person support group, perhaps among people who do what you do, in and outside your organization.

Or join a ready-made group. For a listing, check `www.shersuccess teams.com`.

Find a fun hobby

Build a cool avocation into your after-work life. One of my clients, a Fortune 500 manager, works during his lunch hour on a screenplay he hopes to sell to Hollywood. Another client takes an hour during most workdays to hit a bucket of golf balls. "It makes me feel like I have a great job — I can go to the driving range in the middle of the day."

Weave your hobby into your job

More often than you may think, you can incorporate your hobby into your job, like these people did:

- ✔ Ann Flexer, who works at the Edelweiss jewelry store in Berkeley, California, plays the guitar when business is slow — it passes the time while attracting customers.

- ✔ An interior designer who liked photography took before-and-after photos not only of the job but also of her clients and families, posted them on the company site, and sent 8-x-10-inch prints to her clients as a thank-you.

> ✔ Way back when I was a teacher, I felt out of place with the mostly female faculty. In the break room, conversation typically centered around such matters as Cuisinarts and toilet training — not high on my interests list. One of my hobbies is breeding roses. One day, I brought a bouquet into the faculty room to the oohs and ahhs of the teachers. From then on, I brought in a fresh arrangement each week. Before long, I developed a reputation as the school romantic and became a favorite of the teachers and the principal.

Can you think of a way of incorporating a current or past hobby into your worklife?

Make a lateral move

Sometimes, your current job is hopelessly dull. Can you make a lateral move? Examples:

> ✔ A biologist had spent years on bacterial biofilm but saw that another division of the company was working on a cool mouse gene project. He pitched his boss and the mouse-project boss, and got his transfer into a whole new job. *Note:* You're more likely to get to do new work within your current organization, where you're trusted. An outside employer is likely to hire you to do what you've been doing.

> ✔ An admin had always wanted to spend some time in Europe. When she heard the company was expanding into Spain, she begged her way into getting to help open their Barcelona office.

The World's Shortest Stress Management Course

I'm prone to being stressed. I believe I secrete more adrenaline than the average person. That scared me because I knew that high-stress people die younger. In addition, I saw that being a high-stress person was hurting my career and personal life. No one wants to be around someone who's stressed out.

In contrast, I saw that most successful people appear calm. For example, when watching C-SPAN, I noticed that most congresspeople and expert witnesses, among the nation's most influential people, remain calm, even when negotiating the world's most important issues. So I figured that to get what I want, I too need to be calm.

So, I've worked hard to figure out how to keep my stress under control. Here is what I've learned. I'll never be a laid-back person, but the following strategies have helped me, and subsequently my clients.

Stop rushing

At age 20, I visited Europe for the first time. I recall standing in the Louvre around 2 p.m. thinking, "If I can get through the Louvre in an hour, I can probably fit in Versailles before the end of the day." That was typical. My addiction to adrenaline, fed by always trying to cram in as many activities as possible, kept me from enjoying whatever I was doing and made me a more stressful person.

Lesson Learned: Do everything at a comfortable pace. Rarely is rushing worth it. Even good emergency room doctors rarely rush — they proceed with focus, but without rushing.

Be accepting

Live by the serenity prayer: May I have the serenity to accept the things I cannot change; courage to change the things I can; and wisdom to know the difference. In the workplace, everyone has projects they'd rather not do, but must. Yet some workers get stressed about it while others accept the inevitable.

On a related note: Accept people's fallibility. Everyone encounters people who are stupid, thoughtless, and even mean. You may even be married to one. People are incredibly hard to change — even PhD-toting psychologists often fail to fundamentally change their clients. If you can't cut the person out of your life, try to view him with charity rather than judgment: "We all have flaws. He's doing the best he can." People who are angered by or try to fix other people usually live stress-filled lives, and rarely change them much. You can refine but rarely remold.

Conserve your emotional energy units

You can often reduce your job stress by being conscious of how you expend your emotional energy units. Every day you start out with a full supply, but if you expend your energy units too rapidly, you're burned out before the end of the day. As you feel stress, ask yourself, "Am I expending my energy units wisely?"

Susannah, a home health nurse, came to me complaining of burnout. On questioning, it was clear that most of her burnout was caused by just three of her 30 patients. Those three refused to cooperate and their families were unhelpful and often loudly drunk. I asked her to consciously try to conserve her energy units while visiting those patients. A few days later, Susannah called and excitedly told me that the simple technique reduced her burnout enough that she no longer felt a need to change jobs.

Find support from someone fun

In ever-more-pressured workplaces, without a fun person to break things up, you can gyrate yourself into a whirling work dervish. The funmeister offers badly needed respites: a joke he pulled off the Internet, gossip about who's seeing whom, or a recipe for Last-Request Chocolate Cake. Recruit a funster onto your support team.

Decorate your workspace with flair

Many people feel less stress if they have an attractive workspace. Even all cubicles aren't alike. Want one near the window with the view? Far from the elevator? Near the chatterboxes? Away from them? Even if your cube is run-of-the-mill, your job may feel a bit less stressful if you decorate it to suit you. I recall one cubicle with an Oriental rug on the floor, oil paintings on the walls, and an Asian fountain on the desk.

Get permission to bring your pet to work

Fourteen of Vermont's Small Dog Electronics' employees bring their pets to work. And to boot, the employer pays 80 percent of their veterinary insurance. Workers and management rave: Not withstanding the occasional piddle, flea visitation, and dog-phobic employee, pets at work reduce stress, increase employee loyalty, and save employees the time and cost of a pet sitter. Pet perk — a great idea. The Web site www.dogfriendly.com/server/general/workplace lists hundreds of employers with pet-friendly policies. See whether your boss will bite.

Watch for early signs of stress

My neck starts to feel tight when I'm stressed out. When that happens, I take lessons from the yogis: I make sure my posture is good and take a few slow deep breaths. I may get up and stretch. I also often take a walk around the block or put on some music.

The next time you lose your cool, ask yourself, "What was the first clue I was getting stressed?" From then on, promise yourself to take preemptive action, even if it's just to remind yourself that it's only 15 minutes until your lunch break.

Think less and act more

When I'm already stressed, I ask myself, "Is there anything I can do right now to fix the problem?" If yes, I try to do it. If the answer is no, I immediately divert my attention by asking myself, "What do I want to do now?"

So many people analyze a problem to death: analysis paralysis. After a moderate amount of thinking, try something, anything. Figuring out an alternative approach is easier when you get feedback on what you've tried. Think less; act more.

Take three breaths and leave

Some people have short fuses — they go from calm to explosive in one second. So often they find themselves looking back and thinking, "I wish I hadn't said that." If that sounds like you, take the time to develop the habit — the *second* you *start* to feel angry — of taking three slow deep breaths, and if another person is the target of your anger, leaving the room. When you leave the room, ask yourself, "In the long run, will I be better or worse off if I get angry about this?" If, on reflection, you conclude that exploding is worthwhile, fine. You made a conscious choice to do it instead of letting your adrenaline dictate your behavior. But fact is, you will rarely decide it's worth getting angry.

Be in the moment

Everyone has reasons to be upset about things in the past. Thinking about them rarely helps. Rather, it usually increases your stress. Likewise, you shouldn't look *too* far ahead. When writing my first book, I focused on getting it done. I lived for the moment when I could see the book finished. That looking-forward orientation gave me one moment of pleasure but deprived me of thousands of good moments during the writing process — most work is filled with many little interesting problems to solve. Since then, I strive to stay *in the moment,* trying to derive pleasure in whatever I'm doing that minute. I find that makes work less stressful . . . sometimes.

Winning at Office Politics without Selling Your Soul

Employees often complain, "I can't take the politics," when they really mean, "I can't win at the politics." Here's a top-ten list for keeping your star rising and your back unstabbed.

✔ **Be powerfully placed.** Here's the ideal: You're in a department that's central to the organization, well funded, involved with a core or hot product, and led by a rising-star boss. If not, can you angle for a transfer?

✔ **Get tasks that are high priority and visible.** For example, it's usually better to be on the team that's creating a new joint venture with a big Chinese firm than to be on a team in charge of maintaining low-priority accounts. Usually, the people on that China project team will be the organization's best, and your contribution to the project's success is more likely to be noticed. To boost your chances of getting on the team, you might, in this example, along with your request, submit a little report you did on similar joint ventures.

✔ **Even if you're a clerk, think like a CEO.** Think of a way to streamline a procedure, build the bottom line, or make employees' lives easier.

✔ **Don't wink in the dark. Cautiously self-promote.** To get ahead, higher-ups must know how good you are. How do you let them know without press releases? Career coach Kate Wendleton recommends having a one-sentence message ready. For example, when your boss's boss sees you in the elevator and asks, "How are you, Sam?" instead of the usual, "Fine, Ms. Moneybags, how are you?" occasionally try something like, "Great. I just closed a deal with Astrogel." As writer Angela Durden says, when you work hard without promoting yourself, "it's like winking at a girl in the dark — you know what you're doing, but no one else does."

Unless you decide it's wiser for your boss to get the kudos, get credit for your brainchild. When you come up with a good idea or have drafted an impressive document, run it by a trusted colleague to be sure it isn't stupid. If it passes muster, bring it up at a staff meeting or e-mail the staff "to get feedback" on the idea. That way, everyone knows the gem was yours.

Don't rub your good work in co-workers' faces, especially weak employees'. They can be saboteurs. Instead, keep a record of everything good you do — useful at salary review time or if enemies try to build a case against you.

✔ **Make your boss look good.** Support him where you can. When you do a project, be sure to give due credit for your boss's assistance.

- ✔ **Use the keys to excellent communication** (I describe them in the earlier section "Developing wonderful communication skills").

- ✔ **Get feedback.** Ask co-workers how you're doing. Anything they wish you'd improve? Early feedback gives you time to fix things before you're a marked person.

- ✔ **Befriend a wise old soul.** Having a confidant who knows the political ropes really helps. Often these wise old souls no longer are interested in climbing the ladder. They'd rather play an avuncular role, passing on words of wisdom to the next generation.

- ✔ **Make friends in low places.** Often, employees such as receptionists and janitors know what's going on, and may be more likely than higher-ups to give you the inside scoop.

- ✔ **Perform unrandom acts of kindness.** Bake cookies for the office, look for legitimate reasons to compliment others, or throw a TGIF office party. Not only will doing such things help you politically, but you'll also enjoy your job more.

This list is all well and good, but in the real world, even if you play positive politics perfectly, employees can gang up on you: They may be threatened by you or dislike you, if only because you dress too nicely. Suppose that, as in *The Apprentice* TV series, three officemates decide, if only subconsciously, to form an alliance against you. They do plenty to make you look bad: keeping you out of the information loop, never supporting your proposals, not prioritizing getting your projects done, never offering to help you. And they bad-mouth you: "That Linda. She really gets more credit than she deserves." And if you dare show even a hint of frustration with them, they run to your boss complaining that you have a bad attitude that's destroying office morale. Even though you're a good employee, you can see that their machinations can get you fired. What should you do?

Assuming you prefer not to quit, in addition to positive politics strategies, you can:

- ✔ **Store your ammunition.** Keep a list of everything you do to try to build relationships with alliance members — from helping them out when they're overworked to those brownies you bring in. Brownies are potent political weapons.

- ✔ **Try to neutralize your enemies.** Ask them about things they're interested in, take coffee breaks with them, and so forth.

- ✔ *Gently* **confront the group.** Convene a formal meeting with them. Recount your efforts to work well with them. Ask what *you* can do to improve the office environment. Don't expect them to offer to change anything. That's okay. Often, over the next few weeks, they'll cool down. Don't threaten to go to the boss; it's implicit that you might, and making it explicit can motivate them to go to the boss first. That could force you onto the defensive.

✔ **Have one of your powerful allies intervene.** Perhaps your wise old soul or another respected employee can gently let the alliance know that top management likes you, and that if they continue to mess with you, they — not you — will suffer.

✔ **Go to your boss, perhaps with your ally.** Show your documentation of your peacemaking efforts and, if necessary, evidence of your on-the-job accomplishments.

✔ **Decide that you can accept the status quo or go to your boss's boss.** This rarely works, so you should also start looking for a new job.

Staying Current the Smart Way

Staying current keeps you competent and confident, and increases your employability. But with the information explosion, staying current isn't easy. Before going back to school for a course, let alone a degree, see whether these *just-in-time learning* approaches can help:

✔ **The Hey Joe School.** When you're stuck, simply ask someone in your office, or by phone, "Hey Joe, how do I . . . ?" This simple approach can be powerful. Unlike in a class, where you're amassed with information with no real-world opportunity to apply it, at the Hey Joe School, you learn what you need when you need it. Just-in-time learning.

Most organizations have experts at various things — for example, the computer wizard or the nut who can recite all your company's product specifications in his sleep. Because they're so good, they're likely in demand. If you expect them to return your e-mail within the decade, go out of your way to help them when you can. And when they help you, a thank-you note or little present doesn't hurt.

✔ **The tutor.** For most people, the best way to learn something complicated, such as a computer program, isn't from a course, but a tutor. Who might tutor you? A savvy co-worker in your office, a community college instructor interested in moonlighting, or someone who answers an ad you place on an online discussion group or even on craigslist.org.

Set up your tutoring this way: Keep track of all your questions and use them as the basis for the next tutoring session. Ask whether you can call your tutor for help between sessions.

✔ **The mentor.** Find a respected person in your field and agree that you can call her for counsel. Or create an online version: Form an e-mail group with colleagues in which each member can post questions for the group's consideration. It's easy to set one up. A great free service is at groups.yahoo.com. An appropriate group may already be available — check the groups tab on google.com.

✔ **The article.** Articles are wonderful — they offer condensed expertise on virtually any topic at minimal cost and require minimal time. And thanks to `google.com` or links from your professional association's Web site, finding on-target articles is easy and fast.

✔ **The book.** How terrific to have a large quantity of an expert's best thoughts, available 24/7 for the cost of a large pizza, or free from the library. And you can search `Amazon.com`'s database of 3 million books to find precisely the title you're looking for, often including reviews by readers and experts.

✔ **The electronic discussion group.** Of the hundreds of thousands of groups, one is likely to provide you with an on-target education. That may be the best way to stay up on current issues and trends. Find groups at `groups.yahoo.com` or by searching on Google's groups tab.

✔ **The workshop.** Professional associations and university extension programs offer workshops that focus on the basics or cutting-edge issues. Ask your colleagues which workshops they find most useful.

✔ **Certifications.** In thousands of specializations, you can earn a respected certification by taking a few courses or via self-study. Check local colleges and `certificates.gradschools.com`.

✔ **How good an employee are you, really?** I have counseled hundreds of fired employees. Barely a handful said it was their fault. My sense is that many of them had good self-esteem but in fact were weak employees. Could you be one of them? A way to find out is a *360-degree evaluation:* asking people all around you (for example, boss, supervisee, peer, customer, vendor), "As part of my professional development, I'd like some feedback. What would you say are my strengths and weaknesses?" Requesting a 360-degree evaluation is scary, but perhaps less scary than a stalled career.

✔ **The world's fastest self-improvement strategy.** On your refrigerator, desk, or computer monitor frame, write, "I need to stop *(insert something).* I need to start *(insert something).* I need to continue doing *(insert something).*" Every time you drink something, read those words aloud to keep your goals front and center.

✔ **Continual self-improvement . . . give me a break!** A client of mine says that he can experience ongoing improvement without being overwhelmed by remembering a Japanese car company's motto. Instead of, "How can I improve?" he asks, "How can I be just a little bit better?"

Sometimes, I wonder, though, whether everyone deserves an even easier approach — giving yourself a total break from self-improvement. Is there not a point at which, at least for a while, you deserve to say, "I'm good enough!"?

The Three-Minute MBA: The World's Shortest Management Course

Many employees hold their breath when those oh-so-confident MBAs march in. Alas, those mathematical models, simulations, and case studies that seemed so clever in graduate school rarely work as well in the real world. MBA programs do teach some valid principles, but it's easy to lose sight of those needles in the haystack.

I attempt to remedy that here. All these principles are real-world proven. At the risk of hubris exceeding that even of new MBAs, I believe that if you follow just these principles, you will improve more as a manager and leader than if you had that $100,000 sheepskin.

- **Hire smart.** The best managers hire wisely:

   - Encourage your respected employees, colleagues, and friends to refer truly outstanding candidates.

   - Generally, value intelligence and drive over experience and degrees.

   - Rather than asking standard interview questions such as "What is your greatest weakness?" put candidates in simulations of situations they're likely to face on the job.

   - Instead of calling three references, who rarely criticize a candidate, ask your finalist candidates for ten references. Call all ten at night, when they won't be at their desk. Leave voicemail messages explaining that you're hiring for an important position and want the reference to call back only if the candidate is truly outstanding. Unless you get at least seven callbacks, you probably should move on to another candidate.

- **Cut your losses.** If, within one to three weeks, you get the sense that a hire isn't excellent, and attempts at remediation or clarifying your expectations don't quickly bear fruit, it's usually wisest to let her go. She's unlikely to become excellent. Great managers spend their time on higher-payoff tasks than the remediation of weak employees. Examples of these tasks include developing strategy, acquiring resources, and supporting strong supervisees to do their jobs better (see the next bullet).

- **Inspire; don't micromanage.** Develop a truly worthy agenda for your work group and, if possible, incorporate your supervisees' input, which inspires them to act on the agenda. That doesn't just mean giving motivational speeches. It means being a role model — you gotta walk that talk. Also, be liberal with deserved praise, sending copies of attaboys to higher-ups. Don't micromanage. Do the opposite: Free up your supervisees to do their job with a minimum of rules, policing, and accountability paperwork.

✔ **Communicate wonderfully.** Most people think they communicate well but don't. You must be so clear that a junior high school student would understand and appreciate what you say. You must be so concise that someone with ADD would still be paying attention at the end of your utterance. You must listen more carefully than you ever have before. When you must criticize, do it in a way that allows the person to save face. For example, "I've noticed *(insert problem, stated very briefly)*. Do you think that's a valid concern? And if so, what you do think should be done?" (I discuss developing communication skills in detail earlier in this chapter.)

✔ **Master meetings.** Meetings cost a fortune. Even assuming no travel costs, you have the participants' salaries and benefits, and they have to stop their work to attend. So, call meetings only when that cost is truly justified (for example, when a problem requires instant group brainstorming). Meetings in which people give non-urgent reports usually aren't worth the money. That should be done by e-mail.

When you have meetings, send a tight agenda to participants in advance. Inviting only the few people likely to contribute the most not only saves money, but also produces better results. You can always e-mail the meetings' results to others. At the meeting, if at all possible, keep to the agenda and its time limits.

✔ **Be absolutely ethical. Always.** Ethics are crucial, not only because you and your supervisees will feel better about their work, but also because unethical leaders lead to the devolution of civilization. Everyone wants to feel like they leave the world better, not worse. The test: Would you be proud to tell your child what you're doing?

Enjoying Success at Every Career Stage

A lot of career advice is just as applicable to someone starting out as it is to someone starting to think about retirement. But some counsel is stage-specific, as I explain in the following sections.

When you're just starting out

In your first career years, of course, you're probably still working on becoming technically competent. But perhaps as important, don't ignore the soft stuff: communication skills, developing a powerful network, and entrepreneurial skills. This section shows you how to do all three.

Strengthen your one-on-one communication skills

You probably think you already have them, and you're probably wrong. (See the section "Developing wonderful communication skills," earlier in this chapter, for tips that you can use now.)

Network now

Developing useful contacts takes time. Networking probably won't help you land your first job, but it will help you later.

First, develop a few-second self-commercial. For example, "I'm having a good time as an assistant manager on a small Wi-Fi project, but I think I'm ready for something bigger." Self-commercials are useful when you run into a boss in the elevator, and during networking activities. Keep your self-commercial ready to use when you

- ✔ **Start an *Insider's Group*.** These groups are made up of people in your line of work who communicate via a Yahoo! group (check out `groups.yahoo.com`) and perhaps periodically in-person.

- ✔ **Join your professional association.** Volunteer for its program committee or even to serve as an officer. You'd be surprised how often organizations are searching for leaders.

- ✔ **Attend gatherings.** To maximize your networking opportunities, be on the greeting committee. Or act like the host: Find out about people and offer to get them a drink or food, or introduce them to someone else. Start conversations, perhaps about the host, the event, or something in the news.

Even if you take part in these activities, you probably won't develop a useful network unless you create deep connections with people. The key to successful networking: deep connection. You must get your protagonist to discuss his or her passion or problem. How do you do that? With probing questions. Follow these steps when you meet someone new, and you're well on your way to networking successfully:

1. **After introducing yourself and making an *environment comment* (about the venue, food, speaker, weather, and so on), start with work.**

   For example, you may say, "What do you do at work?"

2. **Listen carefully.**

   Often the answer reveals a passion or a hint of a problem. That hint may be as subtle as a tone of voice dropping while your new contact describes what he does.

3. **If he reveals a passion or a hint of a problem, ask a follow-up question.**

   If you pick up on a potential problem, you may say, "Sounds like maybe your work isn't so thrilling." Keep listening carefully.

4. **When the person runs out of things to say on the subject, express empathy before asking another question.**

   Asking another question too soon may make the other person feel interrogated. Instead, try telling him about, for example, your employee from hell. Then consider asking another question or two to better understand his situation, and perhaps you can gently guide him to a solution.

5. **If your initial question about work doesn't suggest a passion or problem to discuss, move to a question about family.**

   Ask, for example, "Do you have a family?" Again, listen for a sign of a passion or problem.

6. **If that yields nothing, move to outside-of-work interests.**

   You may say, for example, "Outside of work, what do you spend a lot of time on?" That can reveal such things as a home remodel project that he loves or is a pain, or a health problem.

7. **When you're ready to end the chat but would like to continue the relationship, say something like, "I've enjoyed our chat. Would you like to continue the conversation sometime?"**

People love to talk and too rarely are listened to carefully about what's important to them. As Fran Leibowitz says, only half joking, "There is no listening. There's just waiting for the other person to stop talking." So, if you listen actively to a person talking about his passion or problem, you increase the chances of him wanting to befriend you or help you. And at minimum, you'll have had a more rewarding experience than if your conversation focused on the weather. Chapter 8 has more information about networking.

Develop entrepreneurial skills

School rarely teaches entrepreneurship, but it's key in many middle- and upper-level positions in both the non- and for-profit sectors, and even in some areas of government. And of course, entrepreneurial skills prepare you for self-employment.

Of course, you can learn in an MBA program, but before spending the big bucks and big time, try learning at the elbow of a good entrepreneur, even if you're just filing and making coffee. As long as you watch carefully and ask questions, you should pick up some good lessons. Or use the services of the Small Business Administration (www.sba.gov), which offers courses in entrepreneurship and one-on-one free coaching from retired executives.

When you're mid-career

Mid-career is when most people start to top out or burn out. Want to avoid both? Follow these tips:

✔ **Plot out your career arc.** Perhaps rethink what you want to be. Set goals and sub-goals. Say you're an optometrist and think you'll be bored if you spend the rest of your life asking, "Better with lens A or lens B?" So your goal may be to teach part time at the local optometry school. Your sub-goals might be to read a book on the art of teaching and then to teach a workshop at the next optometry association meeting.

✔ **If you want to continue moving up, continue to grow your skill set.** Leaders read leadership-oriented magazines when exercising on the treadmill, find role models and mentors, and engage career coaches to help them navigate choppy waters. Areas of particular importance as you move up:

- **Strategic thinking,** incorporating large amounts of data, but ultimately relying on good intuition.

- **The ability to inspire employees** to work hard and smart, both in their own and in the organization's interest.

- **Delegation.** Take the time to train people to handle delegated tasks or find people to whom you can more confidently delegate.

- **Running a meeting** in an efficient yet inspirational way.

- **Public speaking.** Key is the art of storytelling. Consider taking a storytelling workshop or joining Toastmasters, a club with chapters all over the world in which members give talks to each other to improve their public speaking and to make connections.

- **Conversance with all aspects of a business.** The technology, finance, sales, marketing, and so on.

✔ **Derive more meaning from your work.** Most people want to do this, but they don't know how. Many people think the only answer is a career change into a "make-a-difference" career. Especially after age 30, however, this change can be difficult to do while meeting your expenses. Easier is to ask yourself, "How can I make more of a difference in my current job? Do I want to mentor a younger employee? Learn a new skill? Speak my truth about a political issue? Take a leadership role in an employee fundraising effort? Speak out against unethical practices in my workplace? Volunteer for a charity that could really use my help?"

When you're in your final years on the job

Ever wonder whether you're considered deadwood? I'd feel terrible if my co-workers thought so, even if my job was secure. And these days, ever fewer jobs are.

The more yeses, the more likely you're considered deadwood:

✔ Compared with years past, you're working on less important projects.

✔ You've been reassigned to a less powerful boss.

✔ Your co-workers rarely seek your professional advice.

✔ Your peers' raises are larger than yours.

- ✔ You're not current on best practices or technology.
- ✔ You deride those who work harder than you.
- ✔ You're eagerly awaiting retirement.

Especially if you think you may be perceived as over-the-hill, and even if you're not, the following sections present strategies if you're in the late stages of your career.

Learn something new

Acquiring a new skill or knowledge is energizing and demonstrates to your boss that you're not just going through the motions until retirement.

When you're ready to learn something new, choose something that you feel you can enjoy learning, is valued by your employer, and would be visible to your boss and others. For example, if your company is planning to upgrade its project management software, you might check out the various packages and recommend one to your boss. If you can't learn something by reading on your own, the process is often much easier with a tutor than a course. (See the earlier section "Staying Current the Smart Way" for full details.)

Brand yourself as a wise elder

You may no longer work 14 hours a day or know Version 8.0 cold, but your many years in the workplace may enable you to prevent and solve problems that even the most eager newbie can't. So, rather than compete with the young fire-breathing dragons, establish yourself as a Wise Elder. Here's how:

- ✔ With young upstarts or others who may welcome counsel or mentorship, say things like, "I notice you're working on a challenging project. I've had some experience with that sort of thing, so if you have a question or simply want to kick it around a bit, I'd be pleased to do that."

- ✔ Help people, especially young ones, to network — introduce them to the power people and others who can abet their careers.

- ✔ In your memos, reports, and proposals, mention any relevant lessons you've learned from past experience.

- ✔ In meetings, say things like, "I faced a similar problem awhile back. We tried an approach similar to what's being contemplated here, but it didn't work. Finally, we tried X and it worked well. I'm wondering whether we should consider trying that here. What do you think?"

Angle for jobs in which age is a plus

In certain jobs, age is a plus. For example, you may be the ideal candidate to become a rainmaker (someone who brings in lucrative clients), internal or external consultant, or to work on a product aimed at older customers. Sometimes, to get the okay, all you need to do is make the case to your boss.

Consider changing careers

Even if you don't have much fire in your belly and you're no longer the sharpest tool in the shed, you're not doomed to staying in that same old job you're tired of. Consider senior-friendly workplaces. For example: traditional industries such as banking, transportation, food and wine, nonprofits serving the aged, senior housing, teaching, architecture (mainly older people are in a position to hire architects), the government (which makes great efforts to hire people of all ages), fundraising (big donors are generally older and prefer dealing with their age peers).

Also consider self-employment. Want to use your lifetime of experience as a consultant? Run an espresso cart (with a name like "Grandma's Grind") in a carefully selected location? Or consider one of the few ways to earn while you sleep — affiliate marketing on the Internet (check out www. superaffiliatehandbook.com).

Mind your personal appearance

Most people look at least acceptable when they're young, but with time's ravages, it becomes increasingly important that you make the most of what you have left:

- **Have good posture.** Sit and stand up straight, and walk with a bounce in your step. I know, sometimes you don't feel like bouncing. Bounce anyway.

- **Get enough sleep.** It's easier to bounce when you get seven or eight hours of sleep. Also, you'll look younger — everyone looks older when sleep-deprived. Even if you have to do it in your car, consider taking a half-hour nap in the afternoon. Nothing makes you look more like deadwood than appearing fatigued.

- **Use caffeine judiciously.** Mainstream medical research has come to consensus that one to three cups of coffee a day isn't harmful and may even be helpful. Caffeine certainly increases energy and cognitive function. But people do build tolerance to caffeine, so drink as little as you need to maintain your energy.

- **Stride; don't trudge.** Plod down the hall and you look like deadwood.

- **Avoid a hang-dog face.** Smile as much as possible. Bonus: Your smile distracts people from the part of your face that most reveals your age: your eyes.

- **Wear glasses.** Speaking of your eyes, glasses cover a multitude of sins: red eyes, glassy eyes, raccoon eyes, and crow's feet. Don't need glasses to improve your eyesight? Get a pair with plain glass lenses.

✔ **Dress well.** No need to look like a 30-year-old, but dress smartly and neatly. Wearing an old, tight-fitting, brown suit is like wearing a sign that says, "I'm deadwood." Clothing tips:

- Think three times before buying clothes meant for 20-somethings. The contrast between your clothes and your age will accentuate the very thing you're trying to distract from.

- Soft colors make most people look younger.

- Choose clothes that hide your bad features. For example, if you have flabby arms, wear ¾ sleeves in the summer.

- Be sure your clothes are pressed. The rumpled look doesn't work, even if you're a professor. There's no faster way to look burned out.

✔ **Groom your hair.** For most women, a medium-length cut works best. Older guys, keep your hair relatively short. Both men and women can consider coloring their hair; your original color usually looks best. Guys, that beard may have looked cool when you were younger, but now, it probably just makes you look older.

✔ **Whiten your teeth.** Get your teeth whitened or do it yourself. It costs little and makes a difference.

Examine your finances carefully

If you're eager to retire, see whether you can cut your expenses and afford to retire earlier. The following tips may help:

✔ Estimate how much money you'll need for retirement and how much more money you'd have if you waited a year or five. The Retirement Center at vanguard.com offers useful tools. (Click on "personal investing," then "planning and education," then "retirement planning.")

✔ Consider selling your house and moving to smaller digs or a place in a less expensive location. I was amazed to discover that a home that, on either coast, would cost a half million dollars, could be had in the fast-growing university town of Austin, Texas, for $150,000.

✔ You can safely cut costs on your kids' and grandkids' college education. There's no compelling evidence that attending a low-cost college will impede success and happiness. I have a PhD from Berkeley in the evaluation of education and have written three books on higher education, and I truly believe there is no need to shell out the big bucks. At minimum, insist your child help pay the way.

✔ Reconsider all big purchases. For example, would you really get that much more pleasure from a $2,000 plasma TV than from the TV you already have? From that flying vacation staying at deluxe hotels than from a driving vacation staying at moderate motels? Do you really need more clothes, jewelry, or a new car?

Create an exciting vision for your retirement

When you devise cool plans for your retirement, you have something great to look forward to instead of just dreading your current existence. For example, might you want to tutor illiterate adults? Write that novel? Create the ultimate garden? Learn how to play the piano? Get involved in a community political issue? Serve on your local school board? Become the world's best grandparent? Get involved in your local community theater? Renew the relationship with your spouse or child? All of the above?

Dream away, but don't assume that retirement will necessarily be preferable to working. A few months after retirement, many people wish they were back at work. Too often, after the first few months of retirement, you run out of things to do. If you're contemplating retirement, vacation for a few weeks and ask yourself how you'd like 10 or 20 years of that. Will you soon feel irrelevant, out to pasture? Lay out a plan for how you'll fill the next five years. Will you really fill the time with volunteer work, golf, reading, gardening, and friends? Or will that get old? When in doubt, cut back rather than retire.

Also, retirement apparently isn't good for your health — the average person lives only two years after retirement. I plan to work until I drop, while still trying to squeeze in the enjoyable things that many people save for retirement. For example, I had never been in a play before. So, after a few acting lessons and two unsuccessful auditions, I was cast in a community theater production of Agatha Christie's *Ten Little Indians* and had a ball! I urge you not to wait until retirement to do the things you want to do.

I hope I have many productive years left, but you never know. So, I figure I better use my time wisely before I lose it. I tell myself to take on only clients I truly believe in, and to share with my readers, clients, and listeners as many new and valuable ideas as I can come up with. The old saw, "No one ever died wishing they spent more time at the office," doesn't apply to me. I'd prefer to croak while working.

Assessing Your Chances of Getting Ahead

Up isn't the only way. In fact, many higher-ups wonder whether the extra salary is worth the extra headaches. But for many people, getting ahead is a way to make a career cooler. How likely are *you* to get ahead? After you've been in your new career for a few months, hopefully having followed the principles in this chapter, try this self-test. Or take it now to give you goals to shoot for. Many of these items are from a *Fortune* magazine inventory.

Score yourself on each question, then just add them up to get your total score:

_____ 1. Compare your work with that of your peers. If you think you add more value, give yourself 1–3 points. If you're less productive, take away 1–3 points.

Can't figure out how valuable you are? Think about, or even ask, your peers, suppliers, or customers how much they value what you do.

_____ 2. Do you play a leadership role in tasks and projects central to the organization's success? If so, give yourself 1–3 points.

_____ 3. Do you perform a worker-bee task that is so crucial to the organization that they can't afford to promote you from there? If so, subtract 3–5 points.

_____ 4. If at least one of your suggestions for improving the organization has been adopted and you got credit, give yourself 1–3 points.

_____ 5. If your organization or department is ripe for downsizing, subtract 1–3 points.

How do you know? Here are some clues:

• Your department's product stacks up poorly against others in the organization or among your competitors.

• Morale is low and office politics are high.

• You're involved in cutting costs rather than building market share or creating new products.

_____ 6. Are you known for your enthusiasm? Give yourself from minus 3 to plus 3 points.

_____ 7. Do you have long-term career goals and specific strategies to achieve them? If so, give yourself 1–3 points.

_____ 8. If you've already received a promotion, give yourself 4 points.

_____ 9. Are you pampered? For example, if you still need an administrative assistant to do your word processing and spreadsheets, you look like a dinosaur and a high-maintenance one at that. Subtract 2 points.

_____ 10. Do co-workers and bosses frequently seek your counsel? Give yourself 1–3 points.

_____ 11. If your co-workers and bosses were polled, would all or almost all of them say that they like you? Give yourself 3 points.

_____ 12. Have you cultivated important allies in and outside your department? If so, give yourself 1–3 points.

_____ 13. Do you regularly ask friends and colleagues for feedback on how you're doing? If so, give yourself 1 point. If you've then improved, give yourself 2 more points.

_____ 14. Are you actively upgrading your skills in areas valued by employers? If so, give yourself 1–2 points.

_____ 15. Do you build your reputation by writing articles, speaking at industry events, or being active in your professional association? If so, give yourself 1–3 points.

_____ 16. If you lost your job today, could you tap a network of people for advice and job leads? If so, give yourself 1–4 points.

_____ 17. Do you have portable skills such as technical or management know-how? If so, give yourself 1–3 points.

_____ 18. Listen to your boss during a performance review. If she talks to you about your role in the organization's big picture, give yourself 1–3 points.

_____ 19. Is your boss's star rising or in a death spiral? Give yourself between plus 2 and minus 2 points.

_____ 20. Do you dress like someone in the position to which you aspire? Give yourself between minus 2 and plus 2 points.

_____ 21. If you were the boss, would you hire you? If yes, give yourself 3 points. If no, subtract 3 points.

_____ 22. If you were the boss, would you promote you? If yes, give yourself 5 points.

Scoring:

10 or fewer: You may be downsizing material. Is this a wake-up call to start working on some of the items on this list? Would you be more motivated to do so in a different job? In a different career?

11–25: You may be safe . . . for now.

26–35: Star potential.

36–45: Superstar potential.

46+: Send me your resume.

Think twice before aspiring to management

In the past, it made sense to want to go from worker bee to manager, because it meant more money, more prestige, and a launchpad to even more prestigious job titles. Things have changed. The hierarchy is flatter, so fewer opportunities for promotion exist. Senior management demands ever-more productivity, and at the same time, new laws make firing incompetents tougher. In the book *Gig,* Chad Finlay, a video game designer turned manager, said, "When I first got into games, you're making stuff and you get to read cool reviews about it. . . . Now I'm walking around, 'How's this going? Are you getting this done? I need this by Friday.' It got old."

When you're promoted to manager, your camaraderie with your former peers tends to decline. Your credibility with your former peers also is likely to slide because staying current is hard when you're a manager. For example, few programmers have the time to keep up with the latest programming languages when their full-time job is to manage other programmers.

Even more dangerous, management requires different skills than those required of worker bees. The Peter Principle often raises its ugly head — the great classroom teacher may not be a great principal.

And don't forget about money. Managers usually work longer hours than worker bees and, because managers don't get paid for overtime, they often earn less per hour than the people they supervise! With a 40 percent to 60 percent marginal tax rate, the after-tax benefit of a promotion to management probably won't improve your lifestyle.

The final kibosh: At a time when most people wish they had more spare time, managers work long hours.

An often smarter move than aspiring to management: a lateral move to one of the company's cool areas.

Chapter 12

Light My Fire, Please! Overcoming Procrastination

In This Chapter

▶ Discovering how school turned you into a procrastinator

▶ Checking out a quick plan for curing procrastination

▶ Using custom-tailored cures for excuse making

▶ Trying some all-purpose cures

▶ Knowing what to do if you can't stop procrastinating

*L*et's come back to this chapter later. (Just kidding.)

But you can get into this gradually. I start with some surprising truths about procrastination.

Most independently wealthy people continue to work. For example, Fortune-500 CEOs stay in their jobs even after they have more money than they could spend in five lifetimes. You say, "That's not surprising — they have a cool career." Well, consider this: 100 workers at a cheese factory bought a lottery ticket and ended up winning the largest prize in the history of the Wisconsin lottery — $208 million. They were cheese cutters, packers, and maintenance workers, and many of them worked the night shift, not widely considered cool careers. Yet many of them came to work the very next night (Sunday) and plan to continue working indefinitely.

Many people find that work is key to feeling they have value. I've had many clients who complained of depression, and when they found a good job, that depression subsided. I call work Prozac without side effects.

Yet a surprising number of my unemployed clients admit to doing everything possible to avoid work: They procrastinate in their job search, and when they're on a job, they spend as much time as possible chatting, playing on the Net, and so on.

No surprise, procrastination devastates one's career. When I give a speech to successful executives, I often ask, "How many of you think of yourself as a procrastinator?" Only 15 percent raise their hand. Yet when I ask the same question of groups of unemployed people, about 85 percent do. Procrastination is a career killer. In this chapter, I show you how to turn the tables and defeat procrastination.

In the Beginning: How People Develop a Habit of Procrastination

Psychotherapists offer a variety of explanations for why people procrastinate: fear of failure, fear of rejection, fear of success, and so on. With many of my clients, procrastination is simply a bad habit caused by their teachers. See whether this sounds like you:

At some point in school, for the first time, you waited until the last minute to get started on a paper or studying for a test. Pumped by adrenaline, you managed to get it done. And lo and behold, you got a decent grade.

You promised not to procrastinate again — the experience was too stressful — just as the person who gets drunk for the first time gets a horrible hangover and swears, "I won't do that again."

But unconsciously, a little voice within you said, "Hmm, that was kind of cool: I got to avoid that big ugly project until the last minute, and then the adrenaline of the deadline pumped me up — kind of a fun drug — and I did okay!"

From then on, when an unpleasant assignment came along, you wondered whether you could get away with cramming. And at some point, when an assignment felt especially odious or your friends invited you to par-tay, you figured, "Well, okay, I'll take the risk. It worked before; maybe it will work again." So, you delayed the task until the adrenaline rush of the fast-approaching deadline kicked in, and miracle of miracles, again, another decent grade!

Slowly, like the budding alcoholic or drug addict who comes up with ever-more flimsy reasons to get drunk or high, you, the nascent procrastinator, came up with ever-feebler rationalizations for getting your adrenaline fix: "There's this great TV show on" or "I'll be more in the mood tomorrow." And thanks to rampant grade inflation (almost 40 percent of college students had an A average in high school, double the rate of just 20 years ago), a reasonably bright student can get good grades with last-minute work. By the time you finished school, you became a full-blown adrenaline junkie: Procrastination had become your normal response to an assignment.

Alas, in the real world, you won't find as much grade inflation. To succeed in all but low-level careers, many employers insist that to get a mere passing grade, projects be completed to high standards. Unless you're exceptionally bright, that last-minute crap doesn't cut it. You'll probably be the one who gets downsized, offshored, outsourced, or automated. And, of course, if you're self-employed, procrastination will likely kill your business because you have no one to pick up the slack if you, well, slack.

Most people are fully aware that procrastination hurts them. They know it's like a credit card: fun when you use it, but painful when the bill comes in. Nevertheless, they admit that they're unlikely to change. They accept their procrastination as an immutable weakness, much as a blind person accepts his handicap. If you're convinced that you won't change no matter how many strategies for overcoming procrastination I offer you, this chapter still has something for you: ways to increase your chances of success assuming you're an incorrigible procrastinator; see the later section "Advice for the Incurable Procrastinator." If, however, you want to improve upon your tendency to procrastinate, I can help you. Keep reading.

The World's Shortest Course in Overcoming Procrastination

If you're fed up with the way procrastination is hurting your work and personal life and you're ready to stop, this chapter contains dozens of ways to help you. You won't need them all. Think of this chapter as a smorgasbord of procrasti-cures. Try one. Doesn't do the trick? Try something else.

How your humble author controls his procrastination

I try to stay in the moment. I don't think about what fun thing I could be doing instead, or how much work is ahead of me. I try to stay focused on whatever my next few-second task is. When I feel a compelling urge to play instead of work, I usually indulge it — guilt-free. For example, I take a few minutes to play on the Net or walk around the block and smell the roses (literally), but I try to keep my breaks short so that I have plenty of time to accomplish my work.

Prefer not to bother reviewing dozens of options? Try this plan. It amalgamates the strategies that have worked best for the largest number of my clients. To start:

1. **Decide whether you really want to do the task.** Maybe its benefits aren't worth the effort. If you decide you want to do the task, do you want to do it now or schedule it? Consciously choosing makes it more likely that you'll actually complete the tasks you decide to do.

2. **Picture the benefits.** If you decide to do the task, picture the benefits of getting it done: a benefit could be as small as an attaboy from your boss or spouse or simply the pleasure of getting the task done and off your to-do list. Or the benefit could be much bigger — bringing you a step closer to being able to buy a home, for example.

3. **Build in reminders.** Procrastinators tend to repress thoughts of doing the dreaded task. To make sure you don't forget, write an alphabet letter on your hand, set a timer to go off when you should be starting the task, or simply schedule the darn thing on your calendar.

   Tell people your goal and deadline. For example, you can say, "I have an important report due on Friday." Often, that can motivate you; when they later ask you whether you got it done, you won't have to say no or lie.

   Find someone to compete with. Suppose you're both looking for a job. Make a bet: The person who lands an in-person interview first wins, for example, a dinner at a favorite restaurant.

4. **Identify the moment of truth.** This is the moment you're consciously or unconsciously deciding whether to work on the dreaded task or not. Perhaps the moment is at the beginning, or maybe it's when you reach a hard part of the task. At that moment, say aloud, "Stop!" Literally pinch yourself for sliding back into your wicked ways, and muster the energy and discipline to get started or keep moving. That's the moment of truth, the moment where you have to believe that "Right now, it's in my interest to be productive rather than to have fun." Get through it and you'll find it easier to continue. If that doesn't work, proceed to Step 5.

5. **Ask yourself, "What's making me reluctant to do the task?"** Your response, for example, may be "It's going to be hard," "I'd rather do something fun," or "I don't know where to start."

6. **What would your wise twin say in response?** For example:

   • If you're afraid the task will be hard, your wise twin may say, "You can divide it into small bites and get help when you need it."

   • Don't know how to break it up into little steps? Your wise twin may say, "Who could help you do that?"

- If you're procrastinating looking for a job because you believe you're not qualified, your wise twin may ask you, "Is that true? If so, get training or change careers." If you *are* reasonably but not perfectly qualified, your wise twin may say, "You'll get even better as you work on the job. But you won't have a chance to get better unless you make those phone calls."

- If you're tempted to do something fun instead of the task, your wise twin may ask you, "Is the short-term relief worth the long-term consequences? Your call."

7. **Struggle for no more than one minute.** Sitting stuck is the most painful part of a task. The fear of staying stuck makes many people procrastinate the entire task. My clients have found the *one-minute struggle* to be an invaluable rule. When you reach a hard part, struggle for no longer than 60 seconds. If, at that point, you haven't made progress, you're unlikely to make progress even if you sit there for an hour. So, at the one-minute mark, stop and get help or decide that you can do the task without that hard part.

8. **Commit to a small amount of effort (for example, three phone calls).**

Work at being efficient during that small amount of effort. Frequently ask yourself, "Is this the straightest line to getting the task done?" Perhaps give yourself a reward for getting it done; an example is working all the way through a commercial break, and then letting yourself watch the next segment. Achieving even a small success will motivate you to do more.

9. **Look back and ask yourself whether it was worth the effort to get the task done.** That can make you less likely to procrastinate on the next task.

10. **Block out some time for pure, unadulterated, guilt-free fun.**

Cured? If not, read on.

Cures for Every Imaginable Excuse

Some procrastinators can be helped by a cure tailored to their particular excuse for procrastinating. The following cures for making excuses apply both to job seekers and to those who have already found cool careers.

The fear-of-failure excuse

In other words: "I'm afraid of failing." Sometimes, fear is a sign you shouldn't tackle a task. But if you think doing the task is probably in your best interest but you're too scared to try, one or more of the following tactics may help.

Feel the fear and do it anyway

If, rationally, you believe that the potential rewards of doing the task justify the risk, do as author Susan Jeffers says, "Feel the fear and do it anyway."

Sure, if the cost of failure is huge, don't risk it. For example, if you've been doing mediocre work and your organization is in financial trouble, you probably shouldn't ask for a raise — that could get you fired. But if the risk/reward ratio is good, feel the fear and do it anyway.

Not trying usually means greater failure

If you don't try, you're a guaranteed failure. If you give it a shot, you have at least some chance of succeeding, and at minimum, you'll learn from your failure. You'll also gain self-respect and the esteem of others. People who try and fail are respected more than people who don't try at all.

Think less and do more

As a child, I'd lie awake worrying about dying. As a young adult, I interpreted every twinge as a sign of an impending heart attack. Doctors tried to reassure me that nothing was wrong, while therapists tried to find the cause of my hypochondria. But nothing worked. I was a worrywart. But at age 30, I suddenly stopped worrying. Who cured me? My wife. "Martin," she ordered, "the more you think about your health, the more in knots you are. From now on, every time you get a hypochondriacal thought, force yourself to think of something else." Within two weeks, I was cured. That was years ago. Of course, now I worry about little green men from Mars coming to destroy the earth. Just kidding.

Why did I tell you that story? Because too often, people procrastinate by thinking a problem to death — *analysis paralysis.* This, of course, usually leads to a worse result than if they had tried something, even if it ended up not working.

If you stay at the source of a river until you figure out the precise route to its mouth, you'll never arrive there. Most successful people do minimum planning, try something, and then revise, revise, and revise again. Start down the river and then make midcourse corrections.

Avoiding analysis paralysis is particularly important for career searchers. Rarely can you make progress just sitting there and thinking. Read something, write something, phone someone, or visit someone.

I've found analysis paralysis to be a particular problem with clients who have had psychotherapy that focuses on the childhood roots of their problems. Many of these people appear *more* paralyzed as a result. They seem stuck in the past, more interested in talking yet again about what their parents or siblings did to them decades ago than in doing something to get unstuck.

Stop your downward spiral

Fear is usually better and worse at different times. Often, what makes things worse is momentum: One unproductive thought triggers another, which triggers another, and before you know it, you're overwhelmed.

The key is to stop unproductive thinking before it builds momentum — stopping a rock that's just starting to roll down a hill is easy, but if it gains speed, it can knock you over. So, as soon as you recognize an unproductive thought, just say *Stop!* to yourself and do something productive. That sounds simplistic, but it often works.

Each time you complete a small part of a task, you're starting the spiral upward.

Don't wait until you feel more confident

It works the other way around. The more you do, even if it isn't very successful, the better you'll feel. The less you do, the worse you'll feel.

Try affirmations

I used to make fun of affirmations. So did a weekly segment on *Saturday Night Live* that featured the affirmation: "I'm good enough, I'm smart enough, and doggone it, people like me!"

But fact is, I've seen affirmations work with a number of clients. My hypothesis: Just as repeated negative self-talk likely creates hard-wired physiological changes in the brain, those thoughts can be rewired by consistent positive self-talk. So, what's an affirmation you'd like to say aloud ten times, three times a day for at least a week?

The live-for-today excuse

An example of this excuse is "Searching for a job is yucky, no fun at all. I always find something I'd rather do." Try the following cures if you often use this excuse:

- **Remember that you'll actually have more fun if you don't procrastinate.** When you procrastinate, you suffer from the following:

  - Ongoing guilt: Even when you're watching your favorite TV show, a little voice whispers in your ear, "You should be working."

  - Staying in the same miserable situation that made you want to find a cool career in the first place: the low pay, the lousy work, your lack of success.

  - Enduring your family's searing questions: "When *are* you going to find yourself, Melvin?"

If you truly like pleasure more than pain, the key is to get your work done as efficiently as possible so that maximum time is left for pleasure without guilt or negative consequences to spoil the fun.

✓ **Make the task as pleasurable as possible.** When you're doing the task, keep asking yourself, "What's the fun way to do this?" If, for example, you know you need to cold-call prospective employers, ask yourself, "How can I make these phone calls fun?" That can simply be a matter of not taking it too seriously if a hirer blows you off: "The heck with him. There are plenty of others I can call."

✓ **Beware of focusing only on the fun parts or of creating fun side activities that you rationalize are important to completing the task.** For example, many job seekers spend hours playing with their resume's format or researching companies on the Net, rather than contacting potential employers. Solution: While you're working, keep asking yourself, "Is this the most direct path to my goal, or am I fooling myself?"

✓ **Make a deal with yourself.** For example: "Okay. I've decided that doing this stinkin' task is in my best interest, but I want a reward. So, here's the deal: If I work on it for 15 focused minutes, I'll take a few minutes to answer that e-mail from my girlfriend."

✓ **Accept that you have an addiction.** Like drug addicts, live-for-today procrastinators accept a damaged life in exchange for the momentary relief of deferring work. Are you finally willing to say: "That's it. I'm ready to kick my addiction. I'm ready to be disciplined; I'll be happier if, during the workday at least, I make myself value productivity more than fun"?

A client of mine, Dave, in his early years, was a procrastinating nonachiever. One day he simply decided he'd had enough. Today Dave is a successful fundraiser, having won a number of achievement awards, and is a happy guy.

The spacey procrastinator's excuse

Here's an example of this excuse: "I just can't seem to focus." Spacey people often have big ideas but can't stay focused long enough to accomplish even little things. These folks can benefit from the following cures:

✓ **Becoming more time-aware.** Many spacey people are oblivious to time. Set a timer to go off every three minutes. Each time it buzzes, ask yourself, "Is this the most direct approach to achieving my goal?"

✓ **Being alert to early signs of spacing out.** When you feel yourself *starting* to fade out, say aloud, "Okay, focus!"

- ✔ **Picking a productivity place and time.** Can you think of a place you're least likely to procrastinate? A time? Use that place and time when you have an important task you're likely to procrastinate.

- ✔ **Taking a drug for ADD.** If you have a long-standing inability to focus, even on important things, a trial course on a drug such as Ritalin *may* be worth considering. Originally used with children, these drugs have more recently been found to help some adults. Of course, before taking any prescription drug, discuss it thoroughly with your physician.

The perfectionist's excuse #1

The first variation of the perfectionist's excuse is "It takes me a long time, but I want to get it right." What to do? Know when good enough is good enough and when you need to be perfect. It usually takes a long time to get from good to perfect, so you want to spend that time only when it's worth it — for example, in crafting a good answer to "Why have you been unemployed for the last nine years?" In nearly every other task in a job search and in most tasks in work and life, shooting for perfection is time that you can spend more valuably.

I've seen many clients waste weeks agonizing over the fine points of their resumes, the design of their business cards, or their cold-call script. Their job prospects would be better if, instead, they started contacting employers. One reason people are perfectionists about things like their resume is that fiddling with inanimate things is more comfortable than risking embarrassing yourself. Be aware of that tendency. Ask yourself, "Is this the most direct route to achieving my goal?"

The perfectionist's excuse #2

Related to the previous excuse is "I'd rather not do it than do it poorly." That high-minded talk can be fear talking. Such people are afraid that if they make a mistake, others will think they're stupid.

Fact is, most successful people don't let fear of mistakes stop them. They dive in, make errors (sometimes appearing stupid), and learn from them. Unsuccessful people are much more likely to plan, plan, plan, hoping to achieve perfection and giving up before implementing much of their plan. Or if a project *has* to be done, they find themselves at the eleventh hour, forced to crank out something far worse than what they would have produced if they hadn't procrastinated. Sometimes a procrastinator's motive is to protect his ego: "I could have done it well if I had taken the time." For that cold comfort, they pay a huge price. Sure, surgeons and diamond cutters must be perfect, but almost everyone else, especially job searchers, needn't be.

Advice from Tiger Woods

Golf requires an extraordinary degree of perfection. Mis-hit a ball by a tenth of an inch and it can end up in the woods. Tiger Woods is arguably the most perfect golfer in history, and even he doesn't strive for perfection. He aims for what he calls "professional excellence," a competent effort on every shot. If it's good enough for Tiger, it's good enough for everyone else.

Another difference between winners and losers lies in how they react to failing. Winners don't waste time on self-pity. They focus on learning from their failure so they can succeed the next time.

The fear-of-imposing excuse

This type of excuse is "I don't want to contact them because I don't want to impose." The cures:

- ✔ **Recognize that you may not be imposing.** Many people enjoy giving advice. Plus, if you're phoning for a job and the employer happens to need someone like you, you're doing him a favor. If not, you waste ten seconds of his time. Big deal. You've stopped people on the street asking for directions, right? Asking whether an employer is willing to talk with you requires no more time.

- ✔ **Clue in to the karma concept.** Even if you *are* imposing, recognize that asking for help is okay as long as you remember to be kind to people who ask you for help.

The fear-of-success excuse

An example of this excuse is "I'm not sure I want to succeed. If I do, I'll pay a price." Try these cures to beat this excuse:

- ✔ **Remember that you can set limits.** Accepting more pressure than you want is unnecessary. For example, many successful executives have decided that the stressful 70-hour weeks aren't worth it no matter how high the salary, so they quit to do something low-key like teaching college. Others are strongly committed to family, and they usually, with persistence, find a family-friendly job that allows them to preserve most of their evenings and weekends.

> ✔ **Be aware of the martyrdom tendency.** Some people avoid succeeding because they're afraid their spouse or parent will feel inferior in comparison. You shouldn't sacrifice yourself to protect someone's ego.

The adrenaline addict's excuse

Here's an example: "School got me into the habit of waiting until the last minute to do assignments. I was able to get good grades even though I didn't start working until the night before."

As I mention in the earlier section "In the Beginning: How People Develop a Habit of Procrastination," alas, except in dead-end jobs, last-minute work usually doesn't cut it in the real world. Fine, blame the schools, but now you have to cure your adrenaline addiction.

Realize that adrenaline addiction is dangerous. It's bad for your health and leeches pleasure out of every task.

If you're not ready to kick your addiction to adrenaline, try these palliatives:

> ✔ **Create an artificial deadline.** For example, say, "I'm going to create a networking list by 9:00." Set a timer.
>
> ✔ **Give yourself an absurdly short deadline.** For example, say, "It's 11 a.m. and I want to have lunch at noon. Let's see if I can write a draft of my resume by then."

A client of mine who supervises a cancer clinic was overwhelmed by the task of creating his annual budget. I told him: "You have three minutes. Draft a budget." The absurd time limit forced him to focus only on its key components and to identify the fuzzy areas. Three minutes later, he had written a ton about the budget and was eager to fill in the blanks.

The high-potency version of this cure: Hand a friend a $100 check. If you don't finish the work by the agreed-on time, he cashes it.

The resent-authority excuse

Heard this one? "You're not going to make me do that." You're right. Neither family nor societal pressure can make you do anything, but recognize that if you make the choice not to succeed, you, not the authority, will suffer.

The don't-have-time excuse

Does this sound familiar? "I can't get started on my career search until I clean my desk (or get my divorce finalized, quit my job, whatever)." The cures:

- ✔ **Realize that these are delaying tactics.** Yes, they're also legitimate problems, but millions of people with piled-high desks, who do full-time jobs, and yes, are even in the throes of divorce, have found new careers or done great things on the job. Often, the search for a better career actually provides rays of hope and distraction from the stress of a breakup. If you wait until all the stars are aligned, you'll never get started.

- ✔ **Admit that a career- or job-search does take time.** Starting now, as you contemplate beginning an activity (including turning on the TV), ask yourself, "Should I be working on my job search?" Pull out your appointment book or PDA and schedule blocks of time to devote to your search.

All-Purpose Procrastination Cures

The excuse-specific cures in the previous section often help procrastinators, but some general cures can also be of real benefit. Pick out a few of the following cures that may work for you.

Doing your work without becoming stuck

The following cures can prevent you from getting stuck on a task:

- ✔ **Attach a sense of urgency to the task:** "I *have* to do this."

- ✔ **Create a highly visible to-do list** that you can't avoid seeing throughout the day, perhaps on your desk.

- ✔ **Don't put short tasks on your to-do list — do them now.** If a task is a quickie, getting it done is often wiser than putting it on your to-do list — you avoid adding to that mass of tasks hanging over your head like Poe's pendulum in the pit. Also, doing those quickie tasks now tends to keep you from being overly perfectionistic about them, and, of course, you avoid procrastination — you've gotten it done! So instead of the guilt, you'll start hearing from others, "Wow, thanks for the fast response!" That feels so good.

✔ **Just do it. Do it now, even if you don't feel like it.** If you work on your career only when you feel like it, you won't feel like it often enough. Don't expect it to be fun. As those obnoxious but correct people say, "No pain, no gain." Fight through the discomfort and just do it. Think how good it will feel to have put in a good hour. Think of the benefits you'll derive. Then make yourself start working.

✔ **Pick a specific time to start on your big task.** Put it on your schedule, just as you would a doctor's appointment or a date with a friend. You wouldn't fink out on a friend. Why fink out on yourself? Choose the time of day you're most likely to actually do the task.

✔ **Figure out *where* you're least likely to procrastinate.** If at home you play too much with your dog, consider working somewhere else.

✔ **Draw a thermometer and tape it to your desk.** Instead of numbers on its side, write the little steps you need to take to get the task done. Every time you complete a step, color in that part of the thermometer. This technique helps churches raise lots of money. When my wife was facing her PhD dissertation, we posted on the refrigerator a hand-drawn thermometer with all the milestones on the side. Each time she passed one, we had a coloring-in ceremony. She says that was key to her getting her dissertation done.

✔ **Use a few-second task to get you rolling.** Before you start or when you reach a hard part, you may be tempted to grab a soda, call your friend, or trim your nails. That's when you have to force yourself to get working (on the task, not your nails). Ask yourself, "What's my next few-second task?" An example of an answer: "I have to open my address book to see whom I need to call."

✔ **Don't think about how much work you have ahead of you.** That can overwhelm you into procrastination. Instead, think like a mountain climber. Just put one foot in front of the other, and when you get to the top and look down, you'll be amazed at how far you've gone.

Before I began to write this book, I knew 400-plus pages lay ahead of me, but I never let myself think about that. The task would've felt overwhelming. As soon as those thoughts entered my mind, I immediately replaced them with, "What's my next few-second task?"

✔ **Be aware of the moment of truth.** When tempted to procrastinate, you face a moment of truth when you're still not over the edge, like when you're on the brink of losing your temper. At that moment, you can consciously suppress the desire to procrastinate. When you feel that temptation arise, force up your energy, your discipline, and ask yourself, "What's my next few-second task?"

✔ **Turn on pump-you-up music.** That works for some, not others.

✔ **Recognize that you build momentum.** The more you accomplish, the more you want to accomplish. The less you accomplish, the less you want to accomplish.

✔ **Think of your workday as a series of one-minute blocks.** That mindset proffers many advantages. Many one-minute blocks go wasted — for example, when you're on hold, while waiting for the boss, or before a meeting begins. You'd be amazed how much work you can get done in one minute. Work during those one-minute periods and you may wring an extra half-hour out of your day without putting in any overtime. Another benefit of the one-minute mindset is that it keeps you from being too perfectionistic or becoming overwhelmed by the size of a task. After all, you can do only so much in one minute.

Getting unstuck when all else fails

If, despite taking all the previous cures I offer in this chapter, you're still procrastinating, try one or more of the cures in the following sections.

Remind yourself of the benefits of not procrastinating

Pick the benefit most motivating to you. For example, years ago, I tried to get my wife to quit smoking. I told her it could kill her. No impact. I told her people think smokers are losers. No impact. I told her it didn't look sexy. She stopped that day and hasn't taken a puff since.

Can't think of a motivating-enough benefit? These may trigger something: When you find a job, you can support your family, feel useful, afford that vacation you've fantasized about, and rid yourself of the guilt that you're letting life pass you by.

How do you keep your key benefit in mind? One way is to cut a picture out of a magazine of that benefit — a car, a home, whatever — and hang it next to your computer or on your refrigerator. Or write a benefit of doing the task on your palm. For example, one client wrote "GWOMB." It stood for "Get Wife Off My Back."

Embarrass yourself

Recognize that choosing to procrastinate says, "I value fun more than being productive, even when I'm supposed to be working." Do you really want to define yourself as a shirker? Do you want others to see you that way?

Look back

Although focusing on the future is helpful, also take a moment to look back. See whether you can find a procrasti-cure among your reflections:

- ✔ **Think back to times you've procrastinated.** What were the consequences? Has it hurt your career? Your relationships? Your self-esteem? Sometimes, looking at the price you've paid for procrastinating can make you angry enough with yourself to say, "I'm tired of sabotaging myself. I'm not going to let this happen again."

- ✔ **Think back to a time you *didn't* procrastinate on an unpleasant task.** What kept you from procrastinating then? A rigorous schedule? Someone nagging you? Does that give you a clue as to how to beat your current procrastination?

Grow up

How will you feel tomorrow about having procrastinated on a task today? Ask yourself, "If I were my grown-up self, what would I do?"

Get advice from your twin

What would you say to get your twin to quit procrastinating? Often, people know the solution but are too close to themselves to see it. Imagining that you're giving advice to someone just like you can enable you to see the forest through the trees.

Focus on small changes

People often underestimate the effects of small changes. A client of mine, Dianne, lived wracked with guilt because she paid little attention to the accounting part of her photography business. I said, "Commit to 15 minutes a day working on your books." She did that and what a relief! Next session, she said, "Fifteen minutes isn't a big deal, but it turns out to make a big difference, psychologically as well as practically."

Brand yourself with a scarlet letter

This tactic is a bit draconian, but what the heck. Write the letter "P" (for procrastinator) on the outside of your hand so that everyone can see it. Unlike in Hester Prynne's case, no one's forcing you to do it. That P, which follows you everywhere you go, is an ongoing reminder that curing your procrastination is Job One. The P is also embarrassing, so it may motivate you to overcome the problem so you can honorably remove it.

Find someone to check in with

Some people can tackle projects without support. But many people, especially procrastinators, find that having someone to check in with is helpful. Regular check-in is a key to the success of Weight Watchers and 12-step programs. It can be of equal value in your career. Here are some options:

- **Get one-on-one support.** Some people prefer one-on-one support. Find a friend you can phone every day. Richard Bolles, author of *What Color Is Your Parachute?*, suggests finding a "loving taskmaster" — someone who can meet weekly or even daily with you, giving you a gently dispensed hard time if you've been a slacker. I allow procrastinating clients to e-mail me nightly to report their progress. One client said, "Knowing I'll have to report to you each night makes me feel like Marty Nemko is at my side all day urging me on."

- **Seek support from a group.** Would you prefer group support? Ongoing groups are available in most large cities. For example, the 5 O'Clock Club has branches in a few major cities plus virtual branches — online groups (www.fiveOClockclub.com). Also consider Forty Plus. To find your nearest chapter, visit www.40plus.org/links/. To find other local job-search support groups, check out www.job-hunt.org/job-search-networking/job-search-networking.shtml or check with your chamber of commerce, college alumni association, church, or unemployment office.

- **Take the initiative.** You can even start your own support group. Here's an approach adapted from Barbara Sher's *Wishcraft*. Recruit members by asking friends, relatives, or colleagues, or by placing an ad in a local newspaper. Just write, "Forming a career-related support group. For information, call *(insert phone number)*." Your group should have four to six members. Meet weekly or at least monthly. At each session, each person gets ten minutes in the hot seat. That member starts by telling the group her goal(s). Then group members offer advice on objectives for the next week. Before moving out of the hot seat, each person ends by saying what she commits to accomplishing by the next meeting. Consider using this book as the group's "textbook" to help ensure that all members are knowledgeable about career issues.

Members of job support groups generally do well. They feel accountable to the group and come away with ideas and encouragement from group members, as well as inspiration from seeing people arrive unhappy and leave with better worklives.

Fall in love

I'm not sure why it works, but a number of lifelong procrastinators report being cured after falling in love or having a baby.

Advice for the Incurable Procrastinator

I'll be honest with you. Some people, despite knowing all the techniques in this chapter, will still procrastinate, even if it means getting fired or going broke.

These individuals probably won't find a cure in another book, workshop, or therapist. I had a discussion with an eminent psychologist who has spent his life writing and giving workshops on procrastination for a prestigious organization. In confidence, he admitted that he believes many, if not most, chronic procrastinators are incurable. If you feel that's you, this section's advice is for you.

You may not be able to change, but you can change your environment. Incurable procrastinators thrive best in work environments in which tasks

- ✔ Don't take long to complete
- ✔ Aren't inordinately difficult
- ✔ Are structured, with a clearly laid-out, step-by-step process
- ✔ Are closely supervised
- ✔ Require being part of a team; the sense of obligation to the team motivates procrastinators to get their part of the task done
- ✔ Must be completed on a tight deadline with no room for procrastination

Example: One inveterate procrastinator who is very bright and made a great first impression had been hired three times by Corporate America and fired three times by Corporate America. She's finally found a job she can succeed at: barista at Starbucks. That job meets all the above requirements. Making coffee drinks doesn't take much time, isn't difficult, requires a step-by-step procedure, has close supervision, involves teamwork (the barista makes the drink and hands it to the sales clerk), and has tight deadlines — people want their caffeine NOW!

The good news is that a permanent barista at Starbucks makes a reasonable living with full benefits. Although this procrastinator lost the status she had working in corporate offices, she no longer feels like a loser. She's productive and making a living. You can too.

Don't want such a low-level career? I've scanned the 500-plus in Chapter 2's *Cool Careers Yellow Pages* and picked out a few that many people find appealing yet can often be done successfully by procrastinators: accountant, audiologist, electrician, librarian, locksmith, massage therapist, nurse occupational therapist, optometrist, psychologist, physician assistant, and speech therapist.

Chapter 13

The Keys to Successful Self-Employment

In This Chapter

▶ Finding the idea

▶ Being aware of the downsides

▶ Creating a successful business

▶ Knowing how to handle challenges

*T*he coolest career may be the one you create for yourself.

Who's going to give you a salary to be a ghost hunter, peacock farmer, prairie preservationist, collector of antique furniture, musical instrument maker, horror aficionado, nature poet, Mediterranean culinary historian, backcountry adventurer, boot maker, video biographer, surfing photographer, or Web cop? Those are only a few of the thousands of cool careers people have created for themselves by becoming their own bosses.

I'm not talking about building an elaborate business, as a classic entrepreneur might. If you were one of those, you probably wouldn't be reading this book. I'm simply talking about creating a job for yourself in which you find customers who are willing to pay you to pursue your cool career. You don't need to have employees unless you want them and can afford them. You probably won't need to get bank loans or venture capital. You may not even need to shell out the big bucks for an outside office. Many self-employed people do just fine, thank you, working from home.

In this chapter, I show you the six essentials of self-employment. I also outline potential disadvantages of self-employment and how to overcome them.

But What about the Downsides of Self-Employment?

People contemplating self-employment often get teased: "So you're considering trading job security for the freedom to work 70 hours a week with no benefits?" Or "Being self-employed is being on a perpetual job search." Or "When you're on your own, you only have to work half-time — whichever 12 hours a day you want."

With a little luck, and if you follow the advice in this chapter, you have a good chance of enjoying the freedom and control of self-employment along with healthcare and other benefits, reasonable vacations, and at least as much job security as you can get in a so-called real job. But first, here are the potential downsides of self-employment (and ways to get around them):

- ✔ **Job insecurity:** Many people equate being your own boss with job insecurity. Fact is, self-employment, *well done,* offers a good shot at a life-long paycheck. No one can fire you on a whim. You'll never be offshored, merged, purged, right-sized, or downsized. And with the average job lasting only three and a half years now, isn't job security more nostalgia than reality?

- ✔ **Insane hours:** Conventional wisdom says that the self-employed work harder and longer than anyone else. Yet scientists, corporate managers, and nonprofit managers routinely work more than 50 hours a week. In fact, many in the high-tech and biotech sectors think a 50-hour week is for shirkers. Remember also that a 50-plus-hour corporate workweek doesn't even count the ever-lengthening commute time. Seventy-three percent of people working in offices of 100 or more must work on weekends, and to make ends meet, many people are forced to request overtime or to take a second job. The savvy self-employed often needn't work longer, especially if she's working from home.

- ✔ **You're on a perpetual job search:** If being on your own feels like a perpetual job search, you're probably not doing it right. At first, yes, you'll be busy lining up clientele, but stay with it awhile, and if you're good and you listen to your customers, business will start coming to you.

So you may be wondering: "If all this is true, why isn't everyone self-employed?" The answer is that many people aren't suited to or interested in being their own boss. But I'm assuming you score high on the self-employment test in Chapter 3. If so, you're likely to do just fine in self-employment if only you know how. This chapter will show you how.

What Are the Six Musts for Successful Self-Employment?

Mountains of books have been written about how to become successfully self-employed. Yet, when I really think about it, the keys to success reduce to only six things, which I explain in the following sections.

Coming up with a good idea

People think the key to a successful business is coming up with *The Idea*. Actually, that's the easy part. Good ideas are everywhere:

- ✔ Chapter 2 (the *Cool Careers Yellow Pages*) lists dozens of my favorite self-employment ideas, including, for example, owning a chain of well-located carts selling coffee or soup. That's a low-cost, low-risk, high-profit business.

  Sure, those businesses have been done before. That's actually a huge plus. When you innovate, you're a guinea pig. If you replicate, your odds of success are much better because you're copying a proven winner. Don't innovate; replicate.

- ✔ Your own regular Yellow Pages lists virtually every kind of business. Scan its index, and in the space of an hour, you'll be exposed to hundreds of business ideas that are already up and running. Find one you like? Visit a few businesses of its type, incorporate their best features into your version of the business, and aim yours at a particular geographical location (or online), age group, or ethnic or gender market.

- ✔ Think about your current work. Is there a problem you frequently hear co-workers or customers complaining about? Could you start a business that would solve it?

- ✔ Do you believe in a product or service that you may like to sell?

  All things being equal, service businesses are safer than product businesses. Service businesses have no costly inventory, no theft problem, and no spoilage. Plus, they're usually easier to run from your home, which saves you commute time and thousands of dollars in rent.

- ✔ Start a franchise. www.entrepreneurmag.com lists 500 prominent ones.

✔ *Barbara Sher's Idea Book* contains a wealth of fun, easy-to-start small business ideas, from gondolier to doll repairer. Her ideas generally pay poorly but offer good quality of life. They're a good balance to my more practicality first/passion second approach to business.

✔ Paul and Sarah Edwards' book *Home-Based Businesses For Dummies,* 2nd Edition (Wiley), offers many ideas plus a bookful of strategies on how to make a home business successful.

While you're searching for good ideas, beware of the following:

✔ Don't be tempted by advertised get-rich-quick schemes. You probably won't get rich and it certainly won't be quick. Whatever they're selling will take time, energy, and money, just like whatever it is you really want to do. So don't fall into the trap of thinking, "Well, I'll just buy their envelope-licking business 'opportunity' until I make plenty of money and then I'll do what I really want to do." Instead, save time and figure out how you can make money doing what you really want to do in the first place.

✔ Three of the top ten scams on the Internet involve work-at-home offers and business opportunities. So, be extra skeptical of e-mail solicitations. The old saying "If it sounds too good to be true, it is" has never been truer. Scrutinize each offer with a careful eye. For example, does the solicitation, as required by law, state the number and percentage of previous purchasers who achieved the touted earnings? If the business "opportunity" still seems interesting, check with the Better Business Bureau: www.bbb.org. But just because nothing askance is reported doesn't mean a business offer is legitimate. Most people don't report being scammed; they're embarrassed or think it's their own fault.

Putting your toe in the water

A business idea may sound great, yet in practice, it's a flop.

Sometimes an idea may, indeed, be sound, but you may not have the ability to make it succeed. To reduce that risk, before choosing a business, watch someone who's already doing it. For example, if you're thinking about being a Web site designer, watch one for an hour or two. Can you see yourself, with training, doing that for 40 hours a week and producing wonderful sites? If so, try to learn a bit of the necessary material — for example, PHP, the Web development language — on your own or with a tutor. (See Chapter 5 for more details about preparing for a career without a degree.) Are you catching on quickly? If so, chances are you'll develop the skills needed to succeed.

Other times, a business succeeds only because of Herculean effort — an owner willing to work 80 hours a week or invest a fortune to ensure its success. Last time I looked, you didn't look like Hercules, nor did you have a fortune to invest.

Still other times, the idea is good, but its heyday is over. Open yet another bagel, frozen yogurt, or Hawaiian barbecue joint in your city and you may face a double whammy — a market that's already saturated, and you're buying into a fad that may be fading.

A risk-reducer: Catch people in front of a store, call people out of the phone book, arrange a get-together of friends, whatever. Describe your product or service and ask them how likely they are to buy it. Beg them to be brutally honest — "Better to know now than after I've opened the business." Ask them what they'd comfortably be willing to pay for your product or service and how the product or service could be enhanced so they'd pay more.

Creating your mini business plan

Preparing a simple business plan helps you decide whether to be self-employed. Don't be intimidated by the term *business plan*. There's no need for a massive document. You probably can say all that's necessary in fewer than ten pages. Your business plan just needs to include

✔ Evidence that a market exists for your product or service (based on the marketing survey you'll do as described in the previous section)

✔ A description of your target customer

✔ What you'll do to reach your market

✔ A list of your business's strengths, weaknesses, opportunities, and threats (A little research, even a simple Google search, can be helpful here.)

✔ A rough budget for the first two or three years, and where you'll get the money

After developing your business plan, ask yourself, "Would I invest in this business?" If yes, show the plan to your business-savviest friends or a commercial lending officer at a bank. Ask them the same question. If everyone gives you the thumbs-up, you probably can proceed with confidence.

For more guidance on developing a business plan, go to `www.sba.gov/starting_business/index.html`. You can also check out *Business Plans For Dummies,* 2nd Edition, by Paul Tiffany and Steven D. Peterson (Wiley). And for business plan templates, see `www.score.org/template_gallery.html`.

Having an entry plan that keeps the cash flowing

You shouldn't need a lot of money to launch your independent career. The myth that you need a bank loan, venture capital, or rich friends and family keeps too many people from becoming their own boss.

Creating a job for yourself isn't like starting a traditional business. The average person starting a business spends just $5,000, according to the Small Business Administration. Today, much of that money goes for a computer and office equipment — which you may already have, and the costs of which keep going down. Most of the self-employment opportunities listed in this book's *Cool Careers Yellow Pages* (see Chapter 2) require only a small investment. Before spending big, think hard about ways to launch your business less expensively. If you can't cut costs, before getting into hock, consider another business.

In the following sections, I explain the components of an entry plan that won't break the bank.

Keys to controlling costs

The old axiom "It takes money to make money" may be true in big business, but in creating your own little business, being a cheapskate actually helps. You're going to make errors in the beginning. So if you have low monthly costs, you're more likely to survive those errors without going bankrupt. Here's a list of ways to keep your costs low:

✔ **Start your business at home.** You can save thousands of dollars each month on rent and other costs. If you need to meet with clients and your place is a pigsty, offer them the convenience of meeting at their place, at a quiet restaurant, or at a rent-by-the-hour office in an executive center.

✔ **Provide a service rather than a product.** Products must be produced or bought, and usually require you to maintain thousands of dollars of inventory.

✔ **Learn how to be a businessperson.** The small-business battlefield is littered with former business owners who had a great idea but lacked the knowledge or willingness to run it, and especially to market it hard and smart. Unless you love techno-minutiae, don't bother getting technical expertise; you can always hire that. *You* learn how to run a business. That's a skill that never goes out of style, that many people find doable and more fun than learning endless arcana, and that opens the door to making serious money. In contrast, most technical types work long hours to earn just a moderate wage.

How should you learn business? Volunteer or work for successful businesspeople. Don't try learning it in school. If those professors were such good businesspeople, they'd probably be running a business, not teaching. Remember that most professors are hired based on how well they do research, not how good of businesspeople they are. One of my clients is a business professor. He teaches entrepreneurship yet has never, ever run a business. Indeed, the only jobs he's ever held other than professor are used car salesman and clerk at Radio Shack.

✔ **Avoid the temptation to buy expensive stuff.** Office furniture, state-of-the-art techno-equipment, and pricey ads all cost money. You need that cash for more important things, like your training, computer, marketing, and perhaps a Web site. The guy who created mine (www.martynemko.com) is Matt Nicholas (nicholassolutions.com).

✔ **Avoid hiring help.** If you need help, see whether you can hire other self-employed people on an as-needed basis. Not only does that avoid the ongoing overhead of employees, but it also saves you from paying hefty payroll taxes and reduces the risk of someone suing you for wrongful termination.

✔ **Consider using a small business incubator.** These are sets of adjacent offices that allow you to share equipment and administrative-assistant services, and provide a professional environment. With 1,000 incubators in the United States and 4,000 worldwide, one is likely to be near you. Beyond the cost-savings, the proximity of other budding entrepreneurs seems to inject a pioneering spirit among everyone. A University of Michigan study reported that 87 percent of businesses incubated by "mature incubators" still were in business after five years. To find an incubator, look in your Yellow Pages under "executive suites" or at the National Business Incubator Association Web site: www.nbia.org.

Transition plans

Here are common ways to transition into self-employment:

✔ **The Moonlighting Plan:** Keep your full-time job and develop your business as a sideline. When it takes off, you can go whole-hog. Be sure to work at least eight hours a week on a sideline business.

✔ **The Part-Time Plan:** While you're building up the business, work a part-time job to provide a base income. When your business equals the base, drop the part-time job.

✔ **The Spin-Off Plan:** Turn your previous employer into your first major customer or, when ethically and legally possible, take a major client with you from your previous job.

- ✔ **The Cushion Plan:** Of course, there are obvious cushions like savings, divorce settlements, or severance packages, but think about less obvious assets. Benjamin funded his new business by selling his grand piano, saying, "I wasn't playing it anyway. It was just a very expensive piece of furniture." Your cushion should be large enough to cover your expenses for the cash-poor startup phase, often 6 to 12 months, depending on the business.

- ✔ **The Leave Plan:** Start your independent career while on leave or sabbatical.

- ✔ **The Piggyback Plan:** If you have a working spouse or partner, cut back your expenses so you can live on one salary until your business gets going.

- ✔ **The Key Client Plan:** If you have sufficient stature in your field, line up one or more retainer contracts with clients for the first year to provide you with assured revenue in exchange for a discount rate.

Smart pricing

Of course, when you're first starting out, charging top dollar is unfair, but as soon as you feel it's ethical, consider charging at least mid-range, if only because many prospective clients will be turned off if you charge too little. They believe that you get what you pay for.

Many new businesses charge too little, either because they're desperate for customers or because they fail to take into account all the costs of doing business. In setting your pricing, start by figuring out what yields you a reasonable annual income. On top of that, you must factor in all your costs — for example, setting up your office, your Web site, training time, equipment, materials, travel to clients, phones, accounting fees, utilities, marketing costs, your benefits, and, importantly, the 30 percent to 70 percent you'll typically pay in federal, state, local, self-employment, Medicare, disability, business license, and other taxes.

Do you lament that employed people get benefits but the self-employed don't? You simply have to build the cost of sick leave, vacation time, retirement, and health insurance benefits into what you charge. Here are a few resources to help you out:

- ✔ The Web site `insure.com` makes finding good insurance values easier.

- ✔ The Web site `www.allbusiness.com` links you to services for the self-employed: insurance, legal services, even potential customers.

- ✔ Check with your state's health insurance commission for special programs for the self-employed. To find yours, enter "state health insurance" into the search engine at `google.com` and the name of your state.

Don't base your fees on the assumption that you'll be able to bill out a 40-hour week. Few people can. The number of billable hours you can expect to generate each week depends not only on how much business you can line up but also on the nature of the work. A medical transcriptionist may bill 40 hours a week, while a consultant may average no more than 15. Talk to others about the norm in your field, but soon, your own experience will be your best guide.

Finding money

Okay, I've done what I can to keep you out of debt, but sometimes it's unavoidable. If you really need to borrow money to get underway, here's the straight scoop on the most often considered sources of startup funds:

- ✔ **Banks:** Banks are eager to give loans to small businesses and self-employed individuals for expansion. The problem is, they're looking for a two- to three-year track record.

   The U.S. Small Business Administration can make it easier for you to get a good bank loan, especially if you're a woman or minority. Take a look at www.sba.gov/financing/index.html.

- ✔ **Equity loan:** If you have significant equity in your home, banks will gladly lend you money at a decent rate, but beware. You don't want to risk losing your home on a risky business.

- ✔ **Friends, relatives, and other personal contacts:** This may be your best bet, but before hitting up ol' Uncle Albert, consider what would happen to your relationship with him if, somehow, you aren't able to repay.

- ✔ **Credit cards:** Usually the easiest approach, but it's expensive unless you're careful. Here's how you might do it. Get at least two cards while you still have a job: one for personal use and one for your business. Find cards with low introductory interest rates. Currently, some offer 0 percent for the first year. After that, you can switch cards for a new introductory rate.

   To find the best credit card deals, check out www.bankrate.com/brm/rate/brm_ccsearch_lowrate.asp.

- ✔ **Venture capital:** Generally, forget about it. Venture capitalists want to invest at least hundreds of thousands of dollars for a piece of some action that promises them millions. They're not interested in helping someone create a great little career. Still curious about venture financing? www.vfinance.com has lots of articles, plus links to 1,500 venture capital firms and 24,000 *angel investors* (see the next bullet).

   Beware of firms offering to find you venture financing for a four-figure fee. They rarely work. If you need help tweaking your business plan, hire a consultant for an hour or two.

✔ **Angels:** Say you're not established enough for a bank loan, too small for a venture capitalist, without friends and family, and holding too many maxed-out credit cards. Maybe you need to be touched by an angel — a financial angel, that is. *Angels* are individuals looking for projects to invest in. How to find one? Light a candle and pray at www.angelnetwork.com and www.vfinance.com. Just be sure you have an irresistible one- to two-page summary of your business plan (which I cover earlier in this chapter) and a compelling 30-to-60-second verbal summary ready to go.

✔ **Other sources:** *Inc.* magazine (inc.com) and *Entrepreneur* magazine (entrepreneurmag.com) often have features on financing your small business.

Acting like the CEO you are

When you're self-employed, you suddenly go from subordinate to CEO. To succeed, you have to act like the chief executive. Here are common no-nos:

✔ **Never use a resume.** Prepare a bio, brochure, and/or portfolio. Have professional-looking letterhead, business cards, stationery, and probably a Web site.

✔ **Never refer to yourself as a freelancer.** If you want to command good fees, don't represent yourself as less than the head of your own company. Freelancers routinely get paid less and are paid last. Also, never put the word *just* in front of what you do — for example, "It's just a home business" or "I'm just a one-man shop." Be proud of your one-person operation. After all, your clients never have to work with an underling. They get the personal attention of the firm's principal.

✔ **Never ask for an interview.** Interviews are for jobs. *You* are getting business, lining up customers, serving clients. Therefore, you arrange for a meeting, offer to make a presentation, make a bid, provide a quote, or submit a proposal.

✔ **Never ask what someone pays.** Tell people what you charge. However, don't announce your fees first thing, even if that's the first thing they ask for. Explain that you need to better understand their needs before you can quote a price. That gives you the opportunity to learn their needs and explain how they'd benefit from your work. Build value for what you do before announcing the price and customers are more likely to be relieved to hear that your fee isn't higher.

✔ **Never work without an agreement.** Before you begin working with a new client or customer, get an agreement in writing as to what you'll be doing, the price, payment arrangements, and so on. Depending on the nature of your work, your agreement can be a simple order form, a purchase order, or a contract.

You will often be the one to provide the contract, but large organizations usually have their own standard forms. Beware when you get one of those babies — their attorney probably wrote it to benefit them. If you're nervous, hiring your own legal eagle to review it is a good idea. And remember that even though those corporate contracts look official, they're not set in stone. Don't hesitate to negotiate.

When extending credit, remember that it's always a privilege, no matter how big, well-known, or established the customer. Take the time to check credit references. Big companies go bankrupt, too. Remember that United Airlines, Macy's, and Bethlehem Steel went Chapter 11.

✔ **Never complain.** Your customers have enough problems of their own. That's probably part of why they want to work with you. So don't add to their problems. If you're having business or personal difficulties, commiserate with family and friends if need be, but don't moan and groan to clients. Ever hear a CEO complain to a customer?

Getting business to come to you

It's every new businessperson's biggest question: How do I get customers? Eventually, if you're good, repeat business and word of mouth may largely sustain you, but for now at least, you have to get the word out. People have to know not only what you do but also how you're different from others who do similar work.

The good news is that you have plenty of ways to market, and you need to choose only the method(s) you feel comfortable with. If cold calling makes you sweat, pick something else. Chances are, you won't do a marketing activity you hate. Here are several of the quickest, most effective marketing activities, and they're also low-cost:

✔ **Schmoozing:** Otherwise known as networking, schmoozing is the most popular way for self-employed people to get business. You can schmooze at professional and trade association meetings, in business organizations and Chambers of Commerce forums, and through formal networking groups like linkedin.com and Business Network International (www.bni.com), which has chapters nationwide.

If business gatherings aren't for you, schmooze colleagues, friends, and associates. Pick up the phone, do lunch, or go to lots of parties. Or browse Web sites and user groups, leaving helpful information along the way. Add a tag line to your online signature so people know what you do and can reach you by e-mail.

Even social networking sites such as match.com, facebook.com, myspace.com, friendster.com, and even youtube.com can be used for business networking. In your profile, describe what you do, with enthusiasm.

✔ **Conduits:** *Conduits* are business owners whose customers need what you offer. Make a list of everyone your potential customers do business with. Those are your conduits. For example, if you have a cleaning service, commercial real estate agents can be conduits for you because their clients need property cleaned before sales. Let all relevant conduits know about you and what you offer. Sometimes, referrals from one or two good conduits can keep you busy full time.

A variation on the theme: cross-referral. Figure out categories of businesspeople you can cross-refer with: "I'll send you mine if you'll send me yours." In my case, as a career counselor, I may target headhunters. I'd, for example, attend a local conference of headhunters and, during breaks, chat with people until I found at least one to whom we both felt we could honorably refer clients.

✔ **Cold calling:** Some hate it, some love it. But if you're good at it, it can be very effective. Why do you think companies do so much telemarketing?

✔ **Your Web site:** Creating a site that will be picked up by the search engines is an art, and it's often best left to a pro. When interviewing candidates to create your site, ask what they do to optimize your site so it appears high in search engine rankings. In addition, Google's AdSense ads may, depending on your business, be a cost-effective way to drive traffic to your site.

✔ **Online ratings:** If you provide a service in a major metropolitan area, get a free listing on popular rating services such as `local.yahoo.com`, `angieslist.com`, `citysearch.com`, and `insiderpages.com`. Ask your satisfied customers to rate you.

✔ **Consultant sites:** If you're a consultant, try posting your availability on these sites: `www.elance.com` and `www.guru.com`.

✔ **Flyers:** Post flyers where your target customers will see them. If I were looking for new clients, I might post flyers near a college's career center saying:

Want more career help?

I pick up where college career centers leave off.

✔ **Sampling:** Your work can be your own best sales force. Let people see what you do. Give them a taste and whet their appetite for more. You can provide samples of your work through your Web site, photos, portfolios, brochures, business cards, demonstrations, DVDs, free consultations, speeches, and seminars or by passing out actual samples.

✔ **Articles:** Write an article for a trade publication or have someone write an article about your business. I enjoy doctors as clients, so I could see myself writing a piece for the local medical society's newsletter called "When Doctors Have Necrotic Career Syndrome."

- **Giving a talk:** Libraries and service clubs such as Kiwanis and Rotary are always looking for speakers. Or speak at a professional conference. For example, if you run a bookkeeping service, give a talk called "The Seven Keys to Doing Your Own Bookkeeping" at a small business owners convention. Be sure to give attendees a handout that lists the major points of your talk, plus your contact information. Many of your attendees will try to do their own bookkeeping but later decide that outsourcing it to you is wiser.

- **Being interviewed on a talk show:** Especially on small stations, getting on the air is easier than you may think. Just call the radio station, ask to speak with the producer of *(insert name of talk show)* and give a 30-second pitch about why listeners would be interested in you. For example, "I run a crime scene cleanup business, and you wouldn't believe the stuff I see. There was this time when a girlfriend pushed her boyfriend and all his stuff out the window. He's fine, but you'd be amazed what was among his things. So I think your listeners might find it fun to have me on the show."

Please, if you need more customers, whenever you're not doing paying work, make marketing your number one priority. This may be the most important sentence in this chapter.

But What If I Fail?

If you fall on your face, corny as it may sound, force yourself to congratulate yourself for having had the courage to try, regroup, and put together another plan for crafting your cool career. Winston Churchill once said that success is moving from failure to failure with grace, composure, and confidence. Being more optimistic than that, I would add: until you get the hang of it. If you're willing to learn from your experiences, you probably will get the hang of it; you'll find a way to make your cool career work.

And of course, deciding at any point that being your own boss isn't for you is perfectly okay. As you can see in the *Cool Careers Yellow Pages* in Chapter 2, there are plenty of great salaried careers.

Part V
The Part of Tens

The 5th Wave   By Rich Tennant

ARMANI

In this part . . .

In working with more than 2,500 clients over the past 20 years, I've found that there are only a small number of important career musts. Many of them are usually conveyed only privately, either by a career coach, or more often, by a wise parent to a child.

In this part, we share them with you. Note that I said "we." Some of these career musts apply to everyone, but others are — like the hair dye — just for men. Others are just for women. As a guy, I figured I wasn't the right, well, guy, to write about career musts for women, but I found the perfect person — my amazing wife.

Don't miss The Part of Tens.

Chapter 14

Top Ten Career Musts for Women

In This Chapter

▶ Being true to yourself while maintaining a sense of humor

▶ Getting paid what you're worth

▶ Keeping your personal life from infecting your worklife

▶ Handling hormones at work

*O*pportunities for women in the workplace have never been greater. Often, if a woman doesn't succeed, it's not because a cabal of men has erected a glass ceiling; it's because she's shot herself in the foot. This chapter's ten career musts can ensure you don't.

Note: Barbara Nemko contributed this chapter. She is the Napa County (CA) Superintendent of Schools, recent Northern California Schools Superintendent of the Year, and wife of author Marty Nemko.

Being Who You Are

Today, some women subvert who they are to prove that they can do anything a man can. For example, some women endure physics and calculus for an engineering major and a construction-site engineering career, not because they love engineering, but mainly because society or their parents encouraged them to pursue a nontraditional career. Not surprisingly, women engineers leave the field at twice the rate of men.

Other women do the opposite: hiding their competence for fear of appearing too strong. That, of course, devastates their career.

Be who you are. For example, if you do love and are talented in engineering, go for it, certainly. In fields with fewer than 50 percent women, you often find special efforts made to court you. But being courted isn't worthwhile if a frog (a misfitting career) is doing the courting. Choose a career that's right for you.

Similarly, after they're on the job, some women, in an attempt to show how tough they are, try to act like stereotypical men — all bottom-line. And they'd never dare to do anything as stereotypically female as baking cookies for the staff. Be yourself. If you're all business, that's fine, but if you're more comfortable blending a bit of traditional femininity into your workplace, that may be even better. If, for example, you enjoy baking cookies, bring 'em on in — food is love.

I had a male supervisor who warned me against bringing in home-baked goodies because he was afraid I'd be regarded as a lightweight. I've never found that to be the case. In fact, people seem to like my Jewish-mom caring. Plus, last year, I was named my region's Schools Superintendent of the Year, so I don't think the Death-by-Chocolate brownies I bake and serve at meetings hurt my career.

Being Self-Effacing

Conventional wisdom is that women should never be self-effacing. It reinforces unfair stereotypes that women are weak. But I've found that if you're already viewed as competent, occasional self-effacement is a plus, especially when done in a lighthearted way.

For example, I always make fun of the fact that I can't sing, am terrible in sports, and even that I'm technologically challenged. Remember, more than anything, people want to feel good about themselves. If you're in an even moderately powerful position, it helps to admit things you can't do. When you're self-effacing, the people who work for you may feel better about themselves and therefore be more open to what you have to say.

You don't want to be self-effacing in a job interview. There, you haven't yet established your credibility. For details on interviewing, see Chapter 10.

Negotiating for Fair Pay

Most employers want to get every employee, man or woman, to work for as little as possible. Employers are more successful at getting women to work for less not mainly because of sexism but because, on average, women are more willing to accept an employer's weak offer and, after being hired, are less likely to ask for a raise.

If you negotiate and do it well, in most cases, you should be able to get equal pay for truly equal work. Indeed, Dr. Warren Farrell, the only man who served three times on the board of the National Organization for Women in New York City, wrote a book, *Why Men Earn More,* which distills a decade of U.S. Bureau of Labor Statistics and other authoritative data. That research indicates that when men earn more, it's usually because more men are willing to do the things that earn higher pay: move all over the country to God-forsaken places to get promotions, acquire difficult-to-acquire skills such as computational biology, work more than 50 hours a week, take additional training at night and on weekends, or accept greater risk — for example, a 100-percent commission-based job. Indeed, the book concludes that for many popular careers, for truly the same work, women earn at least as much as men. The statistic that women earn just 80 cents on the dollar is misleading.

Too many women feel grateful or lucky when offered a big job and just accept a weak offer. Learn how to negotiate.

Competing Healthily

Competing with women (and men) is fine — competition can fuel some people to achieve their best. But some women seem to compete with other women on trivial matters — notably, their appearance. Out of jealousy, some women sabotage an attractive female co-worker: by withholding key business information, spreading false rumors, taking credit for her work, and so on. Please, if you want to be taken seriously at work, don't let petty stuff intrude on your worklife. It's hard to expect people at work to respect you if you're playing those games.

Balancing Work and Family

For societal and perhaps biological reasons, the average woman wants to be more involved in family matters than the average man does. Women are generally more eager to have children, and they want to be more involved in raising them and in caring for aging parents.

If that's you, make a conscious choice. Do you want to be superwoman: deeply involved in family while holding a demanding job in which the norm is a 60-hour workweek? Or do you want to opt for a more balanced life? Choosing the latter is fine, but accept that you probably won't be selected for that job in which a 60-hour workweek is the norm if you're not willing to work that many hours.

There is a way to have it all: hire help. If you're in or even aspiring to a big job, hiring domestic and child-care help can be a terrific investment. For little cost, if you search a bit, you can find someone, perhaps a college student, to pick up your kids, drive them to after-school activities, pick up the groceries and dry cleaning, and start dinner.

Research shows that what counts in parenting is quality time. Don't feel guilty if you're working a very full-time job. Just be sure that you do provide that quality time daily. For example, even though I was working full time, our family usually had dinner together (I would cook up a storm on Sunday and freeze meals for the week), talked about the day, and Marty and I read our daughter a bedtime story. That routine went on long after she knew how to read. It was a wonderful time for all of us.

But to be honest, superwomen rarely exist outside of comic books. Many women find that opting for balance is wise. Especially if you have children, you may want to aim for a 20-to-40-hour-a-week job, leaving time not only for family responsibilities, but also for fun.

In our marriage, we have a bailiwick system. We divide life's tasks according to our preferences and strengths. I'm a neat freak, so home care is my bailiwick; I do those tasks or hire someone to do them. Marty is a lousy cook and thus is prohibited from preparing meals, but he's a whiz at investments, insurance, gardening (I hate getting dirt under my nails), and the like. Those aren't my strengths or interests, so he has 100 percent responsibility for those. Our bailiwick system avoids arguments about whose turn it is to do the dishes, and we each feel a certain pride in having control over our domain.

A bit of advice about maternity leave: After having their babies, many women return to work, but their heart is mainly with their baby. They're also exhausted — having an infant is draining — which additionally diminishes their drive to work. You don't want to ruin your reputation at work, so consider coming back to work part time for the first few months, and when you're at work, be sure you really work. Otherwise, you'll convey the impression that you're permanently going to give your job short shrift. If you're working part time, be sure your hours are clearly posted, including the hours you work from home. And stick to your schedule. That way, people know you're really working.

Harnessing Your Hormones

In my younger days, during the few days before my period, I was sort of a lunatic. I'd get teary from little sadnesses that I'd easily shrug off the rest of the month. Routine annoyances would turn me into the Dragon Lady. Now, in menopause, those hormonal changes aren't as problematic, although they're still a bit of an issue.

Here's how I minimize their effects on my worklife: When I'm feeling cranky, I generally keep it to myself and just try to minimize stressful interactions. At meetings, I'm deliberately quieter. If pushed, I might ask whether we can put the discussion off until tomorrow.

With regard to hot flashes, we're not living in Victorian times. Besides, the entire Boomer generation is going through menopause. So, if I suddenly feel a furnace in me, I just rip off my jacket and fan myself. I even have one of those little battery-operated fans. I believe that being upfront about menopause, indeed joking a bit about it, turns a potential negative into something slightly endearing.

Getting Physical

Even if your job doesn't normally require physical strength, chances are good that you occasionally have to lift something heavy. For example, our daughter is an attorney. She frequently needs to move 30-pound deposition boxes down the hall or store them in an airplane's overhead compartment. She makes a point of not asking a man for help, and instead does such things herself. That's a vivid way to show that — like Rosie the Riveter flexing her biceps — she can do it all. That also conveys the message that she won't use being a woman as an excuse for anything. Men, except for the increasingly rare Neanderthal types, respect that.

Dressing Wisely

Wear what you want — if you're not worrying about your choice impeding your career. For some people, making a fashion statement is so central to their identity that they're willing to let their career suffer. But if you're not willing to pay that price, forget about what's in the fashion magazines. You don't want to look like you're spending all your time and money trying to keep up with the fashion fads. Doing that conveys a shallow image.

In some arty or avant-garde workplaces, anything goes, but in general, dressing for success means dressing in quality, timeless designs — look at what TV news anchors wear. You want to be thought of as a professional, not a runway model. If you enjoy making bold fashion statements or wearing a nose ring, save them for after work. One more tip: A scantily clad or tattooed employee doesn't look professional.

Even if your workplace encourages casual dress, casual doesn't mean sloppy. Leave those flip-flops for the beach. You're safest with high-quality, middle-of-the-road choices.

Flirting to Advantage

Daniel Goleman, in his book, *Social Intelligence,* reports that when a woman makes eye contact with a guy for even a moment, it releases dopamine in him, and in turn, increases his feeling of well-being. Babies flirt shamelessly with everyone, and people love it. Don't you want people to associate you with a sense of well-being? You don't want to be known as a big flirt, but a smile, a bit of eye contact, and an unexpected "How are you doing?" has long made the world go round.

Dating in the Workplace without Disaster

Most advice on workplace dating is equally applicable to men and women, so you can flip to Chapter 16 (which covers career musts for everyone) for details. Here, I mainly want to warn you about the one workplace dating issue that applies more often to women than to men: compartmentalization.

Men, on average, are more likely than women to compartmentalize their relationship issues. For example, Bill Clinton had one of the world's most embarrassing affairs (remember the cigar?) trumpeted all over the media for months. Yet, it seemed to have no impact on his ability to do his job.

Most women I know are less able to do that. If you dated one of your co-workers, would you feel compelled to treat your sweetie differently in the workplace? If you broke up, would everyone in the office know it, even without your telling them? Think about how you'd feel if you broke up and had to see him daily. If you don't think you'd handle it well, don't date anyone at work.

If you think you can compartmentalize your relationship, the workplace may be the best place to meet a romantic partner. After all, at a bar or club, for example, you're judging mainly on looks (and that judgment is likely affected by alcohol). At work, you get to see your prospect in action, day in and day out. Is he kind? Competent? Successful? Chasing every skirt in the office?

Disclosure: I'm not unbiased on this issue. Marty and I met at work and we've been together now for 30 happy (well, usually happy) years.

Chapter 15

Top Ten Career Musts for Men

In This Chapter

▶ Expanding your options at work and at home

▶ Embracing your inner maleness without being a Neanderthal

▶ Working wisely with women

So many books offer career advice for women. The *Women and Business* category at amazon.com lists 950 titles. Yet Amazon doesn't even have a *Men and Business* category. This chapter helps fill the gap. Men need guidance too.

Consciously Decide Whether You Want to Be the Primary Breadwinner

In most families, the man is still the primary breadwinner. Often, that's assumed. Far wiser is for each couple to discuss that crucial issue openly.

For example, in being the primary breadwinner, are you forced to take a job that makes you miserable? Some high-paying jobs pay so well because few people would otherwise take them; examples include traveling salespeople, middle managers in an insurance company, and corporate lawyers.

Would you be happier in a lower-paying but more rewarding career? Women, in general, have been wiser about trading money for quality of life. Should you consider that? Might it be worth living in more modest housing in exchange for working at a job you love? Should your wife assume more of the financial burden even if she's not able to be at home as much with the kids? (The evidence is mixed on whether stay-at-home moms' kids do better.) Should you do more housework? Parenting? Would you enjoy that more than working for a fire-breathing boss, or in a clanging, carcinogenic factory?

Fortunately, you have no rules — there is no more "men's work" or "women's work." Each couple should craft for themselves the division of labor that best accommodates both spouses' strengths and preferences.

Consider Nontraditional Careers

For decades now, women have, appropriately, been encouraged to consider all careers rather than just those traditionally held by women. Similarly, men should consider the full range of career options. Some traditionally female careers can be unusually rewarding: librarian, teacher, editor, nurse, and graphic designer, for example. A real man chooses a career that feels right for him without worrying that it's not a "manly" career.

Use the Power of Deep Connection

Women, on average, are better at connecting with people than men are. They start young. Walk into any kindergarten and you'll see most girls playing together cooperatively, while most boys are playing by themselves or in very uncooperative ways: pushing, chasing, and terrorizing. Fast forward a few years and, in most households, while boys are staring at a TV or computer game, girls are on the phone or instant messaging their friends. Fast forward to adulthood and you'll find nine zillion women's organizations — the ultimate networking opportunity — and barely any for men.

Guys, you gotta recognize the power of deep connection. When you talk with another man, ask about deeper things than his new car, techno-toy, or the score of the big game. I'm not saying you have to "process deep feelings," but guys care plenty about their careers, health, looks, finances, maybe even feelings. Find out what the person you're talking with is most concerned about, and discuss that. Then share a concern of yours. Be careful, however, not to give unwanted advice, particularly to women. The stereotype is generally true: Women mainly want to be heard rather than to have their problem solved. I don't get it, but then again, I'm a guy. Because men do, in general, appreciate advice and don't just need to be heard, when you're talking with a guy, you may offer each other help that solves problems. That's likely to bond you enough that you both want to help each other's careers.

Temper "Male Energy"

Workplaces used to deify "male energy": aggressiveness, competition, individualism. Today, in many workplaces — especially those with a number of female higher-ups — to survive, let alone thrive, men usually must temper male energy. That may or may not yield better business results, but certainly, in recent years, the pendulum has swung to give women's ways of being more respect than men's. The unvarnished truth is that in today's typical workplace, men must usually accommodate to women's ways, not vice versa.

Do you talk too much at meetings?

Rule of thumb: In a meeting, talk no more than 50 percent above your share of time. For example, if you're in an hourlong meeting with six attendees, your share is ten minutes. Your maximum talk time: 15 minutes. And that assumes that you have more of value to say than the other attendees. Normally, you want to talk less than that.

A no-holds-barred approach to achieving a goal may win the battle but will probably lose the war. For example, one salesman wanted to become the head honcho when the boss retired. To put himself in line, he did the following:

- ✔ Hyped product strengths, downplayed product weaknesses, and pushed customers harder to "make the commitment."
- ✔ Unfairly complained about fellow team members to the boss.
- ✔ Dominated the weekly sales meeting. Although six people were in the room, he talked half the time.

This salesman sold more machines but, not surprisingly, didn't get the promotion. Why? Because he pushed some customers so hard that they complained to the boss, and his complaints about co-workers and his dominating meetings were seen as the ploys they were.

Drive is often key to achieving excellence, but please, don't cross ethical lines. And even when ethical, always ask yourself whether the side effects of being aggressive might outweigh the benefits.

Be Tactful and Listen Well

Another form of excessive aggressiveness: bluntness. Many men think of bluntness as a positive: "I'm direct, a straight-shooter." Fact is, if the bluntness decimates your listener, the price may be too great. Women, in general, are better at criticizing tactfully. You can be tactful too.

Occasionally, to shake a person's undue complacency, you must be blunt. But do that often, and you'll probably be viewed not as a straight-shooter but as insensitive. When you must criticize, do it in the most self-esteem-preserving way. For example, "I noticed *(insert your concern)* and wonder whether there's something I'm not understanding." When the person explains, even if it's an imperfect explanation, try to accept it, knowing that you planted a seed — he'll probably make the necessary change.

Poor listening is among aggressiveness's most insidious manifestations. The aggressive person is so eager to prove his point that he listens poorly to what the other person is saying, thereby losing opportunities to find common ground, let alone to have his mind changed. Above all, learn to listen well.

Controlling unbridled aggressiveness is particularly important if your boss is a woman. Many female bosses worry about being steamrolled by male energy, so you'll get lots of brownie points if you temper your aggressiveness with good listening and tactfully made suggestions.

If you find yourself unable to consistently follow my advice to temper your maleness to accommodate to today's typical workplace, you may be more likely to find success in the handful of remaining fields in which male-centricity remains the norm — for example, aerospace, construction, transportation, energy, agriculture, and manufacturing.

Mind Your Health

Men die six years younger than women, and it seems that more men than women in their mid- to late-50s show significant decline in physical and mental capability. That, I believe, partly explains why Boomer men are having a harder time finding jobs than are Boomer women.

Because men are at risk of earlier decline, it's especially important that you take precautions to forestall aging and disease. I'm not telling you anything new here, but perhaps this is a wakeup call to get serious about controlling your weight, not smoking, drinking no more than moderately, and getting regular, moderate exercise. Science is finding that your mother may have been right: Walking may be the best exercise. And despite all the diet books and fads, the best advice can fit on a thimble: Eat lots of fruits and veggies, a moderate amount of whole-grain rather than refined-grain carbs, and little fat. Easier said than done, I know.

Flirt with Your Antennae Out

Flirting is fun, but, in today's workplace, it's risky, especially for men. Women typically have the power in such matters: If you flirt and she perceives it as unwelcome, in most workplaces, her perception is presumed valid unless proven otherwise, which is hard to do. And if you flirt again, you're on the road to a sexual harassment claim. Telling a woman three days this week how great she looks may be innocent to you, yet it can be perceived as "persistent unwanted advances." At that point, no matter how trivial you say your comments were, many HR departments would initiate an inquiry.

I'm not saying you shouldn't compliment women. I'm not even saying that you can't flirt. But the burden is on you: Have your antennae out for even a scintilla of verbal or nonverbal indication that your attentions are unwelcome.

Don't Date Your Supervisee

Note: This section applies to women as well as men, but because more men are bosses, I placed it in this chapter.

In my view, if you're the type who can keep a personal relationship from affecting your worklife, the advantages of dating people you meet at work outweigh the liabilities. (Of course, I'm biased in that I met my wife at work.)

But I beg you, even if company policy doesn't prohibit it, not to date someone you supervise. Your supervisee may agree to go out with you only for fear of hurting her career if she says no. Is that the basis on which you want a date? And if things go wrong, oy! The supervisee often claims the boss abused the power relationship, which can cost you your job. Or what if she threatens to make that claim unless you promote her or let her get paid full time for part-time work? Even if you dodge those bullets, having to supervise your disgruntled ex-lover won't be fun. And just imagine if you wanted to fire her! Even when the relationship is working fine, higher-ups may make you pay. Esteemed Boeing CEO Harry Stonecipher was fired simply for having a consensual affair with a Boeing employee.

React to Reverse Discrimination

I've been career coach to 2,500 clients, almost all professionals. In the confidentiality of my office, a surprising number have asserted that women (and minorities) receive favoritism in hiring and promotion over men who are more competent and/or willing to work longer hours.

If you believe you've been the target of reverse discrimination, you could try a lawsuit, but that's very chancy and exhausting. Or you could make a career of changing today's common belief that reverse discrimination is appropriate.

If you don't want to pursue those options, get over it. In many workplaces and universities, reverse discrimination is a fact of life. It's bad enough that you may be treated unfairly; don't let it also destroy your peace of mind.

Be Proud to Be a Man

In the appropriate attempt to redress past and lingering discrimination against women, society's mind-molders — schools, colleges, and media — are empowering women, but too often at men's expense. Textbooks, college professors, sitcoms, movies, even newspaper and magazine features tend to portray women as the good guys and men as testosterone-poisoned boors, crooks, or abusers. The schools and colleges continually trumpet the contributions of women, while accentuating the evils of men, especially "Dead European White Males." It's easy to see why, today, women's self-esteem, on average, is higher than men's, and why only ⅓ of the college graduating class of 2007 is male.

Let me remind you that, despite what society's mind molders may say, all men are not killers, rapists, slackers, and dolts. Aristotle, Plato, Jesus, Leonardo da Vinci, Beethoven, Monet, the Wright Brothers, Jonas Salk, Steven Spielberg, and 98 percent of the Nobel Prize winners for science are all men. In addition, the key scientists behind every drug from aspirin to breast cancer breakthrough Herceptin, and the leaders behind such advances as anesthetics, heart bypass surgery, refrigeration, heating, the electric light bulb, the radio, the television, the computer, the mapping of human genome, even the birth control pill — all are men. And in the five decades since the women's movement began, 97 percent of science, 92 percent of literature, and 100 percent of economics Nobel Laureates still are men.

Turning to the lower rungs of the work world, almost all people who do such grungy, dangerous, life-shortening work as fumigator, prison guard, coal miner, steelworker, and sewer maintainer are men. And 99 percent of American soldiers killed in Iraq are men. And the only gender required to register for the draft is, you guessed it, men.

The fact is, most men are hard working, goal-oriented, and straight shooting. The world needs both men and women. Don't forget it.

Of course some men (and women) are an embarrassment to their gender, indeed to the human race. And, in my view, you have an obligation, not only to yourself but also to your fellow men and women, to use traditionally male attributes — aggressiveness, drive, and a protective instinct — to positive ends. Indeed, in and out of today's workplace, you have ample opportunities to use your maleness for great good. Many men do. You can too.

Chapter 16

Top Ten (Or So) Career Musts for Everyone

In This Chapter

▶ Getting what you want without becoming obnoxious

▶ Finding a mentor and being a mentor

▶ Dating in the workplace without disaster

▶ Sharing the most important lesson I ever learned

Prioritizing these *career musts* will contribute to your having a cool career, indeed a cool life, more than anything I can think of.

Become a Master Communicator

The key is good listening: really trying to understand what the talker is saying while noticing changes in her tone of voice and body language, imagining how she's feeling, and asking follow-ups to be sure you really understand. It's not easy.

Becoming a better listener is mainly a matter of will. When your mind drifts, for example, to "What do I want to say next?" say to yourself, "Stop! Listen!"

When you're talking, your tone and pace must be pleasant. To experiment, talk into a tape recorder: Try faster and slower paces, the low, middle, and high parts of your vocal range. What's most pleasing? Get in the habit of using that voice.

Don't talk too much or too little. Rule of thumb: In any one-on-one interaction, talk 30 to 50 percent of the time. If the other person is quiet, ask questions to draw him out. Don't *you* like it when people ask you a question?

Work Hard

People tell you it's more important to work smart than to work hard. Fact is — and I'm sorry to break the bad news — most successful people work smart *and* hard. The good news is that most hard workers feel unusually fulfilled. It feels great to be productive. Take pride in your work more than your home, in what you produce more than what you preach.

Treat Chapter 11 as your worklife bible: It shows you what you need to know about maximizing your productivity while enjoying the process.

Even if you're unemployed, yes, work hard in looking for a job, but also fill your day with projects: Volunteer, clean your place, help a friend. You'll find work to be a great antidepressant . . . and it has no side effects.

Don't Overvalue Money

Money helps. Indeed, most middle-class people are happier than poor people. They can afford a safe place to live and decent wheels, and eating out needn't always involve the golden arches.

But a more upscale lifestyle — especially if you have to hold an unpleasant job to afford it — is unlikely to yield more happiness. I've found as many unhappy Jag-driving mansion owners as Toyota-driving cottage dwellers.

As you decide what work to do, ask yourself whether the lifestyle gain from the extra income (after taxes) is worth it. Contentment more likely will come from good work, relationships, and hobbies than from an expensive house, new car, or vacation in Hawaii. Well, okay, maybe keep the nice Hawaii trip.

Prize Integrity

My mouse pad is imprinted with the statement, "Integrity is key." Yes, cheaters often win — in the material sense. Many, maybe even most deceptive salespeople, plagiarizing students, and cook-the-books accountants get away with it, but they still lose. They lose in the bigger game of making their lives meaningful. If you — especially when it's to your detriment — do the ethical thing, you'll be loved and respected on this earth, and if there's a hereafter, honored in that one. And you can go through life with your head high, knowing you're making the world a better, not a worse, place.

Become Beloved

You make yourself a beloved co-worker by practicing *positive office politics:* looking for opportunities to brighten everyone's day, even if it's just to pick a piece of lint off someone's jacket. It shows you like them. Other examples:

- ✔ **Be generous with earned compliments, stingy with criticism.** Many people crave praise more than money — feeling worthy is a primal need.

- ✔ **Think twice before hurting a person's self-esteem.** Ask yourself: Do I need to say that? If so, how can I say it so she feels okay?

- ✔ **Bring in those to-die-for cookies — food *is* love.** The wise employee adds just a bit of such not-necessary activities. Too much looks unprofessional; not enough makes you look too all-business.

Avoid Saboteurs

I'm no Pollyanna. I'm fully aware that you can practice positive politics ad nauseam (as I discuss in the previous section), and still, someone may sabotage you. These strategies can help:

- ✔ **Keep your antennae out for saboteurs.** They're rare in some workplaces, the norm in others. You're especially at risk if you're more capable than other workers, are physically attractive, or have a personality that many people find annoying.

- ✔ **Tactfully confront your saboteur.** If you have good evidence that you're being unfairly sandbagged — for example, important information is being withheld from you — gently confront the person with a statement such as, "Perhaps I'm wrong, but as I understand it, *(insert your concern).* Is that true?" If the person denies it, as he usually will, say something like, "I'm glad, because I couldn't tolerate that." That approach puts the person on notice without forcing an admission. If the person admits it, ask why. If the explanation is unacceptable, say, "Can I count on it stopping? If not, I'll have to see the boss." Then, poison his coffee. (Yes, I *am* kidding.)

- ✔ **Keep your friends close and your enemies closer.** A good way to defuse enmity is to invite your nemeses to work with you on a plum project, or even invite them to a party. That gives you an opportunity to have them bumped off. (Yes, I'm still joking.) Seriously, such invitations are a good idea because most people want to be wanted. And when you're together, there will be chances to create connection.

Ask for What You Want

Most successful people ask for what they want. If they want to work for a company, they try to get a meeting with one of its big shots. If they need advice on whether to pursue a career, they e-mail one of the field's gurus.

Successful people are also assertive on the job. *The meek may inherit the earth, but not today's workplace.* Winners know that politely asking for what you want — advice, training, more responsibility, a revised job description — is usually worth the risk.

Even winners get turned down a lot but realize that costs them nothing. They just ask someone else, and someone else, and someone else, until they get a yes — or until they realize the world is telling them, "Nope, not this time."

Losers, in contrast, don't act; they ruminate. For example:

- ✔ Losers worry they'll sound stupid. Winners realize that with a bit of rehearsal, they probably won't sound stupid, and even if they do, there usually are other people to ask.

- ✔ Losers worry about imposing. Winners realize that the imposition is just a few seconds. If the person feels imposed on, she can simply say no. If she agrees to help, that's her choice — and indeed, many people enjoy helping. Think about it: You've stopped a stranger to ask for directions. Asking someone a career-related question is no bigger an imposition than that.

So, how do you move yourself from reluctant asker to enthusiastic one?

- ✔ Make a list of the benefits versus the liabilities of making the request. Usually, you'll find you have nothing to lose and much to gain.

- ✔ Rehearse. Script your pitch; then reduce it to a few guide words. Use those words as you practice into a tape recorder. Role-play with a friend.

- ✔ Imagine the worst case. Could you survive?

Conquer Procrastination

I devote an entire chapter to overcoming procrastination (head to Chapter 12 for details), but it's so crucial that I include it in this chapter too.

Procrastination really is a career killer. Don't rationalize that you can get away with it. You did in school, but you probably can't at work, unless you're willing to settle for a perennially low-level job. After you decide not to procrastinate, be aware of *the moment of truth:* the moment you — usually unconsciously — decide, "I'm going to do that task later." At that moment, ask yourself, "Would I be wiser to defer this task or do it now?" You'll procrastinate less. Then break the task down to baby steps and, when stuck, get help. Don't know how to break it into baby steps? Get help with that.

Control Your Anger

Anger is a career killer. You can be calm 98 percent of the time, but blow up even rarely and you may be branded a hothead, which is career death. Even if your anger is passive-aggressive, people will feel it and will you.

The problem is that some people go from zero to 60 in one second. If that's you, the *nanosecond* you feel anger rising in you, say: "Excuse me, I need to use the bathroom." In the privacy of that stall, amid the atmosphere of toilet paper and toilet seat protectors, take some deep breaths and ask yourself, "Will displaying anger serve me in the long run?" Rarely will you answer yes.

If you find yourself getting angry often, are you expecting too much from people? Are you working in a workplace with too low-level people or with too problemed clients? Is your anger covering your insecurity? You could change jobs or go into therapy for years to figure it out, but I believe it's first worth trying *a zero-tolerance anger policy:* no anger ever. That's better than giving yourself discretion — by the time you've decided, you've exploded.

Get a Mentor; Be a Mentor

Most people grow up hoping that someone will take them under wing. Alas, it rarely happens — unless you *make* it happen. When you meet a potential mentor, ask for a bit of advice. If he's forthcoming, be effusively thankful and look to repay the favor. Later, ask for more advice. If the person provides it and seems to enjoy the process, you have a budding mentor relationship. And no need to limit yourself to one mentor; assemble a team.

You may think of mentors as older than you, but you may meet someone far younger from whom you could learn. A younger person may particularly be flattered by a request for advice.

Look, too, for opportunities to mentor others. Not only is that fair payback, but you'll grow as much from mentoring as from being mentored.

For more on mentoring, see Chapters 5 and 12.

Date Delicately

Fifty-eight percent of respondents to a Vault.com survey said they had been in an office romance. With people spending ever-more time at work, that's no surprise. Alas, there are ever more minefields. The definition of sexual harassment is broadening and employees are quicker to file grievances.

Here's how to increase your chances of workplace dating without disaster:

- ✔ **Don't create false hopes.** If you're looking for a one-night stand, in your seducing, don't make noises about craving a long-term relationship.

- ✔ **Unless company policy prohibits it, keep your relationship secret as long as possible.** Otherwise, co-workers will scrutinize the two of you for any hint that you're playing favorites.

- ✔ **Stay professional.** Try to treat your lover as you would any other employee. No smoochy e-mails from the office — management can snoop. And, of course, resist the temptation to dive into the supply closet. These tips are easier said than done. For example, 28 percent of respondents to the Vault.com survey admitted to an office tryst.

- ✔ **Give each other space.** If you're together at and outside work, things can get stifling. Allow time apart. Bonus: Maintaining outside interests means that if you break up, you still have a life.

- ✔ **Have fun!** Despite these strictures, an office romance can be fun and more. I speak from personal experience.

Always Look Forward

I learned the lesson to always look forward from my dad. I asked him, a Holocaust survivor, why he never complained about having lost his teenage years and his entire family. He replied, "The Nazis took five years from my life. I won't give them one minute more. Martin, never look back; always look forward."

Everyone has bad things happen to them, but my most successful clients don't wallow. They always ask themselves, "What's the next positive little step I can take?" I can offer you no better advice.

Appendix

The Cool Career Finder

*H*ere are 17 special lists of careers: from the best careers for slackers to the best careers for Boomers. You can read about each career on the listed page.

Make a big difference

Biologist, 35
Book/Magazine/Web Site
    Editor, 53
Computer Security
    Programmer, 44
Engineer, 134
Environmental Analyst,
    39
Epidemiologist, 37
Fundraiser/Development
    Specialist, 31
Geographic Information
    Specialist, 67
Infectious Disease
    Specialist, 114
Investment Banker, 99
Journalist, 52
Librarian, 54
Lobbyist, 90
Meteorologist, 39
Nonpolluting Car
    Developer, 137
Physician, 113
Physicist, 41
Plant Geneticist/
    Botanist, 36
Professor, 100
Terrorism Expert, 37
Toxicologist, 41

Venture Capitalist, 100
Writer, 50

Easy-to-transition-into careers

Celebrant, 88
College Student Advisor,
    21
Copywriter, 51
Dispensing Optician, 128
Diver, 70
Dog Trainer, 69
eBay Trading Assistant,
    48
Employee Background
    Checker, 45
Employment Interviewer,
    28
Event Planner, 33
Export Agent, 49
Farrier, 68
Foreign Language
    Interpreter/
    Translator, 124
Fundraiser/Development
    Specialist, 31
Handyperson, 65
Home Stager, 126
Literary, Artist's, or
    Performer's Agent, 25
Locksmith, 68

Low-investment Food
    Operations Owner, 93
Manager, 73
Massage Therapist, 129
Nanny, 26
Neon Sign Maker, 60
Notebook Computer
    Repairperson, 63
Parking Lot Oil Change
    Business Operator, 94
Pedorthist, 62
Personal Assistant, 27
Personal Chef, 69
Personal Coach, 21
Personnel Recruiter, 28
Photographer, 131
Piano Technician/
    Tuner, 62
Private Investigator, 112
Producer, 32
Proposal Writer, 101
Public Relations/
    Communications
    Specialist, 122
Resume Writer, 53
Salesperson, 29
Specialty Stitcher, 69
Temp Agency Owner, 34
Tile Setter, 68
Trend Spotter, 103
Victim Assistant, 25

For new liberal arts grads

Athletic Coach, 87
Book/Magazine/Web Site Editor, 53
Business Developer, 103
College-Bound Athlete Consultant, 91
College Financial Aid Officer, 96
Employee Trainer, 84
Export Agent, 49
Fundraiser/Development Specialist, 31
Geographer, 106
Government Manager, 74
Journalist, 52
Labor Relations Specialist, 79
Management Consultant, 104
Marketer, 102
Military Officer, 82
Patent Agent, 137
Politician, 90
Public Relations/Communications Specialist, 122
Radio/TV News Reporter, 82
Securities Analyst, 47
Sports Announcer, 83
Teacher, 85
Tutor, 92
Work-Life Manager, 75
Writer, 50

Too much fun to be work

Actor, 88
Artist/Graphic Artist, 56
Athletic Coach, 87
Background Vocalist, 89
Brewer, 140
Casting Director, 28
Celebrant, 88
Cinematographer, 59
Composer, 89
Cosmetologist/Makeup Artist, 130
Curator, 141
Dating Coach, 23
Enologist, 139
Fashion Designer, 130
Filmmaker/Director, 140
Foley Artist, 59
Game Programmer, 44
Garden Designer, 126
Gemologist, 68
Graphologist, 55
Holographer, 60
Home Stager, 126
Image Coach, 24
Lighting Designer, 59
Magician, 56
Musician, 89
Nanny, 26
Newborn Photographer, 131
Organizational Identity Consultant, 104
Park Ranger, 133
Perfumer, 60
Personal Historian/Biographer, 123
Pet Photographer, 132
Pet Sitter, 69
Photographer, 131
Professional Speaker, 84
Pyrotechnician, 70
Radio/TV News Reporter, 82
Restaurant Menu Creator, 141
Simplification Coach, 23
Specialty Cake Baker, 56
Specialty Stitcher, 69
Sports Announcer, 83
Sports Information Director, 100
Sports Medicine, 114
Sports Statistician, 42
Talk Show Host, 83
Textile Designer, 58
Trend Spotter, 103
Virtual Reality Programmer, 43

Impress your friends and family

Administrative Law Judge, 121
Architect, 141
Athletic Coach, 87
Attorney, 118
Awards Entrepreneur, 123
Biologist, 35
Book/Magazine/Web Site Editor, 53
Casting Director, 28
City Manager, 76
Clergy, 87
Corporate Intelligence Officer, 82
Cryptanalyst, 42
Curator, 141
Dentist, 127
Engineer, 134
Enologist, 139
Epidemiologist, 37
Ethicist, 55
FBI Special Agent, 112
Filmmaker/Director, 140
Foley Artist, 59
Foreign Service Officer, 123
Foundation Program Manager, 77
Game Programmer, 44
Genetic Counselor, 72
Ghostwriter, 51
Heart-Lung Perfusionist, 61
Holographer, 60
Investment Banker, 99
Journalist, 52
Magician, 56
Mediator, 18
Meteorologist, 39
Nonpolluting Car Developer, 137
Oceanographer, 106

Perfumer, 60
Physician, 113
Physicist, 41
Pilot, 107
Plant Geneticist/
Botanist, 36
Political Campaign
Manager, 79
Politician, 90
Portfolio Manager, 47
Producer, 32
Professor, 100
Pyrotechnician, 70
Radio/TV News Reporter,
82
Sailboat Captain, 61
School Administrator, 78
Computer Security
Programmer, 44
Seismologist, 40
Sports Announcer, 83
Sports Information
Director, 100
Sports Referee/Umpire,
134
Stunt Person, 134
Talk Show Host, 83
Terrorism Expert, 37
Toxicologist, 41
Trend Spotter, 103
Trial Consultant, 34
Venture Capitalist, 100
Veterinarian, 116
Virtual Reality
Programmer, 43
Volcanologist, 40

Express yourself

Actor, 88
Architect, 141
Artist/Graphic Artist, 56
Athletic Coach, 87
Attorney, 118
Celebrant, 88
Cinematographer, 59
Clergy, 87
Composer, 89
Cosmetologist/Makeup
Artist, 130

Curator, 141
Employee Trainer, 84
Engineer, 134
Exhibit Designer/Builder,
59
Fashion Designer, 130
Filmmaker/Director, 140
Foley Artist, 59
Garden Designer, 126
Health Educator, 85
Home Stager, 126
Industrial Designer, 138
Interior Designer, 125
Inventor, 137
Journalist, 52
Landscape Architect, 126
Lighting Designer, 59
Lobbyist, 90
Magician, 56
Musician, 89
Newsletter Publisher, 45
Perfumer, 60
Personal Chef, 69
Photographer, 131
Politician, 90
Professional Speaker, 84
Public Relations/
Communications
Specialist, 122
Radio/TV News Reporter,
82
Software Designer/
Architect, 94
Specialty Cake Baker, 56
Specialty Stitcher, 69
Sports Announcer, 83
Sports Information
Director, 100
Talk Show Host, 83
Teacher, 85
Tool and Die Maker, 60
Writer, 50

Could lead to big bucks

Actuary, 46
Administrative Law
Judge, 121

Attorney, 118
Audiologist, 116
Business Developer, 103
Computer Security
Administrator, 111
Dentist, 127
Engineer, 134
Executive Recruiter
(Headhunter), 28
Harbor Pilot, 61
Investment Banker, 99
Management Consultant,
104
Manager (can lead to
executive positions),
73
Optometrist, 71
Physician, 113
Portfolio Manager, 47
Producer, 32
Securities Trader, 99
Trial Consultant, 34
Venture Capitalist, 100
Veterinarian, 116

Boomer bests (where being older is a plus)

Administrative Law
Judge, 121
Architect, 141
Business Broker, 81
Celebrant, 88
Elder Lawyer, 121
Estate Attorney, 121
Fundraiser, 31
Funeral Director, 92
Geriatric Care Manager,
19
Gerontologist, 96
Health Educator, 85
Lobbyist, 90
Mediator, 18
Personal Coach
(especially
Retirement Coach), 21
Personal Historian/
Biographer, 123
Politician, 90
Senior Retrofitter, 65

For the brainy

Accountant, 96
Acoustics Specialist, 106
Actuary, 46
Administrative Law
    Judge, 121
Architect, 141
Attorney, 118
Biologist, 35
Book/Magazine/Web Site
    Editor, 53
Business Plan Writer, 105
Chemist, 40
Computer Programmer,
    43
Coroner/Medical
    Examiner, 106
Cryptanalyst, 42
Curator, 141
Economist, 46
Engineer, 134
Epidemiologist, 37
Executive Coach, 24
Exercise Physiologist,
    110
Filmmaker/Director, 140
Geographer, 106
Geologist, 39
Holographer, 60
Indexer, 55
Information Technology
    Manager, 75
Inventor, 137
Investment Banker, 99
Journalist, 52
Librarian, 54
Management Consultant,
    104
Mediator, 18
Meteorologist, 39
Oceanographer, 106
Operations Research
    Analyst, 96
Patent Agent, 137
Physician, 113
Physicist, 41

Plant Geneticist/
    Botanist, 36
Political Campaign
    Manager, 79
Portfolio Manager, 47
Producer, 32
Professor, 100
Program Evaluator, 102
Proposal Writer, 101
Psychotherapist/
    Psychologist, 19
Securities Analyst, 47
Software
    Designer/Architect, 94
Statistician, 41
Systems Analyst, 95
Talk Show Host, 83
Terrorism Expert, 37
Thesis Completion
    Consultant, 101
Toxicologist, 41
Trial Consultant, 34
Venture Capitalist, 100
Veterinarian, 116
Web Developer/
    Webmaster, 95
Writer, 50

Employers are eager

Accountant, 96
Automotive Technician
    (Car Mechanic), 66
Bioinformatician, 36
Biologist (bachelor's
    level), 35
Cardiovascular
    Technologist, 128
Catholic Priest, 87
Child-Care Center Owner,
    26
Computer Security
    Programmer, 44
Criminalist, 140
Database Administrator,
    95
Debt Collection
    Specialist, 81

Diagnostic Medical
    Sonographer, 93
Electrician, 65
Employee Background
    Checker, 45
Epidemiologist, 37
Farrier, 68
Forensic Accountant, 97
Forensic Economist, 46
Fundraiser/Development
    Specialist, 31
Geographic Information
    Specialist, 67
Handyperson, 65
Home Stager, 126
Information Technology
    Manager, 75
Intellectual Property/
    Patent Lawyer, 120
International
    Accountant, 98
Locksmith, 68
Nanny, 26
Network Administrator,
    111
Occupational Therapist,
    93
Operations Research
    Analyst, 96
Optometrist, 71
Pharmacist, 71
Physician, 113
Program Evaluator, 102
Purchasing Specialist/
    Supply Chain
    Manager/Logistics
    Manager, 96
Registered Nurse, 108
Respiratory Therapist,
    110
School Psychologist, 20
Social Worker, 25
Solar and Wind Energy
    Technologist/Installer,
    64
Speech-Language
    Therapist, 90
Systems Analyst, 95

Teacher, 85
Telecommunications Specialist, 64
Terrorism Expert, 37

Under the radar

Accent Neutralization Specialist, 91
Accident Reconstructor, 133
Adoption Attorney, 119
Arborist, 68
Audiologist, 116
Bioinformatician, 36
Biomedical Visualization Specialist, 58
Cartographer, 139
Casting Director, 28
Celebrant, 88
Child Life Specialist, 26
College-Bound Athlete Consultant, 91
College Financial Aid Officer, 96
College Student Affairs Administrator, 74
Corporate Intelligence Officer, 82
Cryptanalyst, 42
Doula, 24
"Dull-Normal" Business Owner, 67
eBay Trading Assistant, 48
Enologist, 139
Epidemiologist, 37
Forensic Economist, 46
Genomics or Proteomics Biologist, 36
Geographic Information Specialist, 67
Geriatric Care Manager, 19
Gerontologist, 96
Ghostwriter, 51
Graphologist, 55
Hearing Officer, 121

Home Schooling Consultant, 92
Hydrologist, 38
Indexer, 55
Industrial Designer, 138
Information Retriever, 54
Lighting Designer, 59
Money Counselor, 20
Muralist/Faux Finisher, 58
Newborn Photographer, 131
Nonpolluting Car Developer, 137
Nurse Midwife, 109
Orthoptist, 71
Patent Agent, 137
Patient Advocate, 72
Pedorthist, 62
Perfumer, 60
Photonics, 41
Physician Assistant, 115
Plant Geneticist/Botanist, 36
Polygraph Operator, 92
Private-Practice Consultant, 105
Professional Blogger, 50
Proposal Writer, 101
Proteomics Biologist, 36
Public Affairs Manager, 77
Pyrotechnician, 70
Reunion Planner, 33
Risk Management Specialist, 111
School Computer Coordinator, 112
Seismologist, 40
Shyness Coach, 23
Specialty Cake Baker, 56
Sports Information Director, 100
Succession Planning Consultant, 80
Surgical Technologist, 128
Toxicologist, 41

Victim Assistant, 25
Viticulturist, 107

Maximum security (and offshore resistant)

Audiologist, 116
Automotive Technician (Car Mechanic), 66
Cardiovascular Technologist, 128
College Financial Aid Officer, 96
College Student Advisor, 21
Coroner/Medical Examiner, 106
Dentist, 127
Electrician, 65
Environmental Analyst, 39
Firefighter, 133
Foreign Service Officer, 123
Fundraiser/Development Specialist, 31
Funeral Director, 92
Government Manager, 74
Handyperson, 65
Librarian, 54
Locksmith, 68
Military Officer, 82
Network Administrator, 111
Occupational Therapist, 93
Optometrist, 71
Park Ranger, 133
Pharmacist, 71
Physical Therapist, 117
Physician, 113
Professor (tenure-track only), 100
Registered Nurse, 108
School Administrator, 78
Social Worker, 25
Speech-Language Therapist, 90

Terrorism Expert, 37
Toxicologist, 41
Veterinarian, 116

Good with your hands?

Art Teacher, 87
Artist/Graphic Artist, 56
Automotive Technician
    (Car Mechanic), 66
Avionics Technician, 66
Computer Repairperson,
    63
Conservator, 59
Cosmetologist/Makeup
    Artist, 130
Dental Hygienist, 128
Dentist, 127
Diver, 70
Electrician, 65
Engineer, 134
Engineering Technician,
    137
Exhibit Designer/Builder,
    59
Farrier, 68
Fashion Designer, 130
Handyperson, 65
Industrial Designer, 138
Inventor, 137
Landscape Architect, 126
Locksmith, 68
Magician, 56
Massage Therapist, 129
Musical Instrument
    Repairperson, 62
Neon Sign Maker, 60
Registered Nurse, 108
Occupational Therapist,
    93
Physical Therapist, 117
Physician, 113
Physician Assistant, 115
Prosthetist/Orthotist, 61
Solar and Wind Energy
    Technologist/Installer,
    64
Specialty Cake Baker, 56

Specialty Stitcher, 69
Technical Illustrator, 58
Telecommunications
    Specialist, 64
Tool and Die Maker, 60
Veterinarian, 116
Veterinary Technologist,
    117

The leading edge

Adventure/Eco Travel
    Organizer, 49
Bioinformatician, 36
Biomedical Visualization
    Specialist, 58
Computer Security
    Programmer, 44
Distance-Learning
    Teacher, 86
eBay Trading Assistant,
    48
E-mercial Salesperson, 29
Engineer, 134
Flying Car Developer, 137
Genetic Counselor, 72
Genomics or Proteomics
    Biologist, 36
Geographic Information
    Specialist, 67
Gerontologist, 96
Green Architect, 142
Holographer, 60
Industrial Designer, 138
Inventor, 137
Intellectual Property/
    Patent Lawyer, 120
Nonpolluting Car
    Developer, 137
Patent Agent, 137
Photonics, 41
Physician, 113
Planetary Geologist, 39
Professional Blogger, 50
Proteomics Biologist, 36
Relationship Acceptance
    Therapist, 20
Retirement Coach, 24
Space Lawyer, 120

Special Effects Artist, 57
Terrorism Expert, 37
Trend Spotter, 103
Virtual Reality
    Programmer, 43
Wireless Device
    Programmer, 43

Slackers' specials

Accent Neutralization
    Specialist, 91
Actor, 88
Appraiser, 50
Archivist, 105
Artist/Graphic Artist, 56
Auctioneer, 32
Brewer, 140
Casting Director, 28
Celebrant, 88
College-Bound Athlete
    Consultant, 91
College Student Advisor,
    21
Cosmetologist/Makeup
    Artist, 130
Curator, 141
Dispensing Optician, 128
Employee Background
    Checker, 45
Employment Interviewer,
    28
Enologist, 139
Expense Reduction
    Consultant, 46
Fashion Designer, 130
Foley Artist, 59
Foreign Language
    Interpreter/Translator,
    124
Garden Designer, 126
Gemologist, 68
Genetic Counselor, 72
Graphologist, 55
Health Educator, 85
Historic Preservationist,
    140
Home Inspector, 127

Home Schooling Consultant, 92
Home Stager, 126
Image Coach, 24
Locksmith, 68
Musical Instrument Repairperson, 62
Musician, 89
Nanny, 26
Neon Sign Maker, 60
Optometrist, 71
Organizational Identity Consultant, 104
Park Ranger, 133
Pedorthist, 62
Perfumer, 60
Personal Coach, 21
Personal Historian/ Biographer, 123
Pet Sitter, 69
Photographer, 131
Relocation Consultant, 34
Restaurant Menu Creator, 141
Resume Writer, 53
Specialty Cake Baker, 56
Sports Announcer, 83
Thesis Completion Consultant, 101
Trend Spotter, 103
Victim Assistant, 25

My favorite shoe-string businesses

Accent Neutralization Specialist, 91
Business Plan Writer, 105
Celebrant, 88
College-Bound Athlete Consultant, 91
College Financial Aid Counselor, 81
Debt Collection Specialist, 81
Doula, 24
eBay Trading Assistant, 48
Electrician, 65

Expense Reduction Consultant, 46
Export Agent, 49
Garden Designer, 126
Ghostwriter, 51
Hard Disk Repairperson, 63
Home Inspector, 127
Home Schooling Consultant, 92
Home Stager, 126
Image Coach, 24
Indexer, 55
Low-investment Food Operations Owner, 93
Money Counselor, 20
Newborn Photographer, 131
Organizational Identity Consultant, 104
Parking Lot Oil Change Business Operator, 94
Personal Coach, 21
Political Campaign Manager, 79
Private-Practice Consultant, 105
Proposal Writer, 101
Restaurant Menu Creator, 141
Security System Consultant, 105
Speaking Coach, 84
Succession Planning Consultant, 80
Thesis Completion Consultant, 101
Trial Consultant, 34
Tutor, 92

My favorites

These careers scored highest overall on my criteria: make a difference, enjoyable to many people, good pay, ease of entry, little-known, and good job prospects.

Administrative Law Judge, 121
Adoption Attorney, 119
Athletic Coach, 87
Audiologist, 116
Biomedical Visualization Specialist, 58
Book/Magazine/Web Site Editor, 53
Business Home Economist, 142
Business Plan Writer, 105
Case Manager (Nursing), 109
Casting Director, 28
Cinematographer, 59
College Student Advisor, 21
College Student Affairs Administrator, 74
Computer Security Programmer, 44
Coroner/Medical Examiner, 106
Dating Coach, 23
Electrician, 65
Garden Designer, 126
Genetic Counselor, 72
Genomics or Proteomics Biologist, 36
Ghostwriter, 51
Handyperson, 65
Home Inspector, 127
Home Stager, 126
Intellectual Property/ Patent Lawyer, 120
Interior Designer, 125
Journalist, 52
Landscape Architect, 126
Librarian, 54
Lighting Designer, 59
Lobbyist, 90
Locksmith, 68
Mediator, 18
Meteorologist, 39
Money Counselor, 20
Musical Instrument Repairperson, 62

Newborn Photographer, 131
Nonpolluting Car Developer, 137
Optometrist, 71
Orthoptist, 71
Patent Agent, 137
Perfumer, 60
Personal Coach, 21
Pharmacist, 71
Photonics, 41
Physician (non-clinical specialties), 113
Physician Assistant, 115
Plant Geneticist/ Botanist, 36

Political Campaign Manager, 79
Producer, 32
Professor, 100
Proposal Writer, 101
Prosthetist/Orthotist, 61
Public Affairs Manager, 77
Radio/TV News Reporter, 82
Registered Nurse, 108
School Computer Coordinator, 112
Social Marketer, 103
Speech-Language Therapist, 90

Sports Information Director, 100
Succession Planning Consultant, 80
Surgical Technologist, 128
Systems Analyst, 95
Terrorism Expert, 37
Toxicologist, 41
Trial Consultant, 34
Tutor, 92
Venture Capitalist, 100
Veterinarian, 116
Virtual Reality Programmer, 43
Work-Life Manager, 75

Index

• Numerics •

5 O'Clock Club, 218, 326
10-second pitch, 226, 232, 234
35 most revealing questions, 160–169
40 Plus (support group), 218, 326
40-plus persons
  as college students, 212
  interview tips for, 275
  retirement planning, 306–307
  success in final working years, 303–307
  support groups for, 218
45-second pitch, 226–227, 232

• A •

Accent Neutralization Specialist, 91
Accessory Design, 131
Accident Reconstructor, 133
accomplishments on resumes
  exaggerating, avoiding, 250
  others, remembering, 252–253
  PAR stories, 225, 252
  quantitative, 251
  references and recommendations,
    251–252
  "soft," 252
  summary at top, 258
  for transferable skills, 253
Accountant, 96–98
Acoustics Specialist, 106
Actor, 88–89
ACT/SAT Tutor, 92
Actuary, 46
Acupuncturist, 118
Administrative Assistant/Secretary, 80
Administrative Law Judge/Hearing Officer,
    121–122
Adoption Attorney, 119

adrenaline addicts, 321
Adult Education Teacher, 86
Adventure/Eco Travel Organizer, 49
affirmations, 317
agencies, job-search help from, 240
aging megatrends, 150–151
Agricultural Scientist, 37
Amazon, searching careers on, 175
American megatrends
  aging, 150–151
  decline, 155–157
  environmentalism, 151–152
  inward turning, 153
  Islam, 154
  Latinization, 154–155
  political, 153
analysis paralysis, 316
angel investors, 337, 338
anger, controlling, 361
Animator, 57
Annual Report Photographer, 132
appearance
  tips for older people, 305–306
  for women in the workplace, 349
application letters
  for target employers, 240–241
  without a college degree, 198–200
Appraiser, 50
apprenticeships, 200
Arbitrator/Mediator, 120
Arborist, 68
Architect, 141–142
Architect, Landscape, 126
Archivist, 105
Area Specialist, 107
Art Teacher, 87
articles
  as career information resources, 174–176
  career training from, 198
  for staying current, 298

Artist/Graphic Artist, 56–58
artistic things-oriented careers, 56–60
Artist's Agent, 25
asking for what you want, 360
Association Manager, 76
atheism megatrends, 153–154
Athletic Coach, 87
Athletic Team Trainer, 127
Attorney
  niche careers, 119–121
  overview, 118–119
  similar careers requiring less, 18
attributes resume format, 248–249
Auctioneer, 32
Audiologist, 116
authority, resenting, 321
Automotive Technician (Car Mechanic), 66
Avionics Technician, 66
Awards Entrepreneur, 123

• B •

Background Vocalist, 89
Bail Bond Investigator, 26
Baker, Specialty Cake, 56
banking careers, 98–100
Bankruptcy Lawyer, 119
Barber/Hairstylist, 129
Big-Ticket Item Sales, 30
Biographer/Personal Historian, 123
Bioinformatician (Computational
  Biologist), 36
Biological Weapons Deterrence Specialist,
  38
Biologist, 35–37
Biomedical Engineer, 135
Biomedical Equipment Repairperson, 64
Biomedical Visualization Specialist, 58
Biostatistician, 41–42
Biotech Instruments and Consumables
  Sales, 30
biotech megatrends, 149
Blink (Gladwell), 230, 268
Blogger, Professional, 50
boldface text in this book, 3
Bolles, Richard (*What Color Is Your
  Parachute?*), 234, 268, 271

Book/Magazine/Web Site Editor, 53
books
  as career information resources, 174–176
  career training from, 198
  for staying current, 298
Botanist/Plant Geneticist, 36–37
Bounty Hunter, 26
Brewer, 140
bringing people together, careers
  involving, 28–29
Broadcast Technician/Broadcast Engineer,
  139
Business Broker, 81
business data-oriented careers, 46–50
Business Developer, 103–104
Business Equipment Broker/Lessor, 133
Business Home Economist, 142–143
business plan for self-employment, 333
Business Plan Writer, 105
Business Valuator, 97–98
business-education partnerships, 193

• C •

Cancer Registrar, 42
Car Mechanic (Automotive Technician), 66
Cardiovascular Technologist, 128
Career Coach/Counselor, 22
career guide book limitations, 11
Career Voyages site, 175, 179
caretaking and coaching careers, 18–27
Cartographer, 139
Case Manager (Nursing), 109–110
Casting Director, 28–29
CDs for test preparation, 208
Celebrant, 88
certificate programs, 200, 298
checklist for career suitability, 185–186
Chef, Personal, 69
Chemist, 40–41
chemistry, creating in interviews, 266–273
Child Life Specialist, 26
Child-Care Center Owner, 26–27
choosing your career
  before choosing a college, 201–202
  committing to a career, 180–185

contacting people in the field, 174, 176–178

ensuring a wise choice, 179–180, 185–186

final check for suitability, 185–186

multiple careers, 185

questionnaire for, 159–171

reading about careers, 173–176

visiting a workplace, 178–179

chronological resume format, 248–249

CIA/FBI Theatrical Effects Specialist, 130

Cinematographer, 59

City Manager, 76

Clergy, 87–88

Client Prospecting Specialist, 105

Clinical Trials Coordinator, 110

coaching and caretaking career category, 18–27

College Administrator, 73–74

College Admission Counselor, 91

College Admissions Recruiter, 31

college courses. *See also* online education and training

for checking out careers, 179

in-person, decline of, 198

college degrees. *See also* You University

application letter without, 198–200

apprenticeships versus, 200

assessing a program's quality, 202–203

author's favorite college, 206

business-education partnerships versus, 193

calculating a program's true cost, 203

career opportunities with, 192, 193

certificate programs versus, 200

choosing a program, 201–203

choosing a school, 203–205

choosing teachers, 210

expense of, 209

famous people without, 192

financial aid, 208–209

gaining admission, 206–208

hope for higher earnings with, 191, 193

identifying your career niche, 201–202

making the most of school, 210–212

for older students, 212

from prestigious colleges, 204–205, 207–208

pursuing, bad reasons for, 190

pursuing, good reasons for, 190–191

reasons for bypassing, 191–193

test preparation, 208

You University versus, 193–195

College Financial Aid Counselor, 81

College Financial Aid Officer, 96

College Student Advisor, 21

College Student Affairs Administrator, 74

College-Based Physician, 114

College-Bound Athlete Consultant, 91

Colleges That Change Lives (Pope), 205

Commercial Banker, 98–99

Commercial Debt Negotiator, 81

Commission Artist, 58

committing to a career

ensuring your success, 182

fear of failure, 182–185

finding a career you love, 181

learning more, 180–181

communication skills, developing, 285–286, 300, 357

competition, healthy, 347

Composer, 89

Computational Biologist (Bioinformatician), 36

Computer Chip Layout Designer, 60

computer data-oriented careers, 43–45

Computer Forensics Expert, 64

Computer Game Tester, 70

Computer Law, 119

computer megatrends, 143–149

computer program limitations for job search, 12

Computer Programmer, 43–44

Computer Repairperson, 63–64

Computer Security Administrator, 111

Computer Security Programmer, 44

Computer Tutor, 92

Concierge, 27

conduits, 340

Conference Recording Specialist, 63

conferences, checking careers at, 179–180

connection, power of deep, 352

Conservator, 59

Construction Manager, 78

Consulting Accountant, 98

Consulting Psychologist, 21
contacting people. *See also* networking
  in the field, 174, 176–178
  leads, 231–236
  recruiters and agencies, 240
  target employers, 240–242
Convention Planner, 34
conventions in this book, 3
Cool Careers Yellow Pages
  approaches for perusing, 16
  categories, 3, 16–17
  criteria for careers in, 15
  data and people-oriented careers, 94–100
  data and things-oriented careers, 105–108
  data, people, and things-oriented careers, 108–113
  data, people, and words-oriented careers, 100–105
  data, things, and people-oriented careers, 113–118
  data-oriented careers, 35–50
  guide to the future, 143–157
  icons, 17
  people and data-oriented careers, 71–82
  people and things-oriented careers, 92–94
  people and words-oriented careers, 82–92
  people-oriented careers, 18–35
  reading entirety of, 16
  things and data-oriented careers, 134–140
  things and people-oriented careers, 125–134
  things, people, and words-oriented careers, 140–143
  things-oriented careers, 56–71
  words and people-oriented careers, 118–125
  words-oriented careers, 50–55
Copy Editor, 53
Copywriter, 51–52
Coroner/Medical Examiner, 106
Corporate Intelligence Officer, 82
Corporate Massage, 129
Corporate Security Consultant, 142
Cosmetic Dentist, 128
Cosmetologist/Makeup Artist, 130
courage builders, 183–185
Court Administrator, 74

Court Reporter, 124
creative careers
  people and words-oriented, 88–89
  things-oriented, 56–60
Credit Risk Manager, 47
Criminalist, 140
crunching numbers, careers involving, 96–100
Cryptanalyst, 42
cultural megatrends, 152–157
Curator, 141
Cytotechnologist, 37

• D •

Database Administrator, 95
data-oriented careers
  business data, 46–50
  computer data, 43–45
  crunching numbers, 96–100
  data and people, 94–100
  data and things, 105–108
  data, people, and things, 108–113
  data, people, and words, 100–105
  data, things, and people, 113–118
  healthcare, 108–111
  other specialties, 111–113
  people and data, 71–82
  scientific data, 35–42
  technical, 94–96
  things and data, 134–140
Dating Coach, 23
dating in the workplace, 350, 355, 362
Debt Collection Specialist, 81
deciding on a career. *See* choosing your career
degrees. *See* college degrees
Dental Hygienist, 128
Dentist, 127–128
Dermatologist, 115
Development Specialist/Fundraiser, 31
Diagnostic Medical Sonographer, 93
Dietitian/Nutritionist, 72
Dikel, Margaret Riley (*The Guide to Internet Job Searching*), 260
Director/Filmmaker, 140–141
discrimination, reverse, 355

Dispensing Optician, 128–129
Distance Education Clearinghouse, 197
Distance-Learning Teacher, 86
Diver, 70–71
Doctor. *See* Physician
Dog Trainer, 69
Doula, 24–25
Drafter, 67
Dream-Career Trainer, 85
dress
  tips for older people, 306
  for women in the workplace, 349
Driving Instructor, High-Security, 62
"Dull-normal" Business Owner, 67

● *E* ●

eBay Marketing Consultant, 48–49
eBay Trading Assistant, 48
Eco Travel/Adventure Organizer, 49
e-commerce megatrends, 146
economic megatrends, 152–157
Economist
  niche careers, 46, 142–143
  overview, 46
Editor, 53
education. *See also* college degrees; online
    education and training
  icons indicating career requirements, 17
  megatrends, 147–148
  resume section for, 256–257
  staying current, 297–298
Education Lawyer, 120
Education/Training Programmer, 44
EEG Technician, 93
Elder Lawyer, 121
Elective Medical Care Clinics, 125
Electrical Component Sales, 30
Electrician, 65–66
Electro-Neurodiagnostic Technician, 93
e-mailing
  contacts in your network, 229–230
  leads, 232
  resumes, unformatted version for,
    260–261
E-mercials Salesperson, 29
Employee Assistance Professional, 25

Employee Background Checker, 45
Employee Trainer, 84–85
Employment Interviewer, 28
Employment Lawyer, 119–120
Employment Tester, 112
Engineer, 134–137
Engineering Technician, 137
English-Language-Learners Teacher, 86
Enologist, 139
Entertainment Architect, 142
Entomologist, 37
entrepreneurial skills, developing, 302
Environmental Accountant, 98
Environmental Analyst, 39
Environmental Economist, 46
Environmental Engineer, 136
Environmental Lawyer, 121
Environmental Manager, 76–77
environmentalism megatrends, 151–152
Epidemiologist, 37
e-populism megatrends, 144–146
errors, overcoming fear of, 183–184
Estate Attorney, 121
Ethicist, 55
Event Planner, 33–34
Executive Coach, 24
Executive Recruiter (Headhunter), 28
Executor, 98
Exercise Physiologist, 110
Exhibit Designer/Builder, 59
Expense Reduction Consultant, 46
Expo Planner, 34
Export Agent, 49
Exporter, 49
Expo/Show Producer, 33

● *F* ●

Facilities Manager, 76
failure
  handling fear of, 183–185, 218–221
  legitimate fear of, 182
  procrastination due to fear of, 315–317
  at self-employment, 341
  worth risking, 183
family, balancing work with, 347–348
Farrier, 68

Fashion Designer, 130–131
Faux Finisher/Muralist, 58
FBI Special Agent, 112
FBI/CIA Theatrical Effects Specialist, 130
fear
  of failure, handling, 183–185, 218–221
  of failure, legitimate, 182
  of failure, procrastination due to, 315–317
  of imposing, 320
  of rejection, 218–221
  of success, 320–321
feedback for resumes, 259
Fee-only Financial Planner, 80–81
field of interest, researching, 225–226
Film Critic, 50–51
Film Marketer, 103
Filmmaker/Director, 140–141
financial aid, 208–209
Financial Planner, Fee-only, 80–81
Financial Services Sales, 30
fine arts, 56–57
Finlay, Chad (*Gig*), 310
Firefighter, 133
5 O'Clock Club, 218, 326
flirting, 350, 354–355
Flying Car Developer, 137
Focus Group Leader, 103
Foley Artist, 59
following up
  after contacting leads, 235–236
  after interviews, 278–279
  after rejections, 280
  a second time, 242
  with target employers, 242
Food Carts, 93–94
Food Operations Owner, Low-Investment, 93
Food Scientist, 40–41
Foreign Language Interpreter/Translator, 124
Foreign Service Officer, 123
Forensic Accountant, 97
Forensic Artist, 59
Forensic Economist, 46
Forensic Psychologist, 21
40 Plus (support group), 218, 326

45-second pitch, 226–227, 232
40-plus persons
  as college students, 212
  icon for careers favorable to, 17
  interview tips for, 275
  retirement planning, 306–307
  success in final working years, 303–307
  support groups for, 218
Foundation Program Manager, 77
franchises, 198, 331
freelancers, 338
Fun Yet Effective icon, 6
Fundraiser for Arts Organizations, 32
Fundraiser/Development Specialist, 31
Fundraising Auctioneer, 32
Funeral Director, 92–93
future trends. *See* megatrends

• G •

Game Producer, 33
Game Programmer, 44
Garden Designer, 126–127
gatekeepers, getting past, 232–233
Gemologist, 68
Genetic Counselor, 72
Genomics Biologist, 36
Geographer, 106
Geographic Information Specialist, 67
Geologist, 39–40
Geophysicist, 40
Geriatric Care Manager, 19
Gerontologist, 96
Ghostwriter, 51
Gig (Finlay), 310
Gladwell, Malcolm (*Blink*), 230, 268
global warming, 151–152
Globewide Network Academy, 197
Golf Course Superintendent, 133
Google, searching careers on, 175
Government Manager, 74
Government Photographer, 131
Government Procurement Consultant, 47
Graphic Artist/Artist, 56–58
Graphologist/Handwriting Analyst, 55
Green Architect, 142

Green Gardener, 126
Green Product Sales, 30
Guerrilla Tactics in the Job Market (Jackson), 220
The Guide to Internet Job Searching (Dikel), 260

• H •

Hairstylist/Barber, 129
Handwriting Analyst/Graphologist, 55
Handyperson, 65
Harbor Pilot, 61
Hard Disk Repairperson, 63
Hardware Engineer, 135
Headhunter (Executive Recruiter), 28
headhunters, job-search help from, 240
Health Educator, 85
health megatrends, 149–152
Healthcare Accountant, 98
Healthcare Administrator, 77
healthcare careers, 108–111
Hearing Officer/Administrative Law Judge, 121–122
Heart-Lung Perfusionist, 61
High-Security Driving Instructor, 62
Historic Preservationist, 140
hobbies, 290–291
Holographer, 60
Home Inspector, 127
Home Remodeling Contractor, 127
Home Schooling Consultant, 92
Home Stager, 126
Hospital Research Director, 115
Housing for the Elderly and Disabled, 125
Human Resources Manager, 78
Hydrologist, 38–39

• I •

icons in this book, 6, 17
illustrator
  Artist/Graphic Artist, 56–58
  Technical Illustrator, 58–59
Image Coach, 24
imposing, fear of, 320

incubators for small businesses, 335
Independent Search Specialist/Information Retriever, 54
Indexer, 55
Industrial Designer, 138–139
Industrial Photographer, 131
Industrial Sales, 30
Industry Publications Writer, 51
Infant Mental Health Counselor, 20
Infectious Disease Specialist, 114
Infertility Specialist, 115
Information Abstractor, 54–55
Information Retriever/Independent Search Specialist, 54
Information Technology Manager, 75
integrity, prizing, 358
Intellectual Property/Patent Lawyer, 120
Interior Designer, 125
Interiorscaper, 127
International Accountant, 98
Internet resources. *See* Web resources
interning, checking careers by, 180
internships, 212
interviews
  addressing employer's needs, 269–270, 273–274
  arriving early, 266
  asking questions during, 265, 269, 271–272
  being your best self in, 270
  bringing up a weakness in, 272
  creating chemistry in, 266–273
  day-long job simulation, 275
  ending, 268, 276
  enjoying, 267
  first ten seconds, 268
  fitting job description to your strengths, 274–275
  following up, 278–279, 280
  for 40-plus persons, 275
  handling rejections, 280
  length of answers during, 271, 274
  listening and watching in, 270–271
  mannerisms to avoid, 268–269
  mindset for, 267–268
  by panels, 272

interviews *(continued)*
  portfolio for, 265
  practicing, 265–266
  preparing for questions, 264–265
  references for, 278
  relaxing for, 267
  report card after, 276–277
  responding to job offers, 279
  salary questions during, 269
  studying before, 263–264
  thank-you letters after, 277–278
  tips for, 243
  video, 273
  winning strategies for, 273–276
Inventor, 137–138
Investment Banker, 99–100
Investor Relations Specialist, 122–123
Irrigation System Specialist, 62
Islam megatrends, 154
italics in this book, 3

• J •

Jackson, Tom (*Guerrilla Tactics in the Job Market*), 220
Jewelry Maker, 57–58
job offers, responding to, 280
job search
  answering want ads, 236–239
  being real, 217
  contacting leads, 231–236
  contacting recruiters and agencies, 240
  contacting target employers, 240–242
  creating your pitch, 226–227
  creating your resume, 225
  eliminating resentment, 222
  finding time for, 223–224
  first ten days, 224
  following up, 235–236, 242
  handling fear of rejection and failure, 218–221
  having six balls in the air, 217
  interviewing, 243–244
  negotiating terms, 244, 269
  networking, 228–230
  recognizing your skills, 219

  researching target employers, 228, 239
  researching your field, 225–226
  staying upbeat, 215–218
  support groups for, 218
  targeting specific employers, 227–228
  30 days as realistic goal for, 223
job-hopping, handling on resumes, 254
Journalist, 52–53
Judge Judy technique, 184

• K •

Kaiser, Henry (industrial magnate), 276
Kennedy, Dan (*No BS Marketing Newsletter*), 236
keywords in resumes, 255–256

• L •

Labor Relations Specialist, 79
Laboratory Animals Vet, 116
Landscape Architect, 126
Latinization of America, 154–155
Lawyer. *See* Attorney
leads, contacting, 231–236
Lee, Linda (*Success Without College*), 191
letters of reference, 251, 252
Librarian, 54
library, career help from, 174–175
lifelong learning, 200
Lighting Designer, 59
listening
  in interviews, 270–271
  by men in workplace, 353–354
Literary Agent, 25
Lithograph Cameraperson, 132
live-for-today excuse, 317–318
Lobbyist, 90
Location Expert, 107
Locksmith, 68
Logistics Manager, 96
looking forward, 362
Low-Investment Food Operations Owner, 93–94

• M •

Magazine Editor, 53
Magician, 56
Makeup Artist/Cosmetologist, 130
making the most of school, 210–212
making the most of your job
  assessing chances of getting ahead, 307–309
  developing communication skills, 285–286
  disadvantages of promotion to manager, 310
  handling office politics, 295–297
  hothead boss, 286
  lazy or incompetent boss, 286
  maintaining interest, 289–291
  maintaining moderate workload, 287–289
  management tips, 299–300
  managing your boss, 283–286
  micromanager boss, 286
  self-promotion, 295
  staying current, 297–298
  stress management, 291–294
  success in final years, 303–307
  success in mid-career, 302–303
  success when starting out, 300–302
  tailoring the job to fit you, 284
  telecommuting, 287–288
  time-efficiency for, 288–289
management
  disadvantages of promotion to, 310
  in a fun business, 74
  tips for, 299–300
Management Consultant, 104
Manager, 73
Marketer, 102–103
marketing by self-employed people, 339–341
Marketing Researcher, 103
Massage Therapist, 129
Mediator, 18–19
Mediator/Arbitrator, 120
Medical Examiner/Coroner, 106
Medical Writer, 51

megatrends
  computers and technology, 143–149
  health and science, 149–152
  politics, culture, and economics, 152–157
Menopause Counselor, 110
men's career musts
  being proud to be a man, 356
  being tactful and listening well, 353–354
  considering nontraditional careers, 352
  dating your supervisee, avoiding, 355
  deciding about being the primary breadwinner, 351
  flirting, advice for, 354–355
  minding your health, 354
  power of deep connection, 352
  reacting to reverse discrimination, 355
  tempering "male energy," 352–353
Men's Therapist, 20
mentors. *See also* You University
  developing at work, 290, 361
  finding, 195–196
  learning recommendations from, 196
  mentoring others, 361
  for staying current, 297
Meteorologist, 39
Microscopist, 106
Military Officer, 82
Millwright, 65
mindset for interviews, 267–268
mindset for job seeking
  eliminating resentment, 222
  handling fear of rejection and failure, 218–221
  staying upbeat, 215–218
mission statement, personal, 289
Mobile Auto Repairperson, 66
Mobile Car Detailer, 66
Money Counselor, 20
money, overvaluing, 358
Mort, Mary-Ellen (librarian), 174
Muralist/Faux Finisher, 58
Music Teacher, 87
Musical Instrument Repairperson, 62–63
Musician, 89
musts. *See* succeeding

● *N* ●

Nanny, 26
nanotechnology megatrends, 150
negotiating
    for fair pay, by women, 346–347
    terms of employment, 244, 269
Nemko, Marty (author)
    credentials as higher education expert,
        203–204
    technique for controlling procrastination,
        313
    Utopia College article, 209
    Web site, 209, 335
Neon Sign Maker, 60
Network Administrator, 111
networking
    e-mailing contacts, 229–230
    phoning contacts, 230
    by self-employed people, 339
    sources for, 228
    time needed for, 229
    in your career, 301–302
Newborn Photographer, 131
Newsletter Publisher, 45
Nicholas, Matt (Web site creator), 335
No BS Marketing Newsletter (Kennedy), 236
Noise Control Specialist, 65
Nonpolluting Car Developer, 137
Nonprofit Manager, 77
Notebook Computer Repairperson, 63
Nuclear Engineer, 135
number crunching careers, 96–100
Nurse Anesthetist, 108–109
Nurse Informatician, 110
Nurse Legal Consultant, 110
Nurse Midwife, 109
Nurse Practitioner, 108
Nurse, Registered, 108–110
Nutritionist/Dietitian, 72

● *O* ●

objective on your resume, 247
Obstetric-Gynecological Nurse, 109

Occupational Medicine, 114
Occupational Outlook Handbook
    described, 174, 175
    icon for careers profiled in, 17
    Web site, 17, 175
Occupational Therapist, 93
Oceanographer, 106
Ocularist, 58–59
Oil Change Business Operator, Parking Lot,
    94
older persons
    as college students, 212
    icon for careers favorable to, 17
    interview tips for, 275
    retirement planning, 306–307
    success in final working years, 303–307
    support groups for, 218
one-minute struggle rule, 315
one-on-one people and words-oriented
    careers, 90–92
online education and training
    for adult students, 198
    overview, 147–148
    Web sites, 147, 148, 197
online groups, for staying current, 298
Online Marketer, 102
Operations Research Analyst, 96
Optician, Dispensing, 128–129
Optometrist, 71
Organizational Developer, 104
Organizational Identity Consultant, 104
Organizer, 24
Orthoptist, 71
Orthotist/Prosthetist, 61–62
overcoming procrastination. *See*
    procrastination

● *P* ●

Packaging Designer, 138
Packaging Engineer, 135
PAR stories in resume, 225, 252
Paralegal, 121
Paramedic, 117
Parenting Coach, 23
Park Ranger, 133–134

Parking Lot Oil Change Business Operator, 94
Patent Agent, 137
Patent/Intellectual Property Lawyer, 120
Pathologist, 37
Patient Advocate, 72–73
Patient Discharge Planner, 109
Pedorthist, 62
people-oriented careers
  bringing people together, 28–29
  caretaking and coaching, 18–27
  creative, 88–89
  data and people, 94–100
  data, people, and things, 108–113
  data, people, and words, 100–105
  data, things, and people, 113–118
  one-on-one, 90–92
  other, 32–35
  people and data, 71–82
  people and things, 92–94
  people and words, 82–92
  political, 90
  public speaking, 82–84
  sales-oriented work, 29–32
  things and people, 125–134
  things, people, and words, 140–143
  training and teaching, 84–88
  words and people, 118–125
perfectionism, 319–320
performance evaluations, quoting on
    resumes, 251
Performer's Agent, 25
Performing Arts Manager, 74–75
Perfumer, 60
periodicals. *See* articles
Personal Assistant, 27
Personal Care Facility Owner, 35
Personal Chef, 69
Personal Coach, 21–24
Personal Digital Assistant Repairperson, 64
Personal Historian/Biographer, 123
personalization megatrends, 143–144
Personnel Recruiter, 28
Pet Photographer, 132
Pet Sitter, 69–70
Peterson's Online Learning, 197

pets, bringing to work, 293
Pharmacist, 71–72
Photogrammetry Technician, 67
Photographer, 131–132
Photojournalist, 131
Photonics, 41
Physical Therapist, 117
Physician
  niche careers, 114–115
  overview, 113–114
  similar careers requiring less, 18
Physician Assistant, 115–116
Physicist, 41
Piano Technician/Tuner, 62–63
Pilot, 107
pitch
  creating, 226–227
  leaving on voicemail, 232
Pizza-by-the-Slice Business Owner, 93
Planetary Geologist, 39–40
Planner (urban), 112
Plant Geneticist/Botanist, 36–37
Political Aide, 90
Political Campaign Manager, 79–80
political megatrends, 152–157
Politician, 90
Politician's Writer, 51
politics, office, 295–297, 359
Polygraph Operator, 92
Pope, Loren (*Colleges That Change Lives*),
    205
portfolio, 265
Portfolio Manager, 47
practice interviews, 265–266
Precision Agriculture, 67
Private Investigator, 112–113
Private Librarian, 54
Private School Founder, 79
Private-Practice Consultant, 105
procrastination
  adrenaline addict's excuse for, 321
  advice for the incurable, 327
  all-purpose cures for, 322–326, 360–361
  author's method for controlling, 313
  don't-have-time excuse for, 322
  fear-of-failure excuse for, 315–317

procrastination *(continued)*
  fear-of-imposing excuse for, 320
  fear-of-success excuse for, 320–321
  getting unstuck, 324–326
  how the habit developed, 312–313
  live-for-today excuse for, 317–318
  perfectionist's excuses for, 319–320
  resent-authority excuse for, 321
  spacey people's excuse for, 318–319
  strategy for overcoming, 313–315
  surprising truths about, 311–312
  working without becoming stuck, 322–324
Producer, 32–33
Product Manager, 76
Product Tester, 70
Professional Blogger, 50
Professional Speaker, 84
Professor, 100–101
Program Evaluator, 102
Program Specialist, 86–87
programmer, 43–44
Project Manager, 75–76
project work, for checking careers, 180
promotion
  assessing your chances of, 307–309
  to manager, disadvantages of, 310
Proposal Writer, 101–102
Prosthetist/Orthotist, 61–62
Proteomics Biologist, 36
Psychotherapist/Psychologist
  niche careers, 20–21
  overview, 19–20
  similar careers requiring less, 18
Public Affairs Manager, 77
Public Health Administrator, 77
Public Relations for High-Tech and Biotech
    Companies, 122
Public Relations for Travel and Tourism,
    122
Public Relations/Communication
    Specialist, 122–123
public speaking, careers involving, 82–84
Purchasing Specialist, 96
Pyrotechnician, 70

• *Q* •

Quality Assurance Specialist, 111
questionnaires
  assessing chances of getting ahead,
      307–309
  need for, 159
  35 most revealing questions, 160–169
  tips for taking, 160
  using your answers, 169–171
Quick-Thumb Gardener, 126

• *R* •

Radio Guide Publisher, 55
Radiologist, 115
Radio/TV News Reporter, 82
Railroad Engineer, 108
Real Estate Photographer, 132
recruiters, job-search help from, 240
reference letters, 251, 252
references for employers, 278
Registered Nurse, 108–110
Regulation Compliance Consultant, 125
rejection
  handling after interviews, 280
  handling fear of, 218–221
Relationship Acceptance Therapist, 20
relaxing for interviews, 267
religious megatrends, 153–154
Relocation Consultant, 34
Remember icon, 6
report card after interview, 276–277
Reporter, Radio/TV News, 82
researching
  field of interest, 225–226
  for interviews, 263–264
  target employers, 228, 239
resent-authority excuse, 321
resentment, eliminating for job search, 222
Respiratory Therapist, 110–111
Restaurant Menu Creator, 141
Resume Writer, 53–54
ResumeMaker program, 225, 245, 250

resumes
  accomplishments on, 250–253, 258
  attributes format, 248–249
  attributes on, 259
  chronological format, 248–249
  current employer on, 249
  doing without, 246
  education section, 256–257
  electronic scanning of, 255
  getting feedback, 259
  guidelines for creating, 225
  human story on, 259
  imperfect work history, handling, 253–255
  information checked by employers, 250
  Internet help for creating, 224
  interview questions about, 266
  keywords in, 255–256
  listing highlights at top, 258–259
  name and contact information on,
    246–247
  objective on, 247
  optional sections, 258
  PAR stories in, 225, 252
  personal section, 258
  reference letters quoted on, 252
  references on, 250
  ResumeMaker program for, 225, 245
  selecting model for, 250
  sending after contacting leads, 235
  steps for creating, 246–261
  time to spend on, 225, 245
  transferable skills for, 253
  unformatted version for e-mail, 260–261
  vague language on, avoiding, 254
  Web site on, 247
  white paper instead of, 236
  writers for help with, 245
Retirement Coach, 24
retirement planning, 306–307
Retreat Leader, 86
Reunion Planner, 33–34
reverse discrimination, 355
Riley Guide Web site, 176, 239, 244
Risk Management Specialist, 111–112
risking failure, 183
Robotic Engineer, 136
Robotics Technologist, 64

• S •

saboteurs, tips for handling, 359
Sailboat Captain, 61
Sales Engineer, 136
Sales of E-mercials, 29
Sales of Instruments and Consumables to
    Biotech Companies, 30
sales-oriented work, 29–32
Salesperson, 29
SAT/ACT Tutor, 92
schmoozing. *See* networking
School Administrator, 78–79
School Computer Coordinator, 112
School Guidance Counselor, 26
School Photographer, 132
School Psychologist, 20–21
School-to-Work Coordinator, 28
science megatrends, 149–152
scientific data-oriented careers, 35–42
Secretary/Administrative Assistant, 80
Securities Analyst, 47
Securities Trader, 99–100
Security Sales, 30–31
Security System Consultant, 105
Seismologist, 40
self-employment
  acting like a CEO, 338–339
  controlling costs, 334–335
  downsides of, 330
  entry plan for, 334–338
  failure, 341
  finding financing, 337–338
  finding ideas for, 331–332
  icon for careers with potential for, 17
  marketing, 339–341
  mini business plan for, 333
  musts for success, 331–341
  no-nos to avoid, 338–339
  pricing, 336–337
  scams, avoiding, 332
  service versus product businesses, 331,
    334
  testing your idea, 332–333
  transition plans, 335–336
self-promotion, 295

selling information online, 48
seminars, checking careers at, 179
Senior Housing, 142
Senior Retrofitter, 65
Service Dog Trainer, 69
Show/Expo Producer, 33
Shyness Coach, 23
sideline, trying new career as, 184
signs that a career is right, 185–186
Silviculturalist, 107
Simplification Coach, 23
Small Business Administration site, 197
Small Business Consultant, 104–105
Social Marketer, 103
Social Worker, 25
Software Designer/Architect, 94–95
Software Trainer, 84–85
Solar and Wind Energy
    Technologist/Installer, 64
Sound Engineer, 63
Space Lawyer, 120
Spacecraft Engineer, 136
spaceyness, 318–319
Speaker, Professional, 84
Speaking Coach, 84
Special Effects Artist, 57
Special Effects Makeup Artist, 130
special projects, proposing, 289–290
Specialty Cake Baker, 56
Specialty Stitcher, 69
Speech-Language Therapist, 90–91
Sports Agent, 119
Sports Announcer, 83
Sports Information Director, 100
Sports Medicine, 114
Sports Physical Therapy, 117
Sports Psychologist, 21
Sports Referee/Umpire, 134
Sports Statistician, 42
Statistician, 41–42
status quo, comparing new career to, 184
stress management, 292–294
structured procedures, careers involving,
    60–71
Student Travel Service, 49
Stunt Person, 134

succeeding
  in college after 40, 212
  developing communication skills for, 300
  developing entrepreneurial skills for, 302
  ensuring in your new career, 182
  everyone's career musts, 357–362
  fear of, 320–321
  in final years on the job, 303–307
  men's career musts, 351–356
  in mid-career, 302–303
  networking for, 301–302
  self-employment musts, 331–341
  when starting your career, 300–302
  women's career musts, 345–350
Success Without College (Lee), 191
Succession Planning Consultant, 80
Supply Chain Manager, 96
support groups
  for job search, 218
  for procrastinators, 326
  for work, 290
Surgical Technologist, 128
Surveyor, 67
Systems Analyst, 95

• *T* •

tactfulness, 353–354
Talk Show Host, 83–84
target employers
  contacting, 240–241
  following up, 242
  identifying, 227–228
  researching, 228, 239
  revisiting sites to find ads, 242
Tax Attorney, 121
Teacher, 85–86
Teaching Company site, 194
technical data-oriented careers, 94–96
Technical Illustrator, 58–59
Technical Support Specialist, 94
Technical Writer, 52
Technical/Vocational Teacher, 87
technology megatrends, 143–149
Telecommunications Engineer, 136
Telecommunications Specialist, 64

telecommuting, 287–288
Temp Agency Owner, 34
10-second pitch, 226, 232, 234
Terrorism Expert, 37–38
terrorism megatrends, 152
test preparation, 208
Textile Designer, 58
thank-you letters
  after contacting leads, 235
  after interviews, 277–278
Thesis Completion Consultant, 101
things-oriented careers
  artistic and creative, 56–60
  data and things, 105–108
  data, people, and things, 108–113
  data, things, and people, 113–118
  people and things, 92–94
  structured procedures, 60–71
  things and data, 134–140
  things and people, 125–134
  things, people, and words, 140–143
35 most revealing questions, 160–169
Thomas Edison State College, 206
Tile Setter, 68
time
  don't-have-time excuse, 322
  finding for job search, 223–224
  length of interview answers, 271, 274
  for networking, breakdown for, 229
  to spend on resume, 225, 245
Time Management Coach, 22–23
time-efficiency at work, 288–289
Tip icon, 6
Tool and Die Maker, 60
Toxicologist, 41
Toy Designer/Inventor, 138–139
Trade Show Planner, 34
trade shows, checking careers at, 179–180
transition plans for self-employment,
  335–336
Translation, 124
Transplant Coordinator, 109
Trend Spotter, 103
Trial Consultant, 34
trial period for new career, 184
Troubled Teen Consultant, 91
Tutor, 91–92

tutors
  learning from, 198
  for staying current, 297
TV Newswriter, 53
TV/Radio News Reporter, 82

• U •

Umpire/Sports Referee, 134
Unconventional Wisdom icon, 6
unemployment, handling on resumes,
  253–254
University of California, Berkeley Career
  Site, 175

• V •

Vault.com site, 175, 226, 362
Venture Capitalist, 100
Veterinarian, 116
Veterinary Cardiologist, 116
Veterinary Dentist, 128
Veterinary Technologist, 117
Victim Assistant, 25–26
video interviews, 273
videos, career, 179
Violence Prevention/Resolution, 142
Virtual Assistant, 27
Virtual Reality Programmer, 43
visiting a workplace, 174, 178–179
Viticulturist, 107
Vocalist, Background, 89
Vocational/Technical Teacher, 87
voicemail, pitching yourself on, 232
Volcanologist, 40
volunteering, checking careers by, 180

• W •

want ads
  answering, 239
  deciding how much to use, 238–239
  value of using, 236–238
Warning! icon, 6
Web Developer/Webmaster, 95
Web Programmer, 44

Web resources. *See also specific careers*
  address conventions in this book, 3
  apprenticeship information, 200
  author's Web site, 209, 335
  biotechnology, 149
  career information, 175–176, 239
  certificate programs, 200
  comparable salaries for positions, 244
  degree program databases, 202
  e-commerce, 146
  entertainment, 145
  e-populism, 144
  financing for self-employment, 337–338
  franchises, 331
  internships, 196
  Latinization of America, 155
  military careers, 202
  nanotechnology, 150
  networking, 339
  no-emission vehicles, 152
  Occupational Outlook Handbook, 17, 175
  online education and training, 147, 148, 197
  online groups, 298
  personalization, 144
  researching employers, 239
  for researching your field, 226
  resume writers, 245
  ResumeMaker program, 225, 245
  for self-employment, 336
  support groups, 218, 290, 326
  Teaching Company, 194
  Thomas Edison State College, 206
  tutors, finding, 198
  Utopia College article, 209
  Web site creator, 335
  Wikipedia, 145
  wireless video, 148
Web Site Editor, 53
Web site, yours, 247, 335
Web Store Owner, 47–48
Web Writer, 51
Webcasting Technician, 139
Webmaster/Web Developer, 95
Wedding Makeup Artist, 130
Wedding Planner, 34
Wellness Coordinator, 109

WetFeet.com site, 175, 226
What Color Is Your Parachute? (Bolles), 234, 268, 271
Wind and Solar Energy Technologist/Installer, 64
Wireless Device Programmer, 43
wireless video megatrends, 148–149
Wise Elder, establishing yourself as, 303
women's career musts
  balancing work and family, 347–348
  being self-effacing, 346
  being who you are, 345–346
  competing healthily, 347
  for dating in the workplace, 350
  dressing wisely, 349
  flirting to advantage, 350
  getting physical, 349
  harnessing your hormones, 348–349
  negotiating for fair pay, 346–347
Woods, Tiger (golfer), 320
words-oriented careers
  data, people, and words, 100–105
  people and words, 82–92
  things, people, and words, 140–143
  words alone, 50–55
  words and people, 118–125
work history
  accomplishments on resumes, 250–253
  imperfect, handling on resumes, 253–255
Working Dog Trainer, 69
working hard, 358
Work-Life Manager, 75
workshops, for staying current, 298
Writer, 50
Writing Coach, 52

yellow pages. *See Cool Careers Yellow Pages*
You University
  college degree compared to, 193–195
  finding a mentor, 195–196
  finding what to learn, 196
  learning techniques, 198
  for lifelong learning, 200
  sources of courses, 196–197